MW00531810

Jim's Journey
A WAKE ISLAND CIVILIAN POW'S STORY

L.A. Magnino

Hellgate Press
Central Point, Oregon

Jim's Journey: A Civilian POW's Story
Copyright © 2001 by L. A. Magnino
Published by Hellgate Press

Hellgate Press
a division of PSI Research
P.O. Box 3727
Central Point, OR 97502-0032

(541) 245-6502
(541) 245-6505 fax
info@psi-research.com *e-mail*

Cover design: Mark Hannah
Typography and design: Wordsworth, San Geronimo, CA

Library of Congress Cataloging-in-Publication Data
Magnino, L. A. (Leilani A.), 1951-
     Jim's journey: a civilian POW's story / L. A. Magnino.—1st ed.
        p. cm.
     Includes bibliographical references and index.
     ISBN 1-55571-626-1
     1. Allen, James A., 1918- 2. Wake Island, Battle of, 1941.
3. Carpenters—United States—Biography. 4. World War, 1939-
1945—Prisoners and prisons, Japanese. 5. Prisoners of war—
United States—Biography. I. Title.

D767.99.W3 M34 2001
940.54'26—dc21   2001029897
                                                           CIP

Printed and bound in the United States of America
First edition 10 9 8 7 6 5 4 3 2 1

 Printed on recycled paper when available.

For Pop,

all of the civilian prisoners of war from Wake Island,

all of the military prisoners of war from Wake Island,

and everyone who has shared in Jim's Journey of Life.

A
good man
is immune to misfortune,
for
whatever evil befalls him
leaves him still
his own
soul.

— Marcus Aurelius

Happy is the man who recalls his ancestors with pride,
who treasures the story of their greatness,
tells the tales of their heroic lives,
and with joy too full for speech,
realizes that fate has linked him
with a race of goodly men.

— Goethe

Perhaps no American could cherish our country's liberty more
dearly than those who have defended it and in doing so have
paid the price of capture and imprisonment.

— Ronald Reagan

Contents

List of Illustrations

List of Maps

Preface

This book not only chronicles Jim Allen's journey through "the minefields of life," as he says, but is also a remembrance of those who accompanied him, especially the POWs. Admirals and generals have their experiences, both good and bad, recorded by observers and participants in wars. The common man, who makes up the bulk of armies and navies, is usually lost to history from either ignorance or disinterest. Yet without him, the military leaders, presidents, and emperors would not be able to hold their leadership positions. Only a few names of the hundreds of men who shared Jim's journey can be mentioned in this book, but it is all those unique individual experiences that add up to be the history of the Second World War. It is unfortunate that not all those experiences can be written down for posterity.

Jim's Journey is actually the journey of thousands of American men, born in the late nineteenth and early twentieth centuries, who were swallowed up by world conflict mid-century and tried to regain their lives during their remaining years. Those lives were never to be what they would have been without the advent of World War II. Over fifty years have passed since Jim Allen and others like him were imprisoned by the Japanese, yet they can never leave those prison camps behind, no matter how much they may want to. The POW experience will always be a part of them to their dying day, and a part of their families' lives also. It is an unseen intruder that alters the fabric of the family unit, however slightly, leaving an imprint upon the individual members as well as the ex-POW.

Each POW's experience is different as it is viewed through the individual's sensory filters and based on his past experience. Some POWs might not believe some of the things that happened to Jim or in his camp, but they did. Other civilian POWs who were with him have confirmed many of the things Jim tells of, and mentioned other events he had forgotten. As time passes, much of Jim's POW experience and that of other civilians, will be lost by their deaths. The author hopes this book inspires others to search out and write about the journeys of the POWs they meet and to appreciate the nation and way of life their courage, determination, and sacrifices have allowed later generations to enjoy.

Acknowledgments

I would like to thank those who have helped make this book possible:

James A. Allen, Sr. — the consummate packrat with a great memory, who put up with my incessant questioning about his prison camp experience for many years.

Virginia "Ginger" Genest — without her expert assistance, advice and friendship, this book would be much harder and less interesting to read.

Commander John D. Magnino, United States Navy, (Ret.) for his technical advice.

Margie Allen for her patience.

Joseph Astarita for the use of his wonderful drawings from his book, *Sketches of P. O. W. Life*.

Bill Taylor for the use of the illustration from his picture story.

But especially,
My husband for his unending patience, love and support urging me to fulfill my goal.

1

Prelude

Adversity in life can strengthen some individuals while mortally wounding others. Forecasting its effect is like a game of chance, for the most part. Some unexpected force can change the data and, hence, the results. Throughout history there have been stories of people who, when faced with challenges, found the strength to overcome them and go on to victory for themselves, their people, or mankind. This book is the story of James A. Allen, who had periods of adversity in his young life, but was able to surmount them and went on to face even greater challenges while a civilian prisoner of war in the Pacific Theatre during World War II.

The son of Carl and Viola Bennett Allen, Jim was born in Madison, Missouri, on 14 August 1918. The "Great War," as World War I was called then, raged in Europe with Armistice Day still three months off. His mother was a housewife who grew up on a farm, and his father was a farmer who did not particularly care for the vocation. Carl Allen also tried his hand at work on the Illinois Central Railroad for a few years, but that, too, didn't work out. Money was tight for the family during the Roaring Twenties, which might have been better called the Trying Twenties for Jim's family. In 1922, a brother, Jerald, was born, followed in 1924 by a sister, Hazel. In 1929, when the youngest Allen son, Billie Arnold, was a year old, the prob-

1

Jim Allen, standing, with his parents and brother Jerald, 1924. Sister Hazel arrived soon after this picture was taken. (James A. Allen Collection)

lems of the parents' marriage reached an apex and Viola and Carl Allen parted company. At the time, they were living on her Aunt Lizzie and Uncle John Mount's farm, 15 miles west of Wichita in Sholtie, Kansas. Viola and the four children went to live with her parents, Barbary ("Barbara") and Amos Bennett, in Madison, Missouri.

Returning to her parents' farm was a last resort for Viola. She did it knowing she would be expected to do twice the work of anyone else on the farm in order to keep her children there. The children were expected to help out also, at least as much as their ages would allow. Viola worked to support her family outside the home in addition to doing the laundry, keeping the house clean, and cooking all meals in her parents' home, usually before she left for work

During this time, Jim's grandfather, Amos Bennett, had a profound effect on young Jim's life. A strict disciplinarian, Amos made sure the grandchildren were seen and not heard. He believed they could learn more by listening to the adults and watching them than by prattling aimlessly. This helped Jim develop two skills: the ability to learn through observation, a skill that he would use often in his life, and the ability to relate and work with others by observing human behavior and predictability. Both of these skills, plus an excellent innate memory, were to become invaluable to Jim as an adult, especially during his imprisonment by the Japanese Army. His grandparents and mother also taught him how to grow and preserve food, cook, and make do with whatever materials were available to repair or create needed articles and implements. Unfortunately for Jim, like many other children of divorce, his schooling suffered with his being moved around so much. Jim is the first to admit he wasn't much of a student, a fact he keenly felt and regretted. As an adult, he would make sure his children did not follow his example. But while not successful with formal education, Jim had a mind that soaked up information and retained it, an ability aided by an affinity for reading.

During the 1930s, Jim and his family began traveling between Missouri and California, visiting his mother's uncles in the town of Chico in Northern California and El Monte in Southern California. When she decided to stay in El Monte in 1933, Viola had to register for Los Angeles County welfare to make ends meet. Carl Allen was essentially a "deadbeat dad," never contributing money for the support of the children. Jim, now fourteen, had not seen or heard from his father since his parents had parted, nor would he for the rest of Carl's life. In El Monte, Jim and his family had a very large yard, and with all the water they could use for only a dollar a month, they were able to grow most of what they ate, fresh or preserved. To add protein to their diet, Jim raised rabbits. In this manner, Viola and the children were able to get along.

In 1935, Viola married for a second time to another Carl, Carl West, a widower with a young married daughter. This eased the family's financial troubles a bit, but the country was still in the grip of the Great Depression. Times were tough and would remain so into the 1940s.

As the family moved around, the children went from one school to another, doing the best they could to catch up with their classes; eventually all graduated from high school, a goal of Viola's. In January 1937, after graduating from Downey High School as a class of one and wearing his football letter proudly, Jim moved back to Missouri where his mother, stepfather and siblings had already returned. Viola's older brothers in California had convinced Viola and Carl West that they should try farming back in Missouri. With Viola now stricken with rheumatoid arthritis, farming in the cold Missouri weather would be a challenge, but she and Carl West had decided to give it a go.

Late that winter, Jim went to sign up at the post office for employment with the federal government. Being single during a time of high unemployment made it hard for him to obtain a position. In order to answer the interviewer's questions, Jim had to lie, and one lie then led to another. Jim became so confused trying to keep everything straight, that later he swore to himself that he'd never lie again. "Tell the truth and be done with it," became his motto. "The only time I ever did [lie] was in prison camp. I didn't exactly always tell the Japanese the truth!" Jim has stated.

Not qualified for a federal job, Jim did find work as a stone mason in Hannibal, Missouri, working on a limestone wall that was to enclose the town's Samuel Clemens' (Mark Twain) Field. This was a Work Progress Administration (WPA) job and paid good money. Jim started working on the wall's footing below ground, but in two days found himself promoted to an above ground position. He did well for a week. Unfortunately then the project ran out of money and all single men were laid off.

That spring, his grandparents took him back to Sholtie, Kansas, to visit his Uncle John Mount. In addition to his farm, Mount also ran the town's grain elevator. Jim stayed on in Sholtie to help his uncle with the wheat harvest. Jim and his cousin Kenneth were laborers doing whatever was necessary at the grain elevator, such as starting the elevator engine in the morning, dumping grain from trucks, and shoveling the grain into the back of boxcars. The young men found there was a slight problem with their working around a grain elevator. As Jim recalls, "Every morning you had to pry your eyes open with both hands because the grain dust had glued the lids together."

After the farmers had harvested all the wheat they could with modern machinery, such as the combines used to separate the wheat grain from the straw stalks, the old-fashioned hand-bundled wheat harvest took place. This type of harvesting was much more labor-intensive. Jim left the elevator job and worked in the fields cutting the wheat with a sickle and bundling the long shafts of the wheat plant together. Jim would take the several bundles, or shocks, and stack them upright in the field. One shock was placed on top to keep the rain off the others. Horse-drawn wagons would be brought around and strong-armed men would throw the wheat shocks up into the wagon. The shocked wheat was taken to a threshing machine, which cut the wheat grain from the wheat stalks, now called straw. The grain would go onto the granary and its elevator for shipment by freight train, while the straw would be piled up for farm animals to use as bedding or shelter from the winter wind if left in the pasture all season. Jim plowed for several days with a tractor, preparing the fields for winter wheat.

No more work was available around Sholtie as autumn waned, so Jim traveled to Renaessler, Missouri, where his mother and stepdad lived. At that time, Carl West's boss was one of the county Rural Electrification Project directors. Through his stepfather's efforts, Jim was hired to dig holes for the new power poles that were bringing electricity into the backwoods of the United States. Working for Federal Engineering of Kansas City, Jim earned thirty-five cents an hour for eight hours of work, five days a week. Social Security, which began in 1937, claimed two cents of the fourteen dollars Jim earned his first week.

Deckhand Jim Allen and the sternwheeler *John James* working the Missouri River in 1938. (James A. Allen Collection)

During early 1938 when the ground was too frozen to dig holes, Jim drove cows, fixed fences, and did other general farm jobs that were available until warmer weather arrived. He then went to work on the *John James*, an old sternwheeler. Jim had learned about steam driven engines while living on his grandfather's farm. Amos Bennett ran a molasses mill and used steam to cook down the sorghum cane juice until it eventually became a semi-sugary syrup. Jim's cousin, Tommy Bennett, was already aboard the *John James* and had convinced Captain Van Horn to hire twenty-year-old Jim as a watchman, especially since he knew about steam engines. During the summer and fall of 1938, Jim went up and down the Mississippi and Missouri Rivers, stowing and unloading cargo being shipped upon the *John James* until ice began to form on the Missouri.

Before Jim's return that winter, Viola and Carl West had separated and Carl headed back to California. At his grandparents' farm in Madison, Jim found his mother and siblings waiting for approval of a loan that would allow them to begin farming their own place come spring. Being the oldest son, Jim again assumed the role as the male head of the household and was going to start farming with his mother in order to support the family. Time went on with no word on the loan's approval. Jobs were hard to find that winter. In early 1939, Jim decided to return to California to look for work.

For the journey west, Jim bought a rundown 1929 Model A two-door Ford sedan with a wooden two-by-four as a front bumper and four nearly bald tires. The ten-year-old car had seen a lot of rough use, but Jim patched up and fixed the old black beast up as best he could. On the day before he left, the farm loan returned approved. Although they had already planted twenty acres of wheat, the family gave up the idea of farming and chose to return to California for good: Viola to reconcile with Carl West, and Jim to look for better work. This was a turning point in Jim's life.

With eighty dollars to travel on, Jim, his mother, his fourteen-year-old sister Hazel, and brother Billie, now ten, headed west; sixteen-year-old Jerald remained behind with relatives. The Model A was transporting not just four refugees of the Dust Bowl, but also their worldly possessions. Two mattresses were tied onto the car's roof. Resting on the running board, while tied to the side of the hood, was a two-and-one-half-gallon can of motor oil for the engine. Bedding, suitcases, and household items rode inside with the passengers. John Steinbeck might have used them as a model for *The Grapes of Wrath*. At thirty miles-per-hour, the trip would take five long, tiring days through plains, mountains, and deserts, in a car with four old tires, steering problems and poor brakes. It was more than a trip; it was an endurance test.

Each day around 10:00 AM and again at around 3:00 PM, Jim would stop at the side of the road and put the front end of the Model A up on a jack in order to get underneath and tighten up the wheel bearings. Jim claimed that the steering "wobbled like hell" if he didn't fix it occasionally. One day early in the journey, the car began to heat up. Pulling into the next town, Enid, Oklahoma, Jim found a garage that would put a new radiator in for eleven dollars. Luckily, the car did not have any-more overheat-ing problems for the remainder of

A car similar to the one Jim drove west. However, Jim's did not have the visor over the windshield. (B. M. Glitten Collection)

the trip. There would be enough other obstacles to overcome.

Between Enid and Alamogordo, New Mexico, the family ran into one of the infamous dust storms of the era. Every-thing and everyone in the car became covered with a layer of dust as it seeped into the car's interiors through various small openings. Stopping for the night at Alamogordo, the weary family found there were no rooms available for them.

The family climbed back into the Model A Ford, but when Jim went to start the car to continue down the road, nothing happened. The Model A was still and made not a sound. Tired and dusty, Jim slowly lifted the hood, hoping to be able to eas-ily spot the trouble, even though he was not a mechanic. Jim knew the engine was using quite a bit of motor oil, hence, the large can on the running board. As he looked under the hood, Jim saw where oil had spewed out over the engine and mixed with the heavy dust. Never one to give up easily, an idea popped into Jim's mind to clean off the four thin copper strips that were spark plug wires and hope the clean wires would carry a charge to ignite the cylinders. Being prudent, Jim also cleaned up the engine's distributor in case some of the fine dust had crept in there. After scrubbing off the accumulated dirt and motor oil grime, the Model A started up on the first try.

Back into the car piled Jim, Viola, Hazel and Billie. Con-tinuing to head west through the night, they finally had to stop at 11:00 PM when Jim could drive no longer. Unfortu-nately, the only motel with a room available, as Jim remem-bers, could be described as a "hell hole." After a night's rest, not necessarily a good one, the family started off early the next morning and crossed the border into Arizona, one state closer to their goal of California. They were almost to Bisbee, Arizona, when Jim heard the sound of metal on the gravel road below. The Model A had two long braces that went from the rear axle housing of the car to just in back of the universal joint. The two braces were fastened together at the joint with a bolt that had decided not to continue to California, but to remain along the highway in Arizona. Jim had brought along an extra carriage bolt, but it was two-inches longer than needed. Manipulating the temporary replacement bolt to hold the two braces together, Jim was able to make Gila Bend, Arizona, and a service station before the car completely fell apart.

At this point, a feeling of what else can go wrong settled over the travelers. After a good bolt was in place, Jim decided to avoid other possible problems and bought a retread tire to replace the worst of the Model A's four worn ones. His grandfather's ways had been instilled in him to keep things around; you never know when you may need something. So Jim tied the worn tire to the back of the car. After filling the car's tank with fifteen cents a gallon gas, the remaining travel money added up to only five dollars. However, since they planned to be in El Monte, California, that night with Carl, Jim figured the family was in great shape as they drove west early that morning.

At 10:00 AM, the sound of flapping rubber was heard above the engine. The recently purchased retread had disintegrated. The only thing to do was put the original tire back on and cross fingers the aged threadbare tires would last for another 250 miles of desert roadway. Their luck held, for although the car had lousy brakes, four rotten tires, and a body about to travel in a thousand different directions, Jim's family managed to chug into El Monte that evening to where Carl West was waiting.

Within two days of being back in California, Jim was able to find work with a contractor digging footings for new buildings with a pick and shovel and later using a horse team to dig house foundations; his farm background came in handy. He quickly moved to mixing cement and helping build the wooden forms for the foundations to be poured into. For 1939, the fifty cents an hour for a 44 hour week as a laborer, then carpenter, was good employment for the twenty-one-year-old.

As winter settled in on Southern California, bringing on the rainy season, construction jobs vanished. Jack Huskie, whom Jim had met while working on the home foundations, had taken an interest in the young man. One night he came by Jim's home and told him about a job at the California Store Fixtures Company in suburban El Monte. Huskie was currently working there building cabinets, displays, and other paraphernalia for businesses. The job was also an opportunity to learn carpentry techniques from the much older master carpenter Huskie, who was in charge of the workroom. Jim began immediately, learning how to build the different sales items. Jim did not have many of his own carpentry tools, so Huskie would instruct Jim in a particular tool and let him use it the rest of the work day. By the next workday, Jim needed to buy his own tool because Huskie's would not be available. In this fashion, Jim not only learned and gained skill with many different carpentry tools, but also accumulated a well-equipped tool kit. Jim remained at the store until July 1940.

Now with more finishing work experience, Jim went back to house building during the dry season. He joined the local Carpenters Union, #1507, as an apprentice carpenter. In a short period of time, Jim became a journeyman at double his previous hourly wage of fifty-five cents. Under the union's mothering wing, Jim was assigned an assortment of carpentry jobs until he was sent to Northern California to help build permanent structures at the U.S. Army's Fort Ord. While there, Jim suffered from working around poison ivy. Living in the tent city where the carpenters were housed was not conducive to getting rid of the massive outbreak from the noxious weed. After a month, Jim went back to El Monte, recuperated, and found other work building steam cabinets used to cure concrete pipes for a Metropolitan Water District Project, which would bring the first Colorado River water to a parched Los Angeles.

While World War II raged in Europe at this time, the United States was still not officially involved. However, in September 1940, President Franklin D. Roosevelt signed into law the Selective Service and Training Act in anticipation of the day the United States would need a well-stocked army. Eight hundred thousand men were drafted with more anticipated in the near future. Jim had a low draft number, so he knew it would not be long before he would be called up. Until then the need for additional facilities for the growing American military meant construction jobs and money for many, including Jim who was hired to build barracks at Camp Roberts in California.

The winter of 1940 was an unusually wet one for California, with many roads impassable. Jim, however, was undaunted by the thought of flooded roads between him and his new defense job at Camp Roberts. On 9 January, Jim and a fellow worker, Chuck Royer, headed off for Paso Robles, northwest of Los Angeles, where the army base was located. In preparation for deep water on the roads, Jim rigged up a piece of heavy canvas to protect the car's radiator. The lower edge of the canvas was secured below the radiator and a long, three-quarter-inch iron rod was sewn across the top for weight. A long wire was attached to the middle of the iron bar and brought up through the hood and fastened onto the dash. A metal ring was tied to the end of the wire in order to pull the canvas up over the radiator, keeping water out of the engine. When released, the wire would relax and the weight of the iron bar pulled the canvas back below the radiator. The trick was to drive through the standing water in low gear, as rapidly as possible, while gunning the engine. That way the exhaust would keep the water from flowing into the tail pipe. Jim's idea worked so well that there were times the water was over the headlights, but the engine never flooded. The amphibious journey to Camp Roberts was worth it, for the work lasted five months.

As summer approached, Jim worked on another defense job, this one in Sacramento, before returning to El Monte and building concrete forms for the foundation of an extremely large cement floating natural gas tank in Los Angeles. The tank consisted of an outer sealed cylinder, partially buried below ground level; only the top six-feet or so could be seen of the tank's eighty foot height. The lower portion of its inner wall angled away toward the center of the tank before rising a few feet, forming a trough. Jim thought it looked like a giant donut at this point. The angling allowed for water to be pumped in, which would act as a seal for the natural gas within the inner tank; the gas could not penetrate water. The inner tank, also a cylinder, did not have a bottom, which allowed the natural gas pumped inside it for storage to "lift" the cement inner tank as the gas accumulated within it, trapped by the water "seal" of the outer tank. The massive project presented several unforeseen problems to the carpenters who were constructing the forms and pouring the cement walls and foundation of the inner and outer

A view of the below ground construction of the outer walls of the "floating" natural gas tank Jim worked on as a carpenter in 1941. This was his last job in the States before he left for Wake Island. The construction crane on the right is standing on fill supported by an angled cement trough. (James A. Allen Collection)

tanks. Jim was one carpenter with several innovative ideas on how to overcome the obstacles they met. The superintendent of this project was so pleased with Jim's ideas, that over time he was given more and more responsibility.

Although he didn't have anyone particular in mind, Jim was already thinking of the future and being married in his own home. His mother said that if he waited until he could afford a home, he'd never be married! Owning a home during these years was not easy and most people were renters. Still Jim pursued his goal, saving what he could from his various jobs. This was not an easy task for a young man in a locale where there were enticements to spend dollars at every corner.

One day, back in 1939, Jim had read in the newspaper about the consortium of construction companies that were building military bases in the Pacific on the islands of Cavite, Guam, Johnston, Midway, Palmyra, and Wake, as well as at Pearl Harbor in the Territory of Hawaii. Morrison Knudsen was one of the companies that made up Contractors Pacific Naval Air Bases (CPNAB). Each of the CPNAB contractors were in charge of a particular base, Morrison Knudsen's being Wake Island. They were recruiting skilled workmen in all building trades, including carpenters, plumbers, masons and heavy equipment operators. These workers would be part of the hundreds building the air bases on the small Pacific islands. The islands would become the first line of defense for the United States West Coast and the Territory of Hawaii, especially Pearl Harbor, where the U.S. Navy was consolidated. The pay was outstanding for the time period and best of all, Jim thought, was that out in the middle of the Pacific Ocean, there would be nothing to spend his earnings on. His goal of a house, then marriage, seemed to be closer.

As with most dreams and hopes, there was a problem. Morrison Knudsen wanted carpenters with ten years experience. At twenty-one, Jim lacked the basic requirement. Even with letters of recommendation from two of his job superintendents, it would take Jim several visits to the recruiter's office and two years before he would be hired by Morrison Knudsen to join the workers building the air base at Wake Island. When Jim reported back to his Los Angeles gas tank superintendent that Morrison Knudsen wouldn't hire him, the super was floored. He had written Jim a great recommendation and thought he would do well. According to Jim, his boss' response was to question, "just what the hell kind of carpenters do they want?" He was as mystified as Jim as to just what CPNAB was looking for. In spite of the initial rejection, Jim persevered and was finally hired the first week of September 1941. Jim suspects the company recruiter waived the ten-year policy to make his quota of workers for the next boat out, which was leaving in a week. This time the Morrison Knudsen recruiter didn't ask Jim how long he had been a carpenter, and since it was only two years, Jim didn't volunteer the information. The recruiter told Jim to just put down ten years, but remembering the post office scene in Missouri, Jim wouldn't lie.

Nonetheless, now that he was hired, Jim had to act quickly in order to be ready to leave the following week. Jim applied for permission from his draft board to go to Wake Island. Since it would be a defense job, the permission was assured. The Morrison Knudsen Company wouldn't have honored his contract without a letter from the draft board. Jim was given nine months before he would be returned to 1-A status. With his low Selective Service number, Jim figured this would buy him some time before he was drafted for the war in Europe when the United States officially joined the armed conflict.

The United States Navy at Long Beach, California, gave Jim a physical exam as well as the various shots, including smallpox, required for the overseas travel. Only the very healthy would be allowed to go on to Wake. Regretfully, Jim's medical documentation was lost, requiring him to have another set of shots at Pearl Harbor and Wake Island. With the medical business and draft board out of the way, Jim next rented a garage to house his pride and joy, a four-door, dark green 1940 Ford Deluxe sedan. He left instructions with his mother and sister to pay the five dollars a month rent out of his bank account to which some of his earnings would be sent.

While his mother was not happy with the idea of her first-born child going so far afield, he was a man, not a child, and there wasn't much she could do about it. Viola helped him get ready for his journey. As she washed his clothes to pack for the trip to Wake Island, the washing machine blew up. Realizing his mother and family would need one immediately, whether he was leaving or not, Jim went out and bought Viola a new one. Lacking the cash to make the sale, Jim went to the El Monte Hardware Store, the same store where he had been buying carpentry tools since Jack Huskie had instructed him a few years earlier. Knowing Jim, the store gave him credit to purchase a washer, and Jim arranged with Viola to pay it off out of his future earnings. The replacement washer was still working hard when Jim returned to California in 1945.

Finally, on 11 September 1941 at 1:30 in the afternoon, the moment arrived for Jim to depart upon his grand new adventure. His transportation was docked alongside a pier at the Port of Los Angeles in the coastal town of San Pedro. Sailing Cabin Class with forty dollars in his pocket, Jim walked briskly aboard the SS *Matsonia* for the first leg of his journey to Wake Island. War clouds were gathering as the twenty-three-year-old adventurer waved from the luxury liner's railing to his family on the pier below. When Viola stood on the wharf and watched her son sail out to sea toward the not yet recognized future war zone, she could not have imagined what fate had in store for her oldest son. She would not see her James again for four long years.

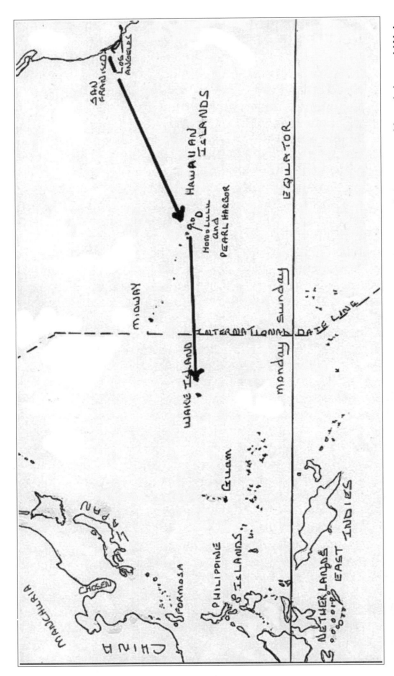

Jim Allen's route from the Los Angeles area to San Francisco, California, and then on to Honolulu and Wake Island.

2

Bon Voyage

The overnight cruise north to San Francisco allowed Jim Allen time to explore his new home of the next five days. In the fall of 1941, air travel was limited and very expensive, so the majority of travelers went by ship. Life moved at a much slower pace. The travelers accepted the standard ten-day ocean voyage to Honolulu (as opposed to the five hours today by modern jet plane) as a welcomed holiday, and the Matson Line's *Matsonia* staff worked to make it as enjoyable as possible. Jim discovered that there was horse racing (by throwing dice rather than live horses) at the Mid-Ocean Race Course in the afternoon, swimming in the on-board pool, tennis on the *Matsonia*'s one court, and a library, as well as lots of excellent food. The view from the ship's deck of nomadic ocean waves that stretched beyond one's sight in every direction, chased by clouds scurrying above, was novel to Jim. For a young man on his first ocean journey, it was "swell."

Jim shared cabin 336 with two other Morrison Knudsen workers bound for Wake Island. Joe Tury, in his mid-thirties, was a merchant marine going to Wake to work as an oiler on the dredging machinery. In his late twenties, Charles Cantry was a carpenter who had already completed a one-year contract with CPNAB on Midway Island and had been back to the States for a visit. Of the three cabin mates, only Jim would make the return

The postcard Jim mailed to his mother from San Francisco. The picture depicts the city and some of the numerous piers and terminals, which made up seventeen miles of berthing at the inland port. Jim wrote on the back that he was "Sure having a swell time seeing S.F." (James A. Allen Collection)

voyage east at the end of the war. During the ensuing days, Jim would meet other Morrison Knudsen employees, from seventeen-year-old laborers from Civilian Conservation Corps (CCC) Camps in Idaho to fifty-year-old carpenters, all with various motives, headed for Wake Island and the air base construction. The names on the cabin class souvenir passenger list included travelers of Oriental ancestry as well as those of European, which made for an interesting pre-war mix.

Jim Allen and Joe Tury found themselves seated at the same dining table that evening and formulated plans to tour San Francisco the next day rather than just staying aboard ship. They knew there would be plenty of time to enjoy the ship during the ocean crossing. At 7:00 AM, 12 September the *Matsonia* tied up in San Francisco for the day. She would sail west at 5:00 PM for Hawaii. This provided more than enough time for Jim and Tury to explore the hilly city. Although Jim had no extra money to spend, he and Joe visited Market Street and rode a cable car. Buying a postcard midday, Jim wrote a quick note to his mother about his experiences so far, something he continued to do whenever possible during the next four years.

Jim and Tury made it back to the *Matsonia* in time for Jim to find a place on the bow and watch the sun set as the *Matsonia* sailed under the Golden Gate Bridge and on into the Pacific Ocean. The view brought back memories of his second grade teacher in Mattoon, Illinois, who had told about her trip to Hawaii the summer of 1925 and sailing out the "Golden Gate" at sunset. The beautiful scene was all he had imagined from her description, plus more. He felt like the luckiest guy in the world according to the letters he wrote home.

Saturday morning at breakfast, Jim didn't even look at the menu. The dining room steward just brought him his meal. In San Francisco, Jim and Tury had tipped him well, with a dollar from each man. This was when pot roast sold for fourteen cents a pound, a loaf of bread a nickel and corn flakes were two packages for fifteen cents. Apparently the world-wise steward had sized Jim up as a country boy who liked just plain food, nothing fancy. Fried potatoes, eggs, and bacon or sausage, which the steward brought, suited him just fine every morning.

During the ocean crossing, Jim added tennis to his new experiences, playing with a young female passenger from Santa Barbara. Jim enjoyed the game so much, he wrote home from Wake Island that he was buying a tennis racket on the atoll. Jim had by now teamed up with Ben Marsh, another construction worker hired by CPNAB. Marsh was the forward type who didn't let anything get in his way. He took pictures of, and got himself introduced to, the college sports star and future baseball Hall-of-Famer Jackie Robinson, who was on his way to Honolulu to join a semi-pro football team, the Honolulu Bears, while working on a

Left to right, Jackie Robinson, Ben Marsh, Ray Bartlett, and Frank Brickner pose for a picture on board the SS *Matsonia* enroute to Honolulu, September 1941. (James A. Allen Collection)

School teacher Norman Wright with his dancing and tennis partner on the *Matsonia*'s tennis court located on the ship's topmost deck between the smokestacks. (James A. Allen Collection)

construction job. Making the introduction was Mr. Francis J. "Brick" Brickner, former coach at St. Mary's College, now a Spaulding Sporting Goods representative. Brickner was traveling on business as well as being the Honolulu Bears' team director who had hired Robinson and teammate Ray Bartlett, an old friend of Robinson's. Ben Marsh later gave Jim two of the Robinson photographs and introduced Jim to Brickner, who offered to take the young men with him on his business stops in Hawaii.

On the crossing, Jim also met a teacher, Norman J. Wright, who was going to Honolulu to research information on the Hawaiian school system in order to write his master's thesis. Wright and Jim Allen were of similar personality and hit it right off. Through this acquaintance, Jim was introduced to new areas of the *Matsonia* as well as some of the "finer" points of an ocean voyage, especially those that might lead to meeting young women.

Although Jim and Norman Wright were in Cabin Class, Wright knew how to get into First Class to go dancing with the girls there. The strategy called for the two young daredevils to ride the elevator up to First Class. This was contrived by each giving the elevator attendant twenty-five cents (not a small sum in 1941) to look the other way. However, the elevator could not be used to retreat after enjoying an evening of dancing the foxtrot, rhumbas, swing, and waltzes with the young ladies in First Class. It was necessary to take an alternate route back to Cabin Class and their own staterooms.

Casually drifting by the kitchen doorway, Jim and Wright would pop through into the kitchen to make their escape. The band and orchestra musicians, sitting in the kitchen at a table eating cold cuts, would invite the First Class dance crashers to join them. After a welcomed snack, it was out the kitchen's rear exit and through the crew's quarters, down over the poop deck to Cabin Class. The surreptitious route added zest to the adventure, but did not fool anyone. The ship's staff knew what the two renegades from Cabin Class were up to, but apparently didn't mind. Nothing was done to stop them during their many excursions into the exclusive realm on the upper decks, perhaps because the First Class women passengers enjoyed the extra dancing partners so much.

During the voyage, the Matson Line issued a daily newspaper containing summaries of the latest wireless reports by the United Press. The newspaper was distributed in all traveling classes for the passengers to read and stay informed while they were at sea. On Tuesday, 15 September 1941, news reports came directly from the front lines of the war seething on the other side of the globe. A portion of the news found in the *Matsonia's* paper that day read as follows:

WORLD AFFAIRS

BERLIN — German troops have entered the outer suburbs of Leningrad and are battling less than 15 miles from the center of the city, an authorized military spokesman said Monday night. He said the battle of that vast city, the size of Chicago, was now in its critical phase; that the Russians were resisting desperately and there was a steady downpour of rain which made it difficult to move up supplies. Leningrad, according to German military informants, is protected by line after line of powerful concrete pill boxes, some several stories deep, built on Maginot line principles. Informants here estimated that 1,000,000 Soviet troops and 4,000,000 civilians were now pressed into an area 130 miles square in the Leningrad sector.

CAIRO — Indications were seen Monday night that the Axis may be preparing a new offensive in the western desert after two strong Italian mechanized columns were driven back across the Egyptian frontier into Libya. The reconnaissance columns had penetrated 35 miles into Egypt before being driven back by British tanks, armored trucks and squadrons of the South

African air force. It was thought in some quarters that the Nazis were testing out British defenses preparatory to start of a new drive into Egypt just a year from the date of the start of Marshal Rudolfo Grazianis ill fated push last year.

LONDON — The air ministry reported Monday night the Blenheim bombers attacked German shipping at Haugesund on the Norwegian coast and off the Frisian islands on Monday. The planes which attacked Haugesund shipping also bombed a factory in the same area.

NATIONAL AFFAIRS
SAN FRANCISCO — John R. Bayless, 25-year-old bank robber, attempted to escape from Alcatraz Island penitentiary by diving into San Francisco Bay Monday, but he was recaptured by a prison guard, Warden James Johnston reported.

MILWAUKEE, WIS. —- Secretary of the Navy Frank Knox declared on Monday that United States warships had been ordered to embark on Tuesday on President Roosevelt's historic "shoot on sight" crusade against Axis shipping. Knox told the 23rd national American Legion convention that naval forces were directed to "capture or destroy by every means at their disposal all Axis controlled vessels encountered in convoy routes from this country to Great Britain," and a message from President Roosevelt appealed for Legion unity behind the government's policy. Mr. Roosevelt's message, delivered to the convention by Nation Commander Milo J. Warner, said the threat to the nation's security and "to our way of life" was "not imaginary but very real." The President summoned "unity of purpose, unity of sentiment and a keen desire to make whatever sacrifices may be necessary in order to obtain our objective." Knox's pronouncement, that the "shoot first policy" would be placed into operation on Tuesday was not explained to a nation which had believed the order effective since President Roosevelt's address of late Thursday night. Knox told reporters informally that "it takes a little time to arrange such things."

NEW YORK — Nazi Germany believed in 1940 that the United States had developed a number of fantastic new secret weapons of war, including a ray directed bomber, fog dispellers and "trench cruchers," and directed its spies here to get details about them, a witness testified in federal court in Monday. The witness was William G. Seebold, German born American citizen, who pretended to accept Gestapo orders to spy but turned the information over to the federal bureau of investigation.

AT THE CAPITOL

WASHINGTON — President Roosevelt is expected next Thursday to ask an additional $5,085,000,000 for land-lease aid to nations resisting aggression, it was understood Monday shortly after the President reported to Congress 90 per cent of the original seven billion dollar appropriation had been allocated.

PRESIDENT ROOSEVELT got down to brass tacks in discussion of plans for accelerating armament output at weekend conferences with his chief war production aides. It was considered possible that as the result of these meetings, which took place aboard the presidential yacht Potomac during a cruise on Chesapeake bay, there may be further reorganization of the defense administrative setup or some action by Mr. Roosevelt to strengthen the authority now possessed by the arms production heads.

ACTING SECRETARY of the Navy Sam V. Forestal advised the House on Monday that the army and navy are working jointly on a plan for censorship of communications between the United States and the rest of the world. He did not say whether the plan was being developed for use before or after any state of actual war.

WASHINGTON — The state department announced Monday night henceforth American ships will be permitted to carry war supplies and passengers to large areas of the British Empire from which they had been barred under previous interpretations of the neutrality act. State department officials declined to define precisely areas in which the new interpretation of the law would open up to shipment of war supplies in American flag vessels.

HAWAII NEI

HONOLULU — The twenty-first Hawaiian territorial legislature convened on Monday for a special session for the purpose of enacting emergency measures. Territorial Governor Joseph Poindexter addressed a brief message to the legislators stressing his wish that the session be held as short as possible and asking senators and representatives to concentrate on preparedness matters. He recommended immediate passage of the so-called M Day bill, which would provide funds for any possible emergency. Following up the governor's request, Senator Harold Rice of Maui introduced the first bill in the Senate calling for an appropriation of $5,000,000.

THE SPORTS PARADE

NEW YORK — The sizzling stretch duel between the St. Louis Cardinals and Brooklyn Dodgers for the National League pennant is strictly according to tradition in the senior circuit. Only nine times in the last 25 years has the flag been clinched before the final week, and in 1934 the Cardinals took it on closing day, Sept. 30. With Brooklyn in front by only one and one-half games and 13 contests still to be played, this year's flag might well go right down to the wire.

NEWS ABOARD SHIP:

CLOCKS ABOARD SHIP were retarded one-half hour this morning and will be set back one-half hour each morning at 1:00 AM en route to Honolulu.

The war in Europe was predominate in the news, but it was still 10,000 miles away from the sunny, peaceful Pacific. Although the legislators in the Territory of Hawaii were reported by the wireless to be making emergency preparations, many Americans, including Jim Allen, were not yet convinced that there would be a war in the Pacific, let alone that it would be a prolonged one.

Tuesday night was the Aloha Dinner aboard the *Matsonia*. It was the farewell event before the morning arrival in Honolulu. At their table in the Cabin Class Dining Room, Jim and cabin mate Joe Tury ate from the following menu.

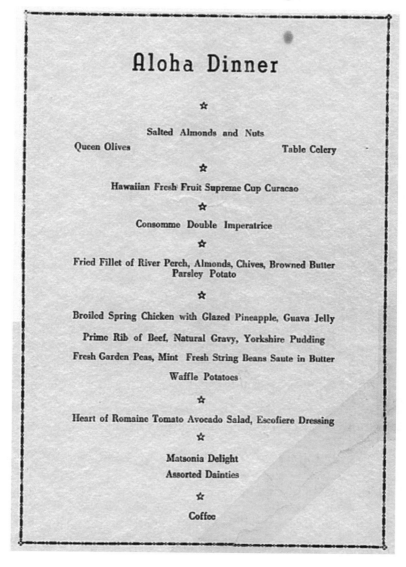

Aloha Dinner

☆

Salted Almonds and Nuts

Queen Olives   Table Celery

☆

Hawaiian Fresh Fruit Supreme Cup Curacao

☆

Consomme Double Imperatrice

☆

Fried Fillet of River Perch, Almonds, Chives, Browned Butter
Parsley Potato

☆

Broiled Spring Chicken with Glazed Pineapple, Guava Jelly

Prime Rib of Beef, Natural Gravy, Yorkshire Pudding

Fresh Garden Peas, Mint   Fresh String Beans Saute in Butter

Waffle Potatoes

☆

Heart of Romaine Tomato Avocado Salad, Escofiere Dressing

☆

Matsonia Delight

Assorted Dainties

☆

Coffee

The Cabin Class menu for the Aloha Dinner was small and not as elaborate or colorful as First Class, but offered basically the same food. (James A. Allen Collection)

Jim had two of the Matsonia Delights, which were ice cream replicas of the SS *Matsonia*. Jim and Tury also bought and split a bottle of wine that night. Jim kept the wine list booklet, with its very colorful drawings of native island men and women in costume, as a souvenir. After the war, Jim wrote in the booklet: "The wine steward had uniform like those in Merry Old England, with a large sash around his neck, from which hung a large key that looked like an old house key. He sure didn't like losing this wine list."

By Aloha Night, several more of the Cabin Class men and women had learned what Jim and Norman Wright had been doing, and getting away with, up in First Class and decided to try it themselves. Dressing up in their finest apparel, the new intruders attempted to crash First Class the same way they knew Jim and Wright had done on previous nights. However, this was not the night to try crashing the First Class Farewell Dinner, and the *Matsonia*'s staff quickly kicked out the gate-crashers. Jim and Wright had already figured out that the last night out of port was not a good time to go upstairs and remained happily in the Cabin Class Dining Room for the night, much to the ire of their imitators.

The next morning Jim and the other passengers could see the Island of Oahu looming in the distance. The tall volcanic mountains provided a lush, green backdrop for the city of Honolulu. As the *Matsonia* docked at the Aloha Tower in Honolulu's harbor, a band played and hundreds of people lined the pier. Island boys swam close to the ship and dived for coins those on board threw into the water for them to retrieve. The color and pageantry of the ship's arrival was a scene that Jim wrote home about saying he "would have bawled if it would have done any good" as he thought about his family back on the West Coast.

When Jim and the other CPNAB workers disembarked the SS *Matsonia*, they were bused to the Bishop Museum where a building was being used to house the men waiting for the next boat to Wake Island. In the meantime, the workers were kept busy on various jobs around Oahu. Jim's luck was with him, as the next boat was leaving in just two days. His wait would be just long enough to see the island, but not so long as to spend too much money.

After putting their bags away where they were assigned to bed down, Jim and Ben Marsh went to see the Honolulu piano repairman the two young woodworkers had met on the *Matsonia*. He had regaled them with stories of what the Hawaiian termites were capable of doing to the wood in pianos in a very short period of time. To hear the man talk, recalls Jim, that hard maple wood used on the baby grand pianos and spinets was like soft angel food cake to these tropical Pacific termites; they zipped right through it. After viewing some of the destroyed instruments, Jim agreed that "what those termites did to the pianos was unbelievable."

On the *Matsonia*, Jim and Marsh had met a woman by the name of Mrs. Dyann Dilly, who befriended the young men and presented them with leis, garlands of fresh flowers, when they alighted on the Honolulu pier. Mrs. Dilly's husband, B. H., played the saxophone in a band at one of the Waikiki Beach nightclubs, and she had been traveling to Hawaii on the *Matsonia* to join him. The three of them had made plans on the *Matsonia* to go to her husband's nightclub across from the Royal Hawaiian Hotel the night that the ship docked. After they had met with the piano man, Jim and Marsh joined some other construction workers from the *Matsonia* and went to the Royal Hawaiian to wait for Mrs. Dilly. Jim vividly remembers the enormous, beautiful green lawn that was all around the hotel and the aged Moana Hotel nearby. By the time he returned to Honolulu in 1985, the lawn had been covered up with cement and asphalt.

When Mrs. Dilly arrived, all of them went across the street to see the show, her treat. Jim later wrote to his sister Hazel from Wake that "while in Honolulu had dinner and danced in as nice a place as in the town." Mrs. Dilly offered that night to keep the young men's good clothes in storage on Oahu until their return. This way the excessive moisture on Wake Island would not ruin the clothes. Having lived in the tropics before, she was aware of how the extreme humidity would ruin them. After Jim became a POW, Mrs. Dilly wrote to Jim's mother and sent the clothes on to Southern California.

Thursday morning, Jim and Marsh met with Mr. Brickner to accompany him on his business rounds selling sporting equipment to the Army. Brickner had rented a car to drive around Oahu, which allowed Jim and Marsh to see much more of the island than they would have otherwise. Jim wrote to his mother:

Here your boy is in Honolulu, Hawaii, having and seeing more than I ever expect. Its wonderful over here just the place for you . . . . Took a ride over the island seen Scoffield Barracks, sugar cane fields, pineapple fields, Pearl Harbor and part of the wilds. Also Red Hills where they are putting those underground oil tanks.

That evening, Jim and Marsh went back to Waikiki Beach and into the turn of the century Moana Hotel for drinks under the massive Banyan Tree in the elegant courtyard. From there, with drinks in hand and a couple of girls beside them, the young men watched the tropical sunset fill the horizon, with the extinct volcano, Diamond Head, as a backdrop. Jim so enjoyed the time in Honolulu that he wrote in the same letter to Hazel that he planned "on staying a week there on my way home." The stopover in Hawaii "turned out to be quite a bunch of fun" for the two nights Jim was there.

Rising early on Friday morning the nineteenth, Jim and the other workers going to Wake Island made their way from Honolulu to Pearl Harbor Naval Station. The new construction workers were scheduled to depart that morning aboard the World War I transport ship USS *Regulus* under Commander J. Kirby Smith. On the Navy dock, Jim found himself in a long line of men waiting to get aboard. The U.S. Navy was taking every precaution to make sure their regulations were not breached by examining all of the workmen's belongings, including tool cases, before they were allowed to

Jim Allen in Honolulu, wearing a Hawaiian lei, or flower necklace, which had been presented to him upon arrival by another passenger. (The Pacific Island Employees Foundation, Inc. [PIEF])

come aboard. The growing pile of confiscated booze behind the inspection team justified the military's suspicions. There would be a lot of men drying out on the ten-day trip to Wake Island, whether they wanted to or not. The United States Navy regulation of no alcohol on board their ships would prevail. Before boarding, the Morrison Knudsen Company took a picture of each of the construction workers, including Jim wearing the Hawaiian lei around his neck that Mrs. Dilly had given him. He looked every bit the Hawaiian tourist, yet disappointingly, he "never saw girls in grass skirts while on Oahu."

Once aboard, Jim found the accommodations less than desirable and definitely far below the *Matsonia's* standards. Regulation United States Navy bunks had been built into the storage hold just below the main deck. This was before climate controlled rooms with air conditioning and the metal enclosed hold felt like an oven in the tropical sun. The heat radiated easily through the steel decking and the hold's stagnant air became hard to breathe. Ammunition was stowed in the hold below the workers, and Commander Kirby was taking no chances with unexpected fires or explosions. A serious looking Navy guard with white leggings and a .45 revolver at his side, was posted in the area twenty-four hours a day to make sure no one smoked around there.

Also unlike the SS *Matsonia*, the *Regulus'* shipboard cuisine seriously lacked flavor and eye appeal. The main course featured liver, liver, and more liver. Jim remembers "it was not even good liver . . . it was cheap too!" The repetitive menu made the men wonder where the money per man went that the Morrison Knudsen Company was paying the Navy to feed the men. Some speculated the good food was being saved for the return trip to Pearl.

It was on the *Regulus* that Jim had his first experience of eating navy beans for breakfast. It seemed strange to him to eat what was usually a lunch or dinner meal instead of the bacon and eggs the old farm boy had been used to. The diet would make the trip seem like forever, let alone the added misery of the heat.

To pass some time, Jim took up an offer of work. The civilian liaison aboard the ship had been told that the navy was offering two dollars a day to any of the civilians who would scrape the old paint off the Captain's Gig, which was a small, official boat for the captain to use when the *Regulus* was in port. The crewmen wanted to varnish it, but needed it scraped first. Being so close to the equator on their voyage made the dirty, hot scraping job even worse for Jim, especially since he was not yet used to the tropical heat. For four days, Jim and other construction workers toiled alongside the Navy crewmen until the gig was scraped down to bare wood.

The plan called for the workers' two dollars a day earnings to be given by the *Regulus* to the Wake Island paymaster, through whom the workers would later collect. Whether the pay was sent or not before the Japanese arrived at Wake, Jim never found out. He never did see the two dollars a day in pay.

Nights aboard the gray ship were barely cooler than the days, with the poky *Regulus* moving stealthily along with all lights blacked out in order to be unseen by other ships traveling in the same area. If the thought of being at war soon had not crossed the construction workers' minds, this helped to push the idea a bit closer towards consciousness.

It was a slow, hot trip with the *Regulus* making about "eight knots with a tail wind," as Jim remembers. The ship's speed was somewhat restrained by the large seagoing barge it towed. Red and green lanterns hung over the port and starboard sides to warn other maritime travelers of the *Regulus'* "tail." Laden with much needed building materials on Wake Island, the added burden on the "slow, old tug's" engines made for slug-like going. Luckily for all involved, no rough seas were experienced on the trip.

3

Wake Island

After ten miserable days, the USS *Regulus* came in sight of the Wake Island atoll the afternoon of 30 September 1941 and anchored off the coral reef that encircled the island like a necklace made of foaming white surf. Located at approximately 19 degrees north latitude and 166 degrees east longitude, Wake Island is 2,301 miles due west of the Hawaiian Islands, but only 1,987 miles from Japan to the northwest. Wake lies farther south than the most southern point of the big island of Hawaii, about the same latitude as Mexico City. An extinct, submerged volcanic crater, three separate islets make up the atoll: Wake, the larger main island; Peale, on the northwest of the crooked V-shaped Wake's upper arm and Wilkes to the northwest of Wake's lower arm. The atoll is very small, only four-and one-half miles long and two-and-one-quarter miles wide, barely the size of a modern airport. In the center of the three islands is a lagoon, which Pan American's Clipper seaplanes used as a landing pad when crossing the Pacific Ocean. Pan Am had maintained a hotel for passengers and a refueling station on Peale Island since 1935, and had built a ramp onto shore for the clippers to use. The arrival of a clipper was a big entertainment event on the remote island. The construction men would pool their bets as to when the clipper's pontoons would touch down on the lagoon's azure water.

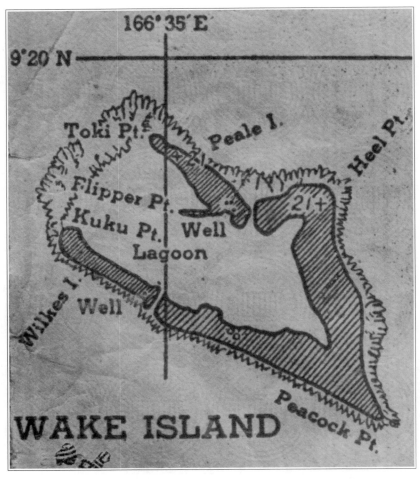

The three islets of the Wake atoll: Peale, Wake. and Wilkes. This map, found on an airmail envelope Jim sent to his sister, shows the high point of Wake at just twenty-one feet above sea level.

Originally devoid of much life other than scrub brush, the isolated atoll was home to sea birds that used it as a sanctuary. With no natural predators native to Wake, thousands of birds of several different species could be found living peacefully, including the strange looking goonie birds. Once explorers discovered the island, part of their stowaway rat population jumped ship, creating hazards for the sea birds and their egg-laden nests. Still, the birds overwhelmingly outnumbered the rats and people.

Wake Island from the air in 1985. Peacock Point is located to the extreme left out of camera range. Wilkes Island is in the middle of the picture, across the lagoon. Peale Island is located to the far right. In 1941 the Contractor's Camp 2 was located on Wake Island (foreground, far right side) just across a narrow inlet from Peale Island. (Albert L. Brueck/James A. Allen Collection)

Jim Allen's first view of the tiny speck of land from the deck of the *Regulus* revealed little from that great distance except to confirm what Jim already knew from geography books and information given by the CPNAB and Morrison Knudsen. Wake Island rose only twenty-one feet above sea level at its highest elevation. As a result, the island's water tower was clearly visible on the horizon. Typhoons of past seasons had occasionally scoured the low-lying island clean of vegetation. The previous year, one traversed the atoll at 135 mph. Jim would see the remains of eight-inch ironwood trees that had been broken off in that storm. The new workers were thankful that typhoon season was just about over.

Jim, later ashore, found Wake to be, "flat, no trees, just brush and humid," and would witness "waves on the ocean higher than the trees' tops on Wilkes Island."

The thick, sharp coral reef made it impossible for the *Regulus*, or any other ship, to come in close to Wake and dock. The *Regulus* and its barge had to lie offshore and transport people and materials by a smaller boat called a lighter. This small boat could pass through the dredged channel between Wilkes and Wake Islands and run to the calm, safe water of the lagoon to a boat landing on the western edge of Wake to offload men and materials. This made for exciting trips back and forth between the ship and shore unloading new arrivals. One could only hope not to capsize and become dinner for the many sharks that swam in the warm tropical waters.

Jim and several other CPNAB workers went down the ladder on the side of the *Regulus* with bags in tow. About thirty feet down, they stood on the small landing platform and watched the rocking lighter and waited until the two boats were synchronized enough for the men to leap into the lighter. Once everything was secured, the lighter turned away from the *Regulus* and headed for shore. In the distance the men could see a Pan Am Clipper land on the lagoon. Jim was impressed with how big the Clippers were. None of the newly arriving men had any regrets leaving the *Regulus*; the "hell" cruise was finally over.

Although the new men seemed anxious to leave the *Regulus* and join the other thousand or so construction workers, Jim would discover the next day that many of the workers on the island "sure wish they were home. They took fifty or sixty back on the boat [*Regulus*] today. More would have went if the boat would of took them." He later wrote a friend, Bill Goodman, that "There's plenty of the fellows that wish they never seen this place."

Once ashore on Wake, the CPNAB/Morrison Knudsen construction men were met by company representatives who took them over to Camp 2, where the civilians were housed in a series of "H" shaped barracks. Camp 2 was close to the point of highest elevation on the atoll, which didn't seem very high when you looked out over the lagoon or over the reefs to the ocean. It appeared that a good wave in a storm could just wash right over Wake without too much effort. The relatively new barracks for the construction workers consisted of two parallel single-story wood frame buildings, which had beds along the outside walls and a passageway down the center. The beds were partitioned off in pairs with five foot tall walls, so the workers had some privacy in the big, airy building. Windows with awnings across were left wide open for maximum ventilation. In addition to the beds, the partitioned spaces had two lockers for the occupants' belongings and provided wall space for individual decorating with photographs and magazine pictures. Two barracks buildings were connected with an enclosed passageway that held in the middle a lavatory with sinks, toilets and showers, all using salt water. A two gallon bucket of fresh water to rinse off with was available for pick up at the powerhouse before the men took a shower. Jim wrote home his first night after work, that when using the salt water "all you taste out of it is fish and it sure makes you feel sticky." Some of the men solved this problem by taking advantage of a passing rainstorm and standing in the rain with a bar of soap to get rid of the "saltwater stickies." As for the drinking water, Jim wrote that it "tastes like cistern water; ice cold everywhere."

Not far from the living quarters was the Contractors Hospital building. The military on the island had their own sick bay, or hospital. The men who made the journey to Wake were exceptionally healthy with little or no illness. However, no matter how careful, accidents and injuries occur around construction sites. Because of this, the Contractors Hospital was well supplied to take care of any emergencies as well as dehydration problems with associated constipation and piles, or hemorrhoids, and circumcisions, as Jim relates, "on the house." Dental care was also available, and Jim was able to have three cavities taken care of within the first two months of arriving. It was fortunate he did, for it prevented worse problems in the next few years.

The new island inhabitants discovered that no matter where you went on the atoll, the sound of the pounding surf was heard, all the louder when whipped up by passing storms. At Camp 2, Jim could look out and "see the waves or spray above the trees on the next island [Wilkes] across the lagoon." The noise of the surf on the outlying reef was loud enough on 8 December to drown out the Japanese attack planes until they were almost directly above their target.

While on Wake Island, part of Jim's life was made easier by the Chinese stewards who took care of the construction workers' barracks. They cleaned, made and changed beds, so that the workers didn't have to do anything but take care of themselves. This was a great change from home and after a few days of the hot and tiring construction work, a welcome one. On the down side of the situation was the laundry. As Jim said when he wrote home to his mother on 19 October, his clothes "all come back the same color."

The Morrison Knudsen Company had started paying Jim and the other workers a salary when they had boarded the SS *Matsonia*. Once settled in on Wake Island, Jim looked forward

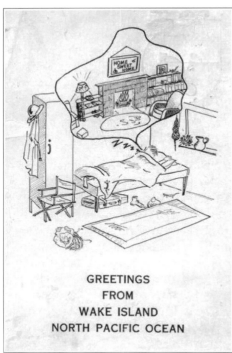

GREETINGS
FROM
WAKE ISLAND
NORTH PACIFIC OCEAN

A standard postcard for the men to send from Wake Island depicting a typical sleeping area in the barracks. The postage cost one-cent to mail to the United States. On the back of this postcard Jim wrote to his brother, "Dear Bill, This is Home Sweet Home. You see it not as good as Hoped. Be good. James." Apparently this card had traveled from Wake aboard one of the Navy vessels bringing supplies and arrived in Hawaii after the Japanese attack since it has a 16 December 1941 Navy Yard, Pearl Harbor, Honolulu postmark, not the regular civilian Honolulu postmark that most of Jim's other letters bore. The card also bears a purple CENSOR stamp indicating wartime restrictions were already in force. (James A. Allen Collection)

to the next day and beginning his new job on the atoll. On Wednesday morning, 1 October, Jim rose at 5:45 AM, eager to start. He had breakfast at 6:00, and at 7:00 began the usual nine hour workday on the hot and humid tropical islet. There followed six day work weeks with Sundays usually off, except for the one or two that Jim worked to complete barracks for the pilots ferrying airplanes to the Philippines.

Jim's first day on the job took him over the small bridge that connected Wake Island to Peale Island, a short distance from Camp 2. Arriving by truck at the two buildings being constructed there, he was assigned to work on the interior partitions of the future Marine barracks. Also at the Peale Island site were the hospital building and a warehouse. Jim had the good fortune to be assigned interior jobs or ones with a roof over his head to keep the sun off the majority of his time on the atoll.

By the time Jim went to bed that first night, he "was so tired my legs wanted to bend." At least there was a good bed "just like the soldiers [had] at Camp Roberts" to fall into. The workers were also provided with innerspring mattresses that when new were very comfortable. But over time being in the hot, humid, tropical climate of Wake Island, as Jim wrote to his friend Bill Goodman, the "beds smell like moldy hay, *no* kidding your dress shoes mold [and are] covered with green fuzz. Clothes mildew."

But that was in the future. At 7:00 PM on 1 October Jim was quite content with what he found on Wake and wrote:

> Well, mother, am the luckiest guy in the world, I do believe. I have had nothing but the best of it. I sure hope it holds out. Am doing all right really at a better job than if I'd of been working for the fellows before. Well, guess will close and write when the next Clipper takes off for Los Angeles.
>
> As ever
>
> James A. Allen
>
> The luckiest fellow in the world I do believe for the present. Address all as James A. Allen as there's a James S. Allen here.

Jim was definitely content with his lot at that moment. Writing on 19 October, though, Jim was concerned because he had only received one letter from his mother. Far away from family and friends, mail was a lifeline of information and continuity for the construction workers and Jim was impatient to hear from everyone, which he would eventually do. In the meantime, he was "glad to hear you [Viola] are [feeling] better. Just keep your chin up & you'll see a light some of these days. The Old World will settle down & we'll all be back together." Part of Jim's concern about his mother's well-being was the fact that Viola had been plagued with rheumatoid arthritis since 1935, getting a bit worse each year. By the time Jim left for Wake Island, her condition had deteriorated to the point that she was using a stool to sit on while washing dishes or preparing vegetables at the kitchen sink.

On Wake Island, keeping hard-working construction men happy required lots of good food and the contractor's cooks and bakers did an outstanding job. The Morrison Knudsen Company cooks had the most modern equipment available and the ingredients to make almost anything. From a poor family during the

Depression, Jim was always appreciative of good food, especially after the USS *Regulus* voyage. Jim found the answer to his prayers at the Civilian Mess Hall with an unlimited supply of meat, vegetables, fresh bread, and desserts to build the bodies up after working at the laborious construction jobs. In the construction workers' Civilian Mess Hall at Camp 2, the men sat on benches at long tables and the food was served family style on big platters. During a meal if a serving platter became empty, the workers would hold it up in the air and one of the Chinese waiters would grab it. Or if the diner happened to be towards the middle of the table, the platter would be passed hand to hand in the air until it reached the table's end where it would be placed into the hands of the watchful waiter. In a flash, the waiter would have returned with the replenished platter, food piled high, to be passed back to its point of origin. Jim's first experience with lamb and mint jelly, which he thoroughly enjoyed, was on Wake Island at the Camp 2 Civilian Mess Hall. "You could eat all the mint jelly you wanted and they'd just bring you more," Jim remembers nostalgically. But it is the pies that Jim remembers most, even after almost sixty years. The excellent bakers prepared pies, especially coconut crème, which would melt in one's mouth. According to Jim, "You didn't have to chew it. Just put it in your mouth and it went down. It was effortless, believe me." Jim wrote home to his family in his 26 October letter that he had added fifteen pounds to his former 160 pound, five feet eleven and one-half inch frame, in spite of the hard work, heat and humidity. No wonder that mess hall was the scene of many a Wake Island worker's dreams in the coming years as a prisoner of war.

When not working, there were many things for the thousand-plus construction men to do on the atoll. For recreation there was shell or shark hunting along the ocean front, outdoor movies six times a week, sports such as baseball, a recreation room with games like checkers, a library, tennis courts, and, of course, swimming. The swimming pools were basically big holes on the Wake side of the gap between the Peale and Wake islands. Big gravel screens were employed to keep the sharks and octopus out. After every storm, the men used nets to get rid of the intruders that found their way into the pool.

The outdoor movies were popular even though it rained most every day or night. The men would wear a poncho to stay dry while the film was running. One evening, Jim joined the other men to watch Dorothy Lamour in *Hurricane*. At the same time, a real hurricane, known as a typhoon in the Pacific Ocean, was blowing by one side of the island with accompanying heavy rain and strong winds. Since the workers had already tied down everything loose that afternoon, they just sat through it all in ponchos and enjoyed the entertainment of seeing a woman, even if it was only on a screen. The only women on Wake when Jim arrived were the Pan Am manager's wife and construction General Superintendent Dan Teters' wife, Florence, as opposed to over 1,500 men. When the Pan Am Clipper flew in, the number of women might climb one or two for the night, depending on the gender of the plane's passengers and crew. By Thanksgiving, the women would all be evacuated back to the States before hostilities broke out.

After the movies, a snack was always available. The Camp 2 kitchen had a long window with a shelf on it and the bakers would set out whole, uncut pies for anyone who was hungry to take and eat. "You couldn't take a piece of pie, you had to take a whole pie," Jim has recalled. The Camp 2 men could eat what they wanted of the pie and then leave the rest in the barracks, where it always disappeared. Jim doesn't "remember a pie not being completely eaten."

By 8 November even the delicious pies grew a bit stale for Jim. He wrote to his mother that "Just as I had planned the food heres like at Camp Roberts or a restaurant good for a while but its not like home cooking. It gets old." Although reality had hit with the food, Jim was content with the employment. He also wrote in that 8 November letter:

> The job and work here is just like in the States. You like it today and tomorrow you cuss it. And wish you had a different [job] but its OK . . . . don't get me wrong I'm not sorry I'm here for [I'm] not. Of course I'll be glad to get back home that's understood but Mother I can make a lot of good money here.

Jim was pleased with work overall and apparently his bosses with him. In an addendum to the same letter before it was mailed, Jim wrote:

> Here it is Sunday 4:15 PM. Another day done. Heard good news today & it looks as though within six month I may get a foreman's job. I don't know but things are

shaping up very nicely. It doesn't pay very much more. But will be able to get a start and work on up because I can do it so don't be surprised if I write & tell you I am a foreman telling the other fellows what to do Ha! Ha! Like I did Billie Hazel & Jerald once in a while Jerald if you do take & want to come sign up as Carpenter's helper not labor [or] for it pays a little more money & if it does come to pass that I do get to be foreman I can get you stepped up to carpenter. Understand Write & tell me what you think about it and all about yourself.

As ever

James

P.S. don't say anything about this foreman stuff because I'm a long Ways from it yet but I have hopes.

On his days off, Jim was eager to enjoy and explore the atoll. The role of beachcomber suited him just fine. The first Sunday he had off, Jim went shell hunting and found a few "nice ones" to send home. Later in the day, he was the umpire for a baseball game, always an under-appreciated job. Jim wrote his mother that the "game lasted 4 innings and one team didn't like the way I was calling the balls and strikes." Another activity he tried normally on Sundays was shark fishing at Wake Island's Peacock Point. Jim wanted to make a swagger stick, similar to the ones other men on the island were making, using a hooked shark's backbone. Popular with the British Officers in India, swagger sticks were carried there when in uniform and, it was thought, lent a dashing air to those who held one.

Using just a heavy line and hook but no rod, Jim threw the baited line out into the reef's sparkling sapphire blue water. After a shark was hooked, Jim backed up on the beach with the line around his rear. Once on the beach, Jim sank the hunting knife he had bought on Wake Island through the tough hide and into the belly. Removing the liver, Jim would throw it out into the water.

When you did that, that really got the sharks coming in. No great big ones, but lots of them. And a five foot shark, all he needed was a foot of water and he could go like the wind. I'd stand on a piece of coral and see them going all around that piece of coral and I'd only be about a foot out of the water."

After chumming the water with the liver, and later the rest of the hooked shark, it was easy to get another shark to take your baited line. Hoping to hook at least an eight footer, the largest Jim caught was a five, too short for a swagger stick.

Jim and the other construction workers were also able to fish from a large floating construction barge off the reef and did so on Thanksgiving Day. When out in the sun and without shade, even fishing was hot labor in the tropics and not all that enjoyable. Still the men were able to catch three foot electric eels and tuna, although the tuna would usually be half eaten by sharks before it could be landed.

By Thanksgiving Jim was thinking ahead to Christmas and instructed his mother by letter to:

"<u>take and draw out five dollars out of the bank</u> [Jim's account Morrison Knudsen put wages in automatically since there was not a bank on Wake] <u>for Xmas and buy food for a nice dinner. Shorty, Dorothy and all that you'd like to have there for dinner and</u> [throw] a <u>big time for me</u>."

Apparently Jim knew his mother well and underlined so she should follow his directions. But during the entire time he was gone, Viola never took any money out of Jim's account to use. His earnings were intact when he returned to the States in 1945.

Jim also had his siblings on his mind and had written earlier for Viola to take money out of his account in the spring for his sister and brother to have gifts and new clothes for their graduations and "fix them up first class <u>all</u>. Spend up to 100 dollars if you have to. Don't forget." In some ways being the oldest in a single parent family, and one who took his responsibilities seriously, made Jim act more like a father than a brother. He had also admonished Viola to get the siblings' teeth fixed with his money. He'd been grateful for the dental care and three fillings that the company dentist had done on Wake and knew that the family needed help since money was scarce.

Wake was a beehive of activity by the time Jim arrived in October 1941. The airfield was partially completed with one runway in place, enabling military planes to begin landing on the hard-packed crushed coral surface and setting up support facilities. A fuel dump was already in position nearby and additional roads around the island were being bulldozed. Dredging continued in the lagoon and between Wake and Wilkes Islands. Planners looked forward to the day when large ships, and possibly submarines, would be able to anchor in the lagoon's protected waters. All the necessities for a naval air station were in place or being constructed by the CPNAB workers.

Routine as life soon became for Jim on Wake, international events continued to churn, especially between the United States and Japan. For those who were interested, news was available in the *WigWag*, the island's newspaper put out by the Marine Wake Island Detachment. Of course the scuttlebutt circulated much faster than the official news. Scuttlebutt is an old navy term, referring to the butt or small cask of water that the crew of sailing ships drank from. The butt was located on the ship's gun deck above a drain called a scuttle. Like the watercoolers of yesteryear, or the soda machines of today, the butt on the scuttle was a place where the sailors would congregate and pass on information, both true and erroneous.

Jim wrote his mother on 19 October, "as far as the Japs are concerned well nobody seems to be the least bit worried about them in fact." But by the 26 October, a letter Jim wrote to his sister, Hazel, gives a different perspective and makes it relatively easy to piece together what the military leaders were thinking by their actions.

> This little island home of ours out here in mid Pacific Ocean is sure a busy place theres 4 or 5 ships lieing out off shore waiting for the sea to quiet down so they can unload you see we haven't any harbor here yet will have someday besides there an Aircraft tender, two subs & battleships out over the horizon You just see their steam & Army bombers they've been coming & going the last three days. Things are getting bad for United States I'd say as we have went to 10 hours a day & two shifts day & night building temporary barracks for Army pilots & staff Officers there coming before long because we are to finish 5 barracks in 5 days.
>
> The wind blows & rains terrible out here but I feel better and Getting fat 180 lbs stuffed. 15 lbs since I seen you it's not bad here at all. Have lots of fun. Get alfull tired it's the climate not use to it but will be before long.

I'm in a 5 inch gun crew out here we practice twice a week will shoot them before long show every night. I sent you a letter by boat three weeks ago you'll get it before Xmas I hope. Its got my bank book in it. I plan on staying my nine months and am going to sell my car & if you want to go to school next fall I'll lend you 4 or 5 hundred dollars to go but you must pay it back full no interest just pay back the principal that's up to you if you go to school.

Please keep good record of my bill & get a receipt for everything pay everything off just as fast as you get enough money. The old gal where the car is pay her by the month I gave her two dollars one month rent don't pay any in advance. Be a good girl & help mother study hard. Write me all the news. Am sending you a special envelope of Wake Island. Its getting close to show time [for] *Reckless Living* [a movie].

Hazel we have the most beautiful moon out here & its warm & balmy most of the time. Just sleep in your pajamas a sheet sometimes along in the morning. Had two teeth filled one more to go. Guess this is all for now.

Your Brother
James

The Marines stationed on Wake Island for its defense had more than enough equipment on hand in the event of attack, but lacked the men to use it all effectively. An official request was made to the civilian construction General Superintendent, Dan Teters, for volunteers from among the civilian construction workers. They would be trained to help out with Wake's defense twice a week in their free time. Not all the roughly 1,100 civilians were eager to play soldier on their day or evening off, but a few hundred, including Jim, were game to volunteer.

About one of his early training experiences Jim wrote home to his family that, "we volunteer for different gun and etc. The [Marine] officers are swell. In fact they have to be, I guess. The Lt. [Clarence "Barney" Barninger] wanted me to say bore clear. I kept yelling clear bore. He just smiled. I finally got it straight. You see I am what they call a plugger."

As a "plugger," Jim was to take a swab, a long stick with a bit of wet cloth at one end, and wipe out the large gun's barrel after the gun was fired. The wet cloth would extinguish and pick up any of the coals left behind by the silk material that encapsulated each load of gunpowder. After the plugger, or rammer, cleared the barrel, the load of powder and the projectile would be loaded by others on the gun crew and then fired. The process would be repeated as rapidly as possible for as long as needed. Practice makes perfect, or at least a bit faster. Jim wrote the following about his plugger efforts to his friend, Bill Goodman, on Thanksgiving Day.

> I am busy all the time there's a show 6 nights a week & the other night we go practice with our 5 inch gun at dark. lots of fun I am the rammer we loaded in 6 seconds last time out getting better but the Marines can load in 2 seconds they're really good.

Jim's group was to handle live ammunition and really fire the five-inch gun for the first time at the scheduled practice for Thursday, the 11 December. Up until that day, the volunteer gun crews were to practice with dummies and substitutes.

Jim continued to drill with Battery B and the five-inch gun located at Toki Point on Peale for the next several weeks, getting more proficient all the time. The five inchers were broadside guns off World War I battleships. The Marine Defense Detachment also had three-inch anti-aircraft gun emplacements, with four three-inch guns each, located around the island for defense. The civilian volunteers could practice their newly acquired skills twice a week on these guns, under Marine supervision. As the weeks went by and relations between the United States and Japan continued to deteriorate, it began to appear that the volunteers might really be put to use.

Time for the men on Wake Island was running out as the Japanese attack fleet grew closer. Whether he was trying not to worry his mother or just plain oblivious, Jim's letter home on 4 December revealed little concern over a future war.

> Dear Mother,
> Will start a letter now & finish when mail closes. Never felt better in my whole life its swell here quiet last two days no wind but its very unusual the wind was in [the] southwest for about 4 hours Saturday & we expected we might get a blow. But not yet maybe later [hear they're] having a storm off the coast.
> This is Sunday Eve didn't work today played ball &

sharpened 4 [saws] in the morning cut out paper dolls [pinups] out of my December Esquire got it sat night also got a letter from Al Brown nice letter remember Mary his niece from Ill. He sent her address Ha! Ha! Won 7 dollars today on the wind. I bet the boys the wind wouldn't blow 45 miles an hour in twenty four hours & it didn't Ha! Ha! Again.

Its about show time now. So will be closing before long. You had ought to see my stall pictures every where whiskey bottles women & horses have Whirlaway [the racehorse] too. Sure peps up the looks of the place all the fellows stop by & make comments about the pictures. You can guess what they say.

Here it is Tuesday [meant Thursday, December 4] night & everything o.k. Bombers [United States military] arrived today 12 in all they are to be stationed here. Last night Lt. [Barninger] gave a talk on the 5 inch gun of which I am a member of the crew. About what it would do In fact all about it. Sure interesting.

We are getting a lot of Service men here on the island.

Its been very hot here the last two days and my veins are very big nothing to worry about made $268.00 last month. Worked 186 hours regular time and 40 hours overtime 8 hours straight overtime. Not bad eh! We had our first blackout last night sure seems funny all the lights on the island are out it had happen at 9:30 just a practice one. Am getting more & more use to this place & like it more everyday. Am a lead man now getting in better every day am making more & more friends. guess had better close

James

Will be sending a box home with clothes in it of what have you [souvenirs]. Look at them & keep for me.

This would be the last letter Viola received from Wake Island.

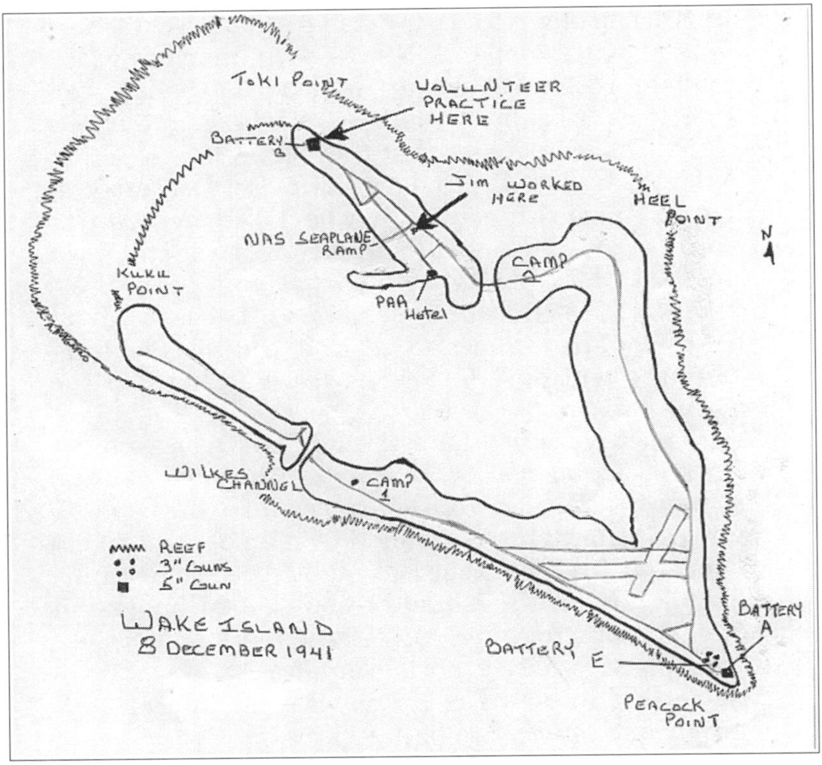
TOKI POINT
VOLUNTEER PRACTICE HERE
BATTERY B
JIM WORKED HERE
HEEL POINT
N
NAS SEAPLANE RAMP
CAMP 2
PAA Hotel
KUKU POINT
WILKES CHANNEL
CAMP 1
REEF
3" GUNS
5" GUN
WAKE ISLAND
8 DECEMBER 1941
BATTERY A
BATTERY E
PEACOCK POINT

Wake Island before the first bombing raid. Jim had a moderate walk from Camp 2 and his living quarters on Wake Island to Peale Island where he worked on the interior of a new barracks for the military personnel.

4

Besieged!

Located to the west of the International Date Line, Wake Island is always one calendar day ahead of the Hawaiian Islands and North America. The slogan, "Where America's Day Begins," would be used for Wake in the future. It was a peacefully routine Sunday morning at 7:50 AM, 7 December 1941, at Pearl Harbor, Hawaii, and at the exact same time the construction workers on Wake Island, approximately 2,000 miles to the west, were getting up at 5:50 AM, a day later. Monday morning, 8 December 1941, was a regular workday on Wake, not yet so different from any other. That quickly changed.

Years later Jim recalled, "The Japanese weren't supposed to hurt us. Not with all that propaganda [the United States Government] give all them years." The government had been publishing a line about the United States' (read between the lines as "Western white men's") superiority to the Japanese and had succeeded quite well with the effort. The majority of the American public was gullible, wanting to believe they would not be involved in the ongoing worldwide war. They did not want to suffer the deprivations those in Europe, and elsewhere, were enduring. This was one of the reasons the well executed attack on Pearl Harbor was such a shock to U.S. citizens. Jim remembers that he was told "they [the Japanese] couldn't see . . . our navy could whip 'em in nothing flat, it was awful."

Prior to the Pearl Harbor bombardment, nobody believed the
"inferior" Japanese Empire could ever beat the United States,
either literally or figuratively.

Although the Navy men and Marines stationed on the atoll
might have received information about Japan's early morning
attack on the U.S. Naval Fleet at Pearl Harbor, the average construction worker, like Jim, heard only the normal scuttlebutt.
As Jim climbed into the back of a flatbed semi-truck, used to
transport men around the island, to go to his Peale Island work
site, he noticed that the Marines driving past in their jeep wore
metal combat helmets. Sitting on the benches in the back of the
truck gave Jim a vantage point from which to survey the island
and to see if anything else was going on out of the ordinary. Jim
spied more busy activity going on at that time of the morning
than he had in the past two months. Others had also noticed
the deviance from routine, and the scuttlebutt started flowing
while the construction workers went about their normal jobs.

The truck/taxi dropped Jim off on the Peale Island main
road and he walked down the side road toward the new Marine Mess Hall to continue working on the interior. At 10:00
AM, Jim heard the engines of Pan Am's "Philippine" Clipper
coming in to land at the lagoon and tie up at the Pan Am pier
near the hotel, a few hundred yards away. Having heard it
take off in the normal manner earlier that morning, the Philippine Clipper's return announced something was wrong. From
a window, Jim watched the Clipper dump its fuel load in preparation to land and knew that bad weather, a broken part, or
something else had forced the seaplane to turn around.

At a few minutes before noon, Jim put down his tools and
headed out the door to catch up with the others who had
already left for the truck/taxi to go to lunch at the Civilian
Mess Hall at Camp 2. As he rounded the southwest corner of
the building to walk towards the pick-up point, Jim remembers, "The island started shaking and the glass windows in
the warehouse across the road began quivering." Jim looked
toward the airfield across the lagoon and saw a formation of
Japanese bombers heading toward the uncompleted mess hall
and him. Jim turned around and ran about seventy-five yards
before he dived for cover under a nearby bush and remained
as still as possible. The bush was not much protection. When
another bomb was dropped, a small shrapnel fragment ripped
into Jim's back.

The attacking planes, with the bright red Rising Sun painted on their wings, were flying low over the buildings, strafing them with machine gun fire. One plane flew so low that Jim could see the "crewman in the clear plastic nose . . . [and he] could have thrown a rock at him."

After a moment or two, the first wave of Japanese bombers were gone and Jim got up to start running for better cover. As he got up, Jim saw a second wave of bombers headed his way.

During times of severe stress, thoughts can come into consciousness that might seem strange at that particular time, but may also be useful. In an instant, as Jim Allen was running, a trivial conversation from the past came back to him.

In 1940, when Jim was working at the California Store Fixtures Company on Long Beach Boulevard, he and his boss, Jack Huskie, were eating their lunches on the sidewalk in front of the store when a one-armed man selling pencils came by. A conversation ensued and this man claimed to have been with other American airmen as part of the Flying Tigers, or *Fei Hui* as the Chinese referred to them. Although not officially backed by the U.S. Government, the Tigers were helping the Chinese resist the current Japanese aggression. Back in the United States because he had lost his arm, the man related how, as a machine gunner in the tail of a plane, he had fun shooting the Japanese army officers as they ran for cover during a raid. The man explained that their running made the soldiers all the easier to see and be picked off than if they had remained still.

As fast as the thought came to him, Jim dropped on to the crushed coral surface beneath him, scrapping his belly on the sharp pieces of stone. Lying still so as to be invisible, the atoll continued to shake with bullets and shrapnel landing around him, but he wasn't hit this time. The attack itself had lasted only about twelve minutes, but it seemed much longer to Jim. Later, when all the destruction was tallied, Jim would realize how lucky he was. Of the eighty-five dead that day, there were twenty-three Marines, two Navy men, ten Pan Am Chamorro employees from Guam and around fifty civilian construction workers.

Jim continued to lie motionless on the ground until he could no longer hear or feel the vibrations of the low flying enemy bombers. Then he began to walk the short distance to the crushed coral main road. In a few minutes, Jim saw the labor foreman, John L, Clelan leading a group of men down the road. Since the foreman always called the construction workers under his supervision his "lambs," it was very appropriate for him to be leading a "flock" during a traumatic episode. Noticing that Jim was bleeding, the foreman opened the first-aid kit he always carried and put a temporary bandage on Jim's back wound. That completed, the group of agitated construction worker "lambs" continued to follow their "shepherd" and walk toward the bridge for Wake Island.

Before long, the men met the truck/taxi coming their way and rode back over the bridge to Camp 1 where they found hundreds of other workers gathering and talking, excited and angry. The construction workers had been told by the Morrison Knudsen Company that, in the event of hostilities, military ships would evacuate them immediately to Hawaii or the States. Unfortunately for the men that counted on this rescue, the closest ships were over 2,000 miles away. There was also the problem that some of those U.S. Navy ships had just been damaged or destroyed while at anchor in Pearl Harbor and couldn't get underway. On 7/8 December 1941 a civilian rescue was not in the forefront of Navy leaders' minds.

Jim and the others in his "flock" went inside the mess hall just as the contractors' General Superintendent, Dan Teters, was beginning to address the workers. Over the din of disgruntled men, Teters told all those who had previously been trained to use the military's equipment to head out to Camp 1, the tent city where the Marines were billeted. Camp 1 was basically in the same position on Wake's lower arm as Camp 2 was on the upper. They were separated by the lagoon and about five miles of road.

Upon their arrival at Camp 1, Jim and the men with him were told to go into a supply tent where U.S. Marines would issue each construction worker volunteer a new .30-06 rifle and twenty rounds of ammunition. Once there, all the workers were told to reach into a rifle box and grab one. The new rifles were completely covered in a heavy, greasy, sticky, caramel colored substance called cosmoline, which preserved them from the excessive humidity. The Marine in charge instructed the group to get a piece of rag and some gasoline that was stored nearby to clean their guns. Jim's group of volunteers began the difficult task of getting the sticky mess off each gun's parts. Even with the gasoline to help break down the cosmoline, cleaning the guns was a long and difficult process in the hot tropical sun. An added discomfort was not knowing when the

Taken from the Japanese propaganda magazine *Freedom*, this photo shows Wake Island from a Japanese plane, probably during the first attack wave. On the left are the barracks and storage buildings at Camp 2, The large white square in the upper part of the photo belongs to Pan Am. The new barracks Jim was working on just prior to the attack are just to the right of the white square, under the black smoke. Jim also was under that smoke, dodging aircraft when this picture was taken. (*Freedom*/James A. Allen Collection)

next bomber would be overhead, which made many of the men anxious. Since the roar of the breakers on the atoll's reefs was so loud and constant, the Japanese bombing planes could be almost directly overhead before the men would hear them. This made many of the men anxious, constantly looking up and over their shoulders to see if any planes were coming.

Holding clean rifles, civilian volunteers Jim Allen, Jack Hoskins, Ira Ellis Stoddard, Floyd F. Forsberg, Thomas L. Fenwick, Nerbert H. Gilbertson and the two Goodpasture brothers, Dorles Dewey and John Ivan, started walking down the hot coral road. Taking the right fork, the volunteers headed southeast toward Peacock Point and Battery A, not quite a mile away. Lieutenant Barney Barninger was the officer in charge of the five-inch gun there. They had all drilled with the lieutenant twice a week at Toki Point since they had volunteered in October. However, the volunteers had not necessarily been assigned to a specific location in the event of a crisis. So, not having been instructed to do otherwise, they headed to where they would find Lt. Barninger and do what he told them.

A few yards to the north of Battery A, the civilian volunteers were hailed by some Marines at Battery E anti-aircraft gun emplacement. The Marines of the Gun One crew hung over the top of the sandbag wall that protected the anti-aircraft gun and pleaded with the rifle toting civilian volunteers to help them out.

The anti-aircraft, or AA, batteries consisted of four, three-inch AA guns grouped together in one location, protected as well as could be. Although in the same area, each gun was a short distance from the others in an effort to keep them from all being destroyed by one bomb. Battery E was short ammunition passers for their gun crews and desperately needed the civilian volunteers to fill in on Gun One, passing ammunition hand over hand until it reached the Marines on the gun platform where it would be loaded into the AA gun, aimed, and fired at a target. The civilian volunteers were tired of walking miles around the atoll in the hot afternoon sun and took up the Battery E Marines offer. Lt. Barninger and Battery A couldn't possibly need them as much as Gun One at Battery E.

Lieutenant William Wallis "Wally" Lewis was the Commanding Officer (C)) of Battery E, with Gunnery Sergeant Krawie. Once the civilian volunteers were inside Gun One's sandbag enclosure, the Gun Captain, Sergeant Gilson A. Tallentire, went over in general terms what they could expect to be doing. The men would be in a line, passing the ammunition, hand over hand, from its storage area inside the sandbag walls. As Jim recalls, Tallentire went over things in general since, "We were not a bunch of dummies, it was no big deal mechanically." Jim, for one, had seen a three-inch gun fired before in 1940. He was assigned by Tallentire to stand next to the gun platform and hand the ammunition up to the Marines.

Once at the three-inch gun placement, Jim did not leave for the next sixteen days unless given permission by Lieutenant Wally Lewis via Gun Captain Sergeant Tallentire. Food would be delivered to battle locations by a civilian volunteer cooking group headed by Dan Teters. Unlike the majority of the civilians (only 312 could be cited by name after the war as helping in the defense of the island), Jim had volunteered and would help as long as necessary. Some civilians had headed into the brush to hide at the first sign of trouble. They only slunk back to the camp to get

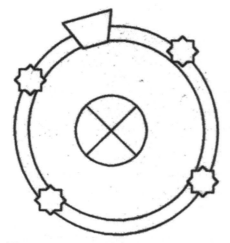

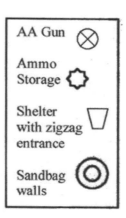

AA Gun	⊗
Ammo Storage	⬡
Shelter with zigzag entrance	⊽
Sandbag walls	◎

Diagram of the Battery E Gun One site. Sandbag walls were about six feet high with the ammunition storage areas built into them. Each gun site was made of hundreds of sand-filled burlap bags. (L. A. Magnino)

supplies before returning to their hiding places.

Late in the afternoon of the eighth, when Lieutenant Lewis was convinced that the Japanese would not be returning that day, he gave Jim permission to leave Gun One and get his wound treated. Jim headed for the hospital and was tended by the Navy doctor, Lieutenant Gustav Mason Kahn. Luckily the coral scrapes Jim suffered during the attack were minor while the shrapnel wound, located mid back on the left side, was a clean one and not large. The wounds would

This three-inch anti-aircraft gun emplacement in Samoa during World War II, was similar to the one on Wake Island that Jim Allen helped defend. Jim recollects Gun One's sandbagged walls were higher than this one. (Heinle, *The Defense of Wake*)

heal quickly. Jim would not have the added concern of infection as a prisoner of war, although that prospect was far from his mind at this time.

Five of the civilian volunteers at Battery E. (left to right): Jack Hoskins of Okanogen, Washington; Tom Fenwick of Pocatello, Idaho; Ira Ellis Stoddard of Prosser, Washington; Floyd Forsberg of Hollywood, California; Nerbert H. Gilbertson of Portland, Oregon. (All photographs PIEF)

Back at Battery E, Jim took his place with the Gun One crew, which was made up of eight Marines: Gun Captain, Sergeant Gilson Tallentire, Corporal Michael N. Economou, Private First Class Rudolph M. "Rudy" Smith, Private First Class Lynn W. Frost, Private First Class George G. Giddens, Private First Class John F. "Porky" George, Private First Class George W. McDaniel, Private First Class Raymond C. Switzer. Another Marine at the Battery E emplacement that Gun One worked with was Staff Sergeant Charles A. "Charlie" Holmes, who was in charge of the battery range finder.

New to combat, Jim anxiously awaited the Japanese return. It was hard for Jim to discern incoming aircraft because of the roaring surf on the reef, a noise that the men had been used to blocking out. Moreover, the ever-present Wake Island wind blowing around him and down the barrel of the AA gun sounded like the drone of approaching planes. Upon hearing the droning wind in the gun barrel, Jim shouted that the Japanese were coming again. (Years later, in a letter sent 17 August 1971 from Albany, Georgia, Sergeant Tallentire would write to the now much wiser Jim, "don't let the wind blowing down the gun barrel trick you into thinking that Jap planes are on the way.")

In these days before radar, the Wake defenders relied mostly on visual identification. The thousands of birds that resided on the atoll suffered from the percussion of the bombs detonating around them. Following the first two bombing raids, the birds were seen moving slowly, some staggering, as they tried to regain their equilibrium. After that, as soon as the birds perceived the approach of large numbers of aircraft, they soared by the thousands into the air, creating a blanket of white in the sky. As well as a beautiful sight to behold, it also became a welcome one to the Wake defenders. The escaping birds gave the island an early warning system for approaching Japanese bombing squadrons. "We'd see those birds rise up and the white leaving the ground going up [into the air]. You wouldn't hear [any] motors or anything, but you knew damn well the Japanese would soon be there. I don't know if the military used it or not, but some of the civilians out in the brush did," Jim recalls.

As day lengthened into night, news of the "infamous" day's events traveled around the island. Jim heard on Lieutenant Lewis' military radio the scuttlebutt that the Philippine Clipper had been stripped of everything that was not absolutely necessary to fly in order to carry more aviation fuel. Instead of the usual stop at Midway Island, the goal was to fly straight to Hawaii, normally too great a distance for a Pan Am clipper. Seats and cargo, including the United States mail, were dumped to make the plane lighter. Even passengers, crew, and evacuating Pan Am employees lucky to be able to leave for the daring flight did not travel in the conventional fashion. Those that were to be aboard the Clipper, according to what Jim heard, stripped down to their bathing suits. Years later, Jim heard that the Clipper made its historic flight, stopping at Midway Island first before landing safely in Hawaii.

Just before noon the next day, 9 December, the Japanese came back to give Wake another beating. Jim's construction work site on Peale Island was apparently a main target. The hospital, with the injured from the previous day's bombing inside, was hit and quickly turned into an inferno, along with the warehouse. The new barracks and mess hall with Jim's handiwork were hit as well as much of Camp 2 on Wake Island proper.

At this point Jim Allen and the other Gun One volunteers were conducted through the United States Marine Boot Camp training in sixty seconds, with Master Gunnery Sergeant Krawie "doing all the damn hollering. The dust was flying, the gun was firing, and he was yelling, you could hear him" above the din of planes, bombs, guns, and destruction. Jim feels he must have done all right, for he never saw Krawie again until they were in Woosung, China, as prisoners of war.

Battery E had another serious problem in addition to being undermanned. It did not have a height finder to assess the bomber planes in order to aim the AA guns with the correct

The Contractors Hospital after the Japanese had bombed it. Many of those inside the hospital died when it was destroyed 9 December. (Joseph J. Astarita)

trajectory to hit them. Lieutenant Lewis judged the height of a target plane using binoculars or just his own eyesight evaluation. Sometimes the F-4 fighters of Marine Squadron VMF-211 stationed on Wake would fly near enough to the target bomber planes to match their altitude and radio back that information to the anti-aircraft guns. But most of the time, it was just point and shoot, relying on previous training and experience.

This time, the Japanese were precise with the bombs and apparently had the Battery E gun emplacement identified. They'd be sure to hit and destroy it on the next raid. A new plan of action was designed and during the night of 9 December, the Marines and civilian volunteers, with the aid of trucks, moved each of the four one-ton guns in Battery E to a new location about one thousand yards back up the road towards Camp 1. Dummy guns replaced the real ones so the Japanese would not become suspicious when they didn't find weapons at the previously identified site. Although the Japanese bombers had also marked the location of the five-inch gun of Battery A with Lieutenant Barninger close by at Peacock Point, it was too large to be moved. Battery A would later take extremely heavy enemy fire in its fixed position.

A third raid took place on 10 December, again around noon, and the original Battery E position drew heavy concentrated enemy fire. The dummy Battery E was pulverized. Although firing at the approaching planes gave away their position, the new Battery E location was not hit. Bombs fell close and it looked for a while as if they would eventually strike the Battery E site. The Japanese bombers apparently ran out of ammunition just prior to reaching Gun One, but a bomb fragment did damage the gun slide.

In relocating Gun One the night before, not enough sandbags had been moved to make a zigzag at the entrance to the emplacement. A bomb fragment was able to come through the opening and hit "Porky George on the belly." It was, luckily for Marine John George, merely a scratch, but the value of the zigzag was proven.

Cleaning up after the latest raid involved more heavy gun moving. Gun One's damaged slide meant that the entire barrel of the AA gun would have to be replaced in order to prevent leaking oil when it was fired again. An AA gun on Wilkes Island was moved over to Wake Island and the barrel exchanged for Battery E Gun One's damaged one. It would be discovered that the damaged gun barrel was still capable of firing without problems on 23 December when the grounded aviators fired it at a runway location close to where the Japanese invaders were landing.

On 11 December, the Wake Defenders learned that the bombing raids were just the hors d'oeuvres for the battle banquet the Japanese had in mind. In the darkness of early morning, the main course appeared on the horizon in the form of a fleet of Japanese ships: one cruiser, six destroyers, and two troop transports.

Surprise was the Wake defenders main weapon and they used it well. The small force on Wake held off firing their five-inch broadside guns until the Japanese ships were as close as possible to shore. As the Wake guns started answering the Japanese guns, the Japanese ships tried to turn and escape into deeper water further away from shore as fast as they could. Fortunately for the men on the Wake atoll, they were able to inflict severe damage to the fleet before they were out of range, and when they were, VMF-211's remaining fighters took over from the air. The destruction the Wake Island defenders wrought would buy them a few more days of freedom and, for some, life.

Once the dust cleared from the raid, battle information was passed along via the communications phone line. Only after the war would the causalities be assessed and the defenders of Wake learn of their true toll that day: one destroyer sunk by shore batteries, one destroyer sunk by VMF-211 planes, and most of the remaining seven ships damaged.

The small force of both air and land based firepower at Wake had held off the Japanese and additionally gave them such a bloody nose that they retreated for repairs and reinforcements. The Japanese would wait for another week-and-one-half and endure heavy losses before the atoll would be theirs.

The following days were filled with preparation and anxiety for the Wake Island defenders as more Japanese bombing raids blasted the island. Busy as they were, the men of Wake were

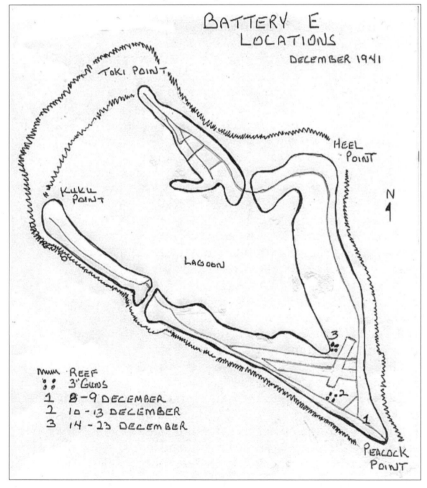

BATTERY E
LOCATIONS
DECEMBER 1941

TOKI POINT

HEEL POINT

N

KUKU POINT

LAGOON

REEF
3" GUNS
1   8-9 DECEMBER
2   10-13 DECEMBER
3   14-23 DECEMBER

PEACOCK POINT

Battery E was mobile during the early part of the siege, first moving closer to the crushed coral runway and then further away to a spot on the edge of the lagoon. The moves were necessary since the Japanese had pinpointed the Battery's position.

fighting a two front war — the secondary battlefront being nature. The men were joined in their sandbag defenses at night by the Wake Island rats, which crawled all over the tired men trying to sleep in the sand around the gun emplacements. Having jumped ship years ago, the rats had adapted to living on the atoll and had done fairly well until driven from their homes by the bombing raids. Homeless and as disoriented as the Wake Island birds, some of the rats sought a safe haven and food around the sandbagged mini fortresses. An abundance of hermit crabs with their borrowed shells also crawled about the gun area and would be quickly tossed out over the thick sandbag walls. But the most miserable of the varmints to join the "party" were the thousands of flies. Prior to 8 December, all fly breeding areas such as garbage dumps or toilets/latrines were taken care of to eliminate the winged pests. But with the start of the bombing raids, fly abatement was low on the Wake defenders priority list; hence, the population multiplied exponentially. It was not just the Japanese making life miserable on the Wake atoll.

On the night of 13 December, it was decided to move Battery E again, this time a thousand yards due north to a position on the lagoon. Jacking up the two thousand pound guns and trucking them one-by-one across Wake was bad enough, but the defensive sandbag walls and camouflage had to be moved and be recreated also. After this last move, Jim remembers, it was decided that Battery E would "stay in one place come hell or high water!"

Not knowing how long they would be holding out in their new location and realizing that the Japanese bombers would soon know exactly where they were, it was decided that a survival shelter, or dugout, was needed for protection. In order to get some tools to work with, Jim walked the four and one-half miles around the lagoon and the still standing channel bridge to his old work site on Peale Island where he'd left all his tools. The eighth of December seemed like years ago now, not just days. As he journeyed down the island's coral road under the hot tropical sun, he viewed some of the destruction that the Japanese bombers had wrought. The island's appearance had been changed from a construction site to one of destruction. Arriving at the remains of the mess hall, Jim collected hammer, saw, nails and a few other supplies that would be needed. Then he walked back to Battery E and started to help build the frame to support the coral that would be piled around and on top of the dugout they were fabricating at the Gun One emplacement.

There was plenty of loose coral available to the builders, thanks to the Japanese bombs. Sergeant Tallentire would write later, again in the letter dated 17 August 1971 to Jim:

> I well remember the night we were building the survival structure and it was you who did most of the heavy hammering on the large timbers. You were also a very good man at the sandbagging, which I'm sure no one really enjoyed except that it was something to keep busy at and would keep our minds off the final result which I'm sure none of us planned.

The Gun One crew in their enthusiasm for safety dug the pit for the dugout too deep, unaware it was low tide. As a result, saltwater seeped in from the atoll's high water table. Jim and the crew used building wood two-by-four's placed on edge with the two-inch side down as floor joists across the bottom of the pit. They then placed large plywood sheets on top and nailed them to the joist as flooring, creating a large platform inside the dugout. This would enable the men to stay four-inches above the pit's bottom and a few inches above the waterline. The crew was lucky that there was not a shortage of building supplies on Wake Island. Thanks to Morrison Knudsen preconstruction planning, there was plenty of lumber available.

More air raids by Japanese planes occurred between 14 and 22 December, and the spunky defenders kept sending shells toward the enemy planes. Hope and the rumors of help coming soon kept Jim and the others going. On the air raid of 22 December, the day before the final morning, the Japanese planes dropped a line of bombs, starting in the ocean on the east side of the atoll, continuing across the island and into the lagoon and the nearby Battery E. Four bombs landed all around Battery E Gun One's sandbag walls, with four thunderous explosions that threw coral rock, dust, and brush into the air, breaking the communications phone line. Large craters marked the area around Gun One. To Lieutenant Lewis, it appeared he'd lost the gun and all thirteen men of its crew. The communication phone he wore only gave him silence from Gun One.

Gun One's crew watched as the line of bombs approached them, with the island jumping up and down underneath them. As the bombs came nearer, Lieutenant Lewis ordered a cease-fire. As soon as Gun Captain Sergeant Tallentire heard it, he hollered "Cease fire!" and told Jim and the others to "make a hole" and take cover. But first, all the ammunition had to be put back into the "safe" storage area in the sandbag walls to prevent it going off when the aerial bombs burst. Hand over hand, the civilians in a line between the ammo storage area and the gun, and the Marines on the

Camp 2 was a main target of the Japanese. Joe Astarita has drawn his eyewitness view of the camp showing the damaged, but still standing, construction warehouse surrounded by bomb craters. (Joseph J. Astarita)

gun platform off-loaded the unfired shells. That done, the crew made for the dugout survival shelter they had built the night before. Once in the dugout, the men bounced up and down, as the bombs grew closer. Sergeant Tallentire was the last one in the dugout. One bomb hit the ground behind him before he had a chance to get completely inside. The blast picked him up and blew him the rest of the way into the dugout. As the dust cleared, Lieutenant Lewis looked over toward the site and discovered Gun One had been destroyed. But to his happy surprise, none of the gun crew was injured, not even the flying gun captain.

It was this combination of skill, luck, and tenacity that the Japanese had not counted on when invading Wake Island. Their plan of a quick surrender had to be shelved as the Wake Island defenders held off the Japanese invaders until 23 December, by which time the Japanese assembled reinforcements to strengthen their sea power for the next try at an amphibious landing.

Finally, on the night of 22 December, in preparation for the eventual enemy troop landing, Sergeant Tallentire told Jim to break out the two small wooden boxes of hand grenades kept in the gun emplacement storage area. The only thing Jim knew about hand grenades was what World War I veterans had told him and what he'd seen in pictures. He'd never actually seen a real one before, let alone used one. He had his hunting knife with him and used it to pry off the wood top of the first box. Inside was a tin box containing the grenades. The tin box's design called for pulling a ring on the top of the box to pull back the lid and reveal the grenades. This was similar to a present day can of nuts or drink mix. As Jim took hold of the metal ring of the first box, it came off in his hand and the box remained waterproof and sealed. Gingerly, not knowing what was immediately beneath his blade, Jim used his knife to make a hole in the metal lid. He was able to cut a hole large enough to lift each of the grenades out. Next, he tried the second grenade box's pull ring; it worked. Jim was able to get out all the grenades and passed them around to the crew of Gun One. "Fortunately, we never did use them." Jim had gained new insight into the reasons for military inspections and appreciated their value. If those grenades had been needed in a hurry, the men would not have been able to get at them. "They might as well have stayed in the United States," says Jim.

The Marines that night also distributed what extra arms they had around the island and dropped off a Browning Automatic Rifle (BAR) at Gun One. The Marines of the Gun One crew weren't familiar with the weapon, but civilian Jack Hoskins had served in the U.S. Army and knew how the BAR operated. Jim volunteered to carry the ammunition clips of twenty rounds each for Hoskins when the Japanese troops came near the gun emplacement. Later, Jim read that because of the weapon's rapid, machine-gun like fire, the BAR operator was usually "zeroed in on quickly by enemy mortars. The weapon and its operator's life expectancy could be measured in minutes." Jim recalls, "I didn't know nothing about the damn thing at the time. I probably wouldn't have carried the ammo for him." Like the grenades, the BAR was never fired before the surrender order was passed down. "I didn't know what I was doing. I just volunteered, defending my country."

As the Japanese fleet came into view, the Wake defenders knew that by the same time tomorrow, they would either be dead or prisoners of war. Through the scuttlebutt, Jim and the others had already realized that help from the U.S. Navy at Pearl Harbor would not be coming. They were on their own.

During the dark, early morning hours of 23 December, the Wake defenders' sixteenth day under siege, AA Gun One fired rounds out in the direction of the landing Japanese watercraft. PFC. Rudy Smith, the fuse cutter on Gun One, began cutting the fuses shorter to go over the arriving enemies and explode, thus changing the gun's intended purpose. Some of the fuses were cut so short there was apprehension that the ammunition might not get out of the emplacement before detonating, but it did.

As the early morning sun shone brightly, the final Japanese assault gained control of Wake, overrunning the tired defenders. Around 7:30 AM on the morning of 23 December 1941, with no hope of help on the horizon from Pearl Harbor, Commander W. Scott Cunningham, USN, Commanding Officer of Wake Island, by phone informed Marine Defense Commanding Officer Major James Devereux, that an unconditional surrender was in order. The major then sent the order to cease fire and surrender via phone to fighting men at their posts, where the enemy had not yet reached. When the order reached Battery E, Lieutenant Lewis ordered the men to sabotage the remaining anti-aircraft guns as well as the rifles, sidearms, and any other equipment that could be destroyed. Blankets were stuffed down the muzzle of the anti-aircraft guns, which were then fired, fouling the weapon. Lieutenant Lewis used his sidearm revolver to destroy the AA battery's fire control by discharging several bullets into the dials. None of the cosmoline-clean rifles had been fired from the emplacement, but now they were to be destroyed. Jim took off the bolt from his rifle and threw it into the saltwater filled bomb crater near the gun emplacement. His rifle quickly followed.

When the sabotage was completed, the men formed up and marched down the makeshift road away from Battery E, out to the main road circling Wake. One of the Marines behind Jim noticed his hunting knife in its scabbard hanging from his pants belt and told him he'd better get rid of it. The Japanese might not take it kindly to finding him with a weapon. Jim immediately took the knife, scabbard and all, and threw it into the bushes along the road.

The Battery E Wake Island defenders marched along the crushed coral road, heading east toward the oceanfront beach and Marine Commanding Officer Major Devereux's command post about 1,000 yards from the final location of Battery E. In a short period of time, the Battery E defenders were met on the road by a group of Marines with Major Devereux in the lead. Devereux's group was carrying a hastily fashioned white flag which flew above them on a long stick. Jim and the other Battery E men fell in and followed Major Devereux down the road, back the way they had just come. At that point, someone mentioned to Jim that under the rules of warfare, he and the other civilian volunteers who had helped to defend Wake Island could be considered guerrillas, or spies. Either one meant death. Execution was not a pleasant thought at that moment for the battle weary twenty-three-year-old carpenter.

As Commander Winfield Scott Cunningham stated in his book, *Wake Island Command,* "Pearl had been bombed only once; at Wake Island we had been subjected to sixteen raids in fifteen days." It was truly heroic what military men and civilian volunteers had been able to accomplish against overpowering forces. In his book, *Wake, War and Waiting . . .,* author and Wake Island civilian Rodney Kephart writes: "We didn't do so badly at that, lost a hundred and thirty-five men and of course all the equipment we had on the island, . . .[while the Japanese lost] . . . twenty-seven aircraft, eleven surface craft, and two submarines. That was about the end of Wake's sixteen days of scrimmage." Adding to that score were the hundreds of men that the Japanese had lost. Also added to the Wake Island defenders honorable record was the fact that the 11 December attempted invasion by the Japanese was the only time during World War II that an amphibious landing had been successfully prevented.

After the war and a review of records and accounts, the Japanese would acknowledge that they were outfoxed by the small fighting force on Wake Island. It was a disgraceful episode for the Japanese to be held off from capturing Wake Island by a small number of men for sixteen days. This was especially true after their surprise raid and subsequent victory at Pearl Harbor, where much more U.S. firepower, both on land and at sea, was located. However, it seems as if it also instilled a bit of admiration for the brave defenders of Wake Island, for the Japanese appeared to not be of a mind to massacre the survivors as a lesson to the world. Rather, by Japanese standards of the time as evidenced elsewhere in the Pacific war theatre and years earlier in China, the treatment could be considered rather humane.

In later years, the surviving Wake Island defenders, both civilian and military men, would take pride in how the Japanese government viewed their efforts. In a memory booklet given to attendees at an October 1983 reunion was the following note:

Considering the power accumulated for the invasion of Wake Island, and the meager forces of the defenders, it was one of the most humiliating defeats the Japanese Navy had ever suffered.

> Masatake Okumiya
> Commander,
> Japanese Imperial Navy

Meanwhile in California, Viola heard about Wake Island being under attack from the radio and President Roosevelt's speech before a joint session of Congress in Washington. On that joyless Monday, 8 December 1941 (California time, a day behind Wake Island) as FDR read through the litany of attack from the previous day, Viola's apprehension grew for her James. As Wake Island's name was read toward the end, one can assume a gasp might have escaped her lips, as she realized her oldest son was in danger, or even already dead. Helpless and thousands of miles away, she could only hope that, as a civilian, Jim would be rescued and home soon. Viola was to be severely disappointed.

The news over the next few days continued to be grim, but there were flashes of hope as news of the Wake Island defenders' brave stand against the whole of the Imperial Japanese Navy reached North America. Comparisons with the stand at the Alamo would even be mentioned. "Remember Wake" would be a battle cry for Americans for a very short period of time until larger and more current battles superseded it.

Concerned about her brother from the radio and newspaper accounts they were receiving, seventeen-year-old Hazel wrote to her brother on 10 December, three days after the Pearl Harbor attack. She addressed her letter in the normal manner, James Albert Allen, Wake Island, T. H., and mailed it off hoping it would reach him. Toward the end of January, Hazel's letter found its way back to her, bringing more unanswered questions with it. The envelope was stamped:

> return to writer
> unclaimed
> moved left no address.

It was stamped with the date, January 21, 1942.

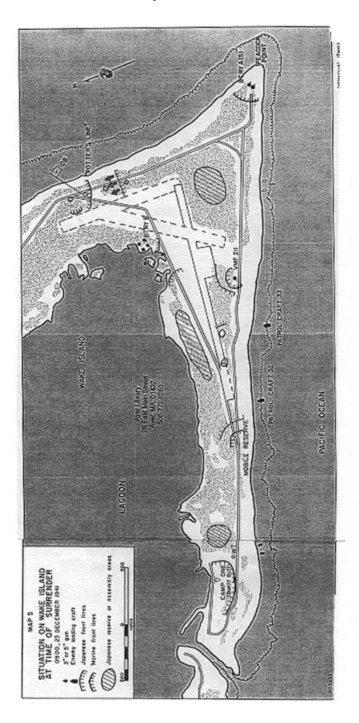

Wake Island as viewed by the military on 23 December 1941 at 9:00 AM. Along the road going between Battery E and Potter's Line (crossing the future runways) Jim and the others were tied up by their Japanese captors while a machine gun was trained on them. (Heinl, *The Defense of Wake*)

5

Prisoner of War

Jim Allen and the rest of the volunteer civilians and Marines continued down the sun-baked crushed-coral main road of Wake Island, following Major Devereux and the white rag flag of surrender. Within a matter of minutes, the tired band of Wake Island defenders met up with a squad of Japanese soldiers, bayonets fixed for action and Colonel Devereux officially surrendered to them. It was only ten o'clock in the morning during a day that seemed a week long. Jim and the Wake Island defenders were now formally prisoners of war of the Japanese.

Immediately, Colonel Devereux was led away while the remaining American men were ordered to remove all their clothing, including hats. In a mixture of English, Japanese, and body language, the captives were instructed to throw their clothes over to the side of the road. Twenty yards up the road, on the seaward side, a machine gun was set up with the new prisoners in its sights. The idea that they would soon be dead crossed Jim's mind, and possibly others' as well. Jim knew that the Japanese had not taken prisoners in China. The new prisoners of war (POWs) were allowed to keep only shoes and socks on. This was one way for the Japanese to eliminate the possibility of any hidden weapons. It also gave the Japanese captors a psychological advantage over their prisoners, a way to be shamed or "lose face" as the Japanese refer to it. As to being embarrassed by their lack of clothing, Jim has said, "We were too scared to be embarrassed."

The next order was to get into one long line and sit in the middle of the road. Jim and the others sat as carefully as they could on the rough crushed coral. "The coral being very sharp," he remembers, "you sat tenderly, facing west" toward the lagoon. The coral on their bare bottoms and legs was as comfortable as an Indian bed of nails to the fatigued and fearful men who had no idea what would happen to them next. As the day grew older, and they sat exposed to the sun's radiation without shade, the coral road became increasingly hot and painful. While the new POWs sat silently, a Japanese dive bomber, evidently from an aircraft carrier offshore, flew above them. Suddenly a Wake Island .50 caliber AA gun fired one burst, hitting the bomber. Apparently there were still some Wake Island defenders who had not yet surrendered. The profusely smoking plane headed for the open ocean, where it dropped all of its payload of bombs before, as the POWs hoped, it eventually crashed.

To make sure they had no trouble from the new prisoners, the Japanese soldiers used pieces of the communication wire that lay uncovered along the side of the road to restrain the Americans. A Japanese soldier had Jim put his arms behind his back, with wrists together. The soldier then tightly wrapped Jim's arms and wrists together with the communication wire. Next, he pulled the arms up as high as they would go and ran the phone wire around Jim's neck, and back to his wrists, where it was tied off. If Jim tried to put his arms down to rest, he'd choke himself. "Your arms got pretty tired," remembers Jim. Soon all the POWs were similarly trussed up.

"I, and all the other prisoners were very concerned and scared. The Japanese had a machine gun set up at our backs, but why they did not execute the entire bunch of prisoners, I didn't know." After his return home, Jim heard from others who were captured that day about the Japanese officer who had come running down the roadway after the new POWs were tied up. This officer told the Japanese soldiers guarding the naked men that they would be taking prisoners. "The more I've thought about it in the years to pass, I think [the Japanese] had every intention of not taking any prisoners," says Jim. "Course they didn't take any Chinese prisoners that I've read about. But due to the fact they took all the clothes off us. They wouldn't have had to have done that. They [the clothing] was all there available for them to bundle up and ship off to Japan, I guess. So, sometimes, I believe that they had all intentions of executing us on the spot."

The new prisoners remained tied up for what "seemed like forever, but it probably wasn't too awfully long, maybe an hour, two hours." Finally, the armed Japanese captors untied the naked POWs and then marched them down the road. The little bit of air movement from walking felt good to the hot and sweaty POWs. The respite from the heat was a brief one, for they were marched to an ammunition bunker, one of two that were being used as hospitals during the siege to replace the one that had been bombed and burned on the ninth.

On the southeastern side of Wake Island proper were four bunkers in a north-south line lying just east of the uncompleted cross-runway for the airfield. Jim had been to the makeshift hospital in one of the bunkers twice before to get his shrapnel wound dressed and knew that they weren't all that large. These bunkers were Quonset hut-like buildings: elongated, domed, and made with reinforced concrete. Partially underground, they provided good protection for the long-term storage of ammunition.

Still very afraid and not sure of what to expect, the POWs stood in a line while a Japanese guard went to the last bunker in the row. Opening the iron door, he fired one shot inside. The soldier apparently "wanted to let people know inside, that he meant business," according to Jim. Ricocheting around the bunker's crowded interior, the bullet struck and wounded a man lying in a hospital bed. Terror filled the captives' hearts, both those inside and outside of the bunker. Yelling in Japanese and using body language, the soldiers pushed the POWs along, jamming them into the enclosed bunker to join those already in the close quarters. The steel entrance door was closed tightly behind them.

Inside the converted ammunition bunker, the air was stale and still, growing hotter by the minute as the men stood naked, shoulder to shoulder. They were jammed so tightly there was no room to move even an arm to fan themselves.

Standing in the dark, stuffy, and hot bunker, a myriad of thoughts crept into Jim's mind and probably those of the other prisoners as well. No one knew what would be happening in the next minute, hour, or, if they lived long enough, day. Jim stated in later years that it was this same continuing fear of not knowing what might happen next that was the most traumatically frightening part of his entire POW experience.

A sudden rush of welcomed fresh air poured into the bunker announcing the return of the Japanese soldiers. Jim, standing near the door, was grateful for the additional air movement, which took the smell of sweat and heat away for the moment. Speaking English, an officer (or uniformed civilian interpreter) asked for a volunteer to help bring in a couple of Marines that had been spotted "running to the bush." Apparently not everyone had received the surrender order.

Realizing this was a way to get out of the hot, stifling bunker, if only for a short while, Jim volunteered to go and inform any of the Wake men still out in the brush of the surrender. He was led outside and around the end of the ammunition bunker. The steel bunker door slammed behind him, cutting off the fresh air for those remaining trapped inside.

Down a beaten path walked Jim, still dressed only in his socks and shoes, while two fully uniformed and armed Japanese soldiers with fixed bayonets walked behind him. Their route took them toward a .50 caliber machine gun, which was not far from the bunker and towards the lagoon. "My God!, there were Japs laying all around there, dead!" Jim remembers. "One of them, half his brains [were] exposed and he was still alive and bleeding. He was trying to talk . . . his mouth was moving. It was awful. . . didn't bother those damn soldiers a bit. Me, I looked and I . . . ." There wasn't anything to be done for the fatally wounded soldier, but this incident gave Jim insight into the Japanese soldier; they were very single minded. Ordered to take Jim and find the Marines evading capture, Jim's escorts ignored the wounded.

Reaching the area where the Japanese had spotted the Marine holdouts, Jim began walking across the roughly graded airstrip, shouting out "Marines, the island has surrendered" at the pugnacious American military men, wherever they may have be hiding. The Japanese soldiers remained at the airfield's edge. After he was about a third of the way across the airfield, heading toward the brush on the other side, yelling every so often, his two Japanese escorts began to holler "O'ou" at Jim. Not understanding Japanese, Jim thought they wanted him to go on farther. So he continued to move away from them a little faster, while maintaining his hollering for the missing Marines. The Japanese soldiers kept yelling "O'ou" together and began to wave at the wandering POW. To Jim, the backhand to face and open palm to the ground wave-like gesture appeared to mean they wanted him to keep going, so he pressed on across the airfield.

With his back turned away from the soldiers, Jim did not see the Army rifles being raised and aimed. He jumped at the sound of the discharging guns and froze. The Japanese soldiers again yelled "O'ou" and this time Jim hurried back the way he had come. "I got the message and went to them." This was his first immersion lesson in the Japanese language, both oral and visual versions.

Giving up the idea of finding the wayward Marines, the two Japanese soldiers directed Jim back to the miserable ammunition bunker to rejoin the other captives. On the way back, the soldiers and Jim came across some cans of food lying along the pathway. "The soldiers offered them to me to eat. I declined, for which I was sorry, because it was a long time before I would get any food to eat." One of the Japanese soldiers noticed some khaki trousers in the dust beside the pathway. Using his bayonet to pick up one pair of pants, he passed them to Jim indicating that he should put them on. Gratefully, Jim quickly put the pants on.

Reaching the ammo bunker, Jim re-entered the cement structure, the iron door clanging sharply behind him. Although it was still hot and stuffy, Jim was a lot more comfortable standing in there dressed in his "gift" khaki trousers. The only other men with clothes on in the bunker were the doctor and a couple of corpsmen, or medical technicians.

After an uncomfortable hour or two in the bunker, the POWs were moved out and herded toward the airfield runway not far from the bunkers, where the Japanese had been bringing all the rest of the prisoners, some by truck, most of them on foot. Jim quickly noticed that the other groups of prisoners were all fully dressed. Apparently, Jim's group was the only one to be stripped of their clothing, further fueling the thought that they were to have been executed back on the blistering crushed coral road.

It was early afternoon and the tropical sun blazed down upon the atoll. Indicating that they should go onto the runway itself, the Japanese guards supervised the approximately 1,500 new POWs as they walked forward onto the runway and then directed them to sit down. While few POWs, if any, understood Japanese, the prisoners did understand the rifles and bayonets pointing in their direction. Jim's group of POWs sat down, mindful of their exposed flesh on the rough, hot sur-

While in prison camp, civilian POW Joseph J. Astarita drew this picture of himself, Jim Allen, and the other Wake Island captives held on the runway. (Joseph J. Astarita)

face. The armed guards remained on the perimeter of the mass of men with machine guns trained on the captives. Talking among the prisoners was not allowed and punishments were quick and severe to those who were foolish enough to disobey, a blow to the stomach or head with a rifle butt being common.

On the first night of capture, 23 December, a squall line came across the Wake Atoll, drenching everyone out on the runway, prisoners and guards alike. Although Wake is tropical, only nineteen degrees of latitude north of the equator and averaging eighty degrees during the day, at night without a large landmass to radiate back captured heat from the day, it can be cold. Even with his bestowed trousers, Jim was chilled. "It was cold at the airport that night we were captured. A squall of rain came by, wind, no clothes on, it was sure cold." Some, including

Jim and the group of men around him, took pieces of coral and dug out a depression beneath them. They used the coral rocks dug up to build a small wall around them with which to deflect the wind. The makeshift wall did provide some relief from the wind and cold, but very little. "I was sure glad to see the sun come up December twenty-fourth." At some point during their stay on the airfield's runway, the rest of the prisoners without clothes received some. Just when, Jim does not remember.

Upon its surrender, Wake Island was renamed Otori Shima, or Bird Island, due to the thousands of birds found on the island. Peale Island was renamed Hane Shima, or Wing Island, and Wilkes Island Ashi-Jima, or Leg Island, a possible reference to the shape and location of the islands in regards to the main island. The time immemorial custom of renaming recent acquisitions, especially land, was a way of announcing to other claimants and the world in general, that the island had changed hands. In a matter of moments, this U.S. territory became part of the Empire of Japan and with it a change of status for the Wake Island defenders. The Japanese captors informed the POWs of their new identity: they were considered soldiers in the Japanese Army. To escape was desertion and deserters were executed.

Dealing with large numbers of prisoners was not something the Japanese had necessarily prepared for. Their culture dictated that it was much more honorable to die for their emperor than to dishonorably surrender. To willingly become a prisoner of the enemy was unthinkable. Decades after the conclusion of World War II, a few Japanese soldiers would be discovered still hiding out on Pacific islands, not wanting to surrender to the Americans and not necessarily realizing the war was long over. Yet this group of American prisoners had fought bravely and held off a Japanese fleet, something the Japanese recognized as honorable. It presented a dilemma for the Japanese Army now in control of Wake Island. Having not signed the Geneva Convention regarding the treatment of prisoners of war, Japan was under no obligation to abide by it. According to Jim, the POWs were often reminded that they were "guests of the Emperor." They were told that everything they had now, even the clothes on their backs, belonged to Emperor Hirohito. Also, Jim recalls being told that, "Anything you were able to have was purely by the pleasure of the Emperor letting you have it," including their lives.

This was a difficult concept for Jim and most of the American POWs. Americans have a tendency to be very ethnocentric, thinking that all other cultures should be like their own. America has stood for liberty and independence with no kings or emperors since 1776. The idea of one giving all or doing everything for a ruler went against all that the prisoners had been taught. It wasn't democratic!

As the sun rose on 24 December, the American men remained exactly where they had sat all night, with the machine guns and Japanese soldiers around them. No one stood up or walked about for fear of being shot. The tropical sun again beat down upon the men as the day wore on. No food or water had yet been given any of the men. All day the prisoners sat or lay in the same spot, not daring to move or talk. When the sun finally went below the horizon that evening, Jim was grateful for the skin burning sun to be gone, but did not look forward to another chilly night on the runway.

Christmas Day, a Thursday, dawned as bright and clear as any other day on Wake Island. The men had not had anything to eat or drink for over forty-eight hours. They remained in their original spots, suffering cold, then extreme heat, as night became day for the second time. It was, to say the least, not a pleasant Christmas for the Americans. They were finally given some sustenance, but nothing close to the previously published, elaborate Christmas menu that the Morrison Knudsen kitchen staff had planned. For Christmas dinner 1941, on the crushed coral runway, Jim and those around him had a small swallow of tomato juice and a small taste of tainted water, which had been stored in gasoline barrels. The rest of the prisoners Jim found out later, had a similar holiday "feast."

Finally, Christmas afternoon, the Wake Island prisoners were moved over to Camp 2 and what remained of the civilian barracks there, now encircled with a barbed-wire fence. All the civilian construction workers were jammed into a barracks with everyone mixed up. The men had to double and triple up in the bunks for everyone to have a space. Some of the men even slept under the bunks in order to have more room. Jim was one of the lucky few to get his own bed, which he shared with another carpenter, Eddie Peres, with whom he had become friends.

The barracks had been searched and the men's belongings and clothing thrown about the beds and floors. Jim and the others who were near their own bed area, looked through their belongings and noticed some things were missing. The most sorely missed for Jim was a new leather wallet containing his driver's license, family pictures, and some money. However, he did find the old black and blue striped tobacco pouch that he had brought to Wake. Apparently the Japanese weren't interested in the cloth item. Cellophane lined, the pouch kept Jim's pictures from the SS *Matsonia,* Carpenters Union Card, Navy medical exam paperwork, and Morrison Knudsen Contract free of mildew. For some unknown reason, Jim also had in the pouch a flat wooden spoon used to eat ice cream from a Dixie cup. Since Jim would never be able to figure out how to make chopsticks work correctly, the old wooden Dixie spoon became his main utensil until he was given a metal spoon much later in prison camp.

Not all the prisoners had their belongings on their mind at the moment. Clarence B. McKinstry, a Marine gunner that Jim knew before the siege, was in charge of a battery on Wilkes Island. He and his men had fought valiantly and kept the Japanese from taking control of Wilkes until after the surrender. The one Japanese survivor of the fight, recalled Jim, "remembered a Marine with a handlebar mustache." Once the POWs were herded back to what was left of the barracks at Camp 2, McKinstry became a man with a serious mission: he needed to quickly shave. "We were in the barracks after Christmas and, man, he come around and . . . he was looking for a razor . . . I don't think he ever found a razor, but I think he got it off with a piece of broken glass."

By this time all the POWs were beginning to look alike with dirty, unkempt, and unshaven faces. Beard stubble was sprouting like corn shoots in Missouri farm fields during the spring. McKinstry would have a better chance of blending in if his mustache was as short and ragged as everyone else's was.

During the ensuing days, the POWs were assigned to hard labor work details to build fortifications and repair buildings. Jim was on one detail instructed to move loose coral from one area to another. As Jim and the others worked on top of an Army concrete igloo, he spotted some color beneath the rock. Moving the coral carefully, Jim discovered a small American flag. Covering it up quickly, Jim waited a second or two to see if any of the guards had seen the flag. Luckily, they hadn't, for showing it to the Japanese at that time would have been "like waving a red flag in front of a bull. You had to think quick" in order to survive.

Going back to the barracks that night, Jim saw the white and red of the Japanese flag flying on the pole in front of Navy Commander Cunningham's headquarters. He had not seen the

American flag lowered after the surrender. Asked years later about his feelings at seeing the Japanese flag flying for the first time, he responded, "You didn't have much feeling — what could you do?" In the middle of the Pacific Ocean on a small atoll, there wasn't any escape or hope of rescue. A lot of changes just had to be accepted.

Another work detail allowed Jim and the others in the group a chance to get back at the Japanese and gave them some self-satisfaction, however small the act of retaliation. The work detail was taken to where the Japanese had off-loaded a two-wheel cannon-like gun. The POWs were ordered to begin piling chunks of coral around it like sandbags. Jim has recalled, I "got the Jap guard to let me line the inside of it all around the gun, [with] real white coral. If you wiped off the dirt and burnt stuff, it was real pretty, white coral." The guard thought that the white coral would look nice around the black gun, so before he could change his mind, Jim worked hard to scrape the black off the coral chunks, making them a brilliant white.

"So," continues Jim, "we lined that thing [the gun] all around with white coral. A plane flying above could spot that sucker a long ways off cause there was bushes and black all around it. Then the black gun right in the middle of it with real white coral all around [looked] just like a bull's eye. I was surprised the guy would let us [do it]." Jim never learned whether or not American planes were able to use that "bull's eye" to take out the gun, but if wishes came true, that gun found itself in a million pieces long before the war was over.

There was a bit of variety for Jim and the POWs in their work details. One of the Japanese four engine flying boats used to transport officers ashore after the battle for Wake, had apparently gotten too close to some coral heads in the lagoon as it was taxiing in. The pilot didn't know where he was and ran over some of the crowns of coral near the surface, knocking out part of the seaplane's bottom. Jim was on the work detail assigned the job of raising the plane from the bottom of the lagoon. There was a stiff-leg crane out on a "big old barge" that had been used by the Morrison Knudsen construction men for various projects. The barge with the crane was floated over to where the flying boat was submerged. The crane was then used to hook onto cable that had been put around the plane to secure it. Slowly lifting the sodden plane out of the lagoon, the work detail "managed to horse it over to the sea plane ramp" on Peale Island where it could be repaired. When the POW crew had manipulated the plane onto the ramp and it was stabilized, Jim's curiosity got the better of him. "I was always curious about how big that red dot [the "Rising Sun" emblem of Japan] was out on the wing, at the end of the wing. So I got up on there and walked out there and laid down in it." The red circle was more than six-feet in diameter, according to Jim's half-inch shy of six-foot body lying across it; "two meters, so it was a fair size wing that was on that old seaplane." He was lucky not to get a beating, or be shot, for desecrating a symbol of Japan.

During their early captivity on Wake Island, the American prisoners were introduced to a revolutionary idea; stopping in the middle of work to drink hot tea. It was during a tea break on Peale Island that an English speaking Japanese soldier excitedly told the POWs about how he and others looked forward to arriving in San Francisco and finding the women there. If the previous years of Japanese occupation in China were an indication, rape and pillage was what the soldier had in mind. Jim recalls that the soldier was pleasant to talk to "and went on about how the short war with America was over with Japan victorious." To that statement Jim replied that "this was only the first quarter of the football game." Jim was not discouraged in the slightest about the United States and his situation. "Always figured I was coming home and the Allies would win." Youthful optimism! Unfortunately, the "short" war of the Japanese dragged on and the United States' victory took much longer than Jim Allen ever expected it to.

December 31, 1941, New Year's Eve, found the Wake Island POWs without the means or desire to celebrate the coming new year. Unknown to the civilian construction workers, the United States Navy canceled the Contractors Pacific Naval Air Bases (CPNAB) contract on that date since they would be unable to complete the project. But although the Morrison Knudsen Company, as part of CPNAB, would not be paid anymore by the U.S. government, they did pay Jim, for example, $100.00 in January and February. Approximately one-eighth of the Morrison Knudsen workers would die before becoming Recovered Allied Military Persons (or R.A.M.P.S), when liberated in 1945. But on 31 December, none of the incarcerated men on Wake knew if they'd ever leave Wake Island alive or see much of 1942. So much for a chorus of Happy New Year!

Life began to take some form of order for the prisoners or, as the Japanese preferred to say, Imperial Guests. Days found work details continuing to refortify the atoll against the expected American attack to retake the island. Nights were hot and stuffy with the men crammed together in the barracks built for a fourth of the number now inhabiting them. In spite of all this, Jim remembers that, "Occasionally there was some laughter."

On the twelfth day of 1942, the Japanese removed most of the Wake Island POWs to a large ship, the *Nitta Maru*, lying at anchor offshore. This would be their transportation to Japan or some other location where they would be held until they were exchanged. The following rules for the trip were printed and handed to the POWs in preparation for the journey.

COMMANDER OF THE PRISONER ESCORT
NAVY OF THE GREAT JAPANESE EMPIRE

REGULATIONS FOR PRISONERS

1. The prisoners disobeying the following orders will be punished with immediate death.
   a) Those disobeying orders and instruction.
   b) Those showing a motion of antagonism and raising a sign of opposition.
   c) Those disobeying the regulations by individualism, egoism, thinking only about yourself, rushing for your own goods.
   d) Those talking without permission and raising loud voices.
   e) Those walking and moving without order.
   f) Those carrying unnecessary baggage in embarking.
   h) Those touching the boat's materials, wires, electric lights, tools, switches, etc.
   i) Those climbing ladder without order.
   j) Those showing action or running away from the room or boat.
   k) Those trying to take more meal than given to them.
   l) Those using more than two blankets.
2. Since the boat is not well equipped and inside being narrow, food being scarce and poor, you'll feel uncomfortable during the short time on the boat. Those losing patience and disordering the regulation will be heavily punished for the reason of not being able to escort.
3. Be sure to finish your "nature's call." Evacuate the bowels and urine, before embarking.
4. Meal will be given twice a day. One plate only to one prisoner. The prisoners called by the guard will give out

the meal quick as possible and honestly. The remaining prisoners will stay in their places quietly and wait for your plate. Those moving from their places reaching for your plates without order will be heavily punished. Same orders will be applied in handling plates after meal.

5.   Toilets will be fixed at the four corners of the room. The buckets and cans will be placed. When filled up a guard will appoint a prisoner. The prisoner called will take the buckets to the center of the room. The buckets will be pulled up by the derrick and be thrown away. Toilet papers will be given. Everyone must cooperate to make the room sanitary. Those being careless will be punished.

6.   Navy of the Great Japanese Empire will not try to punish you all with death. Those obeying all the rules and regulations, and believing the action and purpose of the Japanese Navy, cooperating with Japan in constructing the "New Order of the Great Asia" which lend to the world's peace will be well treated.

The End

Jim kept his copy of the travel rules in his cloth tobacco pouch along with his other mementos and eventually brought it back to the United States as "kind of a souvenir."

Approximately 350 of the prisoners remained behind on Wake, but not by choice. Selected for their individual skills such as heavy equipment operators and some carpenters, the men were used to build further fortifications for the Japanese under horrific conditions. The hospitalized and injured also remained on Wake. One of Jim's *Matsonia* cabinmates, Joe Tury, was among those 350 left behind, possibly chosen because he had been an oiler on the lagoon dredge. Jim learned after the war that Tury had been taken to Omori War Prisoners Camp in Japan, which had been known later for its horrible conditions. Never hearing of Tury again, Jim has assumed that he died in Omori Camp before the war ended.

Eventually, after further transfers, only 100 POWs were left on Wake Island. Two of those men, in a desperate escape attempt, stole a boat and headed out to sea. They were successful with their escape from Wake, but it is presumed that they either drowned or became a shark's meal since they were never seen or heard from again. The other of Jim's cabinmates

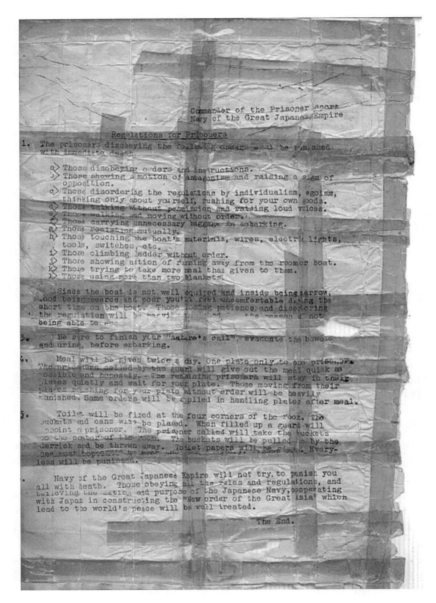

An original sheet of regulations given to the new prisoners on Wake Island before they boarded the *Nitta Maru*. The oversized paper was crumpled and torn from being carried in pockets and baggage for three years, nine months by Jim. After being home for a few years, he cellophane taped it together to preserve it. (James A. Allen Collection)

on the *Matsonia*, Charles Cantry, was one of the last 100 POWs to stay on the atoll. Floyd Forsberg, who had volunteered at Battery E with Jim, also remained on Wake.

On 7 October 1943 the war was going poorly for the Japanese and the POW's services as laborers were no longer needed. Japanese Wake Island Commander, Rear Admiral Shigimatsu Sakaibara, I. J. N., claimed there were problems controlling the POWs and ordered them executed. Sakaibara was later hung as a war criminal in 1947 for this act. The remaining ninety-eight POWs, including Cantry and Forsberg, were marched out to a beach site. The POWs were executed, with their lifeless bodies strewn about the white bloodstained coral sand and allowed to be claimed by the sea.

Five months prior to the murders, one POW, or possibly more, managed to carve "98 U.S. PW, 5-10-43" onto a large coral rock near the water. A large plaque with the ninety-eight names is now in place on Wake Island to honor their memory. The plaque is only a few feet from the POWs' own chiseled monument to their misery.

The large coral rock on Wake Island, which has "98 US PW 5-10-43" carved into it. (Al Brueck/James A. Allen Collection)

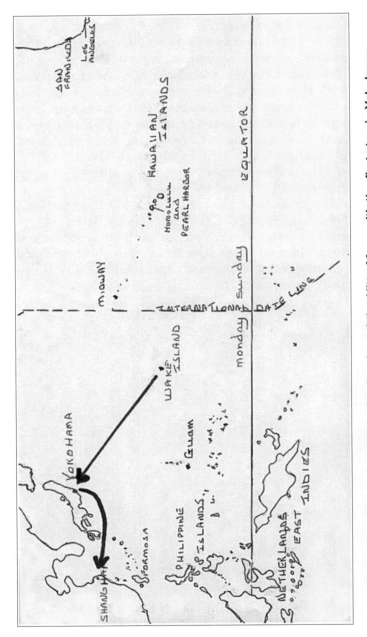

Jim and the other POWs left Wake Island on board the *Nitta Maru*, with the first stop in Yokohama, Japan. Two days later, the ship and its cargo of prisoners headed back out to sea, toward the Asian continent and the international city of Shanghai, China.

6

On A Sea Cruise

The morning of 12 January 1942, the POWs were told they were moving out and leaving Wake Island. This was both good and bad news for the POWs. Wake Island was a known place, home to many of the men for several months. Just what would happen once they left the atoll, none of the prisoners could say. The unknown loomed ahead, sinister and obscure. Apprehension became another piece of luggage to carry along. Each prisoner could take only one small bundle aboard the transporting ship.

Jim packed what few possessions remained, placing them inside a shirt and tying the sleeves and shirttails together to form a bundle. Inside his khaki shirt, he put the blue and black striped cloth tobacco pouch. It still contained his Navy physical form, CPNAB contract, thirty-five cents in airmail stamps, flat wooden Dixie cup ice cream spoon, union card, and the six photographs that had been taken aboard the SS *Matsonia*. The pictures of Ben Marsh, Norm Wright, and the girls they had all met, along with Jackie Robinson and Frank Brickner were a small reminder of more pleasant days such a short time ago. In addition to his khaki work shirt, Jim wore a pair of khaki work pants, silk socks, and J. C. Penney ankle high work shoes. In what was left of his clothes after the Japanese search of the barracks, he could not find any underwear and so went without. Jim's khaki work clothes were good for the tropical weather of Wake Island, but if the ship was heading for Japan as some of the POWs assumed, the khakis would not provide much warmth. It was preparing for a trip without a clue as to where he was going. To be prepared for anything, Jim did the best he could with the little available to him.

Instructed by the guards to line up outside the barracks building, Jim and the other POWs in his barracks scurried outside, formed a line, and waited silently to be counted. The prisoners were all beginning to look more like hobos than military and construction men. The last time they had been able to shave was before the first Japanese bombing run, over a month before. Jim had started growing a mustache several weeks before the 8 December attack and the long ends were beginning to dip down over the sides of his mouth. Once he got this mustache off, he would never grow another.

After they were all accounted for, the POWs were loaded into trucks and driven from Camp 2, along Wake's upper arm on the main road and then back across the lower arm, past Camp 1. The trucks stopped at the boat dock where Jim had first stepped ashore on Wake Island not quite four months ago. Located on the Wilkes Channel, the dock had been where all supplies and people for the atoll were dumped when off-loaded from supply ships by the lighter boats. Now, a reverse exodus of people was underway. Jim and his group were loaded into a former U.S. Navy, now Japanese Navy, whaleboat, a long open utility craft, and ferried to the *Nitta Maru*. Riding out to the ocean barge for transfer to the ocean-going vessel, Jim got his last look at the Wake atoll. The squat chunk of coral rock with no apparent value for centuries except to sea birds, now was priceless to the two nations at war with each other.

The *Nitta Maru* was relatively new, having had its maiden voyage in the spring of 1940. Designed as a modern luxury liner with twin screws powered by oil fueled turbines, the *Nitta Maru* was originally headed for the Atlantic Ocean and the European Continent trade between Yokohama and Hamburg, Germany. However, with the outbreak of war in Europe, the ship stayed in the Pacific. The *Nitta Maru* was pressed into duty as an Imperial Japanese Navy transport vessel, then refitted as an escort carrier (renamed *Chuyo*) as the need arose.

As the whaleboat Jim's group was in came closer to the former luxury liner, the large ship seemed to grow taller and wider, until all that Jim could see ahead was the barge and the *Nitta Maru*, with her black hull and a large Rising Sun painted toward the bow. "It was a fine looking ship and I was glad of it," Jim recalls, thinking that a large ship would make an ocean voyage easier. Jim and the other POWs in his small utility boat, were off-loaded, along with guards, onto the barge and walked to the opposite side of the large barge to board the *Nitta Maru*. Not only were they crossing from one side of the barge to the other, but the POWs were also exchanging the Japanese Army guards for Navy ones. It was not necessarily a change for the better.

The prisoners lined up on the barge, just forward of the Rising Sun, where there was a small, open, watertight door, or hatch, oblong and rounded both at the top and bottom to be sealed tightly against the ocean waves during transit. This type of door is known as a "knee knocker" since the careless will get their knees and shins bruised or scraped if they don't pick their feet up high enough to clear the hatch's bottom when traveling through it.

Scraped shins were a secondary problem for Jim. As he neared the head of the line, he watched the others in front of him try to negotiate traveling between the barge and the ship. Each was rocking to a different pattern with the ocean wave action. As the *Nitta Maru* went up and back on a wave's crest, the barge would travel downward into the trough of the wave and roll to the side. Timing was everything when trying to navigate through the ship's hatchway; to miss would mean being crushed between the two vessels as they came together with the next wave. "When [the *Nitta Maru*] went by one time, you threw your bag of clothes in and that was the last you ever saw of them. The next time, as quick as it got close enough, you jumped in." Jim also recalls that "Of course they had Japanese soldiers with bayonets and rifles in back of you to encourage you to get aboard." Thoroughly frightened, Jim was greeted by a welcoming committee of Japanese sailors on each side of the hatch. "When you went in, they each got you by the arm [so you didn't fall] and then sprayed you with old sheep dip pumps like we had to spray sheep on the farm with. You put your hand on the bucket and you pump, and then you squirt them with it. Well, ... you hit this slick floor and you'd almost go down and then those guys would spray you with the sheep dip. It was exciting! You was scared to death." The passageway was lined by more Japanese sailors who were armed with long, thick pieces of hardwood about

The *Nitta Maru* docked in Yokohama after her arrival on 25 September 1940. Her tall forward mast is directly above the forward hold Jim Allen rode in. This picture gives the viewer an appreciation for the size of the ship. The hatch Jim and others jumped through is on the port/left side of the ship, just in front of the painted Japanese flag on the hull. (U.S. Government U91 7666)

the length of a regulation baseball bat but two-inches in diameter tip to tip. Some of the Japanese sailors would use these clubs to administer a "greeting" to the boarding POWs. One of the civilian construction workers had worn his metal hard hat and received a special "greeting" of having his hard hat beat down about his ears by one of the club wielding sailors.

After the tumultuous welcome, Jim and his group went down several passageways until they reached the forward hold, a large, cavernous room where cargo was stored during a voyage. There were three levels to the hold and they were all filled with prisoners from Wake Island. Jim's level held approximately fifty men, and the lower two levels held a bit less because of the inward curve of the ship's hull. Unlucky Marine PFC Rudy Smith, the Battery E fuse cutter, was on the lowest level right above the keel, Jim found out years later, and would be susceptible to the stale air and cold temperatures as the ship traveled north. Jim's group was lucky to remain on the first level, although the accommodations lacked any bunks or furnishings. The men had to lie or sit on the steel decking of the hold. Jim's Irish luck was still favored, for he found himself on the top of the wooden hatch cover that was much more comfortable than steel and a lot warmer. When removed, the hatch cover allowed passage between the three levels of the hold, but that rarely happened on the voyage.

Jim found out long after the cruise was over that the hatch in the hull's port side was not the route all the POWs took to get aboard the *Nitta Maru*. Some of the Marines had to climb up a rope net on the side of the ship and others were hoisted aboard in a cargo net. Upon reaching the main deck, all POWs were "baptized" with disinfectant from the hand pumps and greeted with the hardwood clubs, then hustled to their assigned places in the ship.

Now in the forward hold, the POWs were informed that they had to lie on their backs or stomachs; they could not sit up unless given permission. Lying on his back in his deck space on the wooden hatch cover, Jim checked his shirt to see if the tobacco pouch was still there. Luckily it had not been jostled loose. The black and blue striped cloth tobacco pouch and the clothes he wore were all that Jim could claim for possessions.

After a considerable period of time down in the forward hold, Jim felt and heard a low dull rumble, clues that the *Nitta Maru* had weighed anchor. The destination of the ship would probably be Japan, or so Jim and some of the others thought. "When I was on Wake Island, I had a lot more knowledge of history and geography of the world than most of them. I know my buddy, Eddie Peres, hell; he wanted to know where Chosen was. That's what [Korea] was [called] under Japan and, of course, I had a pretty good idea where it was." Jim was later dubbed "Knowledge," his best nickname according to ex-POW T. Truman Cope.

Within two days, the tropical warmth was left behind for the January chill of a northern temperate climate winter. The POWs in their thin, tropical clothes were freezing with the extreme temperature change. They did not need a compass to know the direction the ship was heading in. For Jim and those who had studied and remembered their geography, Japan seemed to be the correct guess.

The regulations that were handed out back at Camp 2 on Wake Island were strictly enforced during the voyage. One of the men in the forward hold with Jim found out that the Japanese were deadly serious about the no talking rule. The office man-

John Polak.
(PIEF)

The artist's representation of Polak's beating in the forward hold of the *Nitta Maru*. The arrow indicates the relative location of Jim Allen, beard and all. (Joseph J. Astarita)

ager on Wake Island for the Morrison Knudsen Company, Nebraskan John V. Polak, was observed talking without permission by one of the guards. He was a couple of men over from Jim's spot on the deck hatch. Polak's wrists were tied together with a rope and the rope then was fastened to the overhead, while he was standing. Using one of the baseball bat-like clubs, a guard struck Polak several times on the buttocks, so hard that his whole body was raised up from the deck. Jim remembers that Polak "had the hell beat out of him." Miraculously, Polak survived the beating and lived to tell about it. The shipboard regulations called for immediate death.

As the *Nitta Maru* voyage lengthened, Jim and the other prisoners became an increasingly dirty, smelly bunch, their beards and hair growing ever longer. Lying on the hard steel deck plating in the stuffy, malodorous hold day after day only intensified the men's feelings of being less than hygienic and well groomed.

The sanitary arrangements on board the former luxury liner left much to be desired. Four metal containers that held five gallons apiece were placed in each of the corners of the hold for collecting human waste. They were not permitted to be emptied until they were brimful. When they were full, a guard in the hold would randomly pick one of the POWs to perform the messy task of emptying the excreta, as outlined in the regulations for prisoners. The chosen POW took the offending benjo (excreta) bucket and placed it in the middle of the hold, under the hatch. Then he would climb up the metal ship's ladder attached to the bulkhead or wall in the hold, and began "pulling with a rope, the five gallon benjo buckets and emptying them into a slop chute, evidently a head [lavatory] on the *Nitta Maru*." This was not an easy or pleasant job. It was a case of better to do it than be under it. "That damn bucket would be completely full and man, you couldn't keep from slopping some of it and there were three levels for it to go down. Oh, it was awful," Jim recalls. Some POWs could not avoid being splashed with waste as it was hoisted out of the hold.

If the weather was good, the Japanese would take off the forward hold's hatch cover on the main deck, allowing some air circulation between the hold's three levels and getting rid of some of the stagnant air and fetid smells. Removing the hatch also gave Jim an added benefit. Since he was directly below the main deck hatch, he could look up and see the sky and the forward mast when the hatch was off. Watching the mast lines dance in the wind and the clouds drift by allowed Jim to mentally escape from his steel dungeon for as long as the hatch cover was off. He could also see, not just feel the pitch and roll of the ocean waves as the tall mast would tip back and forward against the heavens. "Yeah, I watched that thing [the mast] the whole way."

The food made the bad liver on the USS *Regulus* seem like filet mignon. Each morning in the forward hold of the *Nitta Maru*, a wooden bucket with a dipper in it would be lowered by rope into the hold just like the benjo bucket was lifted out. Allowed to sit up, each POW was given a dipper full in his bowl of a gruel-like substance made from barley or rice called con gee. (Kon go is the Japanese word for mixture). Jim thought that the con gee was thick enough to hang wallpaper with and about as tasty. It was eaten with the fingers, similar to Hawaiian poi. Con gee was a staple item to the POWs diet during the early months of imprisonment, both at sea and on land.

Each afternoon, Jim and the other POWs in the forward hold received a six to seven-inch dried fish, scales and all. The prisoners would each get one dried fish per day. Although not necessarily a fussy eater, especially after living on Grandpa Amos' farm, Jim went several days before he could touch the fish. "Each day I'd get hungrier [until I] just started at the tail and peel off a little of it. And I give my friend, Eddie Peres [my fish]. Oh, he liked them. He'd eat it . . . he'd eat the head, eyes, everything, tail and . . . by the time we got to Shanghai, the only thing that was left was the head and the bones and Eddie was eating them!" However, hunger is a great appetizer, and within a few days of picking at small pieces, Jim was eating more and more of the little dried fish. "By the time we got to Shanghai, why, I was cleaning everything from the tail up to the gill on both sides and giving [Eddie Peres] the tail, the fins and the head."

In addition to the dried fish and con gee, the prisoners received about a dipper full of water once a day. After thirteen shipboard days of this diet, Jim remembers "you just didn't have much food in you." Dehydration and malnutrition had gained a foothold. There was one advantage to not having adequate food and water available. The men did not use the benjo as often, thereby keeping trips up to the slop chute in the ship's head down to a minimum. "Nothing in, nothing out" was the way Jim saw it.

On the third night out of Wake Island, the routine whine of the *Nitta Maru's* engines shifted into a high pitched squeal. At the same time, the ship's claxon began sounding off with the general quarters alarm. The Japanese sailors remained on guard in the hold, but the hatch cover was dogged down tightly, making the forward hold watertight. The easy roll and pitch of the ship changed drastically. At times staying in their spots became a challenge to the prisoners. The *Nitta Maru* "started really vibrating" with the increased speed of the engines and "just quivered" when she came down from the crest into the trough of a wave. There was an obvious urgency to the way the *Nitta Maru* was being driven compared to earlier in the day. Perhaps it's an American submarine targeting us, was the thought that crossed Jim and other POWs' minds. This thought brought a mixture of emotions, self-preservation being one. Although another sunken Japanese ship was one less for the United States to contend with later in the war, no one wanted to be on board when that ship went down, taking them with it.

As the relatively new luxury liner continued to pitch and roll through the night, the prisoners became more anxious. Each time she shuddered from the impact of crashing onto the ocean waves, they would wait for a second or two to assess if the noise and vibrations were the result of a torpedo finding its mark. While not good news for the U.S. Navy, it was fortunate for the POWs on the *Nitta Maru* that American torpedoes early in the war were not always detonating when hitting their targets. This was a frustrating period for the United States submarines, for they could observe the target in their sights and watch the torpedo zip away on target, only to find out it was a dud. The technical problems would be overcome and the torpedoes did hit their targets with deadly accuracy in the future. But on the night of the fourteenth of January 1942, the *Nitta Maru* prisoners were in no danger from American torpedoes.

Several hours later, the *Nitta Maru* slowed her engines back to a much slower rhythm. The wild ride similar to being on an out of control roller coaster was over. Rudy Slezak, years later, told Jim being in the lowest hold atop the keel was like "straddling a bucking bronco!" The ex-luxury liner, now prison ship, resumed her steady but gentler pitch and roll over the Pacific's waves lulling Jim and others to sleep.

On the sixth day, the *Nitta Maru's* engines ground down slowly and became silent. The prison ship had docked in Yokohama harbor, the port for Tokyo, capital of the Japanese Empire. The seventeenth of January was a cold winter day at the northern latitude of thirty-five degrees. Farther north than Los Angeles, California, it is a great deal colder since the continental westerly winds bring the frigid air from Siberia and Manchuria to Japan. Additionally, the POWs were still dressed in their tropical attire, totally unsuited for frigid temperatures. The freezing steel decks seemed even colder to those lying upon them.

Jim learned much later that some of the prisoners in a different part of the *Nitta Maru* had had snowballs thrown at them through an open hatch while at dock in Yokohama. For Jim, the cold was enough, and he was glad the hatch cover to his hold remained closed to snowballs, for being directly below the hatch, Jim would have been an easy target.

While tied up at the Yokohama dock in Tokyo Bay, it became Jim's turn to empty the benjo buckets. The one bright spot of the job was that the head had a porthole. From the porthole Jim could see the sun shining and a bit of sky, but that was all. It was at least some comfort to know that the sun was still shining somewhere.

After two days of being tied up at Yokohama, the *Nitta Maru's* engines became active once more and the prison ship put out to sea. Crossing the East China Sea, the *Nitta Maru* sailed for the mouth of the Yangtze River (now known as the Chang Jiang), heading for the port of Shanghai, China. Jim, for one, hadn't a clue where they were now headed. Once in the Yangtze River Delta, the *Nitta Maru* traveled toward the mouth of the Huangpu River. Sailing up river, the *Nitta Maru* put in at the port of Shanghai, which had been under Japanese control since captured in 1937.

Just before docking in Shanghai, clothing was handed out to the prisoners. Jim was given a khaki shirt and pants along with a Palm Beach coat, which was a white, lightweight, double-breasted summer linen jacket. Even with this additional clothing, Jim was hardly prepared for the frigid temperatures that awaited him.

Once the *Nitta Maru* had tied up at the wharf that Friday, 23 January, the Japanese in charge had planned on using the POWs for propaganda. They wanted to make a show of parading their captives from Wake Island through the city streets of Shanghai to the suburb of Woosung (Wu Sung) and the awaiting prisoner of war camp. Fortunately for the men from Wake Island, the Japanese "couldn't shake up enough Chinamen to make a showall [display]," recalls Jim. So the captured American military men from the gunboat, USS *Wake* and the British military men, who had all been held in Shanghai, were loaded aboard the *Nitta Maru* for the trip to the prison camp. The ship then sailed back downstream on the Huangpu. The next day, ten miles downstream, the *Nitta Maru* tied up at the village of Woosung, which is located at the confluence of the Huangpu and Yangtze Rivers.

There was a change in the menu on board ship that day from the standard con gee and dried fish. Each POW received a small can of salmon, the *Nitta Maru's* version of an aloha dinner. Even though it was cheap during the Depression and used for meals quite a bit by his mother, Jim "never did eat salmon when I was at home in the States. I didn't like it, didn't want it. But I ate that salmon and, boy, it was good 'cause I was really hungry by then."

That afternoon around 3:00 PM, Jim and the rest of the POWs were herded off the *Nitta Maru,* their uncomfortable abode for the past twelve days, for they knew not where. The former luxury liner also had misfortune in her future. Within three months of dropping her Wake Island prisoner cargo off in Woosung, the *Nitta Maru's* was converted to an aircraft carrier escort; her superstructure was cut off and replaced with an aircraft landing deck. The transformation was completed by 25 November when she was commissioned. Renamed the *Chuyo*, she was intended to be used in a supporting role of transporting planes, but she would also carry war prisoners. Sailing from the island of Truk in late November 1943, as the *Nitta Maru/Chuyo* neared the Japanese home islands, the submarine USS *Sailfish* would sink her on 4 December. Only one POW aboard survived.

Disembarking the *Nitta Maru* was much easier for the POWs than coming aboard at Wake Island. At the Woosung landing, the POWs merely walked off a gangway. Practically none had any belongings to carry. Nevertheless, after remaining immobile on their stomachs or backs for thirteen days, except the few times to get up and use the benjo buckets or to receive food and water, Jim and the others found it very difficult to walk. Their muscles had tightened up from lack of use and each step was painful in the cold winter wind and drizzle. However, those who were slow and did not move fast enough to suit the guards were hit with the hardwood clubs, providing the energy needed to move more quickly. The debilitated POWs walked down the *Nitta Maru* gangway as well as they could to avoid a clubbing and lined up on the wharf before heading toward their new home. Once on the dock, the POWs were back in the hands of the Imperial Japanese Army.

When everyone was finally on the dock and standing at attention, the POWs listened to a uniformed interpreter translate while the officer in charge went over what behavior was expected from the prisoners. Similar to the *Nitta Maru* regulations, orders were to be obeyed, no rebellion or opposition allowed. Escape meant death for desertion since the POWs were considered to be in the Imperial Japanese Army. Jim remembers this lecture on deportment well, standing in the cold and wet of a miserable winter afternoon.

Even though talking was not allowed without permission, the scuttlebutt was still able to permeate through the POWs about the new men taken on board at Shanghai. Last on, it was the men from the USS *Wake*, with Commanding Officer C. D. Smith, who disembarked the *Nitta Maru* first and headed up the column for the walk to the prison camp. The men of the USS *Wake* had not been as confined and starved as the men from Wake Island and were in much better physical shape for the trek to the Woosung Camp. Apparently in an effort to make a good appearance in front of their captors, the sailors from the USS *Wake* led off with a very fast pace that almost seemed like a run to the Wake Island POWs. According to Jim:

> That [walk] pretty near killed us, Smith and his damn USS *Wake* sailors! They walked so fast, it was quite a ways, four plus miles] and we'd [the POWs from Wake Island] been laying on our back, no movement for . . . from the twelfth to the twenty-fourth. . . .so man, they took off. They thought they were in boot camp. Hell, even the Marine Corps, everybody hated them. Damn buggers! They walked real fast and hell, you had to keep up. And it was cold and snow on the south side of the buildings and Glen Church led the way! Boy, the next morning, I could hardly walk, the groins, oh my, it was terrible. Everybody was that way.

The POWs could not protest the pace to the Japanese guards that were herding them along, since in the Japanese's eyes, the prisoners had forfeited all rights or identity when Wake Island was surrendered. In the Japanese culture, the POWs were disgraced, a fate worse than death. "No protest and everything belonged to the Emperor. You don't own nothing when you surrendered and were captured, not even your life. Not a thing, and so they told us" again and again. To protest would have only resulted in a beating with the wooden club or worse. It was a matter of just putting one foot in front of the other and willing yourself to keep walking.

Upon arriving after dark at the Shanghai War Prisoners' Camp at Woosung two and one-half hours later, there wasn't much to be impressed with. The weary travelers were greeted by more guards and an incessantly long speech in Japanese only, given by the camp commander, for whom they had to remain at attention in the cold, drizzling rain. An hour later, the numb POWs headed toward their barracks, drab and dreary old wooden buildings, which had a forlorn air about them. It sure didn't seem like home to any of the POWs that night, especially Jim Allen, but it would be for the next ten and one-half months.

7

Shanghai War Prisoners
Camp at Woosung

The Shanghai War Prisoners Camp near the village of Woosung (Wu Sung) was formerly a base for the Japanese Army after the Japanese occupied Shanghai. In 1937, as part of their quest to create a "Co-Prosperity Sphere of Greater East Asia," Japan seized the Shanghai area of the Yangtze River Delta. A major confrontation between the Chinese and the Japanese occurred at Woosung, with the victorious Japanese erecting a large memorial to their war dead by the barracks.

The "Co-Prosperity Sphere of Greater East Asia" was intended to be a Japanese controlled area from India on the west to Hawaii on the east, and from Indonesia and New Guinea on the south to Manchuria on the north; roughly thirteen percent of the globe. This area would allow the Japanese to gain much needed natural resources, especially petroleum, for Japan's industry, as well as providing expansion room for the small, densely populated country.

There were two roads leading into the Woosung camp proper, which was surrounded by a not yet completed fence with alternating barbed and electric wire. When Jim Allen arrived, the wire was not yet electrified. Four guard towers, one at each corner of the semi-rectangular camp, had a clear

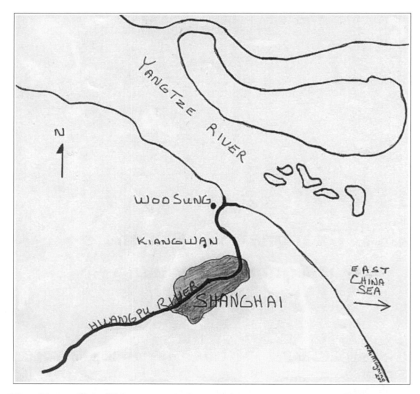

The Shanghai, China area is located near the Yangtze River delta. Woosung, located where the Yangtze and Huangpu Rivers meet, was a small town in 1942 when the Japanese brought the Wake POWs there. Just below Woosung is the village of Kiangwan, where the second camp the POWs lived in was located. It is about five miles between the two camps. By 1999, Kiangwan/Jiangwan had become a section of the giant city of Shanghai. Jim says a shopping mall is now on the site of POW camp.

view of the entire area. There was a second electric fence with barbed wire encircling the seven POW barracks and the associated benjos/toilets, with a small, cold water wash rack area between the two for washing hands, shaving, and so forth. The galley, or kitchen, used wood fires for cooking. The rice, soups, or stews were cooked in several large cast iron cauldrons or kettles, which had fireboxes built around them. Each cauldron had a cold water tap installed next to it so cooks always had plenty of water. The galley, with an attached bathhouse, was to the west of the barracks, outside the inner electric fence along with a teahouse, well pump, and hospital. Close to the hospital were the Japanese offices and the guard barracks. A Japanese shrine was located to the southeast of the camp entrance with a radio station close by. While the barracks were made of wood, they had painted metal roofs and glass windows, if the glass was still in place; broken panes were not replaced. In need of many repairs, the old camp was not adequate for the 1,500 POWs eventually housed there.

Entering through the gate after dark, the POWs were lined up into six groups and stood at attention with the civilians kept separate from the military. It was now time for the official welcome, one Jim Allen and the exhausted POWs could have done without. The interim camp commander, First Lieutenant Takamato, greeted the newly arrived POWs with a protracted speech in Japanese, which few, if any, of the prisoners understood. The drizzle continued along with a cold wind, making Jim and the Wake Island POWs in their tropical clothes extremely miserable. After an hour, Takamato, having worn himself and everyone else out, ordered the POWs to be marched off to their new housing.

After the camp commander's speech, the prisoners were given identification numbers that night. These numbers were to be visibly worn at all times. Jim's number 4428 showed that he was assigned was to Barracks 4, Section 4 and had the individual number of 28. All of these numbers were part of his identity now.

When the preliminary indoctrination was finished, the very fatigued POWs were herded into their respective barracks and sections. Simply getting into shelter was a cause for celebration at that point, if anyone had had the energy. On entering the dimly lit Barracks 4, Jim and his group of POWs were issued four lightweight cotton blankets, which were quite damp. Jim and the others were also issued a small drawstring cloth mess bag, which contained a pair of chopsticks, two bowls, one like a pie plate and the other with higher sides but larger than a teacup, and a teacup for the ever-present eastern beverage. With snow on the ground, no heat in the drafty barracks, and wet blankets, Jim remembers, they, "didn't have a very comfortable night."

There were seven single story barracks at Woosung camp. Made of wood, the barracks were two hundred ten feet long and fifty feet wide; five of them each held approximately 288.

Of the other two, one was used as a hospital and the other was the officers' barracks with fewer men per room, as warranted by their rank. Each numbered building was divided into eight sections with thirty-six POWs to a section. These sections contained four sleeping-platforms in two, approximately twenty-three by seven feet rooms located directly across the barracks hallway from each other. Down the almost six-foot wide hallway either direction there were doors leading into the next section, or if the section was on one of the ends of the building, to the out-of-doors. Some of the barracks had one or two cross-building hallways in the middle of the barracks building, which led outside through double doors.

On arriving at Barracks 4 Section 4, Jim's hopes of a western style bed to sleep in quickly vanished when he saw the sleeping platforms. Instead of individual bunks for the men, there were wooden platforms without mattresses. Raised about eighteen inches off the floor, each sleeping platform was big enough for nine men to sleep on, side by side, with about twenty-four inches of space each. Wooden shelves and pegs ran the length of the sleeping platform above where heads would lie upon rice straw pillows. These shelves were used to store what clothes, hats, blankets, and possessions the men had, or might accumulate in the future. The wooden pegs below held a towel and mess bag. Shoes were placed under the sleeping platform's end, but the rest of the space under the bed was enclosed with boards to keep the POWs from placing anything completely underneath. Eventually the POWs at Woosung camp would have a thin rice straw mattress between them and the hard wood platform, but not on this first night. In trying to make themselves somewhat comfortable, the POWs of Jim's section came up with a way for everyone to have the maximum warmth available that night. "We just laid a bunch of [the damp cotton blankets] out all over on that wooden platform. Then when it got time to get them all spread out and lapped over, we all just got up on top and got it back. We had a few under us and the rest was over us and we all had just one big blanket," recalls Jim. "Well, we survived it and from then on, why naturally things got a little better."

Around midnight, the Japanese brought food to the barracks to feed the starving POWs. Jim remembers getting "one cup of rice and a cup of curry and a cup of tea. Since I was unable to master the chopsticks, I did have in my pocket a Dixie ice cream spoon. I still have the spoon." Within a few

The top drawing shows the interior of a barracks with its sleeping platforms. Note the small empty spaces at the foot of the platform, which served as the dining area. The large can at the left held potable water for the POWs. The lower drawing shows one of the washracks available for the prisoners. The wooden water tank on legs provided cold water via a three-inch pipe, which ran between back to back sinks to several spigots above the crude sinks. Both drawings were sketched by one of Jim's fellow prisoners in the Woosung Camp during March 1942. (James A. Allen Collection)

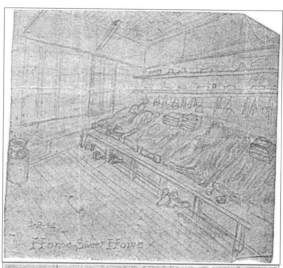

months, much to Jim's delight, the POWs would be issued a metal fork and soup-sized spoon to replace the chopsticks. The stew "wouldn't have been bad without the curry, to my tastes," Jim remembers. "I didn't like curry. That was my first experience with it." However, "Some of the guys thought it was great." Still, there were some men who never liked it. An extreme example of this is one young civilian from Wake Island that Ivan Carden, also a Wake civilian, remembers. According to Carden, this young POW either "couldn't or wouldn't" keep

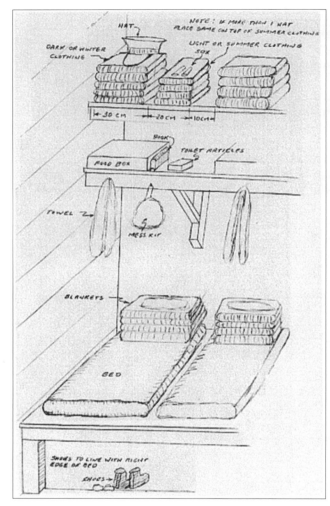

Civilian POW Ernest B. Archer (above [PIEF]) and his drawing of the sleeping platforms illustrating how the POWs had to keep what few belongings they had in a military manner. (James A. Allen Collection — reproduction from the cellophane-taped original)

Japanese food down. He was the first to die in the Woosung camp that Carden knew of.

Jim and the other POWs in Barracks 4 each sat at the end of his individual twenty-four inch wide area of the wood sleeping platform. This is where they would sit for all their meals. There was no dining hall with tables and chairs. The midnight nourishment began to revive Jim and the others a little, but it was still a long, cold, damp night on harsh wood boards. Jim remembers thinking he'd be "sure glad to see spring arrive."

The next morning, and each morning at Woosung camp as well as all the other Japanese prison camps, began with reveille, complete with bugle. "You got up and made your bed in the prescribed condition and then got ready for the morning inspection and count," Jim recalls. The POWs stood at the end of their sleeping space, facing toward the center of the room. They stood at rigid attention in their issued khaki Imperial Japanese Army uniform. For the inspection, "All buttons on your Japanese uniform had to be buttoned. Officers of the Day examined each prisoner. If the buttons were not buttoned, you got slapped or hit." The Officer of the Day would then "stop in front of the section leader who would then bow and make a report of where all those absent were." The section leader, a POW, was required to do all this in the Japanese language, which eventually for most of the POWs, consisted of groups of single Japanese and Chinese words put together. Luckily, the barracks and section numbers were left off; only the last number was used to identify the individual prisoners of the barracks. For example "ichi go-down" would be number one at warehouse or "schichi byöin" number seven at hospital. Bungo (bangö in Japanese), or count-off like a roll call, occurred before breakfast. The men had to quickly learn their numbers in Japanese, especially one through ten. The prisoners were required to use them "for morning and evening inspection. Also going to work and returning from work at the camp guard house." Tenko, the evening inspection and roll call, would happen long before taps. The cries of "ichi, ni, san, shi" (one, two, three, four) and so forth, could be heard throughout the camp at those times, including Jim's ni-ju hachi (pronounced knee jew haw-she), twenty and eight or twenty-eight. Daily bungo and tenko were a permanent part of the POWs' lives as long as they were captive; for some it would be over three years.

Naturally, not all of the POWs could, or would, learn their identification numbers in Japanese. There were two men in Jim's barracks, a truck driver and an ironworker, "one was about sixty, the other thirty-thirty-five," recalls Jim. "I'd give them their numbers and if I give them the wrong numbers, they'd give that number. They'd say I told them [that number]. Right or wrong and of course, if it was wrong, oh boy, the OD [Officer of the Day], he'd just have a fit and we'd have to start over again. And it'd make no difference they wouldn't change. Of course there was some slapping and beating on [the prisoners], when that went on. But they still kept insisting that they wouldn't learn!"

Mealtime at Woosung, or the other POW camps in China, required each section to send men to pick up their ration of food. The galley is in the background with the adjoining bathhouse to the right. In the foreground, the building on the right is the tea house, the one on the left a storage building. (Joseph J. Astarita)

The bowing required by the section leader when making a report grated on the nerves of some POWs, especially the American ones. As Jim explains, "When we first got into prison camp, of course, our idea of bowing to anybody was taboo. But in the Orient, the Japanese, it's the same as our handshake." A simple act of courtesy, the bow illustrates the vast chasm between the Western and Eastern cultures when they met. If nothing else, World War II was a serious clash of two diverse cultures, American and Japanese, each stubbornly convinced that their way was the only correct way for people to behave.

Each morning after the inspection was completed, the POW assigned to fetch the section's tea proceeded to the teahouse beyond the electric inner fence. There he would be given a porcelain teakettle with enough tea for thirty-six men, if poured carefully. But if the POW pouring was too generous with the men at the beginning of the line, he would run out of tea before he ran out of prisoners, and "There would be a big fight," according to Jim. The hot tea "was certainly welcome on a cold morning," Jim has recalled. Tea was an important part of the Japanese culture with the POWs being given tea breaks mid-morning and mid-afternoon, even while working. As Jim says, "This being 1942, it was way ahead of the coffee break in the United States." The hot tea was an important part of the POWs' liquid intake, which was not always adequate.

Meals were served to the POWs in their barracks section. Each section sent one man to the galley to collect a wooden bucket of rice and another to pick up the wooden bucket of thin liquid the Japanese called stew. When they arrived back at the barracks, the food would be divided up among the men in the section. Three times a day, month after month, the POWs usually had the exact same thing: tea, rice, and watery soup.

With thirty-six men in a section, no one wanted to be last to receive his portion, since there might not be any food left by then. Jim remembers some of the worst fights between the POWs being over food. He was finally elected by his section to be the one who divvied up the food and tea. It was then that he came up with the idea of the tea stick.

When Jim started pouring Section 4's tea, he was careful not to fill each cup with too much of the precious hot liquid. He didn't want to shortchange the "guy on the tail end." Jim recalls that "when I ended up, I always ended up with more tea. So then we started seconds. We had a tea stick and you [would] go as far as you could [with the tea] and where you ended up, you [gave] the tea stick to that guy, so that the next time the tea came in, why, you started with him and you went around. Or you started [to pour tea] and when everybody got [their tea], then if you had any left, you started with him. You picked up his stick, went as far as you could and left" the tea stick with the next man in line. The new holder of the tea stick would be the first to receive tea the next time. "I finally did the same thing with the stew or the soup or rice. [We] had a rice stick, tea stick," and so forth, in order to promote even distribution of the item in question. Each stick was a different shape with a different piece of tape. The sticks were written on to identify them. Of

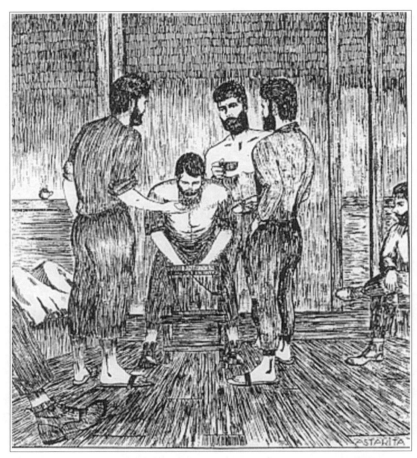

When the bucket of food arrived in the barracks, one man, like Jim Allen, was picked to divide up the food. Note the man on the right seated at the end of his space on his sleeping platform, awaiting his meager meal. On the left, another man is lying down under a blanket with his knees up, perhaps too weary to eat. Soap was hard to come by, so the food buckets were cleaned only with rice straw and cold water. (Joseph J. Astarita)

course, keeping each stick's identity straight was made much easier with thirty-six semi-starving pairs of eyes watching its location and holder. No one wanted to be shortchanged.

Eating their meals at the end of their bunks created housekeeping problems during the meals. After the first meal or two of rice, Jim discovered that it was relatively easy to see the rice worms in his dinner bowl. "They had white bodies like rice, but black heads [that made them] easy to spot. You [would] take your spoon and flip them onto the [barracks] floor along with hulls of rice . . . . We got so we could get the hull in our mouth and just spit them on the floor. You get about eighteen men doing that and the floor gets pretty well covered up at lunchtime or breakfast. But then the Japanese would have us, with the [tree] limb brooms or the rice straw brooms, sweep them all up. Must keep the area clean!" Jim chuckled as he recalled the Japanese Army orders.

The POWs' food got a bit better when it was arranged for the POW cooks, especially those of the construction camp, to be in the galley and prepare the rice, soup, or stews from whatever questionable ingredients were supplied. As the weather became warmer and spring neared, the POWs went to work making a garden just outside the camp fence. It was intended to be big enough to support the camp. But the individual POWs' daily food ration was still meager, even with this addition to their diet. However, by August 1942, the Woosung camp garden was producing well and the fresh vegetables helped improve the routine menu. The POW cooks took a lot of pumpkins from the garden and combined them with the tiny, whole dried fish that the Japanese used as a staple in the POW diet. The final result was what the camp called a stew. "There was one man [a POW]," Jim remembers, "he used to tell about [the stew] in a good way. He said it was much more delicious if they could get a mouthful of that [stew] and then they have to pull that fish bone out between their teeth."

Some of the most vivid memories that Jim recalls have to do with food of some sort. "Used to be some awful fights over tea. One of the bloodiest fights was over one guy giving a fella more tea than another thought he was getting. They had an awful fight. Blood, I mean everywhere! Our section, we had [a big fight] over a stew. It would start with dipping up the stew and . . . a fella by the name of Truman Cope," a civilian who happened to have two brothers, who were Wake Island construction workers and also in Woosung camp: seventeen year-old apprentice carpenter H. T. and slightly older Joseph. Truman Cope apparently, "didn't think the fella was stirring the bucket of stew just right and the guys got pretty sharp, hell, they could stir that [stew] and come up with nothing but water. Or they'd stir it and come up with what little was in it. They'd come up with some of it in the dipper [a teacup on the end of a stick]. Old Truman [and a plumber named Carl] . . . had a pretty good fight over that."

Fifty-eight years later, Truman Cope recalls, "Nobody trusted anybody to dish up food" in Section 4 at Woosung. Then "We finally latched onto Jim." Apparently Jim was considered fair with his serving technique, for Cope claims there weren't any more problems in the section with food distribution.

Jim remembers everyone "was all very touchy. And of course, as the year went on, we got hungrier and hungrier. It was worse in the spring" of 1942. After a while, a constant state of hunger was accepted by the POWs because "They knew they wouldn't get no more. Oh, it was awful!"

One memory of food at the Woosung camp that made Jim cringe calling it to mind, dealt with the camp's miserable mud. In the camp galley, there were cast iron cauldrons that Jim said reminded him of the one "we had on the farm when we butchered hogs to render lard in, heat water, what-have-you." These giant pots would be used to cook the large quantities of rice. The POW cooks had to watch the wood fire closely or, Jim says, "they'd burn [the rice] and it would be just like charcoal. [The cooks would] dig out the rice down to this burnt rice. Then they'd scrape the burnt rice out and put it in buckets and this one time, the only one I remember at Woosung, we hadn't been there too long and a lot of people, in fact all of us, we [were] all pretty hungry. This one time over there at the galley door [the POW cooks] brought a bucket of that burnt rice out and started throwing it up in the air, the cooks did." A large group of hungry POWs had gathered by the door, but few of them were able to catch the rice when it was thrown into the air. The majority of the rice fell onto the muddy ground. When the cooks' bucket of burnt rice was empty, the close to starvation POWs started "diving down after it, over one another like when you feed chickens on the farm and they're real hungry. They're piling all over one another to get into the grain. Well, that's what those prisoners were doing to get to the burnt rice. It was just like charcoal, other than there was some white rice on the inside" of each burnt chunk. Jim was glad he could only remember it happening once because of the health problems the free-for-all presented. The Yangtze River Delta mud in the camp was a breeding ground for some of the filthiest and most vile diseases known to man, such as "cholera, dysentery, and no telling what all."

There were two problems that Jim and the other POWs would try to avoid during their imprisonment, but it was difficult to do so. Dehydration was an issue associated with both. Dysentery or severe diarrhea would be brought on by unclean conditions with food and/or water. It is often a problem today for many people when traveling or vacationing and the POWs were no different. Digestive tracts revolted routinely, making the close quarters of their shipboard journey and now camp life, difficult. It was very easy to become dangerously dehydrated. Jim never did "have dysentery, [at Woosung] I was very fortunate because some of the fellas did."

Clean drinking water, and enough of it, was a problem from the very moment the Wake Island defenders became captives. Going without water out on the hot Wake Island airfield and then receiving an inadequate amount of gasoline tainted water was only the beginning. Now at Woosung camp, the POWs would have to contend with the Yangtze Delta water and its multitudes of hostile microbes. The camp had a well dug to a depth of thirty feet, much too shallow to be considered safe for drinking water. Just how deep a well would have to be dug to be considered unpolluted Jim wasn't sure of, since there was one at Kiangwan that was 210 feet deep and fecal bacteria was still found in it, according to what a POW doctor told Jim. The POW doctors required that all water be boiled for at least twenty minutes in order to kill all the unwelcome microbes. Although this took a lot of fuel and manpower, the Japanese agreed to it. Hot tea would be the only truly potable liquid available at first, which the POWs received five times a day. With time, the water situation would ease, but that would not help Jim and some of the others from the *Nitta Maru* sea cruise, who now had severe cases of constipation with impacted stools.

Several days passed at Woosung with Jim and many of the other POWs not having the urge for a bowel movement and "of course, some of us were getting quite concerned." Since they had not been eating or drinking much, little or nothing was passing through their intestinal system, helpful on the *Nitta Maru* with the benjo buckets, but not a healthy situation for a long period of time. When the urge to finally evacuate their bowels was felt, it turned out not to be a simple task for the affected men. Jim for one, "went out to this Japanese benjo [toilet] and hunkered down, you did. Didn't have no [toilet] stool, just a slot [8" by 2'] in the [wooden] floor [that opened] into these earthen pots that collected the stuff for the Chinese to put on their farms." Once in place, it took a considerable amount of time and effort before anything would be passed. That was if one were fortunate and did not have his stool impacted. This was one time that Jim's luck had not held out, for the stool in his colon had become too hard and big, which blocked any material further up the large intestine from exiting. Laxatives or other treatments may provide relief for some people, but in extreme cases the sufferer usually has to have a doctor remove the fecal material bit by bit with a small probe or gloved fingers. Such relief was not available to Jim and the other unfortunates; they had to do what they could by themselves while sitting or squatting over the slit in the wooden benjo floor. "So you'd sit there with both hands and reach behind there and try to stretch [the anus] and you couldn't stretch it enough," Jim recalls. Consequently, "You'd take your finger, I did, [and] you could dig it out, kinda like rabbit pellets or sheep pellets. Finally got the thing [the hard stool] to where, oh my goodness, it must have been an hour, finally got it to where it started to evacuate and boy, I'll tell you, this was a slow process. It finally started out and it just kept coming and I'll swear that it had to be a foot long and as large as my wrist. And like a club, just as hard as could be!" The misery and pain of this particular struggle was still evident in Jim's voice over fifty years later as he recalled the experience. "There were many of the prisoners that had this experience. And the Chinese coolies when they come to clean out these earthen bowls into their honey buckets to carry to the farms, they just shook their heads at them [the hard stools]." The "honey buckets" Jim refers to were five gallon wooden buckets carried on a shoulder stake, or "yea-ho" pole as the POWs called them, one bucket tied at each end of the pole and then lifted upon one shoulder to tote it along. "It was terrible," Jim remembers, "and a lot of the fellows ended up with piles [hemorrhoids] and what-have-you. I was fortunate, I didn't, but I think I've had trouble ever since over it."

After collecting with wooden handled dippers the excreta from the pots, the coolies would put the dippers into one of their honey buckets and close the outside door to the area. They then lifted their yea-ho pole to their shoulder, transporting the brimful honey buckets to their farms for fertilizer. Jim was impressed by the way the coolies could walk quickly, but "never spill a drop — had a nice rhythm to their walk."

Within a few weeks, the POWs would have clean, clear water available in their barracks. Jim remembers, "We used to have cans that we'd have clear water to drink in the barracks. But you couldn't get a Japanese soldier near clear water even if he saw it boiled for twenty or more minutes." According to Jim, the Japanese soldier "absolutely would not drink clear water. It must have been an army regulation. He'd drink tea, but then that told him it had been boiled." The poor water quality in China and the fear of the spread of cholera kept the Japanese happy to just drink tea.

Settling into Woosung camp took some time, since there was much to be done to make the barren and forlorn looking buildings seem like home. The camp was fortunate to have skilled CPNAB craftsmen. Eventually, Jim and the other "carpenters and the tradesmen from Wake Island, we were able to improve on lots of things," a luxury not found at all POW camps. It especially helped since Woosung camp "was a mudhole, boy, you were on the floor in mud," recalls Jim. The only available brooms were made of tree branches or rice straw and did little to remove the mud from the barracks without a lot of effort.

After the first week, Colonel Yuse replaced Lieutenant Takamato as commander. Colonel Yuse's second in command was Captain Endo, with Lieutenant Akiyama in charge of the guards. Also on staff was the infamous interpreter, Ishihara Isamu, more commonly known as "The Beast of the East." "There was no prisoner who liked him," Jim says. "He was mean . . . beat you up to cause you to work harder." Jim felt that Ishihara was cruel to the prisoners "just because he didn't like Americans. He was from Hawaii and could speak English," so the POWs had to watch what they muttered under their breath to him. A civilian attached to the military and officially known as a gumzoku in Japanese, Ishihara wore a uniform and carried a stick or riding crop, which he liberally used to beat the POWs, occasionally striking them on their Adam's apple. According to Captain James Norwood and Captain Emily Shek of the Liaison & Research Branch American Prisoner of War Information Bureau in their 31 July 1946 report, Ishihara was singled out as being "particularly mean." They wrote that "Ninety percent of the mistreatments reported and protested never reached the authorities inasmuch as such protests had to be channeled through Ishiwara [Ishihara]."

Jim has remarked that he was lucky since he personally was never beaten, just slapped or hit with a clipboard. Nevertheless, he observed many others who were pummeled severely and he grimaces at the memories. Jim also noticed in the prison camp that it didn't take much for the taller prisoners to get severely beaten. Somehow the not quite six foot Jim managed to escape, but men taller than he seemed to be singled out for physical abuse by some of the shorter Japanese. Not all Japanese were the stereotypic short height though, for some were as tall as Jim.

Shortly after the Wake Island POWs settled into Woosung camp, the crew of the H.M.S. *Petrel*, a few British diplomats, and some British gunners from armed merchant ships arrived. Among the new prisoners was Sir Mark Young, governor general of Hong Kong. "Sir Mark was an impressive man," Jim remembers, "slender, but standing ramrod straight." When up against the Japanese, Jim noticed Sir Mark never flinched. The governor general, Jim recalls, "was a lot of help to us. That was when I started to appreciate the "Sir" on the British. I never did have much experience until him." Sir Mark "argued with them [the Japanese]. Don't know that he got a whole lot from them, but he helped."

Sir Mark was one of the many people and situations Jim carefully observed during his young life. As before, Jim carefully tucked the gathered knowledge away in his memory for future use. At the Woosung camp, "I was kind of a pussycat," recalls Jim, maintaining a low profile and learning how things worked. "I seen these older guys wheeling and dealing, how they operate and of course, I had a good buddy [Eddie Peres who had had his fiftieth birthday on 26 January 1942, two days after arriving at Woosung camp] and he was doing it and I didn't have to." Also Jim had to thank his grandfather Amos Bennett for the early training he received about listening and watching others. It paid off for Jim in prison camp by his superior skill of learning via observation.

On the first of February the POW population in Woosung camp rose by about one hundred ninety-two with the arrival of the U.S. Marines captured in North China from their duty stations of Peiping (a.k.a. Peking, now Beijing) and Tiensen (now Tianjin). Better clothed for the cold winter weather of China, the North China Marines weren't suffering as much as the Wake Island POWs. Colonel William W. Ashurst from Peiping/Peking became the ranking POW officer in Woosung camp and the "official" prisoner spokesman. Major Luther A. Brown, who was in charge of the much smaller Tiensen Detachment, became the executive officer, or second in command. Even in a prison situation a hierarchy as to who outranks whom, is quickly established. The Japanese also followed the traditional military role of rank having its privileges, with the officers afforded more room in their barracks than the enlisted men or civilians, with single, double or quadruple rooms or sections, instead of eighteen men together in one room.

The civilians, on the other hand, were in a limbo. For job assignments and barracks, the civilians were treated as enlisted military men, for the most part. Some of the civilian POWs still hoped to be repatriated since they hadn't helped out at Wake Island during the siege or just because they were civilians. At first, when the scuttlebutt of a forthcoming repatriation of some prisoners, such as diplomats and civilians, started circulating, there were those civilians who were positive that the exchange of prisoners would include them. In June 1942 a few prisoners, Marines and the British Embassy staff, were repatriated, again raising hopes among the civilians that they too would be included. They were severely disappointed once more. Later they learned that the Japanese considered them the same as the military since they were on Wake Island constructing a Naval Air Base; hence, they were classified as prisoners of war not civilian internees. The pre-war promises of rescue before hostilities would never be honored.

The civilians did have one advantage over the military POWs. They did not have to necessarily go through a military chain of command to get things done or to complain. If Jim Allen, for example, had been in the Army or Marines as an enlisted man, he could not have spoken directly to the Japanese in charge with his complaints or requests. He would have to go to his corporal or sergeant, with the sergeant speaking with the officer above him and so on until, if necessary, the question at hand reached Colonel Ashurst. The colonel would take the question to the Japanese officials. Jim and the other civilian POWs, however, could go directly to their Japanese guards, sometimes bypassing their barracks adjunct, without repercussions. In time this would prove beneficial to the civilians who would be able to negotiate for things like a carpenter shop garden.

In order to help with communication when the POWs were first at Woosung camp, the Japanese officials set up classes to teach the Japanese language. Although it would have probably proved useful to the POWs to understand the language, as Jim recalls, "In early 1942, anyone who wanted to learn their language would have been a 'Jap' lover, and having plenty of other problems surviving, you certainly didn't need that name. Had we had a crystal ball to see how the political situation changed, we were all foolish for not learning the Japanese language."

The Japanese also tried to institute a morning exercise program similar to what the Japanese Army pursued. It was met with little enthusiasm. As Jim says, "No one was interested, so they gave up on us. [Between] the work they had us do and the amount of food they gave us, you had no surplus energy for exercise."

Early during their Woosung camp residency, Japanese authorities required some of the prisoners, apparently the military, to sign an agreement not to escape from the camp. Jim does not recall the agreement, and says even if he had, "I would not have signed it willingly." There was little need for the signed agreement. A few POWs escaped from the Shanghai War Prisoners Camp at Woosung, including construction superintendent W. Dan Teters and Wake Island Commander W. Scott Cunningham, plus three others. These five, three American officers, one British officer, and one Chinese youth who had worked on the USS *Wake*, were captured within twenty-four hours. The Japanese, Jim recalls, "brought them back wrapped up with log chains and what-have-you to march them down in front of us to show it didn't pay to try and run away." Uncomfortable, but lucky not to have been executed for deserting the Japanese Army, the escapees were eventually imprisoned for several weeks at the infamous Bridge House, the Japanese Army's investigation headquarters in Shanghai. It was not a pleasant place to be with its rather fetid environment and questionable interrogation methods. The Kempeitai at Bridge House was the Japanese equivalent to the German Gestapo. All five escapees were eventually brought back to camp.

At Woosung camp, most of the POWs labored on road construction and the digging of a large canal, although many also worked on polishing empty artillery shell casings. Even though it went against the international agreement of not requiring POWs to work on war-related activities, the Japanese authorities required it of some the healthy, and not so healthy, Woosung POWs. Sergeant Araki was in charge of the artillery shell pol-

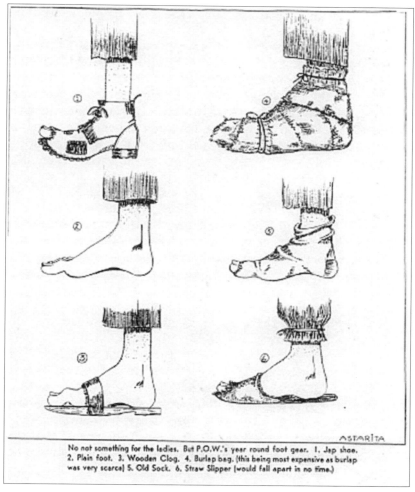

No not something for the ladies. But P.O.W.'s year round foot gear. 1. Jap shoe. 2. Plain foot. 3. Wooden Clog. 4. Burlap bag. (this being most expensive as burlap was very scarce) 5. Old Sock. 6. Straw Slipper (would fall apart in no time.)

Taken from his book, *Sketches of P. O. W. Life*, civilian prisoner of war Joseph Astarita's drawing of POW footwear gives insight into the hardships the men interned in the Japanese Army's Woosung camp, and elsewhere, had to endure.

ishing detail, making sure it was done correctly. The POWs on the other hand, were just as diligent at sabotaging the detail as much as they could get away with. But even working slowly, quite a few shells were polished and shipped out. To polish the seventy-five millimeter metal shell casings smooth, the POWs were given rice straw rope, wood ashes, and plain rice straw. Many prisoners' hands became cracked and bleeding from the work. It was also miserable out in the open air polishing sheds with just a roof overhead and only the ground to stand or sit upon. The rain and cold wind blew through constantly in winter, with heat, humidity, and insects such as malaria carrying mosquitoes in the summer.

Many of the POWs were shoeless, using what rags they could scrounge to wrap their feet in order to protect them. Until the Swiss International Red Cross delivered shoes in the autumn of 1943, those men with large feet had trouble finding suitable footwear from the Japanese issue; everything was too small.

Because of his specialized trade skill of carpentry, Jim Allen never had to do any of the manual or slave labor. Jim and the other carpenters were set up in a warehouse, or go-down as they called it, on the west side of camp. They were charged with creating a carpentry shop with only a few tools. Everything was done by hand; there were no power tools. While at Woosung camp, Jim and the other carpenters did a lot of work to repair the barracks and other buildings in order to make them more habitable. The civilian carpenters especially worked on "the place for the officers to have their little private rooms [in O Barracks] and one thing and another," Jim remembers. Larger areas within the officers' barracks were partitioned off in order to create more of the desired, individualized spaces. The carpenters were also being called on for building special projects from time to time. For example, they made a lab table and a dental chair for the use of the POWs. The prisoners' dental clinic, staffed by POWs including U.S. Navy Captain Pollard, the dentist from the Marine detachment at Peking, would eventually be well furnished with additional equipment donated by the Swiss International Red Cross and people in Shanghai. But initially, the carpenters made the available furnishings.

An extra job that the POWs were assigned to in their barracks was the fire watch. Jim recalls, "The Japanese guards went through the barracks on the hour. If a prisoner fire guard was asleep, he got the hell beat out of him!" Surrounded by old wooden buildings, fires were a major concern to all.

Sundays were a day of rest, with sleeping, reading, and gambling the major activities. The British POWs were able to indulge in a game of soccer for those with the energy and desire to play. Jim remembers attending one or two of the games. However, there were some CPNAB/Morrison Knudsen workers who pursued their own unique ways of using the day of rest, or "yasumi" in the Japanese language. Joe Astarita, for one, chose

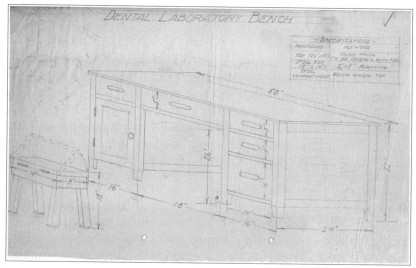

Drawing of plan for a dental laboratory bench for the Carpenter Shop to build. The small bench at the lower left has a hinged top. POW James J. Sweiberg, whose name appears written in at the upper right, was given this task. The two small holes on the bottom are from the shoelaces Jim used to hold several of these drawings together in order to carry them back to the States at the end of World War II. (James A. Allen Collection)

to draw sketches of life at the POW camps, on whatever paper he could find. Astarita hid them from the Japanese throughout his entire POW captivity by putting them in a Red Cross shaving cream tube that had been altered; the metal clamp on the bottom had been taken off, the inside of the tube cleaned, rolled up pictures inserted, and the metal clamp reaffixed to the end. Eventually, Astarita published them in a book after the war. Gurdon H. Wattles was another individual who drew pictures of camp life. A nautically inclined civilian, Ellsworth Graham enjoyed boats and drew blueprints for them whenever possible. Back in the States after the war, Graham eventually built a boat of his own.

Another favorite activity that didn't necessarily occur only on Sundays, was recipe swapping. As time passed at Woosung camp and the POWs became close to starvation, they began to dream up recipes for different foods. They wrote them down on whatever they could find, exchanging them for other POWs' recipes. Everyone was participating, according to Jim, and they came up with all sorts of recipes for every type of food imaginable. Jim doesn't know if anyone ever ended up really making any of the recipes, but it was a good diversion for the POWs as the war lengthened.

When spring finally came to Woosung camp, the warmer weather evidently warmed Colonel Yuse's heart, for he issued three small radios to the POWs. A propaganda picture of U.S. Marine Colonel James Devereux and Raymond R. Rutledge (a civilian who had thrown a multitude of hand grenades at the Japanese landing craft on Wake Island, or so Jim had heard) receiving the radios was printed in the Japanese magazine, *Freedom*. The radios could only be tuned to Japanese broadcasts in English, but any information and music was a welcome addition to prison camp life. One English language newspaper per barracks was also distributed to the prisoners at that time. Since each barracks contained roughly 280 men, there could be a lengthy wait for news if one wanted to read the paper themselves rather than listening to someone read it aloud to everyone.

The Japanese also issued a *Freedom* magazine in early 1942, Jim recalls, one to "every barracks for sure and possibly one to each section for us to look at." The magazine was similar to *Life* or *Look* magazines, but with a very pro-Japanese, pro-Coprosperity Sphere of Greater East Asia slant. One photograph in the magazine uses a picture of city buildings against a backdrop of tall, black columns of smoke. The caption read:

The smoldering fires of the great battle continues days after the fall of Singapore. The City's waterfront was darkened by gushing flames. With Japanese occupation peace was restored to the troubled inhabitants.

As with Wake Island, the Japanese had renamed Singapore, Shonato, or Enlightened South, as a demonstration of its new ownership, as evidenced by this article found on page eight in *Freedom* magazine.

Peace Descends on Shonan
Japanese Citadel of the East.

Singapore was strategic to Britain. Secure of her might, she dictated her polices in East Asia and the peoples of the East bowed to her command. Until Dec. 1941 when Japan Unleashed her military machine and challenged Britain to combat. The result has been decidedly tragic for the British Empire. Under the aegis of Japan downtrodden East Asiatic nations have overthrown the yoke of British imperialism. The victorious Japanese Army had been welcomed by the native population wherever it has gone. For Dai Nippon, creation of a Greater East Asia has set alight a flame which cannot be extinguished. For centuries the East has suffered humiliation and oppression. Today, with Japanese leadership it is united, making East Asia a better place to live. Had Britain, Holland and freedom-loving America tempered their hands of iron with justice, the Asiatic nations would not have arisen.

And so today, Dai Nippon holds the dominant position in the Far East. But unlike her predecessor, Britain, Japan is not out for domination. True, she is wielding a mailed fist, but it is only to gain freedom for the peoples of a Greater East Asia. When Anglo-American resistance is broken, she will set about molding an East which will peacefully spell Co-prosperity and Co-existence in Asia.

Another article in the magazine berated the United States for trying to limit the freedom of other countries. Centered on the page, with yellow lettering and title against a bright red background, the article had a graphic of the Statue of Liberty just above the title. The article is entitled:

HAS AMERICA FORGOTTEN?

To every true American the word "Liberty" is fraught with momentous significance. America shed her life's blood to attain her national freedom and independence from British domination. Yet, what America believes in, and what America fought for, she would not grant to the nations of Greater East Asia! America struggled for independence, but would not willingly grant it to the Philippines.

Today, some few thousand American prisoners are denouncing their government for denying liberty to others thus plunging the nations of the East into a fearful war.

Has America forgotten what Liberty means? Japan has not. Captured prisoners undeserving enemies by every rule of warfare, are given the best treatment allowed every comfort and the utmost personal freedom under the circumstances.

The article may have sounded great to the Japanese propagandists, especially the climax, but as Jim recalls, "Well, that all reads good, but it wasn't exactly like that . . ." his voice trailing off as bitter memories overwhelm him.

Freedom also contained articles about Japan's military might on the sea, in the air, and on land, showing pictures of their military units in control of newly won territory. The following article gives some insight into the general mindset of the Japanese propagandist in early 1942.

JAPANESE DEFENSE UNITS WATCH
THROUGH THE NIGHT

Military and Civilian Population Co-operate
Harmoniously to Ward Off Enemy Attacks

To every son of Nippon, Japanese soil is precious. Love for his country has exerted each valiant soldier at the front to braver and greater deeds. It is only natural then, that the defenders of home bases should feel their duties heavily. For that reason all Japanese in Japan have rallied to the call of arms. Throughout Dai Nippon's towns . . . Should any enemy plane chance to slip past patrol craft . . . modern, efficient anti-aircraft guns will bring them down in a split second.

Although previous to Japan's momentous declaration of war on Dec. 8, bombastic American statesmen claimed America could "Lick Japan with her eyes closed," no U.S. war plane has dared show itself over Nippon soil.

Japanese aircraft on the other hand have made short work of such famed Allied strongholds as Singapore, Hong Kong and Sourabaya. The reason why Nippon has scored such tremendous successes in so short a space of time may be credited to British, American and Dutch misrule of the peoples of East Asia. . . .

American airmen taken captive . . . have testified that Japanese airplanes are in no way inferior . . . Fighting aircraft of Japan are piloted by men who have no fear of death. As a result, British and American warplanes have been powerless when attacked by Japanese air squadrons. . . . Nipponese dive bombers using their planes and themselves as human torpedoes. . . . can never be defeated.

It doesn't take much imagination to know what the POWs in the barracks around Woosung camp had to say among themselves about the "human torpedoes" and the rest of the propaganda articles from the first months of the war in *Freedom* magazine.

Spring in Woosung not only brought radios and periodicals but also the opportunity for Jim and others to get a shave and haircut for the first time since before the Wake Island siege. In April, one of the Marine barbers began offering to cut prisoners' hair and give them a shave, all for twenty-five cents. It was a good deal, if you had the money. Jim was one of those who

Taken for public relations purposes this *Freedom* magazine photograph of a prisoner and Japanese conference at Woosung gives the viewer a glance at what the barracks and other buildings in the camp looked like. The Kiangwan, China camp was very similar. (*Freedom*/James A. Allen Collection)

Referred to as "sanitary washrooms," the washracks between the barracks and the benjo, allowed the POWs some water to wash in. The three-inch water pipe between the sinks brought cold, non-potable water from a small holding tank (rear center left). A larger elevated wooden tank fed water to the entire camp.
(*Freedom*/James A. Allen Collection)

didn't, having lost his wallet to the Japanese on Wake Island, but his buddy, Eddie Peres, gave him the twenty-five cents. Peres could afford to be generous; he still had money he had kept hidden away. Peres had a bad knee that he kept bandaged for support. A veteran of World War I, he had learned how to wrap soldiers' leggings in the army and wrapped his bandages the same way, winding the cloth around both his knee and five twenty dollar bills, which allowed the money to "disappear" from the Japanese's view when searched. Peres was rich by POW camp standards. Thanks to his friend's kindness and the Marine barber's electric shaver, Jim claims that particular shave "was the closest I ever had!" Having the long, scraggily hair and beard off definitely left Jim feeling much better.

Jim remained extremely healthy considering his situation. His luck ran out, though, during the summer of 1942. It was then that Jim made the unfortunate acquaintance of a female Anopheles mosquito, and became infected with malaria, a disease which can be fatal. The initial onset of the red blood cell infection by the single-celled organism called a Plasmodium, species *malariae,* caused Jim to be in the prisoners' hospital

As the POWs' stay in China lengthened, POW barbers like Mike Rice, set up a camp barber shop to try to keep the hundreds of prisoners groomed as best they could with what tools they had available to them. To maximize space, "barber chairs" were set up on an unused sleeping platform. (Joseph J. Astrarita)

for a week. After Jim was bitten, the Plasmodium moved to his liver and began to rapidly multiply. Leaving the liver about three weeks later, the Plasmodium multiplied so prodigiously within the red blood cells, that the cells burst. The onset of this phase was heralded with headache, chills, and fever, causing Jim to shake violently. The camp doctor gave Jim quinine to treat the parasitic disease. However, this treatment was not adequate for the type of malaria that Jim had contracted, for the mature malaria Plasmodium remained in his bloodstream, creating the repetition of malarial symptoms in variable intervals of decreasing severity for years. Even in his eighties, Jim is periodically reminded by his malarial parasites that they are still within him.

Jim received this POW camp rest slip when he contracted catarrhal fever. The slip gave him three days off to overcome it. Rest slips were re-quired when a POW was not ill enough to be in the hospital, but still sick enough not to be able to work. Catarrh is an inflammation of any mucous membrane. In Jim's case, it was most likely a severe cold, sinus infection, or flu. (James A. Allen Collection)

As with anyone separated from their loved ones, concern about what relatives knew or did not know bothered Jim as he rode out his malaria in the hospital. There he had time to think more about his family and whether they knew he was alive. Communication was practically nonexistent as far as Jim knew. The POWs had not received any mail from the States since Wake Island had come under siege. The Japanese used writing letters home as an infrequent reward.

On Wednesday, 3 June, Jim received a piece of the official camp stationary and was allowed to write home for the first time. His letter was stamped in the upper right corner with the official chop mark indicating the Japanese censors had cleared its contents. The rectangular stamp was the inspector's name and/or rank in Japanese characters, much like a signature in the United States. Papers of any type were not official without a chop mark and all mail leaving or arriving at camp needed the authorized chop imprint. The POWs' letters had to be printed clearly with a hyphen between words. Early letters were allowed to be much longer than ones written later in the war when the length of the messages would be restricted.

Unknown to Jim and the other POWs as they eagerly wrote their letters, the Battle of Midway was to begin the next day, 4 June 1942. This was a major turning point in the Pacific theater. Japanese naval superiority in the Pacific Ocean ended with their defeat by the United States Navy in the waters near

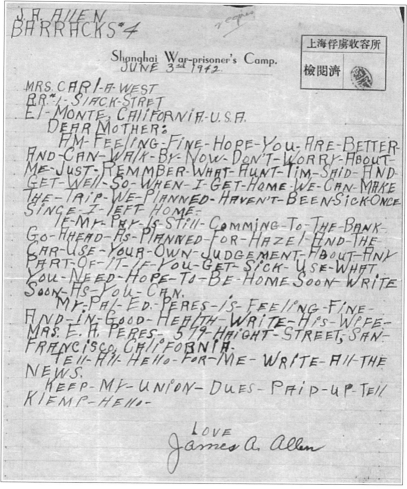

The above letter was the first that Jim was able to write home. Although out of touch with his family for over six months, he is still trying to keep things running smoothly. Note the official chop mark in the upper right hand corner, indicating that this letter was approved to be sent on. (James A. Allen Collection)

Midway Island. The apex of the Japanese Empire had been reached.

When asked about the time he was the most afraid when a prisoner of war, Jim replied, "You never knew when you might [be beaten or killed]. All the time, scared of the unknown. Fortunately, I never got beat up, but [I] saw others. [I]Always managed to do or say the right thing. You had to think over there and think quick; be on your toes and use your head or die. You could argue with them [the Japanese], but you had to know what you were doing!" The longer Jim was a POW, the better he became at negotiating with his captors, which was beneficial for himself and other POWs.

One frightening episode that occurred at the Shanghai War Prisoners Camp at Woosung, dealt with the theft of some Hershey chocolate bars. The Japanese had a "little old shed," as Jim calls it, that they referred to as a canteen. There the Japanese sold items like chocolate bars to the POWs. However, the POWs had hardly any money to spend at the canteen. Nevertheless, Japanese authorities could honestly state to the Swiss International Red Cross representative during visits, that Woosung camp had a canteen with items to purchase available to the prisoners.

The POWs were quite aware of the canteen and its contents, and a conspiracy of a sort was formed by a few of the civilians to obtain a bit of the merchandise without the use of currency. The conspirators had noticed that if two POWs were walking about with a yea-ho pole between them from which hung a half-full rice sack of dirt, none of the guards would bother them. They could go practically anywhere they wanted to in camp. Jim remembers "a couple of wise guys in Barracks 4 Section 6" taking a yea-ho pole and walking by the canteen. More conspirators were on the inside positioned near an opened window. When the first "wise guy" walked past the open window, a couple of boxes of Hershey chocolate bars were tossed out the window and into the partially dirt filled rice sack dangling by grass ropes between the men. The two Section 6 "wise guys" never slowed down. They just kept a steady pace as they walked past the window and received the purloined sweets.

In Barracks 4 Section 4, Jim's buddy, Eddie Peres had secretly loosened some of the wooden horizontal wallboards next to their sleeping platform, exposing a void. It was a great place to hide things. Eddie had done an excellent job of camouflaging the beveled edges of the boards and making them able to be removed and replaced when desired. The barracks' guards had no idea that the wall had been tampered with.

When it came to secreting their illicit goods, the conspirators were not careful enough. While hiding the boxes of chocolate bars in the attic above Section 6 of Barracks 4, they were spied upon by other POWs. When the coast was clear, this new group of POW thieves retrieved the stolen chocolate from the attic. Somehow they had prior knowledge of Eddie's wall and talked him into hiding the chocolate bars inside the wall panel. Eventually, the loss of the chocolate bar boxes was noticed by the Japanese soldier in charge of the canteen, and a massive search begun. Jim never learned how the Japanese found out who the original chocolate thieves from Section 6 were. Unhappily for those men, when they went to retrieve the chocolate bars with an escort of Japanese guards, it was not where they had left it in the attic. They didn't know what had happened and now were "in an awful terrible fix for a while" as Jim puts it. "Here I was, sleeping by it the whole time." Luckily, neither did the Japanese.

So the great hunt for the Hershey chocolate bars was on. All of Barracks 4 was inspected while the 288 POW residents stood at attention near the end of their individual sleeping platform space, but in the center of the walkway. Jim's space was the one closest to the horizontal wallboards concealing the boxes of stolen chocolate bars, and he stood with his back to the hidden sweets. Some of the Japanese guards were crawling through the attic while others rampaged through Barracks 4, throwing bedding off platforms and knocking everything off the POWs' shelves and pegs. Jim recalls, "They took a cheese cutter [Japanese sword], tore everything off the walls."

Being single minded, chocolate was the only thing the Japanese wanted to find at that time. Jim recalls the finding of any other sort of contraband was merely overlooked or disregarded. "I happened to have an onion in my [extra] clothes and they swiped them off the bed. The onion went on rolling across the floor, which was contraband and [I] could have gotten a good beating out of it, but they didn't . . . All they could see was chocolate and of course, they never did find that chocolate. They went all through the barracks and never found anything," Jim recalls with a chuckle.

Coming up empty handed, the persistent Japanese decided to use a different strategy. All food rations for the camp were shut off. Perhaps increased hunger would make the chocolate appear. According to Jim, "nobody was eating and [the prisoners] finally got their heads together." Apparently, Barracks 4's adjutant and assistant adjutant negotiated with the Japanese authorities for the chocolate's return. Somehow Barracks 4's adjutant, John Burroughs, had discovered that the chocolate was hidden in Eddie's wall and came to retrieve it from him. Jim recalls, "They loaded up that damn chocolate out of there and I was damn glad to see it go." Luckily for Jim, the Japanese did not stumble upon the secret space or he might have been considered one of the responsible parties since he slept next to it. Upon securing the pilfered chocolate, the Japanese "beat the fellas up that stole it. They beat them up real good. Kept them in the aneiso [Japanese for guardhouse] quite a while." Eddie's wall was not used again at the Woosung camp.

There was one other time that the Japanese guards went all out and scoured a barracks to find some contraband. That search took place later at the Shanghai War Prisoners Camp at Kiangwan. The contraband was a radio in O Barracks where the officer POWs were housed. Again, some Japanese guards were in the attic searching while others tore through the barracks with the POWs all at attention. As the inspection party proceeded through the barracks, a small second lieutenant by the name of Miyazaki inadvertently discovered a weak spot in the attic floor. He fell right through the ceiling and onto the inspection party. After the inspection ruckus was over, Jim recalls, "We all had a big laugh," especially since the little lieutenant was in charge of the Carpenter Shop and Jim and the other carpenters had gotten to know him. "He was an eager little beaver. He wasn't too bad a Joe, though." Of course, the poor Lt. Miyazaki probably didn't think it was very funny when it happened.

September of 1942 was an eventful month at the Shanghai War Prisoners Camp. On the eighteenth, seventy skilled prisoners, primarily CPNAB/Morrison Knudsen construction workers from Wake Island, were transferred to Japan. It was assumed that since the transfer only involved men with special skills, these prisoners were needed to work on a specific project somewhere. Thinking he might be repatriated sooner in China than Japan, Jim was just as happy staying in Woosung.

Also in September there was an unexpected change in the Japanese leadership of the camp. After being in command of the camp for seven or so months, Colonel Yuse died from malaria. All the POWs were ordered to line the camp road, standing at attention while Yuse's hearse drove by. As Jim recalls, "When his hearse come by, it was an old Oriental [hearse]. We had to line each side of the road as the hearse slowly passed by." The POWs were "paying our respects to him, if there were any!" Woosung camp then welcomed its third commander, Colonel Otera, who was in charge of all the camps in the Shanghai area.

Another major event happened for Jim and the camp in September: mail from home! Jim received his first letter from the States. Up until then, there had only been local mail, which Jim never received not knowing anyone in Shanghai. Jim remembers he "was one of the fortunate ones who did receive a letter from my mother in September 1942. Many prisoners did not receive any [at that time] and many prisoners didn't receive any [mail] the entire war." Now at least Jim knew for sure that his mother, Viola, understood he was alive and where he was.

El Monte, Calif.
June 10-1942

My Dear Son James —
We'll send you another letter. Got to-day the address have sent others hope you get them. How are you everyone is alright. I'm Not well yet. Aim to be when you get home. Well its class night for Hazel to-night. School will soon be out. James is there any business you want tended to here. Your car is paid for. We are just waiting for you to come home. How glad I will be. All will be. Bill's graduation is Next Thursday. Pal is the same old dog. He stay with Bill all the time Uncle Arthurs at Manteca now.
Lucheon isn't home now. Jerald working for the P.E. Car the same old job. Dorthys baby hasn't arrived yet. Looking for hers and Geneva & Carl F. in July. Aunt Barbara's baby is to come in July. Grandma & grandpa are as always. Jack Morgan was in Jail for awhile is out Now and Tom is married last Oct. My dear Son. When you get home will talk then I hope I will see you very soon, I hope. Uncle Mart is at Yuba City Bill [Goodman] Smith in San Diego Now last I heard. Well bye bye you try to get to send me a letter. Hope you get all of mine. Hope you are well and in best of health. So long. From Mother sending you My Love.
From all. X X X X

It was apparently June before Viola found out where Jim was finally interned. Passing along news of family and friends helped keep Jim informed as well as giving Viola something to write about at a time of uncertainty. As the waiting for a letter from her son dragged on, Viola's letters to Jim showed the frustration the anxious mother felt not knowing what was happening to her firstborn.

Aug-6-1942 El Monte
Calif.

My Dear Son James:

How are you. Hope you are well. Everyone is alright. Bill is cook and house keeper now. Hazel and bob was home 2 weeks ago. Got grandpa and grandmas picture for my birthday. They sure look good. Carl Fostner is papa now 9 lb. 6 oz boy. If I could only know just how you are. Manard quit his job has no work now. James I sent you a small package. Wish I could send you what I want to. (cont.- other side)

You know you always say keep your chin up Mother. Bill [Goodman] Smith is in Indiana last time I heard from him Lucheon in Ark. My dear boy I will some day Write what I want to. So I am saying bye bye longing for My boy to come home.

from your Mother

with all my Love. I wish I could get a letter from you. Your hand writing

XXXXXXXXXX
XXXXXXXXXXX
XXXXXXXXXX

A prominent plea of "Do you get my letters?" is found in many of Viola's letters until Jim was able to write that he had received one. Viola had a long wait ahead of her. She would not receive her first letter from Jim, the one written 3 June 1942, until September of 1943: twenty long months without word from her James.

Also adding to Viola's frustration were the draft notices that arrived at her home. The local draft board had not looked closely at Jim's file with its permission paperwork allowing him to work on Wake Island until July 1942. Viola finally wrote and told the Selective Service that if they went and got her James from the Japanese, he would probably be glad to be drafted! That put an end to the draft notices.

Throughout their imprisonment, the POWs were issued ten cigarettes a day. Since Jim didn't smoke, he used to give his ration of cigarettes to the "fellas." By September of 1942 though, cigarettes had become a valuable form of currency. POWs, who didn't smoke them for their nicotine addiction, sold or bartered with them. Around this time, undernourished Jim started to smoke his ration, learning to appreciate a cigarette for the delicious aftertaste it gave to his saliva. With the meager and limited prison camp food, the touch of sweetness produced by the burning tobacco was very welcomed. Of course the sweet taste did not last long, but by then Jim was hooked and smoked cigarettes for the next thirty years.

Fall turned into winter as the POWs kept speculating on how the war was going. Of course, the Japanese told the POWs that their superior forces were smashing the United States Navy fleets. As the tide of war began to turn against Japan, the camp guards were ordered to collect the three issued radios from the POWs. Only contraband ones would be in the barracks to hear the news that the Allies were beginning to get the upper hand in the Pacific as well as in Europe. As the scuttlebutt of American South Pacific victories drifted through the camp, some of the POWs' hopes of being home before much longer heightened.

When the cold autumn weather began to change to winter frigid, the scuttlebutt circulated that the entire camp was relocating, a move welcomed by everyone. The scuttlebutt became reality after the noon meal on Thursday, 3 December. Jim and the rest of the POWs bid a happy farewell to the muddy Woosung camp. Carrying their few belongings and bedding, they began the long walk to their new place of internment, four hours to the southwest at Kiangwan, another small town in the greater Shanghai area. There, the POWs hoped their stay would be a short one and the journey home would be soon.

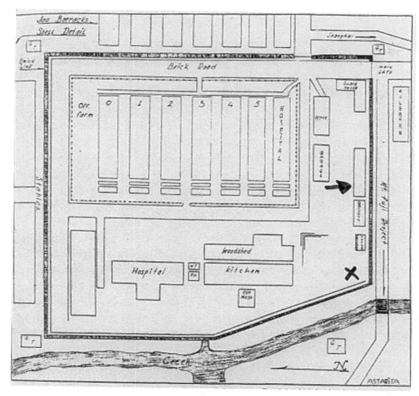

Shanghai War Prisoners Camp, Kiangwan. Against the southern wall is the building, (arrow), which housed the Carpenter Shop and Tin Shop in the east end, Tailor Shop at the west end, with Japanese Lt. Watanabe's warehouse area in between. The X indicates the location of the pig sties. Below each of the numbered barracks are the buildings housing the benjos with the washracks between. Jim Allen resided in Barracks 4. A barbed-wire fence encircled the barracks, benjos and washracks, with a road around its perimeter. A brick wall, eight-feet in height with barbed wire fencing on top and guard towers at the four corners surrounded the entire camp. (Joseph J. Astarita)

8

Shanghai War Prisoners
Camp at Kiangwan

After four long hours of walking through the cold, the POWs and their Japanese guards reached their next home, the Shanghai War Prisoners Camp at Kiangwan (now Jiangwan), China. The early darkness of winter was closing around them as they walked through the main gate and past the thick, nine-foot tall brick walls topped with electric barbed wire that surrounded the camp. Located on the Tazang Motor Road in the small suburban Shanghai town of Kiangwan, the camp was only an hour drive by car north of Shanghai's center. The camp was situated between a Japanese civilian airfield two miles to the north and a military airfield four miles to the south. Jim Allen and some of the other POWs realized if the Allies were to attack the area, those airfields would be prime targets, and they'd have front row seats to cheer them on!

Unlike the Woosung camp, Kiangwan had been built on higher, drier ground, a big improvement that helped the morale of the POWs a little. The Woosung guards and officers, with Colonel Otera as commanding officer, had followed the prisoners to the Kiangwan camp, which immediately gave it a feeling of familiarity. Other than the new buildings and the lack of the heavy mud, Kiangwan camp life was basically the same. Once they had

Artist Joseph J. Astarita of Brooklyn, New York. Astarita "did a damn good job!" with his drawings, according to Wake Island Civilian POW Charles Nokes. (PIEF)

arrived at their new residence, the weary POWs were eager to find their barracks and unload their belongings.

There were not any surprises for the POWs at the Kiangwan War Prisoners' Camp like there had been when they first arrived at Woosung and they were grateful for that. Although the barracks and camp were new to the POWs, the buildings were as old as those at Woosung, but a lot drier. The POWs were assigned the same barracks and section numbers they had had at Woosung, so it was easy to locate their new abodes. Jim went into the new wooden Barracks 4 and found his spot in Section 4 that was basically his same bed space as in Woosung. Bungo and inspection were still before tea and breakfast, with tenko following in the evening. All meals were still eaten in the prisoners' barracks section at the foot of their sleeping platforms. There was some improvement on sanitation; however, drinking water still had to be boiled twenty minutes to be safe.

At Kiangwan camp there were about 1,600 prisoners by 1945, although that number varied from time to time. This included the Wake Island civilian construction workers and a mix of British military, United States Navy, Marines, Army, and merchant marines, including one Jewish sailor, Katz. It could be safely assumed that the Kiangwan camp offered Katz better treatment than any in Eastern Europe under the auspices of the Germans. In the summer of 1943, a group of Italian Embassy soldiers and merchant marines from the Italian luxury liner that Jim remembers being named the *Count Verde*, were housed in Barracks 5. Jim recalls that the liner's captain had ordered the crew to open the ship's seacocks to scuttle it and the ship sank in Shanghai's Huangpo River. Since these Italians remained loyal to King Victor Emmanuel II of Italy and General Badoglio, they were captured by the Japanese in Shanghai and became prisoners of war. Those Italians still loyal to the Fascist government of Benito Mussolini, as part of the Axis powers, were fighting along with the Japanese.

With their second Christmas in captivity coming soon, the

The view was depressing inside the Kiangwan camp brick walls. The two water pits for fire protection are in the foreground. The small gate to the left of the guard tower is the passage to the Japanese Army barracks. To the right of the tower, the perimeter road leads to the main gate. (Joseph J. Astarita)

improvement in camp life by moving to Kiangwan helped pick spirits up a bit. Life began to look even better when the first Swiss International Red Cross boxes arrived just before Christmas 1942. These were a big hit with the starving POWs since the boxes contained food as well as some clothing to replace worn out garments or provide additional ones. A special treat for Jim were the lima beans and ham the Red Cross truck also brought for the POW galley. "Boy, were they good," recalls Jim wistfully. Jim had the job of serving the thirty-six men in

Christmas card, 1942. (James A. Allen Collection)

his section, a job now complicated by the daunting task of dividing a portion of ham thirty-six ways to satisfy everyone with his share and that of the others. "Well, with looks and convincing, everyone was happy. We finally got it figured out." Some of the men in Barracks 4 Section 4 liked the hide of the ham, thinking they would get more than if it were just the meat. Others clamored for the bone so they could suck the marrow out. "Some of us didn't particularly care for that part of the ham." In Jim's section there were "no fights or yelling when dividing up food. It was very much like the town meeting in New England, showing respect for each other."

Soon after the move to Kiangwan camp, Jim received a Christmas card from a Marie Moore of the Shanghai Civilian International Internees Camp. It was addressed on the envelope:

> J. A. Allen, Esq.
> Shanghai War Prisoner Camp.

Jim states, "The only time I can remember being referred to as esquire, was when I was a small boy, about two or three years old. And that was only in a postcard or letter that my mom and dad had had received from his folks in Illinois." The card was designed on the front with a traditional Santa astride a mule while crossing an arched wooden bridge. Inside, the script read:

> Merry Christmas & Happy New Year
> From
> Shanghai Americans to the Prisoners of War.

"It was sure a good feeling, made you feel good to get the Christmas card," Jim recalls. "And of course we had an excellent Christmas dinner furnished by a fellow by the name [of] Jimmy James, [who] was a retired [American] sailor in Shanghai. [Jimmy James] happened to take and be doing quite well. He had a restaurant or two. He sent out all the turkey and all the trimmings. A fine dinner for everyone in camp, about 1200 people, I guess." Jimmy's restaurant at 133 Nanking in Shanghai was still in business in November of 1945. The U.S. Army's Fourteenth Air Force described his restaurant as "the closest thing to Stateside food," in their *Flying Tigers' GUIDE TO SHANGHAI* for the men serving in the Shanghai area after its liberation. Apparently word of Jimmy's food, as well as his generosity, spread through the Western Pacific area. Jimmy James "passed away in Texas [1982 or 83], I guess." (Long after the war ended, Jim had kept up with many of those he had become acquainted with during his prisoner of war days.)

For the past year food had been the main topic of conversation, in fact, just about the only topic, as the POWs became hungrier and hungrier. For most of the POWs, food remained the main focus of their lives: obtaining food, eating it, and then obtaining more food. Memories of long ago meals, like those at the Wake Island Civilian Mess Hall and the whole pies after movies, continued to be recalled and exchanged along with recipes.

As 1943 began, the Kiangwan camp POWs' stomachs were the most content they had been during their entire thirteen months of internment, having been at least partially satisfied with the Red Cross boxes and Jimmy James' generosity. The main topic of conversation around camp was no longer food; conversations now revolved around women and sex. This lasted, Jim laughingly remembers, until "their stomachs were empty, [again, then] it went back about food." Sex becomes a low priority issue when you are starving. Gavan Dawes wrote in his book, *Prisoners of the Japanese*, of one story related to him by ex-POWs, of how a native girl walked by a POW camp in the tropics with a stalk of bananas on her head while wearing only a blouse. After she passed, the interned men were heard remarking about what a fine stalk of bananas that was; the girl's nakedness was not noticed, or at least commented on, but the food definitely was.

Much to Jim's pleasure, the Japanese had issued the POWs large metal spoons, as well as forks, early in 1942 back at Woosung. Jim's wooden Dixie Cup spoon was set aside as another of his souvenirs to bring home. The POWs called the metal spoons "rice shovels" since rice was their main food. They used the metal spoons continuously for three meals a day, everyday, causing the spoons to deteriorate and expose the base metal, resulting in a

rusty appearance. However, in order to preserve the spoons' use-
fulness, the always resourceful Jim and others who worked in
the Carpenter and Tin Shops were recycling materials long before it became popular. As Jim recalls, "We'd eat the original plating off . . . Then [in the Tin Shop] we melted up [the metal]
toothpaste tubes [containing lead] from the Red Cross boxes and
smeared it on [the spoon bowl] and then eat that off" over time.
Luckily, Jim's spoon's base metal slowly became exposed, requiring it to be replated only once.

The Red Cross boxes, which usually arrived at Kiangwan
camp around the tenth of the month, if they came, went a
long way to supplement the camp's regular menu. They were
most appreciated by the POWs, as evidenced by Jim's letter
home shortly after the New Year.

JAMES-A-ALLEN
BARRACKS #4-SECTION #4
MRS-CARL-A-WEST   SHANGHAI-CHINA
RR #1-SLACK. ST.   JANUARY-2-1943
EL-MONTE-CALIFORNIA-U.S.A.

DEAR MOTHER:
    THERES-NOT-MUCH-TO-WRITE-ABOUT-AS-
YOU-PROBABLY-KNOW-OR-UNDERSTAND-BY-
NOW-I-AM-IN-THE-VERY-BEST-OF-HEALTH-AND-
HAVE-BEEN-EVERY-SINCE-CAPTURED-EAT-ALL-
I-CAN-GET-HAVE-BEEN-DOING-VERY-WELL-
SINCE-THE-RED-CROSS-BOXES-ARRIVED-HAVE-
RECEIVED-TWO-CANADIAN-AND-TWO-
AMERICAN-THEY-ARE-VERY-NICE-HAVE-
GOTTEN-ONE-CCC-ISSUE-KIT-
    WE-HAD-A-VERY-NICE-XMAS-AND-NEW-
YEAR'S-THANKS-TO-THE-RED-CROSS-AND-THE-
COMMANDER-IN-CHARGE-OF-THE-CAMP-THE-
JAPANESE-OFFICERS-GAVE-US-SEVERAL-
PRIVALIDGES-OVER-THE-HOLLIDAYS.
    THIS-XMAS-WAS-VERY-MUCH-BETTER-THAN-
LAST. EDDIE-AND-I-ARE-STILL-TOGETHER-AND-
ARE-REAL-PALS-EVERN-THOUGH-HE-HAS-SIX-
GRANDCHILDREN-EDDIE-WILL-BE-51-JANUARY-
26-BUT-DOESN'T-LOOK-A-DAY-OVER-38-WE-
HAVE-BEEN-TOGETHER-FOR-15-MONTHS-

WORKED-SLEPT-EAT-WASH,BATHE-AND-WHAT-
HAVE-YOU-SURE-GET-TO-SEE-ENOUGH-OF-
YOUR-FELLOW-MEN-

WE-HAVE-ONE-CANADIAN-DOCTOR-THREE-
AMERICAN-AND-WE-HAVE-A-VERY-GOOD-
JAPANESE-DOCTOR-WHO-DOES-ALL-HE-CAN-
FOR-US-

WILL-SEND-THIS-LETTER-TO-GRANDMA-
AND-GRANDPA-I-WORKED-VERY-HARD-DEC.31ST
AND-FOR-THOSE-WHO-WORKED-THE-
JAPANESE-LET-US-HAVE-TWO-SHEETS-OF-
PAPER-OR-TWO-LETTERS.

HAVE-ONLY-RECEIVED-ONE-LETTER FROM-
YOU FOLKS. HOPE-YOU-ALL-HAD-A-HAPPY-
HOLLIDAY.

> As ever
> Your son
> James A. Allen

On the left-hand side of the letter near the middle of the page, the word "reported" was written next to the information about Eddie Peres. Either the American military censors or the Morrison Knudsen Company officials did this after Viola forwarded the letter on to them, as requested. By gleaning information from POWs' letters to family and friends, officials gained a better idea of who was alive, where they were, conditions of the camps, and other war information could be had.

Jim wrote on his second piece of paper a letter to his maternal grandparents in Missouri. The Japanese censors apparently felt that some of the information Jim wrote shouldn't be sent out in a letter and so they simply cut out the offending sentences. Years later, Jim has no idea what had been written in that particular sentence that would have required it to be censored.

In his 2 January 1943 letter to his grandparents, Jim wrote that the barracks were now heated by stoves for limited hours, which alleviated some of the severe cold for the POWs. But fuel for the stoves was provided for only a short time. The POWs still marched together in a circular route through their barracks in order to stay warm, a form of line dancing one might say.

The prisoners' work at Kiangwan camp was divided into several projects during their residence. Those prisoners who had

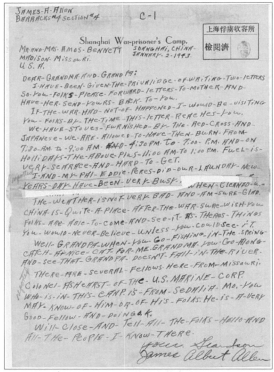

Jim's letter to his grandparents in Missouri has a missing area where a censor, Japanese or American, cut out that information, which was apparently thought to have been sensitive. The word "reported" has been written on the left-hand side, faintly, in two places. (James A. Allen Collection)

mechanical skills, like the Marine ground crew of VMF 211, were sent each day to work on truck maintenance at a Japanese garage. Two Morrison Knudsen metal workers, Don Ludington and Richard Fuller, set up a tin shop and the carpenters had their workshop going. Over time, Kiangwan Camp became a miniature town with the addition of a shoe shop, supervised by Frank Collins, and a tailor shop. All the workshops were located in a building shared with Sergeant Watanabe's warehouse, which stored the Japanese's clothes and other military supplies. In another camp building, POWs such as Mike Rice of California and John Schafferstein, worked as barbers, giving the other POWs haircuts and shaves while their subjects reclined on tilted wooden benches or sat on stools.

One Wake Island civilian, Oral C. Nichols, Jr. of New Mexico, became a typist for the Japanese Army. Nichols had been Morrison Knudsen Supervisor Dan Teters' s typist after the original secretary, Robert L. Yriberry, had been killed during the first day of battle on the Wake atoll. Right after arrival at Woosung in January 1942, Teters had received permission to write to the Shanghai International Red Cross liaison, a Mr. Egle, who became a great help to the POWs. Nichols was instructed to type the official letter and as he was doing so, a Japanese inspection party led by Colonel Yuse unexpectedly came through the barracks. With his back to the door, Nichols did not realize the Japanese had arrived, and kept on typing. According to Nichols, the typewriter was strange to the Japanese and they were very interested in what he was doing. Before they left, they took his ID number and the next day, Nichols was assigned to the Japanese camp office. He was given the job of typing three by five-inch information cards containing the personal data the POWs had already written on scraps of paper. Apparently none of the Japanese at the camp knew how to type and Nichols' special skill was in demand. This "easy job" as Nichols' calls it, saved him from the rigors of the hard labor details. It was also a position in which information could be gleaned and passed on to other POWs.

Those prisoners who were unskilled and not officers drew the hard labor projects, such as burying fifty-five gallon metal drums filled with gasoline, motor oil, and alcohol for safekeeping. This was carried out at the Shanghai Race Course, quite a distance from the Kiangwan camp that the weakened POWs walked twice a day. A "fringe benefit" of working there was the opportunity to siphon off some of the alcohol and smuggle it back to camp to drink, sell, or trade for other items. Those that drank the questionable beverage said it tasted like pineapple. Jim never touched the stuff since he believed it was tainted; some men became ill from it. Jim remembers prisoners so desperate for alcohol, that they drank aircraft engine fluid and died.

By far the largest and most backbreaking project some of the POWs had to labor at while in the Kiangwan camp, was the merciless "Mount Fuji." This project concentrated on building a firing range backstop for the Japanese Army as well as twelve smaller mountains of dirt. Twelve meters or approximately forty feet high, Mount Fuji was created by hand over a two year period by the POWs. According to Jim, "It was hell" for those who worked on it. "It ruined many men's health" since they had to carry heavy buckets of dirt on yea-ho poles and they also had to push small mining rail cars on tracks, which climbed over thirty feet in elevation. "That was a tremendous job and there was a lot of men that ended up with bad legs on that one; varicose veins." The POWs were only "powered by rice," as Jim says.

For their work at the Kiangwan camp, the POWs did receive token pay. The civilians were paid on the same scale as the enlisted military men, which was substantially less than officers. Paid in Chinese Republic Bank (CRB) dollars, Jim received fifty-five CRB dollars a month. "Not enough to buy a pound of peanut butter," says Jim, since a pound cost five hundred CRB. Not much for a month's hard labor, but it was some money that could be spent on extras like food, clothing, or cigarettes between the prisoners themselves.

Although the POWs were not on the front lines of battle, many found ways in which to sabotage the enemy's military capability. The POWs assigned to work in the auto parts warehouses and machine shops managed to decrease the Japanese parts inventory whenever possible. The POWs were required to build sod brick barriers around the individual machines to protect them from damage during bombing attacks. Jim recalls, "A lot of guys threw auto parts out the warehouses into the sod banks to be covered up." The POWs' would take a part off a shelf or a machine when the guards weren't looking and toss them into the dirt wall nearby. The toss would be timed to occur as other POWs were bringing more sod bricks to the barrier, which would then cover the part up. A part or two buried once in a while added up over time.

Those working at the Shanghai Race Course would slightly loosen the bung, or stopper, of each fifty-five gallon drum, or barrel, whenever possible and then stack them upside down. The slightly loosened bung would allow the liquid inside to ooze out slowly, not calling attention to the fact that the barrel was leaking. When this was done to hundreds of barrels, the oozing added up to a lot of missing Japanese fuel without them being aware of it until it was too late. It doesn't necessarily take large or flamboyant measures to sabotage an enemy.

Free time was spent in similar ways as it had been at Woosung, with cards, reading, sleeping, and so forth. Jim was not one to gamble much, so at Kiangwan, he joined three other civilian prisoners, Jack Aikens, Don Ludington, and Miles Glaze, playing bridge in their free time. "We four did not have any money involved in winning or losing," Jim recalls. "Our honor depended on bidding our cards correctly. By doing so, we could have an enjoyable Sunday and evenings."

It was at Kiangwan that Jim began to keep a log of the dates and times, if possible, of where he'd traveled up to that time. Starting with boarding the SS *Matsonia* docked at the pier in San Pedro, Los Angeles' port, Jim had remembered all the times and dates up to Kiangwan Camp. All, that is, except the times of arrival and departure from Yokohama and Shanghai; there wasn't a clock in the *Nitta Maru's* forward hold.

As spring 1943 arrived, some of the POWs improvised on a childhood ditty that became a rite of spring each year. "Spring is sprung. The grass is riz. I wonder where the Allies is?" was wistfully chanted by the prisoners. The reality of the war situation left big question marks about when the Allies would be arriving in Southern China, but it didn't appear to be soon. The hope of a short war had long vanished.

Jim and the POWs received permission to write letters home on the occasion of Emperor Hirohito's birthday, 29 April. In his letter, Jim wrote that he had written a total of four letters at that point, but had received only Viola's letter of the 10 June 1942. Letter writing was used as a reward or punishment. The Japanese revoked the privilege for offenses they deemed worthy. Jim was quick to realize if he started his letters off by writing, "With-the-kind-permission-of-the-Japanese. . ." he stood a better chance of getting a letter through all the hands it had to pass through. "Jap Lover" was the epithet some POWs used, Jim says, to refer to those kowtowing to their captors. But when you are in a continual life or death situation for an unforeseen length of time, one does what is necessary to survive. Also, in this case it was a means of getting information out far beyond the brick and electrified barbed wire walls of Kiangwan Camp. The POWs were still required to print letters with a hyphen connecting all words. Those in the States also were required to do this in their letters as the war dragged on. Viola's early letters were in cursive and lengthy, but within a few months changed to printing with a maximum length of twenty-five words because of the restrictions placed on those writing from the home front. This was a cause of much frustration to Viola, as well as other mothers, wives, and sweethearts.

Her frustration is evident in the repetition of the sentence "Have you gotten any of my letters?" Viola began each letter she wrote with this pleading question, followed by news from home. After continually writing Jim letters and mailing them for a year-and-one-half, Viola, like most mothers, longed to hear how her James was doing. The United States government was not much help, only asking Viola to forward any letters she might receive from her son in the hopes of discovering bits and pieces of information censors overlooked that

Two sides of a postcard written by Jim at the Kiangwan camp. Viola would not receive it until 1944 since it would take over a year for Jim's mail to reach the States. (James A. Allen Collection)

could possibly help the war effort or locate a missing man.

Jim's 29 April 1943 letter home also held news important to a POW, if not to anyone else. According to Jim, the Red Cross had sent into Kiangwan Camp a "fair dinner of chicken and noodles with rice. First since Thanksgiving 1941," which was a memorable pre-war feast on Wake Island.

In the summer of 1943, Jim's malaria flared up with the debilitating chills and fever. Jim required hospitalization for six weeks this time; he also had the misfortune to have severe amoebic dysentery at the same time. The Kiangwan camp POWs were lucky to have Lieutenant Yoshihiro Shindo (later Captain) as the Japanese doctor in charge. Jim recalls that Lt. Shindo "did a lot for us prisoners, but there wasn't a whole lot he could do for his own soldiers, let alone us."

An avid and fast reader when material was available, Jim spent the time in his hospital bed reading books from the camp library. The POWs had been receiving books from time to time from the people in the Shanghai area and the YMCA there, and managed to have a fine library by the time they left Kiangwan.

Jim remembers two books in particular from that summer, since they had a profound effect on his life and the way he interacted with others, especially the Japanese. One was Dale Carnegie's *How to Win Friends and Influence People*, which Jim had heard of long before leaving the United States. Carnegie's book gave Jim some good insight into human behavior. "It was a hell of a lot of help to me with the prisoners. It helped me once I got home, too. It tells you how to talk to people." Being a civilian, Jim couldn't order people around as the military could do with other military men, pulling rank if needed. The civilians and people in general, had to be approached in a way that would allow them to agree with whatever was being asked of them. "Carnegie's book was a lot of help" on how to do just that.

The other book that Jim found of interest was about Chinese history. Though its title has been long forgotten, the content has not. Jim discovered through reading this book that the common Chinese citizen resented the Manchu's rule of China. The thousands of Chinese citizens in the capital city Peking, were put to the task of rebuilding and restoring the Forbidden City, home of the Chinese Emperors, for the ruling Manchus. "Anything [the Manchus] wanted," Jim has related about the situation, the Chinese would bring to them as quickly as possible. "If [the Manchus] wanted a bag of rice, don't argue with them, you give them a bag of rice. Give them whatever they wanted. The Manchus got to where they just stayed in their walled city and the Chinamen carried on outside [the Forbidden City] just as they pleased. But every time they wanted something [the Chinese] got it for them. I thought, hell that ought to work on the Japanese. So that's what I did when I got in charge of carpenter's shop. Always never gave them a hassle and tried to give them what they wanted."

Using his "Manchu Theory," plus being a civilian, Jim was able to follow the Chinese lead. "Try and give them what they wanted and as quick as I could build some damn thing. Didn't make any difference how insignificant it was, get it done for them and then they'd stay up there in their office and leave you alone." This philosophy allowed Jim and the other carpenters to do what they wanted, such as extra projects for themselves or other POWs, within the camp's limitations and without much interference from the Japanese. "Do what they like and they're blind" says Jim, adding it also works in the United States since human behavior is universal and predictable with minor adjustments for cultural differences. By making the Japanese guards happy with his work, especially in the Carpenter Shop, they would leave Jim alone to do what he wanted to do for himself or others.

That same summer of 1943 in August, a group of skilled POWs was scheduled to be transferred to Japan. Jim was on the list along with his pal Eddie Peres. Jim was recovering in

Dr. Kahn.
(Freedom)

the hospital from his bout with malaria and amoebic dysentery when it was time to pack up and leave. The American doctor at the hospital, Navy Lieutenant Gustav Kahn, knew Jim from Wake Island. He had treated Jim's shrapnel wound the day of the initial attack by the Japanese. Knowing that Jim and Eddie were good friends from the atoll, Dr. Kahn asked Jim if he felt up to going with Eddie to Japan. Jim agreed that Eddie was a good friend and a good carpenter. Jim had learned a lot from Eddie. However, if the doctor felt he was not physically able to travel, Jim was willing to stay in China.

Dr. Kahn was apparently able to pull some strings, for somehow he managed to have Jim remain at the Kiangwan Camp. As things turned out, the hospital later reaped many benefits from this change. Jim was very grateful to Dr. Kahn for allowing him to stay at the camp. Jim "did a lot of [carpentry] work for the hospital" in the following months and years.

In preparation for the transfer, flimsy papers with the rules typed on them for the upcoming journey were handed out to those assigned to leave. Since he was on the original list to be transferred, Jim received one that he eventually brought back to the States as another souvenir.

Regulations Covering Transfer of Prisoners

1. Any disobedience of orders issued by Japanese Authorities during transfer will result in strict punishment.
2. Prisoners must keep as quiet as possible and engage in conversation only when absolutely necessary.
3. In case of unexpected accident, prisoners must follow orders given by those in charge as quickly and quietly as possible. Anyone disobeying at this time will be shot.
4. Company Leaders and Section Leaders will be in complete charge, under the Japanese, and must be obeyed without hesitation.
5. Prisoners must salute all Japanese military men.

<u>Regulations on Board Ship</u>

1.   The prisoners must not go outside of assigned areas.
2.   Prisoners must smoke only at assigned place and not walk with lighted cigarette in mouth or hands.
3.   Prisoners are not allowed to touch fixtures or devices without permission.
4.   Prisoners will go on deck only at specified time and then to specified place.
5.   Company Leaders and Section Leaders are responsible for the cleanliness of rooms, which are to be at all times kept clean.
6.   Company Leaders must report any case of sickness or accident to the authorities as soon as possible.
7.   Do not waste water at any time and do not drink water other than that issued for drinking purposes.
8.   Man in each section will be appointed to handle food and clean all dishes.

"There's considerable difference with [the rules above] and the ones on the *Nitta Maru*," Jim points out. "For one [on] the *Nitta Maru* [prison ship] at the start of the war going from Wake Island to Japan, boy, they were [strict]. Pretty near anything you done you weren't supposed to, you would be shot! Course really, right up to the end of the war, they did relax some. By God, I'll tell you, you didn't have to do too much for them to give you a good beating or a hell of a good slapping," on the *Nitta Maru* ocean voyage. Another difference between the two sets of regulations was the amount of responsibility that the POWs in a leadership position were given. Earlier, the Japanese were in charge and the POWs were not given a chance to be in charge of small groups. The POWs could also speak to each other and smoke. This was quite a change from the 1942 regulations.

Before Eddie Peres and the other transfer POWs left camp, Jim and Eddie conspired to keep Jim informed as to where Eddie was being taken. If he had a chance, Eddie would write back to Kiangwan with that information. The two men devised a simple code; whatever port city Eddie arrived in, the first letter of that city would be the first letter of the first word in Eddie's letter to Jim. After a few months, Jim received a letter from Eddie that held the clue as to where he had landed in Japan.

> PAL. Jim.
> O U R - T R I P - H E R E - H A S - B E E N - V E R Y-ENJOYABLE. WE-ARE-PRIVILEDGED-TO-GO-ON-DECK-from 6 am to 6:30 pm-AND-ALLOWED-TO-SMOKE-DURING-THIS-TIME.
> THE-FOOD-IS-VERY-GOOD-THREE-MEALS-A-DAY-WITH-GREATER-VARIETY-TEA-FIVE-TIMES-DAILY. I-HOPE-YOU-ARE-ABLE-TO-LEAVE-THE-HOSPITAL-OR-THAT-YOU-ALREADY-HAVE-AND-THAT-YOU-ARE-DOING-NICELY; SORRY-YOU-ARE-NOT-WITH-ME.
> THE-COMMAND-HAVE-TREATED-US-EXCEPTIONALLY-GOOD-AND-THE-MEN-ARE-VERY-GREATFUL, EVERYONE-IS-IN-HIGH-SPIRITS-AND-HAVE-HAD-VERY-LITTLE-SEASICKNESS-THE-MEDICAL-TREATMENT-IS-100 0/0- A-FEW-ARE-SICK-AND-RECEIVING-TREATMENT. HOPING-TO-SEE-YOU-IN-THE-NOT-TO-DISTANT-FUTURE-
> I-REMAIN-AS-EVER-YOUR-PAL   E. A. Peres

The opening word, OUR, referred to the port of Osaka, which was what Eddie and Jim had figured all along. The letter is very flattering to the Japanese, which may be the reason that it made it into Jim's hands at Kiangwan Camp in China from Eddie's new camp in Japan. In this manner, two POW's were able to exchange information on the movements of POWs by the Japanese. It is from small pieces like this that espionage puzzles are completed; now the men at Kiangwan Camp knew where their comrades had gone and, if possible, could pass that word along to the American authorities. That was the last Jim heard directly from Eddie Peres until December 1945. After the war ended, Jim found out that Eddie "had a much easier life in Kiangwan than he did in Osaka." Eddie lost three fingers in a joiner while doing carpentry work in Osaka, but he did make it back to the States at the war's end.

After Eddie's transfer group left, Jim tried to get that information out to Mrs. Peres through the following letter to Viola.

JAMES-A-ALLEN
BAR#4-Sec #4-

Shanghai War-prisoner's Camp
SEPTEMBER-5-1943

DEAR-MOTHER:
  WITH-THE-KIND-PERMISSION-OF-THE-
JAPANESE-AUTHORITIES-WE-GET-TO-WRITE-
AGAIN-THIS-MONTH-JUST-WROTE-A-LETTER-
THE-25ᵀᴴ-OF-AUGUST-.I-AM-IN-GOOD-HEALTH-
AND-FEELING-FINE-WEIGH-143-POUNDS-
EDDIE-PERES-AND-I-ARE-SEPARATED-NOW. HE-
WAS-FEELING-FINE-AND-IN-GOOD-HEALTH-ON-
AUGUST-21ˢᵀ-1943-PLEASE-WRITE-AND-TELL-
HIS-WIFE-SO-HER-ADDRESS-IS-579-HAIGHT-
STREET-SAN-FRANCISCO-CALIFORNIA.-MRS-E-
A-PERES.
  THERE-SEEMS-TO-BE-AN-EVACUATION-
BOAT-LEAVING-BEFORE-LONG-AND-THIS-
LETTER-WILL-BE-ON-ITS-WAY-SURE-HOPE-YOU-
ARE-RECEIVING-MY-LETTERS-THERE'S-NOT-
MUCH-TO-WRITE-ABOUT-BUT-JUST-TO-GET-A-
LETTER-IS-LIKE-A-TONIC-I-HAVE-ONLY-
GOTTEN-ONE-LETTER-FROM-YOU-GUESS-THEY-
HAVE-BEEN-LOST-ENROUTE-HOW-ARE-YOU-
FEELING-HOPE-ALL-RIGHT-AND-CAN-WALK.-
TELL-ALL-HELLO-TELL-THEM-I-AM-ALL-RIGHT-
WRITE-AND-TELL-BILL-GOODMAN-HELLO-FOR-
ME.HOW'S-JERALD-BILLIE-CARL-AND-HAZEL-?
SURE-LIKE-TO-SEE-THEM-HOPE-TO-BEFORE-
TO-MANY-MORE-MONTHS-I-LEFT-HOME-JUST-
TWO-YEARS-AGO-SEEMS-JUST-LIKE-
YESTERDAY-MERRY-XMAS-AND-HAPPY-NEW-
YEAR-FOR-1944.

YOUR-SON-
JAMES A. ALLEN

  Jim was thinking ahead in wishing holiday greetings in
September. He apparently realized by this time it would take
many months for his letter to travel across the Pacific to
reach the United States. In the two years he had been a
prisoner at that time, he had received only one letter. That
letter was an exception, having taken only three months

Ben Comstock, Jr. (top), and Ben Comstock Sr. of Logan, Iowa. Both men worked as carpenters on Wake Island and in the Carpenter Shop at Woosung before being sent to Japan as carpenter Eddie Peres was. Father and son were assigned to build a hot tub for the Japanese from plans Jim eventually brought back as a souvenir. He presented the plans to the younger Comstock in 1985. (PIEF)

(June 1942 to September 1942) to reach Jim. Subsequent mail to China would be much slower. However, mail traveling west was more rapid, as evidenced by Jim's first letter home, which took fifteen months to reach his mother in Southern California.

The evacuation boat Jim refers to in his letter was probably the Swedish ship *Gripsholm*. The Swiss International Red Cross was the official go-between for the Allies and the Japanese. In the early fall of 1943, the *Gripsholm* sailed to the Gola Region of India for humanitarian reasons. She arrived at the port of Mormugao on the coast of Portuguese controlled India on 17 October. Waiting for her was the Japanese ship, *Teia Maru* which exchanged 1,473 Allied and Neutral Internees for 1,500 Japanese interned in America according to the 18 October 1943 issue of the U.S. Armed Forces newspaper, *Stars and Stripes*, which cited a radio report from Berlin. According to J. Charles Oliver, a missionary in China who was repatriated on the *Gripsholm*, the Swiss International Red Cross unloaded supplies for Japanese held prisoners of war all day from the *Gripsholm* to the *Teia Maru*. The entire exchange of supplies and personnel took five days to complete.

When some of the supplies from the *Gripsholm* shipment finally reached the Shanghai War Prisoners Camp at Kiangwan, the POWs found the large-sized shoes that were desperately needed by some of the men. The Red Cross had sent very large U.S. Army boots. The Shoe Shop reworked some of the larger shoes and boots into smaller sizes that were also needed. The Carpenter Shop made a shoemaker's bench with a shoe vise to aid Shoe Shop Honcho Frank Collins and those working with him as cobblers to rework the Red Cross and Army shoes into useful pairs. One of Jim's souvenirs is a record slip from the Shoe Shop, which shows how busy the cobblers were. For the week ending with 17 March (probably 1944), eleven pairs of shoes were worked on, the following week, twenty pairs. The reworked boots and shoes "weren't stylish," recalls Jim, "but prisoners were darn glad to get them."

Additionally, the Red Cross boxes from the *Gripsholm* included Civilian Conservation Corps (CCC) kits, which contained buttons, thread, and sewing needles. With the CCC kits, the POWs were able to make their ragged clothing last a little longer. Jim used his CCC kit frequently during his internment years, especially to patch a pair of trousers he liked. Jim had sewn patch upon patch through the years until there was little of the original fabric left. He has expressed regret that he left them behind in Niigata, Japan in 1945, saying that nobody would believe how he had patched up those pants.

The Red Cross boxes also contained the metal toothpaste tubes the POWs used to fix their "rice shovels," small blue packages of Gillette brand razor blades, tins of corned beef, and some candy and packs of Old Gold cigarettes. One of the many souvenirs of his adventures that Jim kept was a poem found on the back of the packs of those cigarettes.

> FREEDOM
> Our heritage has always
> been freedom.
> We can not afford to
> relinquish it.
> Our Armed Forces will
> safeguard the heritage
> If we too, do our share
> to preserve it.
> Old Gold
> Cigarettes

"I kinda liked it," Jim says when asked why he put so much effort into keeping a cigarette package through the war and for another fifty plus years in a scrapbook. Whether the Japanese realized it or not, this is an example of the morale boost the Red Cross and Old Gold Cigarette Company were able to pass through to those behind enemy prison fences. It reminded the POWs, and others who might read it, that they were still part of a bigger organization. With everyone working toward that common goal of preserving or regaining their freedom, the goal could be reached. The POWs were an important part of the Allied war effort since they were draining manpower and yen from the Japanese that could have been spent at the battlefront. Instead, those resources were being used to house, feed, and supervise the thousands of Allied POWs. It might not be much, but even one Japanese soldier standing guard duty at a POW camp, or a tiny grain of rice in a POW's bowl, could tip the scales in favor of the Allies.

9

At the Carpenter Shop

Although unofficially in effect since 1942, in the early spring of 1944, an Imperial Edict in line with the Emperor's slogan of no work, no food, was imposed and became known at Kiangwan Camp as "Self Supply, Self Support." The financial drain of feeding approximately 300,000 POWs was taking a severe toll on the Japanese national economy since it was 1/600 of the total Japanese income. Therefore, Emperor Hirohito decreed that the prisoners must grow their own food and pay for their keep. Basically "All prisoners earn their keep or [the Japanese would] get rid of them," is the way Jim Allen paraphrased it.

Everyone had to work in some fashion, even if it was collecting flies while sick and in the hospital. According to Jim, "Self Supply, Self Support; no work, no food. Well, that was the policy of the Japanese Army. [If a] Japanese soldier ever got sick and got in the hospital, they cut his rations. They did the same thing for prisoners. There was so many grams of rice in the hospital and so many if you were working. There was more if you were working." This policy was actually adopted by the Japanese POW camps long before it became an Imperial Edict. Although the Japanese Mess Officer would weight out the grams of rice for each meal, the POW cooks didn't necessarily cut rations as required for the ill.

149

The ten million dollars per year upkeep for the POWs was much more than the Japanese upper echelon wished to pay out. At this same time the same authorities agreed that all POWs, including officers, should be put to work as laborers, not just to grow food or help to support themselves. Ratified by the Japanese in 1912, the Hague Conventions of 1907, which dealt with the treatment of POWs, were circumvented by the Imperial Japanese authorities. Japan had already withdrawn from the League of Nations in February 1933, after being condemned by an overwhelming majority of member nations for their control of Manchuria. The Japanese military's orders for dealing with the POWs concentrated on those dead and, as David Bergamini wrote in *Japan's Imperial Conspiracy*, "left little hope that prisoners taken by Japan would ever return to their homelands alive." After the war, when comparing the number of deaths in POW camps, Bergamini continues that, "Unless you were a Jew in German held areas, the Japanese POW camps were more deadly in WWII." So POW civilians, officers, and enlisted men alike were put to work growing their own food, as well as laboring in factories, on railroads, truck maintenance and repair, roadways, workshops, and, at Kiangwan Camp, the merciless Mount Fuji project.

Since he was a carpenter by trade, Jim Allen missed most of the hard labor projects and was assigned to the Carpenter Shop. According to Jim, the POW carpenters were able to assist with "many small things that could be done to help out. The Japanese didn't have many materials or anything to give you to do anything if you could." The carpenters, or "daikus" as they were called in Japanese, helped make a bad situation a tad better by becoming general maintenance men at the Woosung and Kiangwan camps. Without them, the POWs, as well as the Japanese, would have had even worse accommodations.

Using only hand tools and muscle power, the carpenters "repaired doors different places and roofs if they leaked. Wasn't much you could do." Of the available materials, the wooden International Red Cross crates in which clothes for the POWs or individual boxes were shipped, became invaluable. The wood was stored in the go-down, or warehouse, next to the Carpenter Shop at Kiangwan and was desired by everyone for various projects. Hence, the Japanese kept a close eye on what the Red Cross box wood was used for, requiring that orders for items made of the wood have official chop marks, such as the ones

Some of the carpenters who worked with Jim at the Carpenter Shop: (top row, left to right) James "Jim" Sweiberg of Vancouver, Washington; Earl Burge of Valentine, Nebraska; Claude Hessletine of Knoxville, Indiana; Frank R. Mace of Medical Lake, Washinton; Harry W. Hodgeson of Scottsbluff, Nebraska; (bottom row) Cecil Bouyer of Twin Falls, Idaho; Harry E. Brewer of Omaha, Nebraska; Arthur "Art" Gress of Grandview, Idaho; Kenneth "Kenny" Johnson of McCall, Idaho; John Dustman of Portland, Oregon. (All photographs, PIEF)

found in the upper right corner of Jim's letters home. Some of the official stamped items the carpenters made from the Red Cross wood were ammunition boxes. These were combat related articles that POWs were not supposed to be forced to work on, as with the artillery shell polishing at Woosung Camp.

The Carpenter Shop acquired most of their wood for projects from the old British Army barracks just outside of the camp's electric fence. Work details were sent over to the vacant barracks and systematically dismantled the inside of the wooden buildings. The salvaged materials would then find new life around the Kiangwan camp wherever repairs were needed or whenever projects were desired. Although the quality of the wood was not as good as that of the International Red Cross boxes, it was serviceable.

Since Woosung Camp, those POWs working in the Carpenter Shop were required to have a tool list posted on the wall of the shop, near the tool storage room. The list was in both English and Japanese with the tool name and its number listed. Howard

A. "Art" Gress was the POW in charge of keeping track of all the tools. The inventory always had to be accounted for, matching the official posted list. Sometimes the guards would have a surprise inspection of the shop and tool room and if they were short an implement, everyone in the shop had to remain standing at attention until someone showed up with that particular tool. Fortunately, the missing tools always showed up relatively quickly. "Too many tools," says Jim, "was as bad as one tool short. Just like too many prisoners."

The men used Japanese or Chinese implements that were available in the tool storage room. Since some of the Asian tools operated very differently than Western ones, this presented a challenge to many of the men. They had to learn how to use some of the basic tools they had not worked with in years, or perhaps, never seen before. An example of this was the Japanese hand rip saw that had to be pulled toward the operator's body to cut rather than being pushed forward as with an American saw. This saw caused of a lot of frustration in the beginning. Another challenge for the men was using the metric system. The folding, wooden Japanese Army rulers had millimeters/centimeters on one side and inches/feet on the other, which helped. However, most of the plans for work orders were drawn using the metric system and would have to be converted for those who didn't understand metric measurements. Jim found himself eventually using the metric system as easily as measuring inches, but some of the carpenters never could, or would, master the concept. It was similar to those who couldn't, or wouldn't, learn Japanese numbers for bungo.

Around the end of September 1943, Jim became the third daiku "honcho" (the Japanese term for supervisor). The first honcho, Dennis Bliss, had been sent to Japan the previous summer. The second honcho of the daikus, Earl Burge, resigned the position, choosing to remain only the Barracks 4 Section Leader. By using his "Manchu Theory," Jim had developed a good working relationship with the Japanese officer in charge of the carpenters, Lieutenant Miyazaki, and all the other Japanese that had had work done by the Carpenter Shop, including Colonel Otera. As a result, the Carpenter Shop had a great deal of latitude in what they did with minimal supervision by the guards.

A direct approach to problems was not always the easiest or fastest as one POW officer found out at Kiangwan. The POW kitchen officer, Marine Captain Wesley Platt, wanted cooking

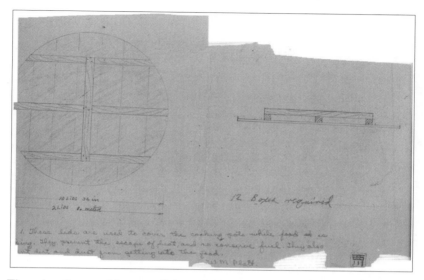

The plan for cooking pot lids submitted by Captain Platt. The official chop mark is in the lower right. A side view of a lid is on the right and a top view is on the left. Captain Platt wrote on the bottom per Jim's suggestion, "1. These lids are used to cover the cooking pots while food is cooking. They prevent the escape of heat, and so conserve fuel. They also prevent dirt and dust from getting into the food. W. M. Platt." (James A. Allen Collection)

pot lids. The concern over dirt falling into the open cooking pots, cauldrons actually, from the open rafters in the kitchen prompted the need for proper solid lids. After several attempts to get materials and have the lids made through proper channels, Captain Platt, whom Jim knew from Wake and liked, spoke to Jim about the situation. As Platt elaborated on the kitchen's unproductive pursuit of lids, Jim began to see an error in the Marines' plan of attack in the situation. Using a cry of non-sanitary conditions when requesting the Red Cross wood for lids to cover the cooking cauldrons, the military officers were, "thinking they're in America. The Japanese didn't care about [the POW kitchen's] sanitary conditions. That was the least of their damn worries. Every prisoner that died, that was just one less they had to feed and that was their thinking."

By now well schooled in POW and Japanese interaction, Jim had the answer to Captain Platt's problem. Over fifty years later the conversation is still clear in Jim's mind. "'Well Captain,' I said, 'when you go up there and ask for Red Cross box wood for

Joseph Astarita's drawing of the Woosung kitchen/galley. Astarita wrote, "The galley was a filthy, smoke-filled room. Fleas, rats, mosquitos, etc. The food was cooked by our own men. It was filthy, but our cooks cleaned it as best they could." The round object leaning against the window is representative of the cooking pot lids the Carpenter Shop made.

lids for your kitchen,' I said, 'don't *never* mention the word sanitation to them [or] about dirt getting on the food from up in the roof. Don't *never* mention that! Just tell them, and emphasize that with holes in the lids, it takes more fuel to cook the food and get it hot. If you get some new lumber and get the new lids, it will conserve and use less fuel.'"

Platt followed Jim's advice and soon returned to the Carpenter Shop with the official chop on his copy of lid drawings. At that point, Jim was able to get the wood equal to twelve Red Cross clothing boxes needed for the twelve new lids. The Carpenter Shop then made all the new lids the POW kitchen needed. "That's what you had to do," explained Jim. "If you wanted anything, it may take you six months to figure out how to approach them on it, but if you approached [the Japanese] correctly," a POW could get what was wanted or needed. "But if it was going to benefit them, not you," Jim emphasized, "you [stood] a chance to get it."

Even with the improved conditions of sanitation and less mud at the Kiangwan camp and the benefit of the International Red Cross food boxes, by 5 September 1943 Jim was still losing weight; down to 138 pounds from 143, a total of forty-two pounds lost since before the first part of December 1941. While Jim had become very thin, he remained relatively healthy considering the situation. Many POWs had lost much more weight, as much as one hundred pounds, leaving some in a severely weakened state.

Death was a regular visitor to the Kiangwan camp and a constant reminder to Jim and the other POWs that their lives were hanging in a balance that could tip at any moment suddenly towards death. One of those for whom the balance tipped was Leo Patrick Driscoll, who was among the first CPNAB workers on Wake Island. The task of making a grave marker was assigned to the Carpenter Shop at Kiangwan, the first spring they were there, 1943. Driscoll's was the first marker of many they were to make.

In planning for a Christian cross-shaped grave marker, the carpenters decided to use concrete reinforced with bamboo, not the usual iron rebar that was not available. Concrete would withstand the high humidity much longer than a wood cross. The form to pour the concrete in for the cross was made by carpenter John Dustman, a fine craftsman according to Jim. The form had metal hinges that folded down and up for reuse. Dustman laid the form upside down with the necessary wooden letters of identification in place. A metal plate with "American Civilian" written on it with a hammer and chisel was

Drawing plan for Driscoll's grave marker, the paper torn and darkened with age. A side view is on the left. Under the name it reads, "American Civilian Employee Contr. P.N.A.B California May 20, 1943." (James A. Allen Collection)

attached to a post on the bottom of the form. The bamboo was arranged in a manner to give the structure strength and then the fresh concrete was poured in. When dry, the carpenters popped off the forms and turned the cement cross over. Leaving the metal plate in the concrete, the wood letters spelling out the dead man's name were delicately removed for future use. According to Jim, cabinetmaker Dustman "carved some beautiful letters [which] imprinted right in the cement." Using six-inch by forty-eight inch long pieces of sugar pine lumber from the Red Cross boxes, Dustman carved all the letters needed to imprint the names and dates on the grave markers, starting with Driscoll's. "We made several of those" crosses for the POWs who died at Kiangwan. The Carpenter Shop also made boxes to hold the ashes and bones of those who died far from home in China.

A rather large project that the Carpenter Shop undertook along with the Tim Shop and the Wake Island masons interned at Kiangwan was building a complete bakery. The masons made the coal-fired oven while the carpenters worked on the main structure to house the bakery, as well as a table with a sheet metal top, flour sifters, and wooden bread peals to remove the loaves from the hot ovens. Making the bread peals turned out to be a continual job since, Jim says, the bakers "kept burning them up." The Tin Shop, manned by civilian POWs Don Ludington and Richard Fuller, was assigned the job of making the baking pans for the bread. Beginning with two sheets of twenty-four gauge black iron to make sixteen bread pans, Jim recalls, "They just kept bringing them [metal sheets] in. I forget how many we made," by the time they were finished with the project. Working together, the carpenters and tinsmiths also made large, black iron-lined wooden troughs for mixing the bread dough.

Although coal was to be used by the bakery for fuel, it was in short supply around the Kiangwan area. Eddie Peres came up with the idea for using the plentiful coal dust from the Shanghai docks rather than large chunks of coal, and mixing it with Yangtze Delta mud as a binder. In order to use the coal dust, the carpenters made wood framed coal dust screens, weaving the fine wire mesh screen by hand. "You take this plain, just plain wire and a frame and you can weave it like chicken wire, any size hole you want" recalls Jim. It was delicate, time-consuming work. A grease strainer for the cooks was also made this way.

By making small balls out of the mud and coal dust then

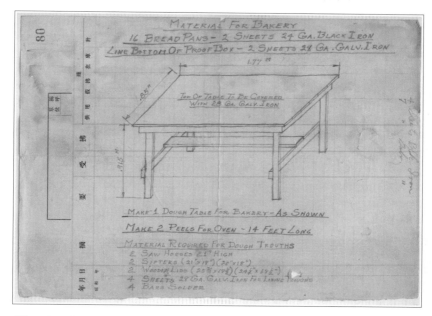

Plan for the bakery table. The required materials for dough troughs are listed at the bottom. (James A. Allen Collection)

drying them in the sun, a sort of briquette about the size of a baseball could be made to fire the masonry bakery oven. The bakers made three small loaves of bread per pan and the POWs received one small loaf, equal to about two hamburger buns, per week; a very welcomed addition to the camp rice and stews. The Kiangwan Camp's bakery was so successful that Jim heard stories about Colonel Otera, in charge of the camps in the Shanghai area, sending loaves to the other Shanghai area internment camp and making money for himself.

The camp bread was also used to barter with. Jim used it to trade for a warm North China Marine fur hat with attached earflaps. Not only did Jim get a hat, but additionally he gained a little revenge. The rather large POW trading the hat worked on Wake Island as a rigger, fastening cables to structural steel in order for a crane to lift them, This man had "belittled my intelligence shortly after I got to Wake. I didn't want a fight, . . . So I swallowed it [the insult], but I didn't forget it." Apparently the large rigger was extremely hungry when the trade was being transacted and eager for the little half loaves of bread Jim wanted to trade. Although the trade had cost Jim twelve little half loaves of camp bread starting with the first one as a down payment, it had been worth it since he had been able to haggle the big man's price down by quite a bit.

On 14 April 1943, a new shipment of Red Cross clothing arrived. Jim was lucky and received a warm overcoat. He wrote home that it helped stop the frigid Gobi wind whistling through Shanghai. Jim could look forward to the winter of 1944-45 as being a bit warmer for him.

With skill and ingenuity, the carpenters helped alleviate many problems with the POW's food. The cooks urgently sought a way to remove the small pieces of gravel in the camp rice. At first wood boxes with nail holes in their metal bottoms had been used as a not so effective way of purging the gravel while rinsing the grains of rice. Then the carpenters were given a work order to make a rice washer, which would vastly improve the cleaning of the camp rice and hopefully eliminate the chipped and broken teeth that the gravel was occasionally causing.

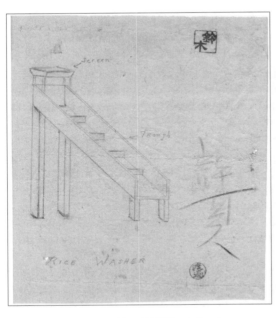

The rice washer was designed along the lines of a sluice box used for California gold mining back in 1849. The idea was for the grains of rice to float along with the water and the heavier gravel to sink to the bottom of the box. This improved rice washer "saved a lot of teeth" after it was operational. During their Kiangwan camp days, as well as at Woosung camp, the carpenters also made many rice paddles, large flat surfaced implements to stir rice

Rice washer used by POW cooks to remove gravel from the rice while rinsing it. The two chops attest this was an official work order for the Carpenter Shop. (James A. Allen Collection)

cooking in the kitchen cauldrons. The POW cooks wore out the rice paddles almost as fast as the carpenters could find time and wood to make them.

Making a noodle drying rack proved to be a tedious project for the carpenters. Jim remembers, "This was quite a project to rip [rough cut] all this stuff up by hand and to plane by hand these boards. It was quite a large rack — two meters high, two meters wide, one and one-third meters deep [with space for] eleven shelves [each holding a] tray one meter by one and one-half meters." The trays were really more like a rack with small wood rods to hang noodles on, allowing them to dry in the air circulating around the rack.

Cabbage was a staple vegetable at the POW camp and the carpenters were given a design, with the official chop mark, of a cabbage cutter to make. "For some reason or other, there were several pairs of ice skates around camp," Jim recalls. "So we beat them out and sharpened them on a brick till they'd cut cabbage." The blades were attached to a wooden board with an opening to allow the sliced cabbage to fall underneath. The board was given sides to help guide the bottomless box that held the cabbage heads to the cutting blade. "The kitchen used it quite a lot."

Among the odds and ends the carpenters made for the Japanese were fly swatters, twig or straw brooms, small glass display boxes for dolls, and foot warmers along with rubbish and garbage boxes, flag poles, tables, chairs, stools, office items for desktops,   sign   posts, sword stands, wooden flower pots, a music stand, and a rat cage ordered by Colonel Otera. The carpenters never knew what they might be asked to make next. The Japanese Pay Master Lieutenant Suzuki, for example, submitted an order for a breadbox. "Now [Lieutenant Suzuki] could

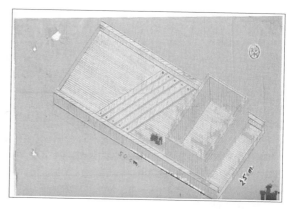

Drawing plan of the cabbage cutter with ice skate blades. (James A. Allen Collection)

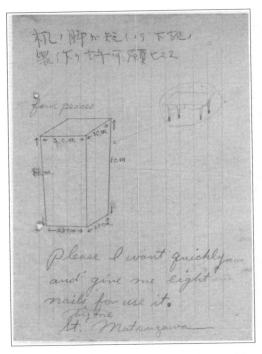

One of the Japanese officers wrote this work order for the Carpenter Shop. Apparently he wanted to repair the legs to a table of his. This work order does not have an official chop affixed to it. (James A. Allen Collection)

speak pretty good English. Excellent English," Jim remembers. "You'd think he was ... you couldn't hardly understand him." Suzuki spoke grammatically better English than Jim and many of the others in the camp whose primary language was English. "In fact, he sounded kind of foreign to me, anyway, with him and his perfect English." Nonetheless, Jim states that Lieutenant Suzuki "was a pretty nice Japanese officer," all things considered.

Hank Brewer was given the job of making a hat rack for Colonel Otera, while Cecil Bouyer and Kenny Johnson made awnings out of grass mats and wood for Otera's office windows. Harry Hodgeson made a small desktop filing cabinet for another Japanese officer. Hodgson and Brewer also made small wooden shipping tags, a quarter of an inch thick, which they ripped by hand. "Not paper tags with string like we had [in the United States]," recalls Jim. One order of tags "used a [Red Cross] box of wood, used a lot of them, too."

In the spirit of the "Self Supply, Self Support" orders, the Japanese required the building of a chicken coop incubator. The POW who took care of the camp chickens and pigs, a man by the name of Fred Ramsey, needed it to increase his flock of birds for the camp's kitchens.

Other POWs also gave job orders to the Carpenter Shop. One elaborate set of plans for a box were drawn in great detail by a U.S. Naval officer, Commander Greer, who had previously seen duty during World War I as a building inspector and had been on Wake Island examining the construction in December 1941. The specifications called for the box to be lined with sheet metal, a material in extremely short supply.

The goal of natural resource-poor Japan's aggression in the 1930s and 40s against China and Southeast Asia had been to gain valuable resource-rich territory. Japan would then have adequate access to materials such as petroleum and metal ores to have their industry and war machine flourish. The country would not be at the mercy of foreign powers imposing crippling trade embargoes against them as the United States had done in July 1941.

"Well, the Japanese didn't have hardly enough sheet metal to make bread pans," Jim recalls, let alone a metal lined box for a prisoner of war. The plans never obtained a chop mark and the box was never made. "I think that the commander and his boys forgot to realize where they were."

Construction superintendent Dan Teters, however, was able to have a desk made with the appropriate chop mark on the design. The carpenters even made a few cloth or leather strapped wooden Japanese sandals, one-inch off the floor, affectionately called "piss quicks," for use in the middle of the night when venturing to the benjo. The wooden clog-like piss quicks were used extensively at night by those who had them. Beginning in 1942 "there was a continuous stream, all night long," of POWs traipsing out to the benjo to relieve their bladders. Although he has no hard evidence, Jim claims that he and the others had to urinate frequently at night because their prostrate glands had enlarged and their bladders couldn't empty properly.

When the International Red Cross representative, a Mr. Egle, would be scheduled to make an inspection of the camp conditions, work orders would come in from the camp office for various equipment to show that the POWs were well taken care of. One such item was a movie screen that eventually showed an Italian movie with English subtitles, which Jim remembers as "not too interesting." High jump stanchions were required once, as well as three tables for ping-pong, and basketball backboards, more to impress the Swiss International Red Cross than for the POWs to use.

Jim saved a typical one day's work list for the Carpenter Shop. Reading down the list is enough to make anyone tired.

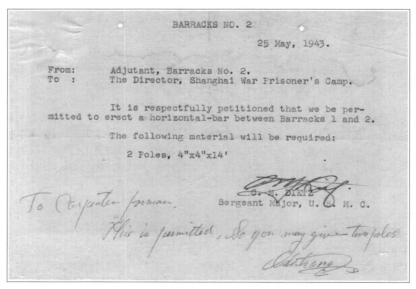

BARRACKS NO. 2

25 May, 1943.

From: Adjutant, Barracks No. 2.
To :   The Director, Shanghai War Prisoner's Camp.

It is respectfully petitioned that we be permitted to erect a horizontal-bar between Barracks 1 and 2.

The following material will be required:

2 Poles, 4"x4"x14'

C. M. DIETZ
Sergeant Major, U. S. M. C.

Work order for the Carpenter Shop with note written by interpreter Ishihara, the infamous "Beast of the East," okaying the request. The Marines apparently wanted to erect a chin up pole. The requesting adjutant, Sgt. Major Dietz, died of wet beri beri while a POW. (James A. Allen Collection)

Repair ping pong table
Repair peel for bakery
Cabinet in the canteen
Bookfile for Officer
Door and gate for stables
Door — galley storeroom
Make fly swatters
Handles for tools
Mats for Japanese Officers bath house
Patch rat holes — Japanese Galley
Repair doors — barracks # 1 & 2
Picture frame — Nakayama
Repair guard towers
Repair window — guard house
Repair urinal box — Hospital

The carpenter honcho, or superintendent, would assign different men to jobs unless someone had a special talent that was needed. The carpenters work list was never short, but

```
Memo to:      Mr. Yazawa        ↓ ↑    17 May, 1944
Subject:      Camp Toilets

              1.  The following repairs and replacements
are needed on the Camp toilets:

Barracks "O"-- 1 door cover repaired. Replace screening.
Barracks  1 -- Replace screening.
Barracks  2 -- 5 door covers replaced. Urinal box re-
               paired. Replace screening.
Barracks  3 -- 5 door covers replaced. Urinal box re-
               paired. Replace screening.
Barracks  4 -- Urinal box repaired. Fit door covers.
               Replace screening.
Barracks  5 -- 5 door covers replaced. Urinal box lid
               replaced. Replace screening.
Hospital    -- Repair urinal box. Refit doors. Replace
               screening.

Materials needed:
10 pounds  small nails (4 cm)
5 pounds   small nails (2½ cm)

                              F.C. Tharin
                              Senior Adjutant.
```

Jim says that this particular work order of Captain Tharin's was really a wish list since a lot of the materials necessary to complete the jobs were not available. This particular request was probably written during the peak of the camp's fly problem. (James A. Allen Collection)

grew longer with each passing day. They usually had more work requests than materials to complete them.

The skilled POWs were not just limited to work in their shop or on camp buildings. The prison camp commander had bigger projects in mind. "Colonel Otera lived in a two story apartment building outside of camp. He wanted the Carpenter Shop to make him a garage alongside the apartment" to house his private car, Jim recalls. " Otera had a four door 1940 Ford sedan just like mine in storage in El Monte. The only difference was that Otera's had bullet proof glass windows and the doors were really heavy."

Close working and living conditions, especially in a life-threatening situation, tend to create a bond between the people in those circumstances. The men in the Carpenter Shop and Tin Shop became good friends as well as coworkers. This was especially true for the core group of men who worked there regularly; extra POWs were assigned to the shop whenever the workload warranted it.

The young apprentice carpenter, H. T. Cope, had a birthday coming up and a group of POWs decided to fix him up with a special present. Tinsmiths Richard Fuller and Don Ludington took a one pound can of Klim, a brand of powdered milk that came in the Red Cross boxes, and cut the bottom of the can out. The two tinsmiths then carefully scooped out most of the powdered milk, leaving the remaining portion in the top of the upside-down can. On top of the powdered milk, some lumps of horse manure were placed and a new tin bottom from another Klim can was carefully soldered back on. Fuller and Ludington then polished the can's bottom so that no one could tell it had been tampered with.

Later in the Section 4 barracks area when the birthday gift was given to H. T., he was very suspicious, at first, of the magnanimous gift and the generous givers. For quite a long time, H. T. carefully inspected the can for any flaws. After looking over the can and not detecting anything wrong, he was willing to accept the gift and thank the givers. When H. T. finally opened the can to enjoy his gift, "He found the powdered milk first and, of course, thought he had something" recalls Jim with a chuckle. H. T. later found his hidden "prize" of manure and realized he had been had. Everyone present in the barracks had a good laugh over the gag, Jim remembers, even H. T. "He took it rather well."

Even nature kept those at the Carpenter Shop steadily employed. On 11 August 1943, a tremendous thunderstorm passed through Kiangwan and the prison camp received quite a bit of damage; this was quite common at Kiangwan. The barracks adjuncts and the Japanese gave long lists of the different repairs needed throughout the camp. Kiangwan's windows, doors and roofs all needed attention, but the major problem was the multitude of roof leaks. The problems were not limited to the camp. Even Colonel Otera's apartment outside of the camp's walls had a leaky roof.

One of the major problems for the carpenters was the perennial lack of materials, which included clay roofing tiles. In order to complete most required tasks, the carpenters always had to be ingenious and open to new ideas and ways of doing things. As Jim recalls, "We'd go out and get some of that Yangtze Delta mud, get it in the bucket, take it on the roof and smear that [mud] over the cracked tiles and what-have-you. That was fine as long as it didn't rain. If it rained a little bit, that old clay would stay up there." Unfortunately long rainstorms or even short downpours created havoc with the clay repairs.

Jim was reminded of the camp's leaky roofs years later, back in the United States, while he was working for a particular Southern California contractor. "I used to get sent out to fix a lot of leaks on the buildings the contractor built," recalls Jim. "I'm telling you, I don't think he built a damn building between Palm Springs and Covina that didn't leak. I smeared twenty-five pounds, five gallon buckets, of Henry's Roof Mastic, wet, in the rain, and what-have-you [on each of the different building's roofs] and don't you think I didn't think of that storm in Kiangwan, China, in 1943!" Thousands of miles and decades later, the experiences of being interned were not to be forgotten.

Jim and the others on the repair work detail would also take along a hammer and a few nails up on the roof to tack down any flashing or roofing that might have come loose in the wind. This would save them a trip back up on the roof later.

During the winter of 1944, Jim, as honcho/supervisor, decided that the carpenters would be able to work better if the shop was a bit above the sub-zero temperatures the unheated building usually hovered near. Jim approached the officer in charge, Lieutenant Miyazaki, and asked if "I could build a wood box, and fill it with dirt for a fire. Over it, hang a hood with a chimney like a Franklin stove, through it, so I could have a fire in the Carpenter Shop." As with the kitchen cauldron lids, Jim mentioned how the carpenters would be able to work more efficiently and faster in a warmer shop, thus producing more completed work. After some thought, the lieutenant gave Jim permission and the carpenters would have a fire for part of the day. Jim chuckles as he remembers the situation and the warmth he was able to finesse for himself and the other carpenters. This victory was especially sweet since even Colonel Otera, the camp commander, did not have heat in his office. "The Japanese used to come out [to the Carpenter Shop] from the office," Jim chortles, "and warm their hands." When asked why the Japanese officers didn't take the makeshift stove to their office, Jim replied that Colonel Otera wouldn't let them. It would have caused loss of face, since Jim, as honcho, had gone through the correct procedure and gotten permission from

Lieutenant Miyazaki, the overseer of the Carpenter Shop. The colonel and his officers might be unhappy with the situation, but apparently not enough to shame themselves by removing the makeshift stove. This victory was affirmation of Jim's skill in applied human dynamics.

Because of their special skills, the carpenters had many opportunities to move around the prison camp without too many questions being asked. One day while working in the guard's barracks, Jim was given the opportunity to steal some grasshoppers and pork cracklings to eat, as well as some Japanese Army soap. Jim relates that he "didn't want to steal too many at one time, just one or two." Possessing the willpower to ignore his constantly hungry stomach, Jim was able to steal just a few pieces of food at a time, which was not enough to be missed. He "never got into trouble. Always felt that if I took a big handful, I'd get clobbered." Thus, Jim was able to avoid spending time in the anieso/jail and/or being beaten and losing his relatively good health. "Just never get too greedy . . . . Other prisoners were too hungry and when presented the opportunity to steal food or such, stole enough to be noticed missing and over time were found out," Jim explains. As Winston Churchill said, "To be good is nice but to live is nicer."

The first priority of any POW was survival; social niceties and emotional desires were abandoned in order to obtain the necessary food. Psychologist Abraham Maslow, in his Hierarchy of Needs, begins at the wide bottom of a pyramid with basic physiological needs that individuals must have to exist: food and water. Once food and water are attained, then an individual can move onto the next tier of the pyramid with the safety needs of feeling secure and having shelter. Surviving is much more important to an individual than the needs of personal growth or the acceptance and approval of peers, which are found higher up on the pyramid. However, once the basic physiological and safety needs are taken care of, then an individual can move on to more of the social needs required for emotional satisfaction and to gain the approval of peers and/ or others. Even a law-abiding person will revert to primitive instincts when necessary to assure their survival. Thus, even though Jim was a very socially civilized person before becoming a prisoner of war, when plunged into a situation where the future is constantly unknown and survival is endangered, he regressed to the bottom of Maslow's hierarchical pyramid. Jim reverted to stealing when necessary in order to obtain the basic needs, such as food and water, required to survive the ordeal of prison camp.

The carpenters and tinsmiths would occasionally be able to scrounge up a bit of extra food due to the Carpenter Shop's location and their connections with the POWs who took care of the camp pigs, which had been given by the Red Cross. Two POWs worked the garbage collection detail around the Kiangwan camp. This meager collection of food waste would then become the pigs' rations. Using a caisson, a two-wheel flatbed cart with a box on top that used to be filled with ammunition, one POW would push from behind while a second POW, rather than a horse, would pull it along by the caisson's two shafts. The cart had two fifty-five gallon metal barrels in place of the ammunition box into which the collected garbage would be placed. The garbage cart had to pass by the Carpenter Shop on its way to the camp pigsty and, the garbage detail POWs would stop the cart by the shop to allow the carpenters to "fish around for something" to eat. The garbage workers were following the maxim of "we'll scratch your back if you'll scratch ours." They were hoping that when they wanted something done in the Carpenter Shop in the future, the carpenters would remember their generosity.

When the carpenters were through "fishing," the garbage cart would then continue on to the pigsty and the carpenters would go inside their shop. Together with the tinsmiths, the carpenters, "Took a one pound Klim can, put the garbage in and cooked it on the hibachi in the Tin Shop," Jim remembers. "It smelled sour [spoiled] even while it was cooking," but the POWs still ate it. Tinsmith "Richard Fuller, he used to laugh and say tongue-in-cheek that anything within five feet of fire was fit to eat."

February 1944 ended with an extra day of imprisonment for those at Kiangwan camp, for it happened to be a leap year. The twenty-ninth of February seemed like one more added obstacle to the end of their captivity,. Unknown to them, events were shaping up to change that. In Europe, a massive invasion, Operation Overlord, was being planned and staged. With the arrival of D-Day, 6 June 1944, and the Allied invasion of the beaches at Normandy, France, the beginning of the end of the European war front was underway. With the eventual de-

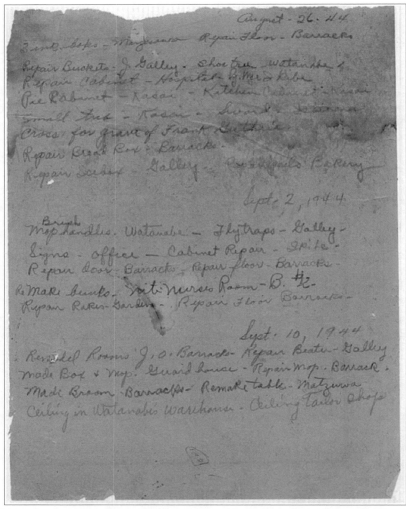

This sheet of paper has jobs for the Carpenter Shop to do listed for three weeks in 1944. The jobs varied from repairing kitchen buckets, doors, rakes, ceilings and bread boxes, to making a pie cabinet, flytraps, mop handles and a "cross for the grave of Frank Guthrie." (James A. Allen Collection)

feat and death of Adolf Hitler, Allied men, ships, and materials would be freed and transferred to the Pacific Theatre, helping to outnumber the Japanese forces.

Spring of 1944 again found the POWs chanting the now perennial questioning rhyme, "Spring is sprung; the grass is

riz, I wonder where the Allies is?" Because of their contraband radio, the POWs were not completely in the dark concerning the ongoing war. However, information was sketchy
at times and always second, if not fifth, hand since the location of the contraband radio and its operator's identity were
kept a well-guarded secret. Apparently the tinsmiths knew
who ran it and where it was, but didn't tell the carpenters.
Jim says that the POWs sometimes would have knowledge of
something or be working on a project and not necessarily tell
the others, even if they were close friends. There are times
when the fewer of those who have knowledge of an incident
makes that information much safer. Jim does recall that the
POWs knew about the siege at Stalingrad, Russia, by the German Army as it was occurring over the months. The POWs
also knew that the Germans were getting pushed back on the
Eastern Front as well as other news events.

Along with the hidden radio reports, the POWs were still
given local English language newspapers printed in Shanghai. They had a definite pro-Japanese tone. On 8 June 1943,
Jim found this article he clipped out and saved as an example
of what a wartime Japanese newspaper was like.

> Death was Fast Chilling His Body
> As Air Officer Makes Last Report
> Comrades Rush to Aid Lieutenant When He Falls
> — Find His Body Icy Cold — Had Been Shot Through Chest

> The almost incredible story of Lieutenant XX who
> made his last report while his body was fast chilling
> under the icy hands of death, is being passed on from
> one Japanese base to another in the South Pacific,
> according to the report of a member of the Navy Press
> Section from an undisclosed base. Lieutenant XX had
> command of the Japanese planes that downed 47 enemy
> planes in fierce encounters over Russel Island of the
> Solomon group. After the combat the sea eagles returned
> to their base about four o'clock in the afternoon. They
> returned singly, in twos and threes with dents of the
> enemy shot visible here and there on the silver wings.
> Lieutenant XX alighted from his plane and watched the
> skies for the safe return of the sea eagles who had fought
> so valiantly with him on this day.

Except for a slight pallor of his face, there was nothing unusual about Lieutenant XX as he stood erect scanning the skies with his field glass. Several hours passed before the last of the wild eagles had reached the base and made his report to Lieutenant XX. Then, Lieutenant XX walked steadily toward the commanding base officer and delivered his report clearly and in detail.

The report finished, Lieutenant XX raised his hands in salute to his superior. The next instant the hitherto erect form of Lieutenant XX crumbled to the ground. The base commander and others rushed forward to assist the Lieutenant. The body they touched was icy cold. Hurriedly they stripped off his life saving girdle and aviator's suit. An enemy bullet had pierced the Lieutenant's breast and the blood streaming downward into his boots was now dripping out from the top. The heavy aviator's suit and the life saving girdle had prevented the blood from oozing outward. None had guessed the Lieutenant's condition.

A moment ago, the Lieutenant had just uttered the last words of his report. Could the body have chilled so instantaneously if death had not already claimed the body even as Lieutenant XX was making his report? His spirit had carried on when his body had failed.

Thus, in the South Pacific as well as in the other battle areas, the glorious virtues of Fleet-Admiral Yamamoto and the indomitable fighting spirit of Lieutenant XX forever lead the sea eagles of the Imperial Navy to victorious achievements for the final crushing of America and Britain.

Whether or not Lieutenant XX was an aviator or apparition, the propaganda was intended to discourage the enemy who might read the article while encouraging allies and supporters. As for the POWs who read the article, it possibly had the intended effect upon the enemy: discouragement. As Jim reflected upon the article, he exclaimed, "That's why we [U.S. Navy/Army] were having so much trouble — they just wouldn't die!"

As the Japanese began to realize during the months after the Battle of Midway that the tide of war had turned on them, damage control took over to remove pro-"East Asia for Asians" propaganda. In 1942 at the Woosung camp, the pro-Japanese Empire magazine, *Freedom,* had been freely distributed to the POWs early in the year. Jim recalls that the POWs had had the magazine "for quite a spell, at least until their [the Japanese] fortunes in the South Pacific was stopped. Shortly after that [the Japanese] collected them all up. They wanted each and every one accounted for." However, Jim was given the opportunity on 10 September 1944 to obtain his own personal copy that would become another of his souvenirs.

Among Jim's souvenirs are some of the Kiangwan Carpenter Shop logs that kept track of work completed. At one point, Jim recalls, "There was a period of time where we had to turn in everything we done that day in the Carpenter Shop." Tool room overseer Art Gress was in charge of writing down what each of the carpenters had done, with explanations if necessary. The entry written for 10 September 1944 in the log is "Ceiling in Watanabe's warehouse and ceiling in tailor shop." Lieutenant Watanabe was the Japanese soldier who oversaw the items stored in the large warehouse that shared the building with the POW shops. According to Jim, "We worked in [Watanabe's] warehouse that day and that is where I appropriated or stole [his copy of *Freedom*] magazine." Although Jim cannot be totally sure this is the date, it is a close approximation.

Jim had to go into the warehouse to supervise the carpenters repairing the ceiling that had been damaged in a storm. While in the warehouse, Jim spied a tall stack of new, unread *Freedom* magazines. Making sure no one was looking, Jim snatched the top magazine off of the pile with one hand while unbuttoning his shirt with the other. Quickly sliding the contraband magazine under his shirt, Jim began rebuttoning while sliding his hand free, casually dropping it to his side. Completely unseen by the Japanese and the other working POWs, Jim completed his tasks with the ceiling crew and carried on normally. Later back in his section, Jim secreted the magazine in his stack of extra clothes on the shelf above his sleeping platform area and the straw mattress he now enjoyed. Not sure what the penalty would be if caught with the stolen *Freedom* magazine, Jim took no chances on finding out and kept it well hidden for the remainder of his internment by the Japanese.

Jim wasn't the only one stealing things from the Japanese warehouse. Jim recalls that "A limey [a Britain] broke into the go-down [warehouse] in daylight. Crawled under the go-down, removed some of the floor boards and stole some of the 'good stuff' there." The daring daylight thief was never caught, but apparently others found out about his reckless action. The imitators were not as fortunate as the first thief and were all caught. They were punished severely for their offense.

10

Winged Creatures, Roosevelt & Mortimer Snerd

Staying alive for several years in a Japanese prisoner of war camp required a strong will to live as well as cunning, quick, and sometimes devious thinking. A prisoner of war learns to be resourceful and imaginative if he is to survive and return home. Jim and the carpenters at the Kiangwan camp were among the best, especially at thinking to the future. Using the Imperial Edict of "Self Supply, Self Support" as a selling tactic, honcho Jim was able to get permission for the carpenters to have their own garden. Located behind the Carpenter Shop and go-down/warehouse, with the camp brick wall nearby, the carpenters' garden was well hidden from hungry eyes. Although other prisoners might already know about the garden, "You didn't broadcast that you had it," says Jim. When asked if there were other personal gardens, Jim responded, "You kept your mouth shut at all times."

Lieutenant Miyazaki, who was in charge of the Carpenter Shop, thought that the garden was such a great idea that "He give me the seeds even," recalls Jim, chuckling. "Well, that's all right. I let him give me the seeds, but we had all the seeds we needed. We got them somewhere or another." Each day after the shop work was done, the ten or twelve carpenters, some-

173

times with the tinsmiths alongside, worked in their garden with the issued seed and tools from the garden tool shed near the Carpenter Shop. Herman "Dutch" Raspe, was in charge of the garden tool shed and had to account for all shovels, hoes, and other tools given out each day to the workers to use in the camp's garden. The carpenters, with the tinsmiths helping out, were able to raise cabbage, carrots, tomatoes, and other vegetables to enrich their meager rations.

The carpenters grew a nice crop of cabbage to harvest that summer and decided among themselves to make sauerkraut as a way of preserving some of it, at least for a short time. The sauerkraut would also be a change from their soup and rice diet. With their combined culinary skills, the men of the Carpenter Shop and Tin Shop cut the cabbage into small pieces. Finding an old wooden soy sauce bucket, the POWs cleaned it up and put the chopped cabbage into it. The chefs "Stole some salt. Someway or another, we had some salt" Jim recalls, and mixed it with the prepared cabbage. They put a lid down inside the bucket, with a rock on the lid to hold it down and slid it all under a workbench in the Carpenter Shop, behind some wood boards, to allow the cabbage time to ferment.

Work went on in the shop with the cabbage brewing beneath the workbench, out of sight. When enough time had passed, "One day we all come to the conclusion [the sauerkraut] was good and ready to eat. So we shopped around and got a can of corned beef that come in a Red Cross box." The tinsmiths had a charcoal fired hibachi, made out of a five-gallon can, "So we put a pot on the hibachi in the Tin Shop and got it bubbling and stirred the corned beef in and divided it all up and we all had, mainly, sauerkraut!," recalled Jim with a laugh. Although the portions may not have been huge, especially the corned beef from a tiny tin, the benefits reaped from creating a different meal other than the ordinary camp fare, and an extra meal at that, was an invaluable boost to their spirits and health.

Even though the carpenters' garden was semi-hidden, there still was a constant danger that they might lose the vegetables before harvest. Late that summer, the carpenters had a close call with their crop of carrots. The Kiangwan camp Mess Sergeant, Nakagawa, was in need of carrots for that day's stew and knew about the carpenters' garden. Sergeant Nakagawa sent four Formosan prison guards to the garden with orders to pull up some carrots and bring them back. (Formosa was what the Japanese called the island of Taiwan. It had been a possession of Japan since 1895.) The four Formosan guards went to the carpenter's garden and diligently began pulling up the carrots. Someone in the Carpenter Shop spied the invaders and an alarm was immediately given. "The carpenters [John Dustman, Cecil Bouyer, Kenny Johnson and Art Gress] all busted out" of the shop, Jim remembers, and began arguing over the carrot patch and bumping the Formosan guards out of the way so they could pull the carrots out first. Dirt, carrots, and bad tempered words in three languages rapidly flew through the air. "Someone got me," Jim remembers, "and I got Lieutenant Miyazaki and boy, he come around the corner and he bellowed out an order." Immediately the guards stopped pulling the carrots up and stood at attention, as did the POWs.

The lieutenant had a dilemma on his hands. The carpenters had permission for the garden and the subsequent food produced while the guards had followed a direct order from Mess Sergeant Nakagawa. "Of course, he had to take and save face too. [Lt. Miyazaki] finally figured it out; he let the Formosan guards keep whatever they had and the carpenter POWs could have whatever they had. There wasn't any [carrots] left in the ground" after the rapid harvest took place. Although the carpenters had lost some carrots from their garden, it was a win-win situation for all involved with no face lost. Japanese cultural ethics of saving face and not embarrassing anyone, especially another officer, worked for the carpenters positively this time.

The carpenters and tinsmiths also joined forces to preserve some of the tomatoes they had grown. In addition to using what materials they had on hand, the resourceful POWs collected shipping cans from the hospital. These cans originally held the glass bottles blood plasma came in. The metal cans, "had a key you wound off like a [old style] coffee can. They had come over on the *Gripsholm* [and were] beautiful cans, shiny and silver on the inside, gold on the outside. The Tin Shop was able to take and fix the can so you could get the lid over the top of it and polished it all up. We stuffed tomatoes in there." The tinsmiths, Ludington and Fuller, "put the lid on and soldered it up. We had a five gallon can set on their hibachi, [put water in it,] got the water boiling" and after placing tomato filled cans in there, Jim says, "we cooked them a long

Civilian POW George Coates drew Jim Allen's birthday card using colored pencils and available paper. Coates even made an envelope to match. The verse inside the card is below.

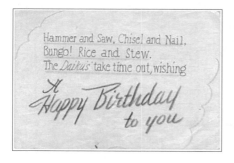

time. Then we [stored] them till that winter, winter of '44." By their resourcefulness and extra work, the carpenters and tinsmiths were able to enjoy some canned tomatoes during the harsh Chinese winter. The processed tomatoes were a great supplementation to the POW diet when other extra food sources became scarce.

August of 1944 found Jim Allen spending his twenty-sixth birthday in the Kiangwan camp, his third as a POW. On that summer Monday, the fourteenth, the carpenters gave Jim a card created by George Coates, Assistant Adjutant of Barracks 4, so they could celebrate the special day with him. On the outside of the card, Coates had drawn in front of a calendar, a seated POW crossing off with X's the days of the month of August 1944. A basket full of old pages from the calendar sits on the floor to the left of the POW. The very appropriate caption read, "DARN IT! ANOTHER BIRTHDAY HERE." Inside the following verse was written:

Hammer and Saw, Chisel and Nail.
Bungo! Rice and Stew.
The Daikus' take time out, wishing
A Happy Birthday to You

"They thought they had a very appropriate verse for me," recalls a very proud Jim. "I thought they did real well, as good as Hallmark, in fact."

Carpenter tool watchdog and friend Art Gress later wrote on the inside of Coates' card the menu for a special birthday dinner he had scrounged up for Jim and himself to enjoy that day. Gress had a very creative side to his personality. The following menu at first glance belies the fact that the two men are prisoners of war.

MENU
Birthday Dinner
Baby Lima Bean Soup
Combination Salad — Butter toast
Sweet Corn — Fried Potatoes
Fried Spam
Steamed Rice A La Gravel
Pumpkin Pie A La Kiangwan
Sweet Coffee — Chesterfields

The sweet corn and salad items were from the daikus'/carpenters' garden, and the cigarettes, sugar and coffee for "sweet coffee" as well as the Spam, something relatively new that some of the POWs had never seen before the war, were from International Red Cross boxes. The rest of the menu such as that garnished with "a la Kiangwan," was traded for and/or creatively cooked or made.

Art Gress also gave Jim Allen a gift of a pack of Chesterfield cigarettes with a long half-inch thin wood shaving wrapped around it like a ribbon. Gress had taken a carpenter's plane to slice off the thin, foot long ribbon of pinewood. Written on the shaving was "Happy Birthday — from Art." Gress apparently thought a lot of Jim to go to so much trouble. After he returned to the United States, Gress named a son Allan after Jim. The fourteenth of August 1944 was an all around good day for Jim, one of the few during the prison camp years. "I don't think we had much hassle out of the Japanese that day," Jim mentions after some thought. Moments of happiness were few and deeply remembered.

The Carpenter Shop was often sought for answers to the ever-present problems around camp, such as broken doors or urinal lids. When Mother Nature was the cause of the problem, the carpenters took her on, building window awnings to keep the sun out of Colonel Otera's office and repairing the damage wrought by severe thunderstorms. But for one major ongoing problem, the Carpenter Shop could only be a small Band-Aid, not the solution. They were continually asked to make fly traps and fly swatters for the Japanese; the POWs were on their own where insects were concerned. And insects, especially flies, were an ongoing problem. Each year with the arrival of warm weather, the insect population grew. Flies multiplied at a rapid pace. Jim and the other carpenters "were quite busy building fly swatters" to combat the pests, Jim recalls. "The [POW] officers and adjuncts had been after [the Japanese] to get screens . . . to get rid of the flies."

The pesky flies became so numerous that the camp commander, Colonel Otera issued an edict. In order for a POW to receive his food ration, he must catch and kill twenty flies a day. At first, "We all laughed at them about it," but the Japanese were serious. The motivation to be a successful hunter was hunger. The POWs had to be crafty and clever to kill the twenty flies needed to eat since no fly swatters were issued. Every way available to the POWs was used. Even the sick had to catch ten flies a day, and some of them didn't have the strength to try to catch one fly, let alone ten. Recalls Jim, "I've seen some of those older men that would get out on the south side of the barracks in the sunshine and try to find something that'd get the flies to come there and [then] wait in order to get their ten flies." Patience would sometimes pay off if the bait were right.

The barracks adjutant collected all the flies caught by the barracks for a day and would then turn the numerous dead bodies over to the Japanese authorities so that the POWs of that barracks would be allowed to eat the next day. With its eight sections of thirty-six men, this meant the men of Barracks 4 had to place 5,760 dead flies in their adjutant's collection can each day; a few less if someone had a sick slip from the guard. With approximately 1,500 prisoners in the Kiangwan camp, the number of flies that had to be caught was roughly 30,000 a day. Jim was quite busy locating and then trying to kill and recover flies for the official daily body count, in addition to his other required work.

With time the hunger motivated fly hunters basically eliminated all the flies anywhere near Kiangwan camp, so the fly bounty was then changed to mosquitoes. The mosquitoes were even harder to catch than the flies. However, Jim and some of the others discovered if they let the mosquitoes land on the water in the bathhouse, it was then easy to drown them and recover the body. As a result, the Japanese camp authorities were able to eliminate two of the insect pests in camp, as well as forestalling the spread of disease.

During the fly edict, and at other times when the Japanese authorities would cut rations for those who were in the hospital or couldn't work, the POW cooks would count all prisoners, even those in the hospital, together when preparing meals. They would then distribute the rice or other food to everyone. The "Americans didn't believe in cut rations," says Jim, especially for those who were sick and needed more calories to help them get better.

One morning during the last quarter of 1944, a couple of Japanese soldiers arrived at the Carpenter Shop with a large framed mirror. It was about two feet wide and six feet long. Colonel Otera wanted the carpenter's to build a stand for the large mirror in order for it to be freestanding and able to tilt. Jim as supervisor of the carpenters, gave the job of making the stand to John Dustman.

The nicest wood available to the carpenters was the Philippine mahogany used for the gun racks found in the barracks. On the walls of each section of the former Japanese Army barracks, gun racks had been installed large enough to hold the nine rifles of the nine men sleeping on the platforms. Dustman was allowed to removed some of the gun racks and used the wood in his design for the mirror's stand. The way Dustman designed the stand allowed the mirror to tilt back and forth, giving the viewer several different angles to look at himself.

The morning the stand was completed with the mirror attached, Jim and John Dustman carried it over to the Japanese interpreters' office and requested permission to see Colonel Otera. The Japanese interpreter led the way to Otera's office. Otera was seated at his desk. "We carried it in and set it down," Jim recalls. "He stood up and we bowed to him. He bowed back, which they always did. I never had a Japanese soldier or officer, that if you bowed [would not return it] . . . It might not be a very deep bow, but I never had one that didn't recognize it." In this instance, a bow was used as a military courtesy in place of a salute.

Immediately Colonel Otera returned the POWs' bow, Jim remembers, "you could tell he was real pleased with [the stand/ mirror]." The Japanese colonel walked from behind his desk and went over to the two POWs. That's when the most incredible thing happened. The Japanese commander of a war prisoners' camp stuck his hand out to the two American POWs, John Dustman and Jim Allen, and shook each of theirs. "I never expected, EVER [that] the camp commander, [a] colonel, Japanese Army, he stuck HIS hand out and shook mine and John Dustman's," Jim emphatically recalls, still marveling at the occurrence. "Course now, there's many prisoner of war of the Japanese [who] find that hard to believe, which I can't blame them. But he DID do that!"

Colonel Otera was extremely pleased with the craftsmanship of his mirror's stand. Following the handshake, he walked over to a cabinet and took out several items, which he then presented to the two POWs still standing at attention. To their surprise, Dustman and Jim each received a carton of Chenmen Grandy cigarettes, which Jim remembers "were as good as you could get over there other than in a Red Cross box." The two semi-starving POWs also received a fairly large can of jam, about ten ounces, which helped supplement their meager food rations. "And it was good jam, real good!" Jim recalls with a chuckle. "So we made out pretty good that morning!"

Over the period of time that Jim was interned as a POW at Woosung and Kiangwan, he had gotten to know which of the Japanese were semi-okay and which to steer clear of. Sergeant Major Kasai was one to keep away from. "He was one mean booger." However, in 1944, a change in personality occurred. The carpenters had dealt with Kasai a lot since he had the Carpenter Shop build several pieces of furniture for his apartment. The carpenters didn't realize at the time what Kasai was preparing for.

A POW camp was like a small town, with most everyone knowing what everyone else was doing, sooner or later. So when unpleasant and mean Sergeant Major Kasai disappeared for awhile, a few prisoners asked why. It was discovered, and the word was passed around, that Kasai was returning to Japan to be married. Upon his return to the Kiangwan Camp, the former Sergeant Major Kasai was now Warrant Officer Nakamura; he had had a promotion and a name change during his absence. Sergeant Major Kasai's bride, Miss Nakamura, had five brothers, all of whom were killed without having children, in the South Pacific area. In order for the Nakamura family name to continue for future generations, Sergeant Kasai took his bride's name. It can be assumed that Kasai was not an only son and his family did not have a similar problem. "Boy, [Sergeant Kasai, now Warrant Officer Nakamura] was a different man," Jim remembers. "He was rather mean before, but she sort of tamed him down." Jim, as honcho, along with some of the other carpenters got to see the new bride when they were sent to Warrant Officer Nakamura's apartment outside of camp on a work order. Jim, and the other carpenters with him, bowed to the new Mrs. Nakamura which she returned. Jim remembers that "She was a pretty little thing . . . cute as a bug's ear."

While some individuals were known for their hostility and inhumanity, others were known for being genial and even chummy at times. Mr. Nishegawa was one of the three Japanese interpreters at Kiangwan Camp. He was also one of those who oversaw the Carpenter Shop for a period of time. Nishegawa was not a true soldier, but a civilian in uniform, similar to Ishihara, the "Beast of the East." Nishegawa was the opposite of Ishihara. Jim recalls, "[Nishegawa] got to where that guys would ask him if they could have a board or something and he'd say 'Jimmie know, okay.'" I told them they could have it and it's all right. I had him snowed pretty good."

Working in close quarters for long periods of time brings even adversaries closer as they begin to know the individual person rather than their government's propagandized enemy. Jim got so he "respected the little bastard and I didn't take advantage of him. It wouldn't have been the thing to do. He hadn't caused us a whole damn lot of trouble." According to Jim, Nishegawa "was a Christian Jap. He knew many of the evangelists here in the United States." Nishegawa "had a son born in Kiangwan. He'd come in . . . telling us about his wife [going] to give birth. Finally he come in all beaming and [told us] the child had been born and it's a boy! We asked him his name and he told us in Japanese." Of course, the carpenters didn't speak true Japanese, only a pidgin variety sprinkled with a few Chinese words. The infant's name was unintelligible to the POWs. But that didn't stop the carpenters. "Well, in the Carpenter Shop, we nicknamed [the infant] Roosevelt Nishegawa," Jim recalled while laughing heartily. "We called him Roosevelt. [Nishegawa] stomped and fussed about it. Then, of course he . . . he was a right nice little guy. He finally got to where that he'd come in and we'd ask how's Roosevelt this morning. Nishegawa [would say] 'Okay, Okay, Okay." He'd speak some English." Apparently, Nishegawa was pleased that the carpenters would ask about his son.

Jim saw the baby in person one day when he had to do some work at the Japanese apartments just outside of camp. "I saw the little fella down in the apartment where I guess him and his mother and Nishegawa lived. His grandmother was home evidently and was out on the stoop [with the baby] and the sun was shining on him. ['Roosevelt'] was all bundled up. I think that was all the heat they had in the damn building, the sun shining." With a smile on his face as he remembers the baby, Jim stated that he has "wondered what happened to him, wondered about him, where the hell he is now, Nishegawa Roosevelt-san?" In May of 1945 when the entire camp packed up to leave the Kiangwan camp, Jim asked for and received Nishegawa's address in Japan. Jim thought he might write and find out how the baby was doing when the war was finished. Unfortunately, Nishegawa's address was lost when Jim turned in some of his clothes and other items to the U.S. Army in Yokohama in 1945.

"Roosevelt" Nishegawa was not the only Japanese to receive a nickname, although his was done in a friendly manner. Other Japanese received theirs for more hostile reasons. Giving nicknames to the Japanese soldiers was an easy task for the POWs. A certain name just suited them as in the "Beast of the East" for Isihara. Another interpreter who was easy to name was Morisako. Morisako looked and acted a lot like Mortimer Snerd, one of the wooden dummies ventriloquist Edgar Bergen used in his pre-war act. As more of the POWs called Morisako "Mortimer," he demanded to know why. "I mean," Jim recalls, "he puffed up like a big toad when he asked somebody who that was or why," the POWs called him that. There was one time that a particular prisoner was put on the spot. As Jim remembers the incident, "The prisoner thought real fast and said, 'Well that's a famous movie star in Hollywood,' and of course being familiar with Hollywood like an awful lot of Japanese were," Morisako calmed down for a while. It took Morisako about a year, but he finally found out who Mortimer Snerd really was and woe to the first prisoner who called him that then. "Oh boy, [Morisako] stood the man at attention," Jim remembers. Morisako "wasn't too strong or husky, but he sure boxed that guy around real good. But the name struck with him. By the time I saw him, that's who he was, Mortimer Snerd."

Sergeant Major Kurakawa was another Japanese soldier who earned a special nickname, One Punch Hogan. "He was a mean bastard," Jim says. "One time he caught us [in Barracks 4 Section 4] not ready for inspection." Jim was the barracks leader at the time and remembers Kurakawa became mad because some of the POWs' uniform coat buttons were not fastened in addition to other offenses. Kurakawa hit the offending men with a clipboard he was carrying and then left. Later when he came back into the section and still found buttons not buttoned, those men were hit again with the clipboard, this time hard enough to draw blood. Furious, Kurakawa finally left and Jim remembers, "We had a rope with a brick to close the door [which would cause it to slam]. [When Kurakawa left,] the door slammed and Shorty Martin's Schnapps bottle he was brewing blew up." Timing is everything and, in this case, the timing of the home brew's eruption saved Shorty from a beating, or worse.

In February 1945, an unexpected event enabled Jim to hide his contraband with relative ease during future inspections by the Japanese soldiers. Colonel Otera called Jim into his office and presented Jim with a citation, written first in Japanese and then in English. In the middle of the paper, to the right of Otera's name in Japanese characters, was Otera's chop mark, making the paper official.

James A. Allen

You, as a member of the inside details have worked diligently according to your special ability for a long time, following the instructions of the Camp Authorities, and have shown a good record. I hereby recommend you and give you a prize.
1 February, 1945

S. Otera, Colonel
Japanese Imperial Army
Director, Shanghai War-Prisoners' Camp

According to Jim, "It says J A and some [of those] chicken tracks [Japanese characters], now that says Aren [instead of Allen] in Japanese. They can't get the 'L' out, so they put an 'R'. Has Otera's chop which was pretty important." Jim was not the only

Jim's citation, or "good boy paper" as he refers to it at times, from Colonel Otera. The square shape in the center right of the citation is Otera's elaborate chop, an indication of his status. This piece of paper enabled Jim to hold onto much of the contraband and souvenirs he brought back to the States. (James A. Allen Collection)

POW to receive one of Otera's citations. Many were given out to different people over time at the Kiangwan camp. But as Jim recalls, "Many prisoners threw them away, but I kept mine." Only decades after being repatriated did a fellow ex-POW from Jim's camp, a Marine, reveal that he also had kept his citation, but had hidden it in camp and for the ensuing years, not wanting others to know.

Jim put his citation to work for him and others. "Well, I'll tell you what, this little piece of paper was invaluable to me. Because [when] we were shook down, [we] laid out all our belongings out in front of us and let the Japanese come along and inspect it. And of course, I had quite a lot of contraband." Jim would just put the citation from Otera on the top of all his belongings, with the contraband under cover on the bottom. The Japanese inspecting the POWs would come along and see the piece of paper with Otera's chop mark, sometimes reading it. The soldier would then turn to Jim and say, "Very good," and move on, never bothering to look at Jim's things beneath the paper. In this manner, Jim was able to keep his contraband from being confiscated and himself from being punished. That small, thin piece of paper would also aid in many other ways as the time drew near for the Kiangwan camp to close.

11

"Air Your Blankets!"

Among Jim Allen's souvenirs, one stands out as a symbol of his resourcefulness and talent: his handmade guitar. Its creation is a marvelous tribute to Yankee ingenuity.

At Kiangwan, the POWs worked six days a week and were given Sundays off. During this time, the prisoners could wash their clothes, play cards, get their hair cut by Jim's friend, Mike Rice, or pursue other available activities. It was during one of those Sunday afternoons in early 1943, not long after arriving at Kiangwan, that Jim took upon himself a personal challenge. He would apply what he had observed and create a tangible product for himself, while at the same time, bring some enjoyment to other POWs.

The peace and quiet of the Kiangwan camp, such as might be found, was broken that Sunday by the civilian POWs from Guam who lived in Barracks 3 directly across from Jim's Section 4 of Barracks 4. They had worked for the Pan American Airline at the company hotel on Wake Island and were stranded there, like the CPNAB workers, when the assault began. The International Red Cross in the Shanghai area had supplied the Guamanians with several guitars, which they played continuously in whatever free time was available to them. "Boy, they really played them over there. They had a ball with them," declares Jim. Since the barracks buildings were relatively close together, guitar music could be heard across much of the camp. Fellow prisoners Faye Belnap, H. T. Cope, Frank R. Mace, along with a few others in Barracks 4 Section 4, Jim remembers, "were grumbling over the fact that the Guamanians had guitars and they didn't." The discord around him caused gears within Jim's memory to begin turning with visions from the past.

In 1938 as a deckhand on the riverboat *John James*, Jim had watched the chief engineer, John Van Horn, make guitars in the stern engine room. Jim thought for a bit about what exactly he had seen Van Horn do. Although interested in how the guitars were crafted, Jim had never played one and had no musical background or interest. However, Jim knew that he, too, could make a guitar. He would simply follow the same steps and procedures he observed Van Horn doing on the *John James*.

Boldly, Jim interjected into the disgruntled Section 4 POWs' discussion of the guitar playing Guamanian prisoners that he'd make a guitar for them to play. The announcement was met with scoffs and jeers, especially from Jim's older and cynical Wake Island buddy, Eddie Peres, who said outright that Jim couldn't do it. So confident in his memory and ability, the other POWs' taunts didn't discourage Jim. He immediately left the barracks to begin accumulating the materials he needed to craft his guitar.

First, though, Jim went over to Barracks 3 to ask the Guamanians if he could use one of their guitars for a model. Receiving an affirmative, Jim quickly looked one over to get a feel for the size, shape and thickness of the materials he would need. Thanking the Guamanians, Jim exited Barracks 3 and began to search out materials.

As he walked around the camp, Jim thought about the type of wood he required. He knew he wanted solid pieces of wood for the front and back of the guitar, which were not necessarily easy to find in a prisoner of war camp. Then he remembered that while doing repairs in O Barracks where the prisoner military officers were housed, he had seen a small table with a top just the size (twenty-four inches by sixteen inches) and thickness (one-and-one-eighth inch) he wanted for the back of the guitar.

The Japanese Army issue table, Jim remembered, was located in Lieutenants Lewis and Barninger's room. Luckily Jim found them there. The three men had known each other since Wake Island when Jim had volunteered with the Marines. The two lieutenants each listened carefully as Jim explained his goal of making a guitar and the integral part their table's top would be. If the lieutenants were agreeable, Jim told them, he would make a false tabletop out of Philippine mahogany plywood to match the original so that the Japa-

Lt. Clarence "Barney" Barninger (left) and Lt. Wally Lewis. (*Freedom/ James A. Allen Collection*)

nese would not realize there had been a switch.

To Jim's grateful surprise, Lewis and Barninger told Jim he could have the tabletop. The lieutenants were taking a great risk, Jim remembers. "I thought that, boy, they were sticking their heads out a mile, 'cause if the Japs had come through there and found out that table top was missing, they'd been so mad, [the lieutenants] would have had to answer where in the hell it went. There'd been a whole bunch of us that'd got the hell beat out of us." Jim knew the stakes were high for what he wanted to accomplish. If discovered, Jim, and anyone else who was near him or in the Carpenter Shop or his barracks section, would have been punished. At the least, they would have had a good beating and time standing at attention at the guardhouse in all kinds of weather for an unknown period of time without food or water. Every precaution was taken by Jim to keep the Japanese ignorant of the guitar's existence and progress.

Now that he had a solid back for his guitar "staked out," as Jim phrased it, he thanked the lieutenants and headed over to the POW kitchen to look over the firewood pile. He might find wood for the guitar's neck among the pieces of hardwood. Another Wake Island civilian, Roy Stevens, had the job of splitting all the stovewood. Apparently Roy, a future Texas rancher, had missed a few pieces of wood the day before because when Jim arrived at the woodshed he found a nice piece of unsplit oak just the right size and length.

Over the next few weeks, Jim was able to acquire the majority of the materials he still needed. The front of the guitar was from a piece of ponderosa pine board three-quarters of an inch thick, thirty inches long, and sixteen inches wide, which was originally part of a Red Cross clothing box from the *Gripsholm*. How that particular piece was acquired, Jim no longer remembers, but since it was pine, "I must have stolen it" from the Japanese.

Jim knew exactly where to find the wood for the guitar's sides. The problem was getting it without a beating or time in the aneiso. The mahogany gun racks along the walls of each barracks section were the correct width and the perfect material for guitar sides. Jim devised a plan to "rip" a thin one-eighth inch strip off the back of one of the gun racks that was lying around the Carpenter Shop. These racks were the same type as those found on the walls of the barracks. The gun racks had to be replaced when the Japanese guard was not around, which luckily, occurred often. Since the carpenters gave the appearance of being productive, they were usually left to themselves for long periods of time while the Japanese guards occupied themselves elsewhere.

Jim smoothed his wood guitar pieces with a piece of broken glass and a wood plane. He used a small gouge, or chisel, and razor blades from the Red Cross packages to shape the front and back guitar pieces. It was slow, time-consuming work done mostly in the barracks at night or on Sundays. As Jim made progress in shaping the pieces, he became more and more confident that he would definitely be able to pull off the trick of creating a guitar from nothing.

Since much of the work was completed in the barracks, after awhile most of the other prisoners in Barracks 4, especially Jim's section, became interested in what Jim was creating and helped keep him out of trouble with the guards. It also protected them since everyone in the section would have been in trouble if the Japanese had discovered the guitar project. There was already an early warning network in place to inform fellow prisoners when guards were near. Cries of "air your blankets" would undulate like an ocean wave through the barracks when the Japanese guards appeared for inspection or just a walk through the living quarters, giving the POWs time to hide any illicit activities.

Those three little words, "air your blankets," would propel Jim into clearing wood shavings, sawdust, and materials off his bed and hiding them on the shelf above his sleeping platform space, where he kept his extra clothing. By the time the Japanese appeared, no signs of woodworking could be found. When the Japanese soldiers left the building and the coast was clear, Jim would go back to carving and smoothing his current wooden pieces.

Slowly the body of Jim's guitar began to take shape as he carved the back, front, sides and neck. To join the pieces of the guitar's body together, Jim used a Red Cross Gem razor blade to carve a deep notch along the edges of the front and back pieces, forming a lip. In carpentry terms, this is referred to as a rabbet. Jim then spread glue he had been given by U.S. Marine Corps Captain Pollard, the dentist, on the rabbeted edges and placed the edges of the guitar's sides against them, clamping them together until they were dry. A piece of glass was then used to smooth the edges and removed any excess glue.

Before the neck was attached to the rest of the guitar's body, holes for the tuning keys were drilled out and the fret board fashioned. Jim needed something to mark the spaces on the fret board. The other POWs' interest in the guitar helped Jim acquire the material needed. While working at the Shanghai Racecourse burying fuel drums, some of the prisoners had dug up a piece of brass. The "strip of rolled-up twisted strap [was] about three-quarters of an inch wide and one-eighth inch thick and maybe eighteen inches long," Jim remembers, and was perfect for the fret bars on the guitar's neck. Since any metal was difficult to come by during the war, Jim was very glad to have the salvaged brass strapping. "I don't remember how or who got it into camp or what I had to do to get it," Jim says of the brass strapping. Chuckling softly Jim added, "Maybe it was given for the cause."

A scrap piece of mahogany from the Carpenter Shop was perfect for the fret board. Jim cut a series of parallel grooves into it at regular intervals. Pieces of the brass strap were cut to size and then inserted into the grooves on the fret board to identify the musical chords.

Jim obtained a large piece of bone from the kitchen to be used as a bridge to suspend the guitar strings from. The bone was "big enough that I could saw pieces out of it," says Jim, in order to obtain a four-inch long piece thick enough to work with. After carving the bone piece into a rectangular prism shape, he placed it on the front, just below the guitar's sound hole. The nut, the rectangular piece that suspends the strings above the fret board at the top of the neck, also came from the same bone from the galley. "I don't know if it was a beef, horse or water buffalo [bone]," Jim says. "Whatever it was, the prisoners had eaten the cooked meat off it."

Although Jim lacked proper guitar tuning keys to attach strings to, he was not deterred. He scrounged up some old violin tuning keys to use instead. Since he had cut a hole in the guitar's neck large enough for guitar-size keys, Jim had to fashion a plug called a "Dutchman." (This was possibly in reference to the story of the little boy who stuck his finger in the dike in order to stop a leak.) This plug made the keyhole small enough to properly accept the smaller violin keys.

As with the glue, Jim was given guitar strings from Captain Pollard, who also had the job of music officer. As such, he had obtained a supply of guitar strings as well as other musical instrument equipment from the International Red Cross. When the guitar was finally completed during the summer of 1943, although not concert quality, the musical notes emitted from the instrument were sweet indeed to Jim's ears. "Frank Mace, H. T. Cope, and Faye Belnap all had lots of pleasure playing the guitar, and I don't believe their fellow men in Section 4 gave them a bad time," Jim recalls. "Most of the men enjoyed listening to them play." A bit of music helped mask the reality of their prison life, at least for a moment.

As with most transactions in a prisoner of war camp, a favor needs to be returned and Captain Pollard was ready to redeem his when Jim's guitar was completed. Jim was now considered the camp's guitar "expert" and the captain had several guitars that were in need of repairs from excessive use. Pollard had saved and stored the damaged guitars and now asked Jim if he would make the repairs. Naturally, Jim agreed to restore them. Luckily, the repairs were nothing serious and were quickly made. Captain Pollard also played the guitar and was happy to have a good guitar back to strum, although Jim remembers he "didn't make points with some of the officers in O Barracks. They didn't appreciate the captain's efforts at making music."

Later on during the fall of 1943, Captain Pollard came over to Jim and said he wanted to check his teeth. Jim agreed and moseyed over to the building that was used as the POW Dental Office. The captain discovered several teeth in need of repair and subsequently filled them. As Jim says, "Luck was with me again." Jim would end up without major decay problems or tooth loss thanks to Pollard's intervention. Dental care was not high on the Japanese's list of required items for their prisoners. Those at Kiangwan camp were very lucky to have a dentist and the necessary equipment from the International Red Cross available to them. Kiangwan was indeed an unusual Japanese POW camp.

For over a year, Jim kept his guitar hidden from the Japanese soldiers, storing it on the shelf above his sleeping area when it wasn't being played. Unfortunately for Jim, during an inspection in the fall of 1944, the guards happened upon it. Immediately confiscating the guitar, the guards took it to the camp office. Luckily, Jim was at the Carpenter Shop during the mid-day inspection and was quickly told of the guitar's abduction by one of his barracks mates. This gave Jim some time to think about what he wanted to do and say about the situation.

"That afternoon," Jim recalls, "I went to the Japanese office to try to get the guitar back." Arriving at the office, Jim was confronted by "interpreter Isamu Ishihara, who demanded to know what Jim wanted. "I said that I came for my guitar. Ishihara wanted to know who gave me permission to have the guitar. I said Lieutenant Akiyama did." This particular lieutenant had left the Kiangwan camp several months before, apparently in disfavor having been reassigned to duty in the war torn South Pacific. He figured that the odds were good that Akiyama had been killed or at the least was inaccessible for any questioning about whether or not he had rally given Jim permission to build a guitar.

"Ishihara knew me quite well and on one [previous] occasion had slapped me — very easy — late one afternoon when the carpenters were doing some work in the Officer's Barracks for new arrivals. He was questioning why it was not done, and I informed him that the carpenters had been working very hard, which was true and he knew it. But for Ishihara to save face, he had to tell me I could not talk that way to a Japanese officer." At the time, Ishihara "was wearing knitted wool gloves, black in color, and he proceeded to lay the palm of his glove easy to the side of my face." Realizing Ishihara's reputation as being savage about beating prisoners, Jim says, "This sea story will be hard for some to believe, but it happened. Anyway, I got the guitar back. The Japanese did not cause any more problems with the guitar." If they had, it would have caused loss of face for the absent Lieutenant Akiyama, and by association, the other Japanese officers.

Again Jim's growing understanding of Japanese culture aided him to successfully avoid serious repercussions. Jim was continuing to win the skirmishes of his private war with the Japanese.

12

"Spring has sprung;
the grass is riz . . ."

For two of their three springs of imprisonment, the POWs had repeated their poem with questioning impatience. But as this fourth spring came into full bloom, the spring of 1945, it brought with it new hope for the war's end to come soon.

The POWs had a pretty good idea based on observation of the activity in the sky overhead, especially from the nearby airport, that the Allies were getting close, and Japan was losing the war. From time to time, the POWs would see Japanese planes in the air traveling to or from the airport. Around early 1944, Jim recalls seeing seventy-five Japanese single engine fighters form up in the sky above the Kiangwan camp after taking off from the military airfield to the south. The fighters then followed two larger planes heading toward the southeast. Fewer Japanese planes returned later. While being cheered with the thought of the Allies "kicking butt," the turn of the tide of war also brought fear; the POWs knew they might be executed in order to remove all evidence of POW mistreatment and war crimes. After the war officially ended, specific Japanese documents pertaining to such an order were found; luckily the orders were never carried out.

Knowing the POWs wanted news, the Japanese would feed misleading information about the war to them from time to time. The information received "was usually a long time after it happened," recalls Jim. "Very much exaggerated." The POWs would then have to determine how much of the lopsided news report was true. The POWs still had their hidden radio, which the Japanese tried to find many times. Unknown but to a handful of POWs, the operator was Lieutenant John Kinney from Wake Island. Kinney had been in the Reserves before the war and had also been a China Clipper mechanic for Pan Am Airlines. The "lieutenant made the radio, had the radio in camp" according to Jim, who only found out Kinney's identity long after the war was over.

The POWs also had their unconventional news broadcasters in camp. As Jim remembers, during the summer of 1944, "Why, there was a Navy chief [who] was putting on an act that he was crazy. We all thought he was [really crazy]." The chief was housed in the hospital, which helped confirm the POWs suspicions. "But anyway, there were several of the prisoners around the inside fence; the electric fence wasn't electrified during the day. Well, [the chief] motioned for some prisoner to come over there [to the fence by the hospital] and talk to him. He was telling several of them [at different times] that . . . the States has flying cruisers." Of course, the listeners really thought the chief had gone over the deep end since he was telling them that the United States had large warships that could fly with eight inch diameter guns mounted on them, almost two-thirds larger than the anti-aircraft guns they had fired on Wake Island.

"Well, we all thought he was nuts. But on Armistice Day [November 11] of 1944, what flew over [the camp], but a B-29. And if you don't think that wasn't a sight to see, the size of it!" For the out-of-touch POWs, the B-29 airplanes looked enormous when compared to the small planes they had seen for the past three years. It was the same as being used to a dachshund as the only dog you had ever seen and having a Great Dane suddenly come running up to you. To the POWs, the B-29 was a reaffirmation of their country's inventiveness and might. "We began to think maybe [the Navy chief] wasn't as crazy as he was letting on," recalls Jim. "That was just one way of his telling us [the United States] had a tremendous large airplane. Because we had shot-down flyers [American pilots who] come in [to the Kiangwan camp] and tell us they had a .75-millimeter gun in the nose of twin engine bombers that was working boats over on the Yangtze River, going along, shooting holes in the [Japanese gunboats'] bottom. So we didn't think [the navy chief] was so crazy after all." Within a few months time, Jim and the other POWs would occasionally spot P-38 planes flying high above Kiangwan. Jim thought they were possibly taking reconnaissance photographs of the Shanghai area for a future invasion.

A very memorable day for the POWs of Kiangwan Camp was 1 April 1945. The American Armed Forces played a terrific April Fools Day "joke" on the soldiers guarded the POWs. The "joke" took place during one of the Sunday softball games that occurred in good weather. The International Red Cross had supplied the softball equipment and the Carpenter Shop constructed a crude backstop for the playing field. Jim would sometimes pitch at the games, but on that first day of April he was solely a spectator. Jim stood behind third base with some other POWs, watching the game. The POW ball games always attracted an audience of off-duty Japanese soldiers. Colonel Otera and some of the other officers were observing the game from the luxury of chairs place along the third base sideline.

The semi-relaxed mood of the afternoon changed in the middle of the game when three U.S. Army Air Force P-51 Mustang airplanes flew over at a low altitude. Hearing and seeing airplanes was not unusual since there were two airports nearby: one a Japanese military, the other a Chinese civilian. But having planes fly over the camp at such a low altitude and going quite fast — definitely not a take-off or landing pattern — was unusual. Even more unusual was the fact these planes were painted with American markings! A single star in a circle with two stripes on either side was clearly visible to the POWs, as well as to their Japanese captors.

While the planes were overhead, Jim looked up and saw the American pilot inside one of the cockpits. This close-up view of a warplane did not fill him with the shock, anxiety, and fear that he had experienced when he had watched the attacking Japanese plane on Wake Island from a similar position. This time, Jim was very happy to see the pilot's face.

The three planes made giant figure eight's in the sky as they continued to make bombing runs on the airport to the north, then circling and coming over the prison camp for another bombing run on the airfield to the south. After the initial shock of the air attack wore off, the Japanese guards blew the camp air raid siren and the POWs had to run into their barracks at once. It was lights out immediately even though it was only late afternoon.

While the POWs were in their barracks, Jim could still hear the planes' bombs landing on targets in the vicinity of the airports. Fifty-caliber machine gun fire was also heard until the American planes apparently ran out of ammunition and headed back to their base in an area of China not occupied by the Japanese. Within seven weeks of the air attack, the Kiangwan camp would be closed and the POWs moved north as the Japanese withdrew the majority of prisoners from the Shanghai area. This only helped confirm the POWs' suspicions that the Japanese were losing the war. This confirmation brought with it new worries of whether the POWs would be alive to see the war's end or annihilated first.

After the 1 April air attack, others followed much to the POWs' delight. Jim remembers one particular incident during the interval between the "Fools" raid and moving from Kiangwan. Snatching a moment now and then to peer out the Carpenter Shop doorway, Jim observed that particular aerial attack at close hand, Jim saw one Japanese "twin engine bomber with a stinger in its tail" escape from the aggressive P-51's, but a second Japanese bomber did not. From the west-facing doorway, Jim heard the gunner firing a burst from his machine gun as the American P-51 bore down on the second airborne bomber. It only took one burst of gunfire before smoke came out of the enemy plane's right fuselage near the rear of the wing with its Rising Sun.

In early July of the previous summer, as the threat of aerial attacks by the allies appeared to be a good possibility, the Carpenter Shop had received plans for a new project: an air raid shelter for the Japanese officers. Using a two-meter long concrete water pipe with a diameter of two meters, the carpenters made a wooden door to plug it. Located in front of the Japanese Officers' building, there was only room enough for a few men and it was never covered over with dirt for added protection; the concrete pipe remained out in the open. Jim says the concrete would have "turned back machine gun bullets as long as they didn't hit the wooden door." As to a direct hit by a bomb, there probably would not have been much hope for any Japanese officers huddling inside.

As the days at the Kiangwan camp waned, Jim confronted some personal changes to his routine of the last two and one-half years, including putting up with a new section and bunkmates. Why this change took place Jim is still not sure, but it left Jim living in a barracks section that included hundreds of undesirable inhabitants.

As with other prisoner of war camps, critters of all kinds could be found in the crowded and less than sanitary conditions. As a POW in the Kiangwan camp during the spring of 1945, Jim became familiar with bedbugs first hand. Bedbugs are small (one-eighth to three-sixteenths of an inch in China or about the size of a grain of rice), wingless, blood-

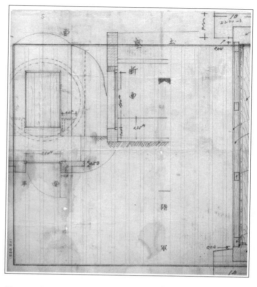

Part of the plans for the Japanese officers' air raid shelter. The wall to the right is part of the building where the Japanese office was located. The bottom of the plans shows the workings of the exterior door. (James A. Allen Collection)

sucking insects belonging to the order *Hemiptera*. A true bug, this little beast makes life miserable for those whose bed, and body, it resides upon. It is hard to sleep when you have throngs of small creatures strolling all over your body,. The wanderlust bugs stop their journeys only to take a bite of the host, ingesting blood. The POWs were vigilant about bedbug avoidance and woe to the one who introduced bedbugs to their community sleeping platform.

Jim had two previous experiences with bedbugs and knew firsthand what miserable creatures they were. When he was eleven and visiting relatives, Jim slept on an infested army cot. Trying to get rid of them, he poured hot water over the cot, but that was ineffective and the bugs remained. The second encounter was on the *John James* where the infestation was so bad Jim claims, "the only way to get rid of them was to burn up the boat."

Luckily, Jim had been able to avoid the bothersome creatures during the past three and one-half years, but his luck

The 3" x 3½" identity badge Jim had to wear. The numbers were stenciled in red onto a tightly woven white cloth. Don Ludington made Jim a metal holder for it with a safety pin soldered on the back to attach it to his clothing. (James A. Allen Collection)

ran out at the end of winter, near 15 March 1945. At that time, Jim was moved to Section 8 of Barracks 4 and given the new identity number of 4 8 17, or shi hachi ju-shichi instead of shi shi ni-ju-hachi (4 4 28). At the new section, Jim discovered the ultimate bedbug habitat existed in the form of a resident of his new section. Although hard to achieve, some form of cleanliness could be obtained in Kiangwan camp by those who wanted it. But it was apparent to Jim that this one man in his new section did not aspire to that goal. Maybe it was something in particular that those pesky critters liked about this one P.O.W., but Jim could only wonder how he stood it. The multitudes of bedbugs associated with this man had a path up the barracks wall similar to the ones made by ants. But unlike ants that leave no trace of their passing, bedbugs do. As they feed on the blood of their host, the bedbug's back end enlarges and as they continue to move along, they pass bits of digested blood that drop upon their trail, leaving a line of little black dots. The more the trail is used, the wider and blacker it becomes. Jim remembers there was "quite a trail on the wall" from this band of bedbugs. Jim watched the trail widen and thicken during the next few weeks. Apparently avoidance and toleration were all the POWs of the section did about the bugs, except for verbal outbursts at the host POW. Fortunately, within two months of Jim's assignment to Barracks 4 Section 8, the Shanghai War Prisoners Camp at Kiangwan was closed.

The month of April 1945 was full of change. Relatively soon after President Franklin Roosevelt's death on 12 April 1945, the POWs learned about it from the Japanese guards who began to question the POWs about the new President,

Harry S. Truman. Jim recalls, "We didn't know who Truman was, but we told them that [President] Roosevelt was a pussycat compared to Truman." The POWs made up anything that would discourage the Japanese. However, this time their fabrication became a reality, in July 1945, when Truman OK'd the use of the new "secret weapon" the United States had developed.

Don Ludington. (PIEF)

Later that April, fifty POWs were sent ahead to the Peking area to prepare a new camp for the Kiangwan camp prisoners. There was no mistaking that the POWs would be moving north soon. The only bright spot was that it meant the Japanese were definitely losing the war.

With the prospect of moving to a new camp, Jim, along with Don Ludington and Richard "Dick" Fuller, the two tinsmiths, began to seriously discuss the forthcoming move. All three men had heard of several British ships being sunk and the survival tales that the British crewmen, now POWs in camp, had regaled them with. Many Japanese ships carrying POWs had been sunk as well, although Jim and the others didn't have knowledge of that until long after the war. Nonetheless, their consternation was well founded, especially since Jim and the others assumed that they would eventually end up in Japan as Eddie Peres and the other POWs had in 1943. It seemed a water crossing could not be avoided. After the horrible *Nitta Maru* voyage in 1942, Jim was ready to do everything in his power to avoid suffering from dehydration and starvation again.

Most important to survival the three men decided, was fresh, clean water. Even in a life raft, survivors of ships that were sunk have been known to die of thirst. Jim recalls, "We three decided to have Don and Dick prepare cans with handles to carry water in." The three survivalists scrounged up some squared five gallon metal cans from around camp to transport a clean supply of boiled drinking water during their forthcoming journey. "Don and Dick cut their cans to two-and-a-half gallons. The one I carried was five gallons. We wanted to be sure to have water to drink on land or on sea," says Jim. In order to withdraw the drinking water from the metal containers, Jim and the others "each got three feet of quarter-inch surgical rubber hose from the hospital. This we wrapped around our mid-section in case our ship was sunk." The plan was that the hose would be used as a tube or straw to retrieve the water in the metal cans. Jim, Ludington and Fuller would have a supply of fresh water even while treading salt water in the Sea of Japan.

Even though it meant a heavier load for him to carry, by keeping his can at the five gallon size, Jim carried only two and one-half gallons of water (about twenty pounds), leaving two-and-one-half gallons of airspace in the can. This created extra buoyancy, which would help keep Jim and his can afloat if he found himself abandoning ship. The longer he could stay alive, the better the chances of rescue by friendly forces. At least that was the plan. "Whether I'd ever been [able] to get in the water with it, I don't know, but I was going to try!" Jim, for one, was not about to give up easily if he could help it, even if a ship were torpedoed out from under him.

The forthcoming journey to a new camp required a lot of preparation on the part of all the camp, especially the Carpenter Shop. As honcho of the carpenters, Jim had extra men assigned to him, without carpentry experience, in order to be able to complete all the tasks required by the Japanese. The number of POWs under Jim's supervision varied from time to time, but "When we got to move [in May of 1945, north to Fengtai], I had fifty working, tearing up barracks [and getting] the lumber. I had two men just straightening out nails." The camp buildings' lumber and nails were reused by the Carpenter Shop to build wooden boxes or shipping crates to pack the furniture and other property from the Japanese offices, barracks, and apartments. Additionally, the POW kitchen with all the cooking implements was to be packed into crates. "[The Japanese] sent out a list of what you could take and what you couldn't take," recalls Jim. "You couldn't take a whole lot that was approved [by the Japanese]. We couldn't take our library or hospital stuff, much," or at least that was the official order from the Japanese.

As the prisoners began to box up furniture, it was discovered that the drawers being shipped were empty. The efficient POW workers of the Carpenter Shop thought it was a shame to let such desirable space go to waste. Jim agreed and put his "Manchu Theory" to the test. As long as the carpenters were working quickly and getting everything done that the Japanese asked for, the guards didn't closely supervise the carpenters. "Well," Jim smiles as he relates the story, "quick as the

Japanese would bring a piece of furniture, desk or what-have-you, down to the Carpenter Shop, outside there, well, the men would get right on it and crate it up real quick. They weren't carpenters, but they learned real quick how to crate furniture. But the one reason they were doing that was [because] all of the contraband we had at the barracks" was being packed inside the crates. Along with the empty drawers, the POWs looked to see if there were any holes or crevices where items could be stashed. These places would be filled with contraband. Then, "They'd crate it up and set it out on the side [of the working area] and [some other POWs] would come and the crew would haul it away. That's the way things was going. Everything's going real smooth. [The Japanese] weren't having no trouble out there. Went along real good. I had one carpenter in the library, boxing up books" in spite of the fact that the POWs were told they could not move the camp library. As supervisor, Jim had "Another [prisoner] over in the hospital and that's all he was doing, crating their stuff up. [The carpenters would] bring a crate down there and [the Japanese] would haul it away. After a while, why, [the Japanese] got to scratching their heads down at the railroad siding. As I understood it, the gondolas and boxcars and everything was full . . . and [the Japanese] was scratching their head; couldn't figure out why. [How had] they made such a mistake," of miscalculating the amount of goods to be shipped out of the Kiangwan camp?

There was no mistake by the Japanese in their calculations. "Well, there was no trouble, so there was no need for [the Japanese] to go inspecting [the crates] or anything. So they just ordered more [train] cars and so we just kept boxing up and hauling." Within days, the carpenters had all the empty drawers filled with the POWs' contraband shortly before the shipping crates were nailed shut. The crates were hauled down to the railroad siding and loaded aboard the waiting freight train with its extra cars. The Japanese unknowingly shipped all the additional weight of the POWs personal goods and the POW library and hospital on to the Fengtai camp near Peking in northern China. In Jim's case, the Japanese eventually transported his personal wooden box of contraband all the way to Niigata, Japan.

While Jim supervised those working for the Carpenter Shop, Ludington and Fuller worked on other preparations for the move, including more false Klim cans. The cans of powdered milk had increased in value because there had not been any International Red Cross shipments since the fall of 1944. The two tinsmiths were lucky to find unopened cans that could be used for their ruse. These new cans were similar to the one presented to young H. T. Cope for his birthday. Instead of containing horse manure, these Klim cans held parts from the POWs' concealed radio. Again the one pound Klim can bottom was cut open and half of the powdered milk removed. The radio parts were put inside in a manner that would not allow them to clang against the metal sides of the can. The bottom was soldered back into place and the can buffed and polished in order to hide evidence of tampering. The altered cans were handed over to Jim for transport to their new location. Jim moved the camouflaged radio parts along with his contraband food, souvenirs, and guitar during transfers, as well as his clothes and the five gallon water can. In order to carry all his acquired belongings of the past three years and four months, Jim had a cloth "pack outfit that Don Ludington had made that I could just strap it on. Put it on my shoulders to carry it. Oh, well, hell, I had accumulated a lot of stuff." The pack outfit was similar to a present day backpack except that it consisted of straps of canvas with two circle shaped buckles made from number 9 wire. Jim strapped in a jute sack with hardtack and other supplies for the upcoming trip.

Jim used a wooden Red Cross clothing box, thirty-six inches square by eighteen inches deep, that had come from the 1943 *Gripsholm* shipment to pack most of his belongings. "I had one of those boxes," says Jim, "and I filled mine. I had it full!" with his Carpenter Shop drawings, overcoat, clothing, and Klim cans. The Japanese carted it to the train station along with the other boxed goods. He didn't have to bother with it during the journey north. Additionally, Jim had acquired "two honey buckets, brand new, one on top of another and lashed them up with rice straw rope just like the Japanese wrapped stuff and [then I] put them in the freight car." Jim hoped the Japanese would think the two buckets were just some of their goods and move it on, which they did. When asked about all that he had packed away for the transfer north, Jim can't identify everything. "I don't remember — useful things. And what would be useful to me then," Jim chuckles, "you would throw in a trash can now!"

13

North to Fengtai

Reveille came early the morning of 8 May 1945. Jim and the others in his section rolled off of their sleeping platform for the last time at the Shanghai War Prisoners Camp at Kiangwan. After a quick breakfast of hardtack and tea, Jim put on his backpack, lifted the guitar onto his shoulder, and picked up his water can. He then joined the other POWs still at Kiangwan and lined up outside of the barracks for bungo.

At 5:30 AM the large group of POWs officially left the Kiangwan camp for the last time. As they marched down the road toward the railway station, Jim fingered the Carpenter Shop door key he had put in his pants pocket the day before; Dick Fuller had given it to Jim as another souvenir. Nicknamed Kagi-woe (roughly "our key man") by the POWs, Fuller had been the prisoners' illicit locksmith, as well as a tinsmith, and was able to make duplicates of all the various keys that were at the camp for whoever needed them. H. T. Cope was one POW who employed Fuller's expertise to make him a new key for the camp chicken coop after the guards had changed the lock. When given the new key to unlock the coop to work for the day, H. T. simply pressed the new key into a bar of soap to make an impression. When given to Fuller, an unauthorized key was made from the soap mold, allowing H. T. to visit the chicken coop at unsupervised times to appropriate an egg or two from the nesting hens.

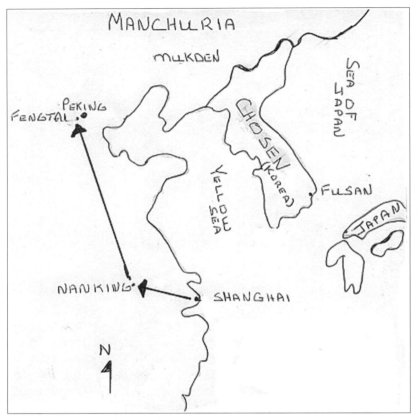

Jim's route in 1945, from Kiangwan to Fengtai, near the capital
city of Peking.

Feeling the key in his pocket caused a number of memorable moments to come to Jim's consciousness, some good and
some bad. It had been a long two-and-one-half years at
Kiangwan and an even longer time since Jim had left his California home and family for the construction job on Wake Island. The short nine month adventure he thought he was on
had now stretched into three-and-one-half years.

Once at the railway station, the POWs were herded over
to the boxcars at the siding. In a single file, Jim and the other
prisoners walked up a ramp and into their transportation to
Northern China. The wooden freight boxcars had been modi-
fied to accommodate prisoners instead of livestock or crates of
goods. Each boxcar had been partitioned into three sections

Cutaway view of the interior of a boxcar similar to what Jim Allen rode. Note the small windows through which civilians Bill Taylor and Jack Hernandez, as well as five military men, escaped from the moving prison train. (Bill Taylor Collection)

separated by a curtain of barbed wire. The two larger sections were for the POWs, one at each end of the boxcar, with a small, barbed wire covered window on each sidewall. Each POW section held twenty-five men with little room to move about in. The men could not all sit down comfortably at once in the small space allotted them; they had to take turns. Their personal goods hung on the boxcar walls or had been stored in another boxcar. Jim kept his guitar with him, hanging on a wall. A benjo bucket was supplied in one corner of each section. Its use continually added to the strong odors that already permeated the wood floor and sides of the boxcar. The POW sections were separated by the smaller Japanese soldiers' section in the middle of the boxcar where the sliding doors were, which were kept open when possible to help remove some of the odors. From this position, the guards could oversee all their charges in each half of the boxcar. A POW corpsman, or medic, was assigned to each boxcar and carried a few first aid items as well as a bottle of iodine. Although at all the train stops the Japanese boiled water in vats to purify it, the POWs took no chances on bad water. The corpsman poured iodine into each container of drinking water brought to their boxcar. It was the only way to be sure the water didn't carry unwanted microbes and was safe to drink. It wasn't only POWs who didn't trust the water. The Japanese guard escort, made up of all the

Japanese personnel from the Kiangwan camp, including Colonel Otera, drank tea exclusively during the trip.

When the prison train pulled out of the station at Kiangwan, it began the long, slow journey north by heading west and staying on the south bank of the broad, yellow tinted Yangtze River. Reaching Nanking, now Nanjing, a little less than 200 miles to the west-northwest, the Japanese soldiers ordered the POWs to leave their belongings in the boxcar and line up on the side of the train tracks. The Japanese herded the 1,000-plus POWs through the city and toward the river while Nanjing's residents watched. The Japanese wanted to show off their captives as evidence of their military might, even if they were losing the war at the time.

Waiting at the water's edge were several small boats that resembled tugboats. The Japanese soldiers packed the POWs tightly on board the boats; there was not a single square inch of space that did not have a human being on it, prisoner or guard. POWs sat on top of the boats' pilothouses and all over the decks. As they set off across the Yangtze River heading for the city of Poukow on the northern bank, these POW "ferries" presented quite a sight.

Jim was one of the many POWs sitting cramped upon one of the small boats' decks. From this vantage point, Jim had a clear view of the river and the other boats. The small boats were very top heavy and had only six inches of freeboard showing above the water line. If the boat were to go "down six inches more, it would have just filled up with water." Jim wished he had his five gallon water can along so if his boat floundered, he would at least be assured of having something he could use to float to shore with. Today there is a bridge at this spot, making crossing faster and safer, but in May of 1945 being ferried across the wide Yangtze River was the only way to cross it; it was an experience not to be forgotten quickly. Jim remembers that at the crossing "There was nothing but yellow mud for water and it was running rather swift. I was sure glad when that tugboat got over on the other side, for my part. They didn't have no problems, they didn't lose no prisoners. Fortunately [the POWs] all got over there and we made our journey up to Fengtai."

Arriving safely at Poukow, the POWs rejoined their boxcar traveling homes. The train, at another crossing point, had taken a larger ferry that accommodated trains. The POWs were taken off the boats, lined up and marched over to their waiting boxcars at the train depot. There were still over 500 miles to travel before they reached Fengtai and the new POW camp.

As the train sped across the Eastern Asian landscape, the POWs with Jim continued to complain, as they had the day before, about not being able to lie down or even sit. But no one would listen to anyone else about what to do, so everyone remained uncomfortable. This went on for three days, but by the third night, the POWs were so fatigued that they were ready to listen to anyone's suggestions.

William L. Taylor. (PIEF)

By trying out different ideas, the twenty-five POWs finally discovered that all of them could lie down on their sides if everyone had someone's feet next to their back and someone else's feet next to their stomach, alternating head and feet across their entire half of the boxcar. This left room in a corner for the ever present, but necessary benjo bucket. With this new arrangement satisfactorily figured out, the POWs in Jim's boxcar section were finally able to be a bit less uncomfortable for the remainder of their trip north.

During two different nights on the train trip, there were two semi-successful escapes by seven POWs. Two civilians from Barracks 4 Section 6, Bill Taylor and Jack Hernandez, removed the barbed wire over the small window in their boxcar section. They climbed out while the two guards were asleep in the center section. Although Hernandez broke his ankle during his drop from the moving boxcar and was quickly recaptured, Taylor managed to avoid the Japanese while making his way through the Chinese countryside. Taylor eventually found freedom in non-Japanese-occupied western China, meeting United States allies Chou En-lai and Mao Tse-tung, and returning to the U.S. before the war's end.

The second escape was made by four Marine lieutenants, Richard M. Huiznega, Jr., John A. McAlister, James D. McBrayer, and John F. Kinney, who had planned their escape in Kiangwan after learning about the upcoming transfer. The four men also climbed out of a window in their boxcar while their guards were asleep. Additionally, a U.S. Navy Ensign, Louis Bishop, had observed the four Marines while they left and since no alarm had been raised, he quietly climbed out the window to join them. They were a bit more successful than the civilian attempt, with all five evading capture by the Japanese and eventually returning to the United States before the war's end.

Lieutenant Kinney would eventually become a Brigadier General in the Marines. "In fact, he was the one who took care of the radio. Lt. Kinney made the radio, had the radio in camp. The Japanese, they tried to get that [radio] and find it many times, but [Kinney] put it together and we were being fed information about what was going on [with the war] that was usually a long time after it happened," Jim remembers adding, "Very much exaggerated [also]." The escape of Kinney made the value of the concealed radio parts that Jim and others carried questionable. Of course that was if and when the POWs would get a chance to get the radio back in operation again when their journey was finally over.

Taylor, Hernandez, and the military escapees had not been the only ones thinking of getting away from their captors. In order to be prepared if the opportunity arose, Jim had pilfered a keyhole saw from the Carpenter Shop before the last tools were packed away. The small saw had a thin, tapered six-inch blade with a tip that Jim filed down to a point. If given the chance, Jim planned to rotate the saw's oblong handle between the palms of his hands, creating a drilling action with the blade's tip. The strategy was for a hole to be formed in the boxcar's wood flooring or wall, into which Jim would be able to slip in the keyhole saw and cut a hole large enough for him to crawl through and escape. Unfortunately, Jim never had an opportunity to carry his plan out. He ended up carrying the small saw all the way to Niigata, Japan.

Unhappily for Jim and all the POWs still on the prison train traveling north, the Japanese soldiers increased their supervision and security details after the escapes. All boxcar doors and windows were tightly shut for the remainder of the trip. With fifty-two or more men, including guards, in each closed boxcar, the air quickly grew hot, stale, and fetid with the warm May weather and benjo buckets.

On Monday, 14 May 1945, the sun rose on the POWs' train as they pulled into the town of Fengtai, only eight miles southwest from the city of Peking, now Beijing. Finally, Jim and the others in his crowded boxcar were able to stretch their arms and legs without hitting someone else or the boxcar walls, as they walked down the ramp from their boxcar. The POWs had a two-mile trek from the Fengtai railway junction to their new camp, and it helped loosen their muscles up after the six-day journey. Memories of the hike to the Woosung camp after the *Nitta Maru* prison ship voyage were relived as the POWs were marched through the streets to a large warehouse, which resembled an airplane hangar from the outside except for the small entry doors. This austere place would be their home for the next thirty-six days, although at the time, the prisoners had no idea how long they were to remain there. For all they knew, it could be another year or more before they could be freed by advancing Allied troops; that is, if they weren't executed first.

Now at Fengtai, all the crates that had been loaded aboard the train at the Kiangwan Camp had to be unloaded, but there was not any lack of willing labor. The helpful POWs wanted to get their contraband out of the crates and furniture hiding places before the Japanese found it. Jim recalls that at Fengtai, "Uncrating all that furniture and everything, that was very easy because here, all those prisoners was out there to get their stuff out of the furniture. So, it got uncrated and carried to the office real quick. It worked out slick, everything got there."

The Fengtai conditions were extremely miserable, especially when compared to those at the Kiangwan camp. The Fengtai warehouse facility offered much less food and even fewer facilities for basic body functions. The primitive benjo at the POWs' new home left much to be desired. Located only one hundred feet away from the warehouse "barracks," the benjo consisted of a large open pit with logs placed across on which to squat. Surrounding the benjo pit was woven grass straw matting, tatami mats, apparently placed there in an attempt to keep the area less muddy from rain and inaccurate feces and urine deposits. When they first arrived, a fire hydrant was the only source of water for the POWs to use, making bathing difficult at best for approximately 1,000 men. Eventually, a trough arrangement with several spigots was made available through the work of the skilled POWs.

The extremely large warehouse, or go-down, as it was referred to in Chinese by the prisoners and their guards, was a big open affair. It was about the size of two and one-half American football fields at 250 yards long, while 146 yards wide and

The inside of a section in the Fengtai warehouse camp drawn according to Jim Allen's recollection. (Linda Spencer/L. A. Magnino Collection)

50 feet high. Familiar with the large buildings of downtown Los Angeles, Jim was very impressed with the sheer size of the structure: "Sure as hell big and I wasn't a kid then!" The only windows were located near the top of the walls, close to forty-five feet from the floor, which allowed little in the way of light or ventilation for those at ground level. The warehouse floor was concrete brick, upon which the POWs slept with whatever bedding or blankets they had brought themselves: no sleeping platforms here. Each POW was allotted a two foot by six foot space on the concrete brick floor, which left very little room to walk around in. Just lying on the bare floor Jim shivered, even though it was May, thinking about the coming winter of 1945-46. He knew it would be miserably frigid in the drafty, high ceiling concrete building without any heat.

The Fengtai warehouse was divided into five sections, or bays, which were partitioned off with walls made of the same small concrete bricks as the floor. There was only one door into each individual bay, which was located on the south side of the warehouse. There were no doors or windows on the north side. Since the Chinese and Japanese relied on abundant people-power to move goods for storage, there was no need for a large door to admit motorized vehicles. There also was no need for shelving, ledges, or other places to put things. Those who hauled the bags of rice, wheat, soybeans, cement or other commodities to be stored in the bays, would create stair steps with their burdens to enable them to pile the bags, layer upon layer, all the way to the ceiling, forty plus feet up. Although the relatively new building might have been a great warehouse, it was a lousy place to live.

Immediately the hierarchy took over and separated the military and civilians, the officers and enlisted men, to reinforce the camp pecking order. The Japanese assigned the POW officers a bay to be shared with the hospital, each in a half. Jim and some of the other civilians were in another bay, with the Carpenter Shop designated for one end.

According to Jim, the senior POW officer, Colonel Ashurst, was not happy with the situation and wanted to move the carpenters out of their bay and into another location. That would allow the colonel to move the hospital into the carpenters' vacated bay. Jim, the Carpenter Shop supervisor, didn't see eye to eye with the colonel on the move. The colonel wanted the carpenters to build a tatami mat shelter outside for them to move into, separate from the warehouse and the other POWs. Jim recalls the colonel, "telling me how cool it was going to be in the summer time" in the new location, out-of-doors on the north side of the warehouse. "But I had already heard the [American] North China Marines telling us down in Woosung and Kiangwan how damn cold it was up that way in the wintertime and I let the colonel know it was going to be the carpenters that was going to take and make anything anywhere near comfortable in this [warehouse and] that I'd be damned if they're going to be out in that damn cold in the wintertime if I had anything to do with it. They were going to be in [the warehouse]!"

By the spring of 1945, the twenty-six year-old Jim had gained enough clout to be able to stand up for his carpenters' welfare if necessary. "In Woosung and Kiangwan, I was just a carpenter there until September of '43," when Jim became honcho of the Carpenter Shop. The POW officers at these camps, Jim claims, were "finagling all kinds of 'goodies' getting made for them in their quarters or Officers Barracks as they called it. I didn't particularly appreciate that, while the rest of us . . . ." Jim's voice trailed off in mid-sentence as memories came into focus. It was obvious by the tone of his voice that, although he thought well of several of the POW officers interned with him, there were a few officers that, in his mind, cared more for themselves than those who ranked below them, including the civilians.

A social hierarchy was still very much a part of American life in the 1940s, as was racial segregation. Place of birth and parentage, as well as shade of skin, pigeonholed individuals whether they liked it or not. It appeared that the civilians were considered by at least some of the POW military to be low in status and thus able to be pushed aside. But they apparently hadn't reckoned dealing with a determined Jim Allen. "I had the upper hand," Jim recalls, for by May of 1945, he had developed a positive working relationship with Colonel Otera and was also known in camp for his integrity, good judgement, and overall fairness. "I'd gotten to where people halfway believed me." Not knowing how long the POWs would remain at the warehouse camp in Fengtai, Jim felt he had to be proactive toward the long term and the possibility of a frigid North China winter or two. Jim also felt, rightly or wrongly, that if he had presented the situation to Colonel Otera, Otera would have backed him up. "Of course, if we'd stayed there very long, I would have lost; the colonel [Ashurst] would have won in the end."

The Fengtai warehouse camp was the only place Jim kept a diary, other than his travel log of dates. Concern over repercussions later because of his disagreeing with the much older, ranking senior POW officer, Jim kept the diary so, "I'd have a record of what the hell actually happened and what all the hell he said." Writing in cursive, Jim wrote in the back of a book and copied it out later onto other paper. An entry near the end of the diary reads, "Hope to never [have] to use." Jim kept the diary up diligently from Monday, 27 May, to 16 June, with descriptions of the day's activities and pertinent interactions among Jim and the other shop honchos dealing with Ashurst. But after the sixteenth with its comments about, "Got our trunks inspected today another hectic day. Tired as hell In Group B," the diary suddenly stops with the last entry written on the nineteenth, which just says, "Left Feng Tai."

Many years later, Jim found out why the colonel wanted the carpenters to move, which would then have allowed room to separate the POW officers and hospitalized enlisted men and civilians who were in the one bay of the warehouse together. According to what Jim was told by another ex-POW, an enlisted man in the hospital area had dysentery and tried to go out to the benjo. The enlisted man had to take a rather circuitous route in the densely populated warehouse. The unfortunate man didn't quite make it and lost some of his bowel contents along the way on one of the POW officers lying on the brick floor. Evidently this was more than enough reason for the Marine colonel to justify in his own mind a move of the carpenters in order to remove the hospital with its low ranking patients from his warehouse bay. From the colonel's perspective, the social hierarchy of the military demanded the separation of ranks at all times and in all situations.

Although the camp was overall worse than the one in Kiangwan, there was a change in diet for the POWs at Fengtai. Since they were now farther north, away from the rice paddies, the main food staple was wheat flour, readily available, which was used for noodles and dumplings as well as bread. Still, as with the other camps, meat was nearly invisible when the ration was divided among a thousand hungry POWs. There was still never enough of anything for the emaciated prisoners. What food was available was served in the warehouse barracks after being cooked in a tatami mat shed about 200 yards away from the warehouse. Cauldrons and wood fires were again used to cook the meals. The kitchen area was by the main road heading west toward the Gobi Desert with camel trains passing by occasionally. As with the Woosung and Kiangwan camps, only the designated POWs went to fetch the rice, tea, and the "questionable stew," as Jim refers to it.

News from home was nonexistent since there was no incoming mail other than local delivery. The POWs were not allowed the "privilege" of writing letters home during their Fengtai sojourn. Most of the men had only six months, maybe year old, news from home and their families or sweethearts. It didn't appear that there would be any mail deliveries for them in the foreseeable future. Jim and the other prisoners could only wait and see what the next day brought to them in the way of news from beyond their prison site.

The carpenters were immediately assigned the task of making the living conditions at Fengtai more bearable. Jim had other POWs assigned to him to help speed up progress on the construction of a wash rack and better benjo facilities. A

Mr. Tomiyama, a Japanese engineer who told Jim that in 1940 he had helped build the building that the POWs were being housed in, was assigned to help build the new and much needed sanitary facilities. Tomiyama gave Jim the plans for the new wash rack and benjo, on a board twelve inches wide and thirty inches long; paper was still hard to come by. However, work progressed expeditiously since Tomiyama had been given one hundred sacks of cement for the wash rack and benjo.

While work continued on these two projects, the carpenters were also called on to build a kitchen and construct furniture for the Japanese along with other projects that the Japanese as well as prisoners wanted done "yesterday." On 10 June, a hot cloudy afternoon, Jim wrote in his diary that several of the officers asked to use some of the carpenters' tools. Jim let them have them, but, as he wrote in his diary:

> "Not for private use the standing Japanese order is to not issue tools without their permission. Yesterday a officer got some tools for use on the farm he told me and [instead] he made a bed. So will have to tighten up."

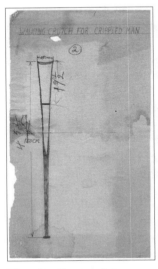

Plan for the crutches the carpenters made. (James A. Allen Collection).

As honcho, Jim found himself caught in the middle between the American military and the Japanese more than once.

Jim's diary records the progress of the construction projects at the Fengtai camp as well as more mundane tasks like laundry. However, his entry from Monday, 11 June, mentions a "Micky Miles, a limey tried to escape. Found him in lumber pile." The next day Jim wrote "two new Pilots arrive in camp." On that Tuesday, Jim had one of his crew making a pair of crutches out of bamboo to help one of the pilots with the broken leg he sustained when he bailed out of his airplane.

While at the Fengtai camp, young H. T. Cope managed to steal a case of

Japanese Army soap from one of the storage warehouses nearby. H. T. had been on a work detail in the warehouse and when presented the opportunity to acquire some of the enemy's fine soap, he took it. "He could talk to the Japanese," Jim remembers, chuckling at the memory of H. T. and his pidgin Japanese. "What a character." H. T. knew that the soap would be excellent to barter with other prisoners as a valuable commodity. Any risk was worth it.

H. T. managed to get the case of soap past the guards supervising the work detail, but needed somewhere to stow the case before it was discovered in his possession. This was not a matter of just looking around and finding some loose board in the barracks. With a brick floor and walls, the Fengtai camp offered very little in the way of hiding places. But there was one place in the camp area that might be able to conceal his soap and H. T. went to it straightaway. The Carpenter Shop, or work area really, offered the only solution to the young POW's problem.

H. T. knew Jim had a small room in one little section of the warehouse barracks for an office. When he found Jim in the work area, H. T. asked him to hide the case of soap and Jim agreed to stash the soap in his office, with one stipulation. "Of course I had to split it with him. I got half of it." Luckily for both men the Japanese never found the soap and, possibly, never even realized it was missing. But H. T. and Jim still had to keep it under cover to avoid being beaten or worse if any Japanese guards ever saw it.

As the POWs' stay in the Peking area lengthened, Jim's diary entries indicate that the POWs expected to be at the Fengtai Camp a long time. Tomiyama set a project completion date of 30 June for the wash rack and benjo and Mr. Egle of the International Red Cross in Shanghai sent word on the thirteenth of June that "regular shipment of supplies will start on June 25th," according to Jim's diary entry. Since it had been over eight months since the last regular International Red Cross shipment, the prisoners joyously welcomed the news of the anticipated return of American cigarettes, Spam, Gillette razor blades, and other items found in the little cardboard boxes that each POW received.

But by Friday, 15 June, change was in the air. For his entry on that date, Jim wrote, "Many rumors today." The rumors, or scuttlebutt, were apparently fed by the Japanese ordering that the camp library, hospital and recreational supplies, which had been supplied mainly by the International Red Cross, be divided up three ways. Jim's diary entry continues for the fifteenth with "Rec Hall and Medical supplies and lib [library] split 40, 40, 20. 40 for old war prisoners 40 for new P.O.W. and 20 per cent for Japanese." But along with the anticipation of an eminent move, Jim's diary entry for that June day continues with a touch of the reality of the moment. "Lt. M tells me to repair and make a total of 45 toilets working on W.C. as usual went to Japanese dump. All same as U.S. everything. Sure wish we could get what we wanted from there."

Jim writes on about progress on the various projects and the ongoing power struggle between Ashurst, himself, and the other shop honchos, but also found it important to end that 15 June entry with "Gave out Red Cross articles today even Pajama's." These were apparently from a supply of Red Cross items the Japanese previously withheld from the prisoners and were given out in preparation for leaving the Fengtai camp. Twenty-four hours later, the scuttlebutt around the camp became real as the POWs were given group assignments in anticipation of departure from Fengtai on the following Tuesday, 19 June. The benjos and wash racks would remain unfinished with only the trusses for the roofs built.

The almost 1,000 POWs at the Fengtai Camp were divided into A, B, and C groups for the upcoming travel. Jim was assigned to B group and became number B 83, his third identity since 23 December 1941. B group consisted of 300 POWs: seventy-two Italians, five Norwegians and 228 American civilians and Merchant Mariners. Group A was made up entirely of military POWs while some civilians were also in group C. At six in the morning on 19 June 1945, all three groups left their warehouse home and, "We were back in the boxcar for another journey to we knew not where," or how long. However, the scuttlebutt said Japan. The POWs could only hope the war would soon end and they would still be alive to see it.

14

On the Road Again

As the POWs got ready to leave their warehouse home on 18 June 1945 they were organized from their larger A, B or C groups into small subgroups of twenty-five men. This smaller subgroup was assigned to half of a boxcar for the new journey.

Jim found himself in charge of his half of the boxcar. In the car with him were some of the Italian POWs from Kiangwan. On the trip north to Fengtai the men in Jim's boxcar had figured out how to let everyone lie down and rest at the same time in the very crowded space, but Jim knew it was useless to talk about it that first night. No one would listen to him so early into this new train ride. This was especially true of the non-English speaking Italians. Jim remained silent while everyone else was "just growling and going on about laying down, doing nothing." Complaining seemed to be the only worthwhile activity for some of the prisoners. By the third night, everyone was exhausted. At that point, Jim spoke up and explained how everyone could lie down on their sides if each person had a pair of feet in their stomach area and a pair in their backs. Even the Italians understood what Jim had in mind, for they lay down quickly. There was no arguing or bickering from any of the very tired men. There was even room left in one corner for the benjo bucket.

Leaving the suburb of Fengtai behind as dawn broke, the POW train passed through the pre-war capital city of free China,

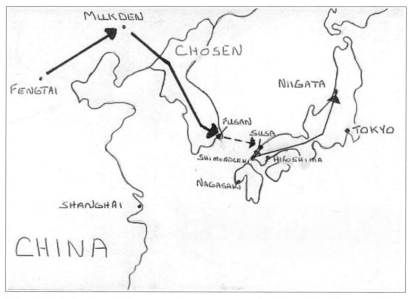

After a brief stay at the warehouse camp in Fengtai, Jim and the other POWs traveled to Fusan, Chosen, via Manchuria. Crossing the Shimonoseki Strait to Japan, Jim's final destination was Northern Japan and the industrial seaport of Niigata.

Peking. The POW train reached a portion of the Great Wall that night, traveling through it by tunnel. Unfortunately, it was dark, so Jim could not get a good look through the boxcar's small barbed wire covered window at the monument built of the labor, and in some cases death, of thousands of Chinese peasants over several centuries. The train continued on toward the Japanese controlled Manchurian Plain and not stopping until it reached the vast industrial city of Mukden, today known as Shenyang. Manchuria had been Japanese territory since the end of the Sino-Japanese War of 1894-1895. China ceded it to Japan as part of the concessions of the Treaty of Shimonoseki. This was the start of Japan's imperialism on the Asian continent, much to the disapproval of European powers.

At Mukden, the POW train changed direction and began heading south-southeast, climbing away from the broad Manchurian Plain into the mountains. Soon the train crossed the border into the Japanese colony of Chosen, known as Korea to the rest of the world. Jim remembers the mountains were beautiful as he viewed them through the barbed wire window of the boxcar. The Japa-

nese had controlled Chosen since
1905. As George McCune states in
his book, *Korea Today*, before World
War II Western countries thought
"the Japanese were . . . performing
yeoman's service to the rationalized
ideals of Western imperialism and
that Japan by her precociousness
had demonstrated that she could be
deputized to carry part of the white
man's burden in the Far East." The
Japanese followed the traditional
imperialistic bent of controlling the
government, economics, and so
forth of the colony, while not allow-

Jim's cloth ID badge during
the trip from Fengtai. It was
the same light colored
cloth and red stenciled
numbers as previous ones.
(James A. Allen Collection)

ing the "colonials" much input into their own country's manage-
ment. It was not a surprise when the Japanese withdrew from
Korea in 1945 that the country's basic structure collapsed.

Entering Korea at Satchu, the POW train continued on to
Pyongyang, which the Japanese called Heijo. Finally Kaesong
was passed before reaching Seoul, or Keijo as the Japanese referred to it. "The [American] GI's in the 1950s fought for this
railroad," Jim recalls, when they were part of the United Nations troops attempting to keep Communist forces out of Korea.
The final leg of the five days of travel took the POWs through the
Korean countryside, passing the towns of Chonan, Taejon, Taegu,
and Samnangin, before finally reaching Fusan, as the Japanese
called Pusan, Korea, on the morning of the twenty-third at 6:00
AM. The strong odor of sea air invaded the boxcar as the prison
train pulled into coastal Fusan's rail station, situated next to the
docks for large seagoing freighters. A torrential downpour greeted
the POWs that Saturday morning as they departed from their
cramped boxcars. The POWs' legs were stiff and sore from dis-
use after the ninety-six hour journey. When Jim saw how hard
the rain was coming down, he was glad he had the Marine Corps
oilcloth poncho he had traded cigarettes and his carpentry skill
for back at the Kiangwan camp. The waterproof poncho kept not
only Jim dry, but also his guitar, which was strapped onto his
back along with his homemade backpack; inside a cloth sack
strapped to it were a few clothes and a meager supply of tooth
breaking hardtack, or ship's biscuit. His large wooden Red Cross
box with most of his clothes, the Klim cans, and other such items

had been taken along with other boxes and crates to be loaded into a freight carrying boxcar.

Walking from the freight train to the new camp's barracks through the streets of Fusan, Jim and his belongings remained dry as he sloshed through the water and thick mud. The Guamanian POWs were not as fortunate. Their unprotected guitar, received during the division of recreational supplies back at Fengtai, became saturated and fell apart. Learning of the other guitar's demise after settling into Fusan camp, Jim "went over and asked them if I could have the [tuning] keys to it" for his guitar. The Guamanians were glad to give Jim the tuning keys since they had no use for them. Jim tucked the keys away inside his backpack until later when he had the opportunity and tools to put them on his guitar.

The Fusan camp was "a big mudhole," Jim recalls, and very unpleasant. What made it even more unpleasant was the work required of the POWs by Colonel Otera, who had traveled with the POWs all the way from Kiangwan. The Japanese Army soldiers who had guarded the POWs in Kiangwan and Fengtai camps were also still with them. Colonel Otera, Jim believes, arranged for the prisoners to be rented out to work on the Fusan docks in order to bring a little extra money into his pockets. Presumably, it was common to use POWs for extra labor and income.

After unloading their baggage in their assigned barracks that wet Saturday morning, the POWs were marched over to Fusan's wharf area. They were now under the supervision of the commanding Japanese officer of the dock area. The POWs were immediately organized into a continuous line of men carrying yea-ho poles with two baskets attached. The men formed a human conveyor belt whose task was to load salt into the cargo hold of a seagoing freighter lying alongside the pier. Wooden boards made a ramp leading up onto the ship's deck and more boards lay across the freighter's holds with another ramp of boards leading back down to the pier with its "great big pile of salt on the wharf," as Jim remembers it. It was from this mountain of salt that the POWs obtained their mineral millstone to be carried upon their shoulders. On the dock, two selected POWs put two or three shovelfuls of salt into both of a POW's baskets, which the POW would then lift with his yea-ho pole upon his shoulders. The POW carried his approximately forty pound load up about fifty feet on the crude wooden ramp to the freighter's deck and over to the open hold. While walking across the open hold on more wood planks, the POW pulled one of the three ropes on each of his baskets, tipping it in such a manner that the heavy salt would fall into the cavernous hold. The prisoners never stopped while unloading the salt or plodding up and down the ramps and dock. They had only thirty seconds to maybe a minute of rest when they put down their baskets while waiting for them to be refilled. This went on for hours.

The Allied POWs weren't the only ones loading salt. Parallel to them was a second human conveyor belt made up of Koreans who were filling another of the freighter's empty cargo holds. The smaller Koreans were quite adept at moving loads from one point to another with baskets attached to yea-ho poles and caused their conveyor belt to move at a speedy pace.

That afternoon and again for the next two mornings and afternoons, the commander of the dock area at Fusan spoke with the honchos of the POWs to motivate them to make the rest of the prisoners work faster. Jim was one of the honchos, and he remembers the "dock CO lined us up every morning and afternoon and yelled . . . at [the honchos] because the prisoners were not loading the salt fast enough to suit him." The commander wore a samurai sword about his waist and while speaking, he would swing it around violently for emphasis. It was "not a toothpick like" today's U.S. military officers might have, but one that could "cut your damn head off in one lick," according to Jim. The thought that one of the honchos' heads would be used for a demonstration of the samurai sword's power as a way to motivate the POWs, came to mind as Jim stood there listening to the ranting Japanese officer.

Between the sword swinging and the camp commander speaking Japanese rapidly at the top of his lungs, Jim had a difficult time following what he was saying. The message was eventually understood to be that the POWs were not loading the salt fast enough. Jim thinks that the commander, whose name he has forgotten or possibly never knew, probably had "some sort of contract" with harbor officials to send prisoners down to the piers to work as slaves filling the cavernous holds of the seagoing ships. Of course, after more than three years of hard labor, disease, lack of medicines, extremely poor nutrition, and weight loss, the POWs from Fengtai weren't in any condition to move fast while performing heavy labor. Jim remembers a Korean Presbyterian minister who, on behalf of the prisoners, tried to convince the dock area commander that the POWs didn't have enough food to enable them to perform such tasks well. The commander remained unconvinced and continued to demand more of the POWs.

The Allied POWs were not even close to matching the speed of the toiling Koreans. During one day's efforts, honcho Jim took a yea-ho and its loaded baskets from one of his men and carried it up the steep wood planks onto the ship. As he walked across the planks over the hold's gaping opening, Jim looked across into the Koreans' hold. The faster Koreans had piled up quite a peak, the pile reaching close to the top of the opening. In comparison, as Jim tugged on his baskets' ropes in order to dump his load of salt, he looked down into the dark interior of the cargo area and could hardly see any salt inside. It's no wonder the dock area commander was angry; he was probably losing money because of the POWs' slow work.

After a couple of days of hauling salt, the POWs stopped going to the wharf and remained in their barracks all day. The samurai sword swinging commander must have decided to cut his losses with this weak group of prisoners and get rid of them.

On Wednesday, 27 June 1945, the fifth day at the Fusan camp, the POWs were instructed to leave all their belongings in their barracks and were marched over to another part of the camp. Since the POWs were sure that the Japanese were close to losing the war, they were uneasy with this turn of events. The wary POWs were herded into an enormous building where they were instructed to remove all their clothing, including their shoes, and tie everything in a bundle. Memories of sitting naked, attired only in his shoes, on the hot, crushed coral road on Wake Island came rushing back into Jim's mind. Thoughts of being executed were as potent now as they were then. Once naked, the prisoners were given a piece of tape with their identity number on it and instructed to put it on their forehead. The POWs were then moved on in neat order into a large tatami mat covered room.

Looking back on the situation, Jim recalls it was similar to a scene from the 1993 Steven Spielberg movie, *Schindler's List*, where the interned Jews were herded, naked, toward the showers where they were gassed. Seeing that movie, long after the war's end, gave Jim an eerie feeling of déjà vu. "We were naked, we didn't have nothing on. We didn't know what was going to happen. When I saw [*Schindler's List*] I could figure what was probably going through their minds. I didn't know, had no idea, what was going to be."

Complete extermination was the Japanese goal that early summer day in Fusan. Fortunately for the POWs, lice and cholera were the targets. The large facility was a delousing and medical testing station for all those returning to Japan from the rest of Asia, civilian and military alike. The Japanese were very health conscious and wanted to stop unwanted vermin and disease from invading their home islands.

As Jim explains the procedure, "You went in on these tatami mats and you lined up in two rows. They had a Jap [medical technician], two of them, sitting on a box with a bunch of culture dishes and little glass rods. As you got up to [the medical technicians], you turned around and spread your cheeks [of the buttocks] and he took this little glass rod, stuck it in [the anus], wiggled it around and tapped it on the dish." The medical technician then removed the numbered tape from Jim's forehead and placed it on the culture dish with Jim's specimen inside. Apparently, the prisoners from Fengtai were a relatively healthy bunch considering the circumstances. Jim doesn't remember anyone being pulled out for cholera and not making the trip to Japan, but says there could have been some.

There was one POW in Jim's group who was well known to be high strung and jittery, "goosey," as Jim puts it. Anxiously, the other POWs waited to see what "Goosey" would do when his turn came to "about face" for the medical technicians. Punishment could be meted out for all the POWs, not only the ticklish one, if the orderly procession to produce the required specimens was shattered. Anxious moments passed as each silent prisoner in line took his turn and about-faced. Jim held his breath as "Goosey's" turn came. "Goosey" jumped when poked, but to everyone's grateful relief the Japanese were amused by his reaction. "We sure had a very good laugh," recalls Jim. Even though he jumped when first prodded, "Goosey" mustered enough will power to perform the required task without presenting any problems to all those involved.

After a fecal sample had been taken, the POWs "Then got a good bath — Japanese style," recalls Jim. A bath, with lots of soap, was something that had been in short supply during the POWs' interment. "We had a bucket of warm water which was splashed on — soaped ourselves — and then used the rest of the bucket of water to rinse with. Then we got into the big community tub." Jim says that it was the best bath he had had since he'd left Honolulu in September 1941; he finally felt clean after years of having poor or nonexistent bathing facilities. After the bath, Jim continued following those ahead of him in line and went to another part of the huge building where he received his clothes back. "You'd come back and there your clothes was or there was a ball [of clothes]." The Japanese arranged for the POWs' clothes to be washed and run through a sterilizer while they were being screened for illness and bathed. Jim and the other prisoners quickly dressed and marched back to camp to be reunited with the rest of their belongings, which were non-sterilized. It is quite likely that the POW's sterilized apparel were reinfested with vermin in a relatively brief period of time. At least they felt a lot cleaner than they had just a short while before.

That evening, the POWs gathered up their belongings for yet another journey. By now most of the POWs had guessed correctly that they were headed for the Japanese home islands. Before leaving his Fusan barracks, Jim wrapped his surgical hose around his waist and carried his five gallon can half filled with boiled water. It appeared that it might come in handy after all on an ocean voyage to Japan.

At 11:00 PM on the twenty-seventh, the POWs were marched out of the Fusan camp and into the Fusan streets, lined with two- and three-story apartment houses. The march to the ship was a repeat of their arrival, complete with rain. Again, Jim was glad he had the waterproof poncho to protect the guitar. The POWs walked quickly through the mud-filled Fusan streets toward the harbor and the possibility of a ship's dry hold.

Whether it was nerves or just poor timing, while marching down the Fusan streets Jim felt the urge to relieve his bladder. "I didn't want to wet my pants," says Jim, so "I asked the Japanese guard about 'Benjo!' and so he run me over to the curb and he told me, [pointing to the gutter] 'There!' That's where I urinated, in the gutter, with people hanging out [the apartment windows] and everyone watching," including the prisoner parade.

Feeling better, Jim hurried along in the rain to catch up with his place in line. Giant freighters loomed in the darkness like frightening banshees waiting for their next victims. Memories of the hellish *Nitta Maru* voyage flashed back into Jim's mind as he clutched his water can tighter. Once again, Jim had no idea what the next leg of his journey would bring. Only time would tell.

15

Into the Enemy's Home

Jim walked aboard the waiting ferryboat just before midnight on the twenty-seventh of June. He had been expecting a larger, ocean-going ship to take the POWs across the Sea of Japan. He was surprised to find a much smaller, and slower, ferryboat tied at the pier. Slowly Jim and the other POWs descended into the ferry's interior until the passageway opened upon a big, flat deck area. Woven grass straw tatami mats were on the deck to sit upon. There the POWs and their guards spent the remaining hours of the early summer night, hot and miserable, within the stuffy boat's interior.

Around dawn, the rest of the ferryboat's passengers joined the POWs. Japanese women, old men, and children entered the lower deck's open area and immediately sat upon the tatami mats for the upcoming journey. The POWs, their Japanese guards, and these civilians composed the group that would cross the Korea Strait to Shimonoseki on the Japanese home island of Honshu in the early morning of 28 June 1945. The atmosphere in the ferry's passenger space was a mixture of excitement, happiness, dread, and fear. The Japanese aboard looked forward to seeing their homeland again. Jim saw the volcanic formed mountains of Japan with a mixture of curiosity and fear — curiosity for the new sights, but fear of being taken deeper into the enemy's territory where it would take much longer for the American Army to free him and the other POWs.

The ferry left the Fusan pier on time at 6:00 AM and continued along its normal navigation route toward the Japanese Island of Honshu. The interior of the ferry had grown stale quickly with the many bodies packed into it. With the ferry now moving and picking up speed, some fresh air began to circulate into the passenger deck area. Halfway into the crossing, the monotonous grind of the engines picked up and the ship began to make a turn to what seemed to be the north. The prisoners wondered what was up and that wonder soon changed to concern, as they realized they were on the open sea. With the ferry sailing through the Korea Strait on its way to Japan, the POWs were probably sailing into harm's way and the United States Navy. The friendlies might not know there were prisoners of war aboard the Japanese transport; an occurrence (unknown to this group of POWs) had happened earlier in the war with the sinking of enemy ships and drowning of allied POWs. "I was sure glad I had my can of water and the hose," recollects Jim. "I had carried it a long way."

After several tense hours, the ferryboat's engine whine slacked off and the POWs realized that they were stopping. The ferry had pulled into a beautiful little harbor; however, it was not their intended destination of Shimonoseki. The ferryboat had gone further north up the coast of the island of Honshu, to the port of Suza, where a Japanese destroyer lay at anchor, in the hope of its offering some protection to the defenseless ferryboat. This revelation confirmed their suspicion that the ferry had been in danger of being sunk.

Three months later on the return journey to the United States when Jim's homeward bound ship, the USS *Ozark*, docked in Pearl Harbor, the POWs' suspicions would be validated. Tied at the pier for the night in Pearl Harbor, no one was allowed off the ship, but one of Jim's fellow CPNAB workers knew his way around shipyards. He had been a Navy enlisted man before the war and getting off a restricted ship was a "piece of cake" for him. While strolling through Honolulu that night, this man ran into an officer who he had served under. Over drinks and discussion of what had occurred since their duty together, the officer, now commanding officer of a submarine, mentioned his location in the Shimonoseki Strait during the previous July and how a boat had barely gotten away. After the two sailors compared dates and times, they came to the frightening realization that the officer's sub had had the POW ferry from Fusan in its periscope's crosshairs. The evasive measures the ferry employed had saved it, and consequently the POW's, from a torpedo. Jim and the other prisoners had been correct in thinking that the ship had changed course to avoid being sunk.

Although the ferry docked in Suza on that Saturday afternoon, 28 June at 4:00 PM, the POWs were left on board in the hull's stale air, until 1:00 PM the next day. Obviously the change of port had thrown the Japanese efficiency machine for a loop. During the long wait, Jim, Ludington, and Fuller siphoned some of the clean water from their cans to quench their thirst. Because of their forethought, they did not have to wait until, or if, the Japanese guards furnished water to the prisoners.

On dry land again, the POWs were marched toward a little brick school near the docks and herded into an auditorium-like room without seats where they spent the night sleeping on the polished floor. There was a small stage at one end of the large room, with a heavy red curtain drawn across it. One of the more curious POWs, forgetting the traveling regulations of no "disobedience of orders issued by Japanese" and "Prisoners are not allowed to touch fixtures or any devices without permission," crawled over to the curtain and started to draw it back. Before he could see what was behind the curtain, the Japanese guards descended on him and beat him mercilessly. When speaking about the incident now, Jim feels that there must have been a portrait of Emperor Hirohito behind the curtain. Since the Japanese considered him a god, it would desecrate the Emperor's image for a foreign prisoner to look upon it. Of course, it could have been simply a case of not following the regulations as well as tired and testy guards.

The next morning around 8:00, the POWs were taken to a train and began traveling southwest along the western coastline of the island of Honshu to their original destination, the port city of Shimonoseki. Seven hours later, the POWs' train pulled into Shimonoseki. At this point, the POWs were split up according to their group letter and sent to several different camps throughout Japan: Group A to the Tokyo area and Group C to the island of Hokkaido, which was north of Honshu. At Shimonoseki, Jim's Group B, consisting of 150 prisoners, was slated to journey to northern Honshu and the western

Joseph F.
McDonald, Jr.
(PIEF)

port city of Niigata. Group B left behind Colonel Otera and the Japanese soldiers who had been their guards since the Kiangwan camp, some for over two years, and acquired a new group of five Japanese soldiers as guards for the train ride to their final destination of Niigata. These five were, according to Jim, "The largest [soldiers] I had seen since the Japanese sailors on the *Nitta Maru* [voyage in January 1942]. They had the best looking uniforms I had seen on enlisted Japanese Army personnel. They sure knew what they were doing. It sure was a good thing all the soldiers were not like these five."

This new group of guards was very businesslike and let the POWs know who was in charge. They immediately divided up the POWs into three groups of fifty. POW Joe McDonald was identified as the overall leader of the prisoners by the new guards. The guards also selected two sub-leaders, Fred Ramsey and Jim, who were appointed leaders of fifty men each, with McDonald also responsible for the remaining fifty. McDonald was informed by the Japanese soldier in charge as to what the POWs could and could not do during the imminent train trip. This information was relayed to Jim and Ramsey, who, in turn, passed it on to their fifty man groups via a POW chosen to be head of a smaller ten man group. This information chain apparently worked well for communication during the trip since everything went smoothly.

By 8:00 on the evening of 30 June, after a change of trains, Group B began traveling northeast through the cities of Hiroshima, Kobe, and Osaka. At Nagoya, the POWs' semi-passenger train headed north, through Nagano and on to their destination of the industrial city of Niigata, 160 miles northwest of Tokyo. The new guards kept watch that the window blinds were tightly drawn as they traveled through the Japanese cities. Although the POWs were unaware, the Japanese guards knew that wrathful civilians had attacked earlier prison trains passing slowly through cities and towns. However, the POWs were still able to sneak occasional peeks by looking through the crack between the window ledge and the blind when passing by train stations. Allowed to have the blinds half up when traveling through the countryside or the perimeters of population centers, the POWs were able to see destroyed buildings and wrecked factories. Jim was amazed how the Allies could burn everything up but the train depot with their bombardments. "Far as you could see, only masonry; everything else burnt up!" As Jim recalls, "We seen many burnt out cities and it was horrible. But then, pictures of Hiroshima didn't look any worse" to Jim in later years. "Only thing was it only took one plane for that and it took hundreds to do all the other burning out."

A small bright spot in the POWs lives during the journey of two days and nights to the Niigata War Prisoners Camp 5B, was their transportation. The men rode in the relative luxury of passenger cars, similar to those in the United States, even though they were far from first class and very crowded. Jim found himself riding in a small lavatory containing only a sink. Across the passageway in another small room was the toilet. Oriental style, it was made of ceramic with 8" x 18" slit in the floor and two platforms for the user's feet on either side of the slit. There were two straps hanging overhead, which allowed the user to straddle, squat, and hang on while the train rocked back and forth. In the close quarters of the lavatory were Jim and a fellow POW. All their belongings, including Jim's five gallon water can, guitar, and his strap backpack were in the small washroom with them. By lying on their backs with their feet and legs up the lavatory's side walls, both men found a bit of comfort during the long trip north.

As the journey continued, the three leaders, Jim, McDonald, and Ramsey were informed by the Japanese soldier in charge that "in a short time we were to change trains," Jim recollects. "We had five minutes from the time our train stopped to be aboard the new train. We were to pick up food and water on the run. We were to have the leaders of [each sub group of] ten men appoint one [man] to pick up ten wooden lunch boxes and [another] man to pick up ten rations of water. The other eight men in the group were to carry the belongings of the men getting food and water."

At the train stop, the supplies had been assembled to be handed out to the POWs. Jim recalls, "There was a long line of Japanese women. The first fifteen women each had ten boxes of food. They were little wooden boxes. [Each contained pressed soybean cakes as a meal.] The next fifteen women each had water for ten men. The prisoners went by on the run. Those

to get water, picked up [ten rations of] water — on the run!"
While the thirty runners picked up supplies, the remaining
120 POWs carried their belongings, and those of the supply
runners, up a long staircase and over a walkway high above
several train and rail tracks. They descended down another
staircase to reach their new train. Everyone hurried as quickly
as possible. One hundred twenty men moved almost as one
giant mass. "When we were aboard, the train began to move
and just five minutes had passed. It was a smooth operation."

Finally on 2 July, the long journey from Fengtai via Korea
was over as the POWs' train came into the northwestern city
of Niigata. When the skyline of the city came into view with
the faint light of a midsummer sunset, the POW's could see
none of the devastation witnessed in other cities and towns.
In the future, the POWs would learn that Niigata had been
left relatively unharmed by bombardments because it was one
of four Japanese cities identified to be the target for a new
American weapon. The strategic planners did not want conventional bomb damage to mask the level of destruction the
new device would be capable of inflicting upon the enemy. It
was hoped the damage would be enough to finally end the war
with less bloodshed on all sides than a full-scale invasion.

Upon arrival at the Niigata rail station at 9:00 that evening,
the POWs were herded off the train. Jim was happy to see
that his eighteen inch square by three feet long wooden Red
Cross box loaded with contraband had made the transfer from
the earlier trains; he had not had seen it since leaving Fengtai.
Luck was still with Jim for when his Red Cross box was unloaded from the freight car. "I had one of those boxes and I
filled mine," says Jim. "I had it full of stuff: overcoat, a half
case of Japanese Army soap and what all. So I didn't even
[have to] carry it from the train station siding. Some Japanese
Army [guards] made guys there carry it up." As it happened,
two rather antisocial men who would continually decline to
help others out in the camp were given the job.

Jim followed the rest of the newly arriving POWs as they
headed down the road on the long trek toward the northerly
edge of the city. There at the side of the dusty road was Jim
and the other POWs' new home, such as it was, surrounded
by sweet potato fields with a small foundry across the road. It
didn't look like much. In fact, it looked worse than anywhere
he had already been.

This Niigata Camp 5B, which replaced an older version, was opened in September 1943 and had earned a vile reputation. Although the buildings had been completed only a year earlier, the new Niigata Camp 5B still had a rundown atmosphere due to overcrowding and lack of maintenance. The sides of the camp's prisoner barracks and buildings were supported on the exterior by long six-inch wooden poles propped against the walls. Camp 5B had not been as fortunate as the Woosung or Kiangwan camps in having skilled construction workers as prisoners who could be assigned to repair and maintain the camp facilities.

A wooden fence about six feet tall encircled the entire camp, with two wooden gates facing the road to Niigata city, forming an entrance. There was no need of electric barbed wire atop the fence; escape was futile since there were no friendlies to go to for aid as there had been in China. There was a guard house and barracks to the right of the gate with the Japanese officers barracks on the left. Walking into camp, there were one and two story buildings used for prisoner's barracks on either side. The galley stood at the back on the left just before the north side fence.

POWs, some in advanced stages of starvation, appeared in windows and doorways to inspect the new arrivals. "There were pot-bellied guys there, fellas selling their rice, starving themselves really," Jim remembers. "But they was pot-bellied, skinny as could be, lots of them and I thought, 'Oh what in the world are we getting into here?'"

Jim and the other 149 prisoners walked through the camp's gates and were quickly told to line up. Bungo was to be taken. Jim spied his wood Red Cross box and went over to stand next to it, with others lining up in the same area. As a group leader at this new camp, Jim was required to give all fifty identity numbers of the men in his group in Japanese; English was not acceptable. However, the Japanese guard who was writing down the count wrote the numbers down in English for his report. This was standard harassment for Camp 5B, Jim learned. Although it was frustrating to be toyed with that way, Jim had no problem reciting the individual numbers of the men in his charge; he was able to write the Japanese numbers into the hundreds of thousands. He had learned by walking down the roads around Kiangwan while on work details and seeing the sequential numbers written upon telephone poles. He had also been able to get his hands on a small book that told what the names were for 100, 1,000 and 10,000. "If you could write to ten, then it wasn't too difficult to write to ninety-nine," Jim says. It was a matter of adding up the different sub-numbers; ninety (kyu-ju) was nine (ku or kyu) and ten (ju) added together, plus nine (ku or kyu) more, to create kyu-ju ku, ninety-nine.

The Commandant, First Lieutenant Tetsutaro Kato, removed any doubt as to what behavior he expected from those under his control. Nicknamed "Four Eyes" by the prisoners, referring to his glasses, Tetsutaro Kato was an impressively big man (on average, the Japanese people were very small in relation to Westerners prior to the second half of the twentieth century). Jim and the other POWs stood apprehensively at attention, with all their belongings, while they waited for their processing to begin. Jim had the good fortune to be standing in front of the camp kitchen's door and was spotted by a fellow Kiangwan carpenter who worked inside. Harry E. Brewer had arrived in Camp 5B before Jim, having left Kiangwan much earlier in 1943 or 1944, and now worked as a cook. Brewer recognized Jim and, as Jim remembers, Brewer "told me that my award [the citation for good work] that was given to me by Colonel Otera would not hold up with this man, Lieutenant Kato. I believed him and started to throw my belongings I thought would be contraband in through the kitchen door, onto the floor: half a case of Japanese Army soap, some Red Cross cans of food, and several socks, because I had an exceptionally large number of socks." The *Freedom* magazine was also tossed onto the large pile of contraband.

During inspection of Jim's belongings, the lieutenant merely batted his "good work award" aside without looking at it. Lieutenant Tetsutaro Kato became angry as he went through the drawings of work plans for the Kiangwan camp Carpenter Shop that Jim had carried along with him "in a folder with a shoestring through them to hold them." Innocent enough pictures and information about tables, bakery equipment and so forth had been drawn on the back of official Japanese Army documents in an effort to salvage writing paper. Lieutenant Kato tore through the thick pile of papers, tearing some out and ripping them up, "especially the ones with chops on them," Jim recalls. "Maybe he saw stuff in there he figured I didn't need." Jim could only stand at rigid attention and hope that nothing would be found that might be serious enough to require a beating, or at worse, execution. Fifty years later, Jim would remark that he wished he had been able to read Japanese then, since he might have learned some interesting information from those papers. Although Jim had lost some of the Carpenter Shop drawings, he still had his guitar intact, the half case of soap and other contraband inside on the kitchen floor. Jim was "sure thankful for this man, Brewer." It could be that Jim owes his life to Brewer, for if Lieutenant Tetsutaro Kato had found the Japanese Army soap or other contraband after the Japanese official papers, it is possible Jim would have been beaten to death or formally executed.

After destroying several of the drawings and papers, Lieutenant Kato moved on to other POWs' belongings, which were also closely scrutinized by the inspecting team. Finally, the lieutenant and the Japanese guards were through with their inspection. The POWs were herded to their new barracks. Each section had its own area opening onto the center passageway. All POWs arranged their bed area in the Japanese prescribed manner, with blankets folded and shoes neatly under the foot of the sleeping platform. Unlike the Woosung and Kiangwan camps, there were no overhead shelves for the men's belongings, since there was a second level of sleeping platforms, accessed by wooden ladders at the end and middle of each room. With the second level of sleeping platforms, the barracks were cramped for space. Extra clothes, socks, hats, and possessions were to be neatly folded and arranged at the head area for each man rather than using wall shelves. Space at the foot was still preserved for a sitting space where meals were eaten, even for those on the second level.

Jim was able to choose the space at one end of the sleeping platform, next to the wall, which was similar to where he'd slept in Woosung and Kiangwan. He later discovered his choice was a serious mistake. The benjo was only ten feet away on the other side of the wall. Although great for convenience, the associated odors would become unbearable in the July weather. It was definitely too close for comfort.

New identification numbers had been given to the men upon arriving at 5-B, but were not necessarily worn prominently as at the other camps. Jim was given another cloth badge with 965 printed on it, his fifth identification number since Wake Island. The rest of the men in his group had following sequential numbers, ending at 1014. At Niigata camp, the last number

The list of the fifty POWs in Group Thirteen at Niigata 5B. Jim and Miles Glaze were designated the group leader and assistant group leader since their numbers were circled in red. Many of those in Group Thirteen worked at the Carpenter Shop, Tin Shop or Shoe Shop in the China-based Japanese POW camps. (James A. Allen Collection)

dictated which two days each month a prisoner would have off from work at the Rinko Coal Yard or Marutsu Dock Yard. There were no Sundays off as at Kiangwan. In Jim's case, his days off were the fifth and the fifteenth of each month since his number ended in a five. The twenty-fifth didn't count and there was no negotiating a change of date. On one of these two days, the POW would be allowed to wash his clothing and take care of personal business. On the remaining day, the POW would be required to join a work group to climb up into the sand hills behind the camp and carry pinewood logs down for firewood. Some of these logs were quite large and were carried on the shoulders. Even though the walk back to camp was downhill, it was still grueling work for the devitalized men.

Jim remembers that the guards "were something else" in Niigata compared to those in China. In China, food would be cut off until whatever was missing showed up. Niigata's guards were just plain brutal. The first morning at bungo, one guard, a sergeant named Ito, beat one of the new POWs in front of the others. Jim suspects that this brutality was to show how tough he was to the newly arriving prisoners. Ito, nicknamed Pistol Pete by the POWs, wore a long samurai sword whose scabbard dragged upon the ground when he walked. Jim was later told by other ex-POWs that Ito was hung for war crimes.

Over the next few days, the new arrivals learned more about their current "home." The city of Niigata, population around 150,000, was located in northern Japan almost on the thirty-eighth parallel, across the Sea of Japan from Korea and Siberia. Cold, arctic winds from Asia blew across the Sea of Japan during winter, bringing snow and frigid temperatures — so much snow, in fact, that a previous winter storm had caused a barracks' roof to collapse, killing eight American POWs trapped inside. Jim "was not looking forward to the winter of '45 at all."

By Jim's arrival, the camp had representatives from just about every venue of the Pacific theatre of war. POWs from other camps had been relocated at 5B when their original camps and/or supporting industries were destroyed by Allied bombing or could no longer be used. Some of the survivors of the Philippine Bataan Death March of 1942 were in the second barracks on the right of the gate, while Canadians could be found in the two story barracks next to Jim's.

A form of "entertainment" when not working was a time consuming task of smoking tusami, which was know by several names among the POWs. The POWs could buy tusami at the camp canteen; it was the only thing available to be smoked. Resembling shredded coconut husks, the name is possibly from the following Japanese words: tsumeru, to cram or stuff; tsumekaeru, to refill or repack; and tusame meaning claw or finger/toe nail. The POWs would use their fingers to stuff the tusami into the bowl of a pipe, which in Jim's case happened to be an old opium pipe he bought after arriving at Niigata Camp 5B. Taking the opium pipe, Jim would make a little ball about the size of a pea out of the tusami and some of his spit. Upon lighting the tusami, "You get about two puffs and then you get to do it all over again," recalls Jim. It was a lot of work for very little return.

The POWs had a band at Niigata Camp 5B. Jim remembers Walt Madkins, a U.S. Army POW from the Philippines, played a base viola with the band. "They had enough musical pieces there, they'd play some pretty good music." Apparently the Japanese officers thought so too, for the band would have to go over to the officers' barracks whenever a party was given. "They'd [the Japanese] have lots of saké to drink," Jim recalls, "and these guys in the band, why they would play music; whatever the Japanese wanted. They were all halfway pretty good musicians, I guess." The Japanese officers would "get all saké'd up and one night, I was woke up," by the exceptionally loud band music. "They was playing, I think, the 'Stars and Stripes Forever,'" Jim laughs as he remembers the night, the first he and the other newly arrived POWs had experienced like this at Camp 5B. "Madkins told me the Japs, they were just having a ball over there over that. It was quite a shock to me to hear "Stars and Stripes Forever." I mean they were really beating it out, just as loud . . . I mean to tell you, it was awful [loud]!" Either the Japanese officers were not familiar with the John Philip Sousa tune, or didn't care, for the martial music promoting the flag of the United States was a hit with the Japanese soldiers.

Jim later discovered that these parties with the loud musical interludes happened frequently. The musicians, "Why they fixed the whole camp up real good . . ." with an evening of music. The musicians would start off with tunes for the pleasure of the Japanese officers, but would eventually change to ones that the POWs could rally behind. Meanwhile, the Japanese Officers would be "having a big time. They could dance, they could march, and carry on and have a big time," all the while not realizing the POW musicians were striking a musical morale blow of victory for their side. Wars can be won in small ways as well as large.

While at Camp 5B, Jim came across a poem entitled *The Exile* that he thought was very interesting. He copied it down so that he would have it later.

The Exile
By Burton Braler

I'm sick of the Mongol and Tartar
I'm sick of the Jap and Malay;
and far away spots on the chart are
no place for yours truly to stay.
I've had enough under-sized chicken,
and milk that comes out of a can.
The east is no place to stick in,
for this one particular man.

I'm weary of curry and rice, all
Commingled with highly spiced dope;
I'm weary of bathing in Lysol,
and washing with carbolic soap.
I'm tired of itch, skin diseases,
mosquitoes and vermin and flies;
I'm fed up with tropical breezes,
and sunshine that dazzles my eyes.

Oh, Lord, for a wind with a tingle,
an atmosphere zestful and keen;
Oh, Lord, once again just to mingle with
crowds that are white folk —— and clean.
to eat without fear of infection,
to sleep without using a net,
and throw away all my collection
of iodine, quinine, et cet.

To know all the noise and the clamor,
the hurry and fret of the west;
I'd trade all the Orient glamour,
that damned lying poets suggest.
They sing of the east as enthralling
(and that's why I started to roam;)
but I hear the Occident calling,
Oh, Lord, but I want to go *home*.

After three and one-half years of being a prisoner of war, a
continent and ocean away from home, Jim felt the same longing for home that Burton Braler had written. "I felt that it
kind of summed up my feelings" at the time, Jim has said.

The Japanese program of "Self Supply, Self Support" applied at 5B as in China, with some of the POWs tending neat
rows of sweet potato plants that ringed the camp. "If the war
hadn't gotten over, " Jim says, "we'd have eaten all those vines
and then we'd eat the sweet potatoes." Nothing was wasted
when it came to food, since there was little food available in,
or out, of camp by now. In fact, according to David Bergamini
in his book *Japan's Imperial Conspiracy*, by July/August 1945
the POWs were actually consuming as many or a few more
calories per day as the average Japanese citizen.

One prisoner, John Glenning, was able to come up with a way to supplement his meager food rations. Glenning had worked as a painter on Wake Island, but also was able to repair watches. The infamous Sergeant Ito learned of Glenning's ability to fix broken wristwatches and asked him to repair some. As Jim tells the story, Glenning replied that in order for him "to repair watches, he had to have good eyes. I'm hungry. I need food for my eyes so I can see to repair a watch. So the Jap brought food whenever he had a watch to repair." Glenning did fairly well with supplementing his food since Jim recalls Ito kept coming back with more watches to be repaired.

Food was not the only desired item. Just as some POWs at Kiangwan were willing to drink the tainted alcohol from the fifty-five gallon drums at the Shanghai Race Course, there were those just as willing to drink alcohol taken from compasses and gyros that were stored in a Marutsu Dock warehouse. "They also drank antifreeze for airplanes," recollects Jim. "They were very sick doing this." Unfortunately, the theft put all the POWs in jeopardy. Jim, for one, was just "squeezing out the time" day by day after learning of the alcohol hungry POWs' theft. He was "very much concerned" that the Japanese would find out and there would have been very serious repercussions. It was a very anxiety-ridden time, but luckily, surrender came shortly after the theft.

Niigata Camp was a definite change for Jim and his carpenters since the camp had no carpentry shop. Their special skills would not keep them from hard labor details. Jim and some of the other POWs found themselves down at the Niigata harbor with yea-ho poles and baskets, loading coal onto gondolas (low sided railcars without tops) from the large piles of coal found under the trestles of the coal cars. Dirty, tiring work, the POWs would begin their day at 5:00 AM rising for bungo followed by hot tea. A meager breakfast of barley soup, rice, or possibly a daikon (a large white radish), preceded a two mile hike down the road toward the main city and the waterfront. A normal workday at the Rinko Coal Yard would start around 7:30 with a mid-morning tea break followed by lunch. A tea break in the afternoon preceded the long walk back to camp when the workday was over at 5:00 PM.

There were cherry trees along streets throughout the march to the Rinko Coal Yard, adding a touch of color to Jim's otherwise drab life, which now included a layer of coal dust.

Jim recollects that "They was pretty, nice pretty green." Since their blooms had long past, the July sun made the cherry tree leaves a brilliant green.

Jim and the other POWs in his work group would also unload cement, large compressed disks of soybeans, and two meter wide newsprint rolls from boxcars. The newsprint rolls were difficult to work with until some of the POWs came up with an easier method. "Those fellas got some four by four's" to use as levers. The POWs would tip the large, heavy newsprint rolls over and roll them out of the boxcar into the warehouse. They then turned them with the short wood four by four's on end, slightly lifting and turning the rolls toward the direction they wanted them to go. The POWs came together to lift the long heavy rolls on end for storage. "It was sure hard on the door jambs of the boxcars 'cause when they'd got to the back end [of the boxcar], they'd bounce that thing out of there and got it going and when it hit down there, it just knock the fire out of those door jambs!" Jim laughs heartily. "Course we didn't mind a'tall." Some of the rolls of newsprint would be torn, as they were unloaded, offering the opportunity to obtain some scarce writing material. Thinking about rewriting his log of dates that he had been keeping since Woosung, Jim would rip off a piece of the torn newsprint to write on later. By rewriting the dates of his travel as a POW, Jim made his log a bit neater than the original paper had been. The folding and refolding of the paper made it hard to read.

Working down at the Rinko Coal Yard, Jim noticed one group of POWs just lay around much of the morning while the rest worked. Loading one of the coal gondolas, which held 22 long-tons (2,200 pounds to the ton or 48,400 pounds), was half a day's work for a four man crew. Two men would load the coal into yea-ho pole baskets while the other two men of the crew would haul the baskets of coal on their shoulders to the gondola. The task required seventeen trips by the men carrying the yea-ho poles. Jim, as honcho for his fifty men, found out quickly why the four POWs were at leisure so much. It seems these four hustled as fast as they could to fill their gondola, usually requiring about fifty-five minutes. They figured their work was over until after lunch. At that time, they'd again complete filling their gondola as quickly as possible, relaxing the rest of the day. It was great for the four of them, but not for everyone else, especially Jim. As honcho, he had to try and talk the Japanese out of demanding that everyone fill his gondolas in fifty-five minutes. The four renegades "just made it rough on everybody," Jim remembers bitterly.

While at Camp 5B, Jim was able to replace the violin keys on his well-traveled guitar with the Guamanians' guitar keys he had received in Fusan weeks earlier. Removing the old violin keys, Jim then cut out the Dutchman of bamboo wedges he had put in the hole to hold the smaller violin keys. Jim slipped the real guitar keys in and fastened them in place. With many musicians in the camp, Jim was finally able to get the guitar tuned. "So H. T. Cope and the fellas, they played it around there," Jim recalled. Jim, of course, still couldn't play the instrument that he had now carried over 2,490 miles and would carry for another 8,680, until he reached home.

One day in the first part of August 1945, Jim's group was at the Niigata dockyard, loading coal, or "yea-ho-ing" it, down to a small barge at the waterfront when Jim was presented with a dilemma. Jim was honcho and honchos in the Japanese culture did not do physical labor like carrying baskets of coal on yea-ho poles. Yet, a Japanese civilian guard in charge ordered him to do so with a brisk cry of "shigoto," the Japanese word for work. Nicknamed "Paddlefoot" by the POWs, this guard carried a large club about the size of a sledgehammer handle. Having had the past four years to study and learn about Oriental culture, Jim knew that if he were to follow that order, he would lose face, or be considered shamed by Paddlefoot and the other Japanese nearby. But if Jim did not haul the coal after being ordered to, Paddlefoot would lose face, which would be considered an extreme insult, especially since Jim was a prisoner. Additionally, for Jim to lose face would mean that he would no longer be in a position to bargain with the Japanese about assigned work or barracks difficulties. "You always argued with them and then you never did finish up [the assigned work]; almost, but never quite what they gave you to do." So, Jim replied to the order to work with "shigoto nai, dame dame" (which roughly translated would be, honchos don't work and its useless to tell me to). Now an imaginary line had been drawn in the dirt between the two willful and determined men, both trying to not lose ground to the other. For even though Jim was a prisoner, he had a Japanese cultural tradition behind him to support his position of only supervising. Paddlefoot continued to insist on Jim working, while

Jim stood at rigid attention and looked at him eye-to-eye. Paddlefoot's "Shigoto! (work)" was answered with "Nai, nai (no)." Paddlefoot then began to swing his club as close to Jim's head as he could come, but not hitting him, for that would cause Paddlefoot to lose face in the situation. Jim remained immobile, looking his antagonist in the eye and not giving way either. A stalemate ensued. More than fifty years later, Jim remarked that this was one of the times he was the most scared during his imprisonment, for he could easily have lost his senses or life being hit in the head with that club.

Finally, the Japanese civilian guard gave way and left, leaving Jim to continue to supervise his group. Jim had won the confrontation, but it could have also meant he would lose in the future since Paddlefoot was the one to lose face. Later on that same day, Jim noticed that Paddlefoot was walking under a train trestle, about a hundred yards from Jim's work group. With Oriental culture in mind, as well as his accumulated information on human behavior, Jim walked over to Wake Island time-keeper Hal Fields, whose yea-ho pole and baskets Paddlefoot had wanted Jim to carry that morning, and asked Fields for it. Then Jim deliberately placed the yea-ho pole with its coal filled baskets across his shoulders and carried it over to the gondola. Making sure Paddlefoot could see him, Jim carried two loads before he handed the yea-ho pole back to Fields. Now the battle-field of argumentation was level again. Jim's actions allowed Paddlefoot to regain his lost face, while Jim's face was intact, which enabled him to continue to negotiate work assignments.

Unfortunately, many POWs throughout their imprisonment did not recognize the differences between the Eastern and Western cultures. The attitude tended to be that his own culture's way of behaving was the most appropriate. The idea that there might be other acceptable and proper ways was not considered. Hence, any cultural trait or action, like the section leaders' bowing when reporting after bungo or tenko, the equivalent of a polite handshake in the West, was considered wrong by the Western culture POW. They considered bowing to the Japanese to be demeaning, yet they would shake hands and not think twice about it. Because of this ethnocentric point of view, Americans caused themselves needless trouble, something slow to change even today.

As before, a new camp and barracks necessitated a few changes to make it seem like "home." After a few days, Jim decided to create a new bed for the hot July weather and give the other fellows on the sleeping platform more room. Conveniently, he was already next to the end wall of his section, which suited his plans well. Taking a piece of rope from among his possessions and a few pine tree limbs he had scrounged from around camp, Jim designed a hanging cot. He attached it to the wall by some of the rope and tree branches. Two rope strands were then hung from the ceiling near the end wall for support and provided the additional convenience of allowing the cot to be folded flat, out of the way against the wall when unoccupied. Another pine branch was secured between the ropes, creating a frame around which Jim wove the remaining rope into a tight latticework similar to the old-fashioned rope beds. By day, this ingenious bed would be out of the way, above the first level sleeping platform, but lowered at night it would provide an airy, comfortable bed free of the ever-present sand fleas. Jim worked on ways to elude the Niigata sand fleas by picking, before dark, all the fleas off the outside and inside lining of a pair of Red Cross coveralls with long sleeves he had received back in 1943. Later, before he climbed into his sling/ hanging bed, he'd put the coveralls on and pull a pair of socks up around each pant leg. Jim then put some acquired mosquito netting over his head and put another pair of socks on his hands, pulling them over his sleeve cuffs. This getup also helped keep the mosquitoes at bay. With his nightly ritual of bug proofing, Jim was able to sleep in relative peace for some of the night. "If the B-29s didn't come over . . . you could rest and sleep till three, four o'clock in the morning before them damn fleas or mosquitoes, especially the fleas, got to you!"

By this time, the Americans had begun dropping bombs and mines into Niigata harbor as well as making bombing runs on other cities nearby. "We'd just experienced [on the train trip north] many towns burned up. [At Camp 5B] You'd see the sky light up at night" from all the fires started by the American bombs landing among the many wooden buildings. Yet Niigata city was left relatively unscathed.

As Jim remembers, the B-29s would "fly over at night and they'd be in the searchlights and you'd see the mines that would be dropping out, that [the B-29s] were dropping in the harbor." Some of the American planes were not lucky in dodging the anti-aircraft fire, or flak. "One night," Jim remembers, "we seen [the Japanese] hit one of the B-29s and saw the parachutes come out.

[The Japanese] had searchlights on and we could see the B-29s plainly. That's how we could see the parachutes open" when the crewmen of the hit B-29 abandoned their craft. In a way, it was like "jumping out of the fry pan into the fire" of the waiting Japanese guns. Jim never saw crewmen from the wounded B-29s arrive at Niigata Camp 5B.

When the American B-29s flew raids over Niigata harbor and kept the POWs up, it was groups of Japanese home guard firing anti-aircraft guns at the planes, sometimes downing them. (The lines in the dark sky are page ripples from age and use of the magazine.) (*Freedom* / James A. Allen Collection)

At night when the American B-29s flew overhead, the Japanese guards would come into the barracks yelling for everyone to get up. Jim, for one, would be just as happy to ride out the air raid in his sling bed. But the guards would not allow that, poking the reclining Jim and others who were slow to rise, with their bayonets. "That was the bad part," according to Jim, having to get up.

After all the prisoners were up and out of bed, the Camp 5B guards forced the POWs to file out of the barracks, head out of Camp 5B and into the tall sand hills behind the camp. There the POWs and their guards found holes dug for the men to stay in, away from possible dropping bombs. The B-29 raids cost the POWs a lot of sleep, for by the time they returned to the barracks, it was almost time to get up and start another day of labor. Additionally, more sand fleas had been picked up in the sand hills and they had to be contended with before the POWs could get any more rest that night.

If there were only one B-29 during a night raid, the POWs would be left in the barracks and not disturbed. But when a group of B-29s were spotted, the guards made the POWs head for the hills. Or at least they had to get up and be ready to leave if it were ascertained that the planes would be hitting the Niigata harbor or city. If they were just passing through on their way to some other target, the POWs might be allowed to return to bed without a night hike out to the foxholes in the hills. Jim recalls, "You'd have to get up and get dressed. Hell, they come out there and jab you with the damn bayonet. . . . You had to get up. Then you'd sit on the foot of your bed." If the sky lit up from bombs being dropped on another city, the POWs knew Niigata wasn't that night's target. "Then after a while, they'd come through and tell you, you could go back to bed. The hell! You couldn't go back to sleep, the damn fleas ate you up!" Jim's first six weeks at Camp 5B in Niigata were filled with uncertainty, brutality, disruption, and very little rest.

16

The End Is Near . . . Finally!

Five weeks after Jim and his group of POWs from Fengtai arrived at Niigata Camp 5B, the new secret weapon that the Americans had been working on was prepared for detonation over Japan. Weather conditions were a major consideration since the chase panes carrying scientists and other observers wanted to have a clear sky to observe the new bomb and the destruction it inflicted. Four Japanese cities had been left untouched by conventional bombing: Hiroshima and Niigata, on the island of Honshu, and Kokura and Nagasaki on the island of Kyushu. All four cities had many factories and other industry supporting Japan's war effort.

When those concerned with the new secret weapon checked the weather on Monday, 6 August, Hiroshima was selected from the four objectives as the target with the optimum viewing area. The destructive power of the single bomb overwhelmed the Japanese, but not their resolve to fight on. Three days later, another target city was selected from the remaining three, and on the ninth an American bomber, again loaded with one atomic bomb, headed for the Japanese city of Kokura. Arriving at the chosen drop site, some clouds obscured the viewing area of the scientists in a chase plane and in mid-flight it was decided to proceed on to an alternate city for better conditions. That summer

Thursday, Kokura survived and the city of Nagasaki was destroyed. This became the final blow leading to Emperor Hirohito's agreeing to surrender six days later, rather than destroy the Japanese culture and have the Japanese people fight on to the last man, woman, and child.

Within the week, the Japanese would have their world turned upside down. For Jim and the other POWs at Niigata Camp 5B, the timing of Hirohito's surrender saved their lives. According to David Bergamini in his book, *Japan's Imperial Conspiracy,* two more atomic bombs were being prepared for use in the next couple of weeks. As one of the two original sites left, Niigata undoubtedly would have been one of the targets.

The POWs had no inkling of the devastation wrought by the two atomic bombs; life was still a routine of work and little sleep. However, the Japanese residents of Niigata heard about the demise of the two cities. B-29's dropped information leaflets, printed in Japanese, on selected Japanese cities hoping the masses would uncharacteristically rise up and demand the Emperor accept the surrender terms offered him. One of the later flyers dropped, AB-12, read as follows:

ATTENTION JAPANESE PEOPLE
EVACUATE YOUR CITIES

Because your military leaders have rejected the thirteen part surrender declaration, two momentous events have occurred in the last few days.

The Soviet Union, because of this rejection on the part of the military has notified your Ambassador Sato that it has declared war on your nation. Thus, all powerful countries of the world are now at war against you.

Also because of your leaders' refusal to accept the surrender declaration that would enable Japan to honorably end this useless war, we have employed our atomic bomb.

A single one of our newly developed atomic bombs is actually the equivalent in explosive power to what 2000 of our giant B-29's could have carried on a single mission. Radio Tokyo has told you that with the first use of this weapon of total destruction, Hiroshima was virtually destroyed.

Before we use this bomb again and again to destroy every resource of the military by which they are prolonging this useless war, petition the Emperor now to end the war. Our President has outlined for you the thirteen consequences of an honorable surrender; we urge that you accept these consequences and begin the work of building a new, better, and peace loving Japan.

Act at once or we shall resolutely employ this bomb and all our other superior weapons to promptly and forcefully end the war.

EVACUATE YOUR CITIES

Whether or not the citizens of Niigata received this exact leaflet or received the information through another source, they took the "get out of town" warning seriously. By the afternoon of Monday 13 August, many of the citizens voted with their feet. By the time the POWs got back to camp from their work details late that evening, "The road into the sand hills by our camp was just a steady stream of people walking through," Jim remembers. The procession of people and possessions continued well into the night. "They had oxen pulling two wheeled carts. There was all kinds of different wheeled vehicles they were pulling and they all had packs on their backs. If it could walk, even a two year-old kid, it had a pack on its back. Damnedest sight you ever saw!"

The day after the evening exodus was Jim Allen's twenty-seventh birthday and his fourth as a prisoner of war, but he spent it as he did all other work days, down at the Rinko Coal Yard supervising POWs for whom he was honcho. Early that morning when Jim and the others left the camp for work, they found the normally busy streets of Niigata deserted. An eerie feeling settled over the town as if only ghosts inhabited it. Shutters on windows creaked in the breeze and a few doors stood open as if someone had left hurriedly. The street where a normally bustling bathhouse stood was strangely quiet in the early morning light, with only the POWs' footfalls heard. The only Japanese to be seen were the soldiers guarding the POWs. Returning to camp that evening, only a few Japanese were seen.

Although Jim spent his birthday working, the following day, Wednesday the fifteenth, was a yasumi for him since his identity number ended in a five. It would be his second, and last, day off for the month and possibly Jim's only chance to wash what clothes he had for another twenty-one days. Even though it was called a rest day, there was to be no catching up on sleep and lying about on their sleeping platform. For the POWs on yasumi at Camp 5B, it began as so many days had for the last forty-five months with a tea and rice breakfast followed by bungo. Then all the prisoners not on yasumi began the long walk to the coal yard for another day of heavy labor. It appeared to be a normal day.

It was not quite mid-morning when Jim and those prisoners remaining at camp made an unusual sighting. The boring routine of laundry quickly was forgotten. As Jim recalls, "About 11 o'clock there was a B-29 flying over real high and that was a scary situation. You didn't know what in the world was going on." This was especially true since the POWs had listened and seen the B-29s coming over Niigata at night, dropping mines in the harbor. The thought that it could now be bombs dropping on land, and POW camps, crossed Jim's mind. "We'd seen him drop something out of his belly. We could see [the dropped payload]. It got into the most weird shapes as it was coming to the ground. Oh, we was out there watching it; we didn't know what it was. It was kind of eerie." As the B-29s' payload continued to fall, it "got into different shapes. My God, they got in different, weird shapes." The falling object seemed to be like the plastic goo children play with, capable of acquiring any shape or dimension.

Finally the falling payload came low enough that Jim and the others could tell that the strange falling object was actually thousands of objects — leaflets! The B-29 crew had "done an excellent job of turning the things loose," Jim says, "because there wasn't any that got into the country [side]. There was a road and we was on one side [of it]. Not one [leaflet] came down on our side of the road. They all started on the other side of the road and they went clear across the town, I mean they covered" the city of Niigata with the leaflets. Jim found out later that the message in the leaflets was advising Niigata's residents to evacuate the city, in an attempt to reduce civilian causalities. But few Japanese were left in Niigata by this time to receive the downpour of leaflets.

Unknown to the POWs, Emperor Hirohito had decided to go against the traditions of his culture and surrender to the American forces threatening his country's home islands. This decision came after millions of Japanese soldiers and civilians were dead, major Japanese cities were destroyed, and the two atomic bombs had been dropped by the Americans in an attempt to shorten the war. On the day before, Tuesday, 14 August, Hirohito had made two recordings of his speech to the Japanese people concerning the surrender of their country and the loss of the war. Hirohito's surrender speech would be an unparalleled event in Japan, for it would be broadcast over the radio for all to hear. Millions of Japanese subjects would hear their Emperor's voice for the first time. This was like hearing God speaking to them over the radio since the Emperor was considered divine by the Japanese people.

In recent years, Jim has discovered, by reading David Bergamini's book, that Hirohito, "is damn lucky he was even alive to make the speech and if they hadn't of made two records of it, . . . they found one, the hot-heads did that wanted to [continue the war] but they didn't find the other one." If the warmongers had found it, or the Emperor who was in hiding, Jim claims:

> Who knows what would have happened! Believe me . . . Top Secret, Operation Olympic [code name of the first invasion of Japan's home islands in November of 1945], . . . I know a typhoon went through in October and they were to land on Kyushu in November. It is very likely that typhoon would have destroyed the U.S. ships staged for the November invasion. They wouldn't have been landing in November of 1945, I can tell you that right now.

Jim strongly feels that President Harry S. Truman shortened the war and saved lives by ordering the atomic bombs to be used. "You can thank Truman for dropping the bomb because that convinced the Emperor," to surrender Jim claims.

Jim's appreciation and respect for Truman is not misplaced if one is aware of Operation Downfall (the code name for the invasion of Japan's home islands), the weather of October 1945 on the island of Okinawa where the invasion forces were staged, and the 1944 Japanese order to kill all POWs in the event of an invasion.

The designated date for the beginning of Operation Down-fall was 1 November 1945. The first invasion, code named Operation Olympic, targeted the southern island of Kyushu. An amphibious assault similar to that at Normandy, France, on D-Day, 6 June 1944, it was generally believed it would take three months to securely hold Kyushu and then make the move north to the next home island, Honshu.

The second part of Operation Downfall, named Operation Coronet, was planned to swing into action during March of 1946. This second invasion was to be aimed at the island of Honshu and Tokyo itself to bring about the fall of the Japanese government, Emperor Hirohito, and an end to the war. Casualties during Operation Downfall were expected to be extremely high on both sides, with armed Japanese civilians including children, as well as soldiers, defending their Emperor and homeland to the death as their culture dictated. Until the atomic bomb was available, nothing but a full-scale invasion was felt to be able to bring about an unconditional Japanese surrender.

Using the files of Operation Downfall, now in the National Archives, as reference, James M. Davis wrote a booklet called *Top Secret: The Story of the Invasion of Japan.* Davis claims that Operation Downfall would have cost hundreds of thousands of American military lives as well as hundreds of thousands of Japanese military and civilian lives. Davis maintains that the weather would have played a significant part in the invasion, perhaps destroying the American invasion fleet three weeks before the first invasion was to begin.

On 9 October 1945, Typhoon Louise struck Okinawa with 100 mile-an-hour winds and fifty to sixty foot high seas for twenty hours before heading out to sea. Two days later, the powerful storm returned for a second attack on the island and the American fleet located there. A large number of the ships, planes and supplies stockpiled for the now unnecessary Operation Olympic were destroyed, as was much of the rest of Okinawa. Had the atomic bombs not been dropped on Hiroshima and Nagasaki in August, bringing an end to the war, the American invasion force of a half million men with associated equipment and materials, would have been on Okinawa in harm's way of Typhoon Louise. A "kamikaze" (Japanese for "divine wind") would have once again probably saved Japan from a foreign invasion as it had in 1281 when the Mongols and their fleet were sunk by an unexpected storm.

A copy of the Japanese orders to kill all POWs was found in the journal of the Taiwan Prisoner of War Camp Headquarters in Taihoku, dated 1 August 1944. The order itself was issued 8 January of that same year and stated that "In any case it is the aim not to allow the escape of a single one, to annihilate them all, and not to leave any traces." It can be deduced that if there had been an Allied invasion of the Japanese home islands, prisoners like Jim Allen would not have been kept alive very long. Long after the war, Jim was told by other ex-POWs that there supposedly was a big cave in Niigata prepared for the final solution to the POW/Camp 5B problem. According to Jim's sources, the POWs "would be run inside it, killed, and the entrance covered over." The Japanese would then not have to watch their backs as they defended their city from an American invasion.

As Jim washed his clothes at Camp 5B the morning of 15 August, the POWs working at the coal yard noticed something was up when all the guards disappeared. The POWs were having lunch on tables and benches in a room. While the others continued to talk and eat their stew, one POW stole over to the guardhouse window and peeked in. Inside the guardroom, the Japanese soldiers all stood at rigid attention. On a silken pillow rested a radio from which came a man's voice. The eavesdropping POW understood a little of the Japanese language, but couldn't understand enough to realize what exactly was taking place other than it was very unusual.

After the Emperor concluded his speech, the guards rounded up the POWs. They then all marched back to camp. Work was over for the day. Once back at camp, word of what the eavesdropper had seen spread like wildfire. The Japanese added fuel to the scuttlebutt when most of the guards left the camp; no one was seriously guarding the prisoners anymore. Dinner time came and the POW cooks whipped up a meal. Used to the camp routine, most of the POWs kept to what they knew and deviated little from it that day. The POWs weren't at all sure what to make of the day's events, but hoped that it meant the end of the war.

The morning of 16 August dawned upon Camp 5B the same as it had in the past, but now new guards were in place rather than the ones who had previously worked there. According to Wake Island civilian POW George Rosendick, camp commander

Lieutenant Tetsutaro Kato gave a speech to the POWs stating that Great Powers said Japan had surrendered to them. The confused but happy POWs wanted to know what had happened, but the answers they were given only caused more questions. Told that an atomic bomb had been dropped, the POWs asked what was that? They had never heard of anything like that from scuttlebutt, but they were glad it had brought an end to the war. However, now the big question was when would they get home, not if.

Though some POWs took advantage of the guards' absence or inattention and left camp, Jim and most of the others remained in camp 16 August. Not exactly sure of what to do next, they waited to see what happened or who showed up, the Japanese or the U.S. Army. It wasn't until the second evening after the Emperor's speech on 17 August, that Jim and five others decided to see what was happening in town. Since Camp 5B's gates were never closed, now the POWs just walked out of camp and went south down the road toward Niigata proper. "We still didn't know if the war was *really* over or not," recalls Jim. Without any hard evidence of the war's end, the survivor in Jim was still wary of the Japanese announcement.

Coming to a barbershop, the POWs went inside and spoke with the Japanese men there. In the crowded shop, some of the Japanese spoke a little pidgin English. "They were all acting nice, just like the Emperor said," recalls Jim. Toward the end of his radio broadcast, Hirohito had instructed his subjects to:

> Beware most strictly of any outbursts of emotion that may engender needless complication, of any fraternal contention and strife that may create confusion, lead you astray and cause you to lose the confidence of the world. Let the entire nation continue as one family from generation to generation, ever firm in its faith of the imperishableness of its divine land, and mindful of its heavy burden of responsibilities, and the long road before it. Unite your total strength to be devoted to the construction for the future. Cultivate the ways of rectitude, nobility of spirit, and work with resolution so that you may enhance the innate glory of the Imperial State and keep pace with the progress of the world.

There was to be no retaliation or situations in which there would be a loss of face to Japan as a country as well as to the individual. Emperor Hirohito wanted to have his people look to the future now that the war was over, begin rebuilding their country, and ensure that their culture would continue by working with the occupation forces, not against them.

As the half dozen POWs continued into town, they came upon a dimly lit intersection. One small bulb of no more than one hundred watts hung over the center of the street. The lack of adequate lighting was a shock to Jim. "That's all the damn lights there was excepting maybe a few buildings, but it was dark!"

By this time, Jim had become thirsty and decided he wanted a drink of water. The group was in front of a hotel and Jim walked up the front steps and went inside. His ringing a little round silver bell on the registration counter received a quick response. From behind a curtain, a young Japanese woman shuffled out in the short steps required of those wearing a kimono. Jim bowed and the woman returned his bow. Jim then asked for "mizu," water. The woman went behind the curtain and returned with a glass of water. Jim drank it thirstily and set the empty glass on the registration counter. Jim recalls "I 'ari-gato-ed' [thanked] her, bowed and left." When questioned about not worrying that the water was not boiled or clean, Jim replied, "I trusted her."

After wandering around for a while, Jim and the group got tired and returned to 5B. The leisurely exploration walk in the darkened city had an eerie feel to it, but the POWs discovered they were in no danger of retribution from the Japanese citizens left in Niigata. They had walked around without any protection. The Japanese people were following Hirohito's instructions and doing whatever the Americans asked of them. According to Jim, it was unbelievable since just two days prior everyone had been bitter enemies.

An airdrop of food, such as C-rations and K-rations, began not long after 15 August and was appreciated as "manna from Heaven" by the starving POWs. With the airdrops, the POWs were eating much better than they had previously at Niigata or in the prior camps. The dropped K-rations, each the size of a present day cardboard margarine box, contained dry foods like cheese and crackers, along with toilet paper, chewing gum, and two American cigarettes. The C-rations contained the moist food, like SPAM, sealed in a small tin. Invented as a cheap meat in 1937, the *spiced ham* in a rectangular can was

something familiar to most POWs, especially since it was being used widely by the military during World War II. It was a
taste of home to some of the prisoners.

Many of the military prisoners weren't necessary excited
by the prospect of eating the same food they had had in the
Army before they were captured. "Of course to me," says Jim,
"they was both delicious. I thought they were great. And one
night we ate C-rations and K-rations, I did, and we had a bunch
of saké. We'd drink that cold saké and that's the bad thing
about cold saké . . . you could drink it and drink it and eat that
stuff and eat it and all of a sudden, the saké catches up!" Saké,
Japanese rice wine, should be warm when ingested and only
sipped sparingly. The wine and military rations on top of their
previously poor diet, was too much for the celebrating POWs
and they paid the price of extreme hangovers and complaining bellies for their over indulgence.

After the first drop of the large parachute-attached pallets,
the POWs realized they needed to identify the camp and desig-
nate a drop point in order to prevent destruction to themselves
and their buildings. Some of the POWs painted the letters PW
as large as possible across the roof of one barracks and 5B on
the roof of another. Way out past the sweet potato fields, the
POWs took white painted rocks and made a sign that read "Drop
Here," which could be read by the American B-29 pilots and
bombardiers dropping the food pallets. If the food was dropping outside of camp, then the buildings that the POWs still
lived in wouldn't be damaged or destroyed. Unfortunately, the
barracks Jim lived in did have its roof hit by a heavy pallet
falling through the second level sleeping platforms, and onto
the first level sleeping platforms. Luckily no one was injured. A
local Japanese woman, though, had not been as lucky when an
airborne pallet landed on her outhouse, crushing her inside.
Jim remembers one pallet of Campbell's split pea soup cans
ruptured on the impact of another pallet, making an "awful
mess." Airdrop pallets were going through downtown Niigata
hotels and other buildings' roofs. "It was a hell of a mess!"

After the B-29's started dropping the pallets of food, they
eventually began dropping clothing also. "Boxes of stuff," Jim
recalls. Some of the now well fed POWs at Camp 5B would "go
down and stay in the hotels and what-have-you." This included
the red-light district with its prostitutes. Some of the POWs
would remain out of the camp until their supply of food and

Niigata 5B, Japan. U.S. aircraft took this photo around the end of August 1945. Notice the main gate, which faced west, is wide open and the POWs (small dots) are milling inside and out of camp at will. Jim's barracks was the one with PW 5B written on it; he was to the left of the P at the end of the building's first floor. The dark roofed structure immediately to the left is the benjo. The kitchen/ galley is just above Jim's barracks. The Japanese soldiers' guardhouse is the first building to the right of the open gates. At the top of the photo a large, white DROP HERE (arrow) was placed to help pilots avoid the camp with their airdropped pallets of food and clothing. Just below are the foxholes for the POWs and their guards to crawl into during the Allied B-29 raids. (National Archives 380376)

clothing, which was used as currency, ran out and would then return to Camp 5B just long enough to stock up again. "A lot of guys had a ball. . . . hell, the only time you'd see them is when they run out of comshaw to give to the Japanese and the whores and what-have-you."

The airdrop food and clothing was very appreciated by the starving Japanese locals. "There's some of them [POWs] would

Jim Allen standing outside his barracks at Niigata 5B Camp days after the surrender. The poles leaning against the walls are actually supports to keep them from falling over. When civilian POW Victor Lane took this photo, the camp had become a mess from the debris of the airdrops and rubbish the POWs threw around as well as wood torn from the camp buildings. (Victor Lane/James A. Allen Collection)

go out and stop a street car and just ride wherever they wanted to go. Walk out in front of the damn streetcar, [the driver would] stop and they'd get on. [The POWs] always paid them though; candy bars or some damn thing. Or they'd stop an army, Japanese Army truck and then [the POWs] of course, gave them lots of food and clothes," as well as the especially desired parachute cloth from the B-29 windfall. Jim recalls some of the POWs remarking that the Japanese soldiers had taken them ten miles from Niigata, out through the northern Honshu countryside. "Hell, you'd never think they was ever mad at one and other. It's funny, really."

The Japanese soldiers were more than happy to drive the POWs wherever they wanted, not just because Emperor Hirohito had said to be courteous, and as Jim recalls "whatever is necessary to make them [the Americans] happy." The now starving Japanese soldiers and people needed the food and clothing gifts to help them survive. Before the surrender, the POWs were receiving more calories per day on average than some of the ordinary Japanese citizens. Now with the B-29s' bonus, some of the Niigata area's citizenry were eating much better.

Around 21 August, the prisoners of war were officially declared free. Of course, that did little to change the POWs' situation of the moment. Although he could walk out of camp and go wherever he wanted, was not assigned work details for the Japanese, and execution was no longer constantly hanging over his head, Jim still felt like a prisoner since he was not out of Niigata and back home in the States.

During the POWs' limbo period, the U.S. Military officials had been sending planes out over the Japanese countryside to locate and identify prisoner of war camps in order to facilitate the repatriation of the men. Ten days after the surrender on 25 August, the first American planes, other than B-29s, flew over Camp 5B and landed at the Niigata airport. The pilots were brought by Japanese Army truck to Camp 5B where they visited with the POWs. Jim was able to

Four of the civilian POWs waiting to be repatriated at Niigata 5B. Left to right, John Pace, a painter on Wake Island and watch repairer John Glenning, who was in Jim's group of fifty. Unfortunately, Jim cannot recollect the other two civilians' names. The man on the far right is wearing a pair of "pissquicks." By this time most of the POWs wore GI clothing from the airdrops. (Victor Lane/James A. Allen Collection)

collect some of their names as more of his souvenirs. The flyers were: John L. Roch of Sullivan, Missouri; Bill Elder of Toledo, Illinois; E. Iglesias of Washington, D.C.; and R. L. Podsednia from Bynum, Texas; along with two pilots from New York, Bill Leacock of Worcester and Don Wagner of Rochester.

Another group of fliers led by the former governor of Minnesota, Commander Harold E. Stassen, were among those who flew their small, battle scarred planes into Niigata airport and visited with the now, at least officially, ex-POWs. Jim, again, got their names and home towns for a keepsake, writing them down in a small notebook he had used as honcho. Along with Stassen were the following Naval Reserve Ensigns: M. S. Harden, 1519 South Paderewski Street, Detroit, Michigan; George Terrien, 33 Bowers Street, Nashua, New Hampshire; L. A. Nordgren, 1027 North 5th Street, Mankato, Minnesota; C. T. Neal of Kenshaw, South

Five of the U. S. Navy airmen who flew into Niigata's airport with Commander Stassen pose for Lane's camera. The truck behind them was apparently their transportation to Camp 5B from the city's airport. (Victor Lane/James A. Allen Collection)

Carolina; W. K. Anderson of 522 W. Lee Street, Wilson, North Carolina; W. L. Sutherland, 920 Carlisle Street, Martins Ferry, Ohio. The POWs enjoyed finally getting to speak with Americans who had not been interned. The visitors were able to fill in the details of the strange days since Emperor Hirohito's speech and the weeks before that.

Two days later on 27 August, planes from Torpedo Squadron 31 flew by, waving and dropping cigarettes and comfort articles to the POWs at 5B. The American-made cigarettes were greatly appreciated by the tusami smokers. Although it was great to see American planes and pilots in the airspace over their camp, POWs like Jim would have rather been able to leave with them than remain in the rundown prison camp. Unfortunately for the prisoners, it would take time to complete the military and diplomatic arrangements needed for their repatriation following even an unconditional surrender. United States Occupation Forces would not arrive on the island of Honshu until 28 August.

One of those POWs who was "having a ball" now that the hostilities were over, was the now twenty-one year-old H. T. Cope. H. T. was not one to stay around the bedraggled prison camp if he didn't have to and so he headed for the Niigata docks with a load of comshaw: food, clothing, and whatever else had fallen from the sky. H. T., "made friends with the [Japanese] captain of a transport/freighter down by the coal yard where we worked," Jim recalls. The Japanese maritime captain and H. T. would sit in the captain's cabin on board his ship and "just drink all the saké and . . . drank everything the captain had on his ship. [The captain would then] lowered a boat over [the side] and sent a crew member to row around the harbor trying to find more saké." As he related the story of his fellow POW, Jim became more and more animated. It is obviously a memory that he enjoys recalling.

"So one afternoon," Jim recalls, "here come H. T. and this little boy who happened to be the damn captain's purser. He was only eleven years old. H. T. and this kid, and the captain with them, they were just

Victor Lane stopped taking photographs long enough to have his own taken by the torn up barracks of Niigata 5B. Lane was one of the fifty men Jim Allen was group leader for at Niigata. (Victor Lane/ James A. Allen Collection)

carrying all kinds of bottles of saké." H. T. led the captain and the young purser into the barracks and up the ladder to his sleeping platform area on the second level. H. T. invited Jim and the other POWs he saw in the barracks to come on up and meet his new friends. "We went up there, course, we had C-rations, K-rations, and all kinds of damn food" to give away or barter with. "So we drank saké and ate that damn stuff. We talked to the Jap captain. I think he had eleven ships torpedoed out from under him. But, he was just up there friendlier as hell," laughs Jim. After the POWs and their guests had drunk the entire supply of the captain's saké and ate what food they had available around the barracks, the captain and the young purser prepared to return to their ship down at the harbor. The captain "got an armload of that damn stuff," Jim remembers, food and other supplies given to him by his new American "friends" and then returned to his ship. The POWs in Niigata were conducting their own post-war diplomacy with great success.

The camp became chaotic during the POWs' weeks of limbo before liberation. "The guys, they was tearing boards off of the shack. They'd go out and get them some ducks or chickens

or what-have-you and . . . . build bonfires or campfires, cooking vegetables and stuff." Jim laughs as he recalls the chaos.
"It was a hell of a mess!" One of the POWs, Victor Lane, managed to get a camera and film with which he took pictures of
other prisoners and the camp. Jim is in one where he is standing next to a barracks building that looks as if a tornado had
recently traveled through the area.

Jim enjoyed his new found freedom by just walking around
outside the camp. On 29 August, fourteen days after the surrender speech, Jim climbed to the top of one of the sand hills
that overlooked Camp 5B. The quiet summer day was peaceful
and Jim was enjoying sunning himself when he heard an approaching airplane. Turning toward the sound, Jim watched
the single-engine torpedo bomber from the USS *Lexington* (affectionately called the Lady Lex) coming closer to him. The plane
came "real low, had his flaps down and his motor just roaring,"
declares Jim. When the POW and naval aviator were practically eye to eye, the pilot, Joseph Tettelback of Cleveland, Ohio,
"threw out a newspaper and a carton of cigarettes. I got it and
I wrote him a letter" of thanks. Tettelback had written his address and name on the newspaper, which was a May 29, 1945,
edition of the *Cleveland Press*. Other American pilots flew over
the camp also, dropping duffel bags loaded with supplies, "right
on the damn doorsteps of the barracks. They'd let loose and
[the duffel bags] would go right into the barracks."

The B-29 drops weren't always quite so accurate, but for a
couple of POWs, the timing of one inaccurate drop was provi-
dential. These two POWs were part of the four who had hauled
coal at the Rinko Coal Yard too quickly, causing problems for
the other POWs. Jim recalls, "The lazy bastards" had refused
to go out into the sweet potato fields and bring in some of the
clothes, food, or other items that were on the parachuted pallets from the B-29's, as the rest of Jim's group of fifty men
were doing. These two just sat in their barracks and let everyone else work, yet they would still get their share of whatever
was available. "This one damn morning," Jim relates, still irritated by the men's actions, "they decided they'd go and take
some of this stuff and walk out into the countryside and look
the countryside over. While they were gone, a B-29 come along
and dropped a pallet full of Campbell's pea soup right through
the roof of [their barracks'] right through the second floor,
right to where those bastards sat for days, one or both of them."

The hours and days passed slowly at times for Jim and the other POWs as they waited in limbo for the U.S. Army to arrive or the Japanese to take them to the Americans. One slow day during their three-week wait, Jim and Kiangwan bridge playing buddy Miles Glaze observed a Japanese soldier loading a truck in front of their barracks with boxes of Japanese hardtack from the kitchen warehouse behind it. For lack of anything else to do at the moment, Jim and Glaze decided to time the loader as he went back and forth between his truck and the

Miles Glaze of Los Angeles, California. (PIEF)

warehouse. Jim recalls "We timed him in our mind; how long he'd go and wouldn't see us. He'd carry [a box of hardtack] on one side going out to his truck" and then he'd return to the warehouse for another box. Jim and Glaze watched, all the while timing how long a complete trip took, especially the amount of time the worker was out of sight.

Old habits die hard and after forty-five months of scavenging to survive, Jim and his old bridge pal couldn't resist taking one of the boxes of hardtack. With careful timing, Jim and Glaze ran over to the truck, entered, and grabbed a box. Putting it between them on their shoulders, they walked quickly over to a nearby open hole dug as an air raid shelter for the POWs. According to Jim, "We dropped [the box] off in the hole and then just walked along the side of the building."

Waiting until the worker had finally filled his truck and driven away, apparently not missing the stolen box of hardtack, Jim and Glaze retrieved the hardtack from the hole and brought it into their barracks. "It was a little bitty box [but] it was awfully good hardtack. Much better than anything the Americans had." Jim and Glaze were joined by Don Ludington and opened the box, which contained many smaller packages. "We [each] took several bags apiece," Jim recalls. "Then the rest of it we just threw like we was feeding chickens to the rest of the prisoners who was out in the hallway. Got rid of it all."

Unfortunately, the hardtack theft led to a confrontation with the senior military officer at Camp 5B, a U.S. Army Major who had been stationed in the Philippines before capture. The major had heard about the hardtack theft and informed the barracks adjutant, an Australian, to turn in the hardtack thieves. The adjutant passed on the request to Joe McDonald, who was the barracks honcho.

McDonald explained the situation to all the barracks' POWs. They then took a vote whether or not to turn in the larcenists. All 150 barracks residents were present, but two of the POWs didn't vote. They were the same two who refused to help bring in materials from the airdrops and made work at the coal yard tougher for the others. "One hundred forty-eight of them says to tell the damn major he could have the whole bunch in his damn jail!" recalls Jim heartily chuckling at the memory of the overwhelming vote of solidarity from his peers. "That was the end of him [the major]." Jim had felt that the major wanted to turn in the thieves in anger since he had not gotten a share of the hardtack. Jim's impression of that particular ranking senior officer during the short time he had been at Camp 5B was the major was out for himself and a few other officers.

One late August afternoon with nothing urgent to do, Jim walked out to the sand hills behind camp and began to climb up one. After a while, Jim heard a B-29 in the area. Then something in the air caught his eye. It was just a second before recognition came into his conscious mind. Falling directly above him were two metal fifty-five gallon drums welded together and hanging below a parachute. But unfortunately, the parachute "looked like it was going to hit me just as sure as the world and I started running. The more I run, the closer," the parachute with its attached drums looked. Exhausted, Jim finally gave up trying to outrun the rapidly approaching parachute and it's cargo. "When it got pretty close to me, I just stopped, which was good I did because if I'd kept a running, [the parachute and two fifty-five gallon drums and Jim] was right on target, boy! I'd of had an armload of that damn thing. But for some reason or other, I just decided that I couldn't outrun this thing, so I just stopped." The two heavy metal drums full of supplies for the POWs hit the ground hard, throwing sand in the air while the parachute followed in its own leisurely way now that it's load was gone.

More supplies continued to fall from the heavens and Jim, as honcho of his fifty-man group in the barracks, had to keep track of what each man received. The Japanese had given Jim a list with the fifty men's names on a sheet entitled Clothing Distribution List and dated 30 August 1945. Jim has kept this list all these years and upon examination, it shows that Jim didn't get many of the clothes from the drop. Nothing fit him; it was all too small. However, he was able to get two pair of trousers to replace his old "patch upon patch" ones. The new trousers lacked hip pockets and were designed for the Marines, Jim has concluded, since that was the uniform style they were wearing in 1945. Jim had gained enough weight while eating the C- and K-rations to be able to fit into the twenty-nine inch waists.

One day as Jim was walking through the surrounding sweet potato fields looking for small airdrop items that might still be out there, he met a Korean man who was also looking for anything of value. The Koreans were treated poorly in Japan and suffered similarly to the POWs. There were usually plenty of items left behind after the POWs had carted off to camp what they could see. They "never got all the stuff" from an airdrop, according to Jim.

While passing time waiting for the American Army to arrive, Jim had made himself a 1940s style swimsuit resembling a pair of underwear, out of some white cloth he had obtained. Since he had them under his old patched pants, Jim asked the needy-looking Korean if he would like the worn out trousers. The reply was "yes" and Jim just "walked out of them and handed them over to the man," since he had his swimsuit on underneath. The Korean had to be desperate for anything, Jim feels, to have wanted that old worn out pair of patched pants. "You ought to have seen the pants [thoughtful pause] patched, my God, I patched them things! I regretted very much I didn't bring those home 'cause there's NO WAY I could tell anybody how they looked! More patch than original [material], patch on patch."

Some of the Japanese soldiers were still around Camp 5B, but no longer guarding the POWs. Their job now was more of overseer. One day, the Japanese gathered all the POWs who were in camp and would cooperate and took a group picture outside of the Canadians barracks, in the main roadway, at the center of the camp. A little over a hundred of the approximate 945 POWs then in limbo at Niigata posed for the snapshot. The small black and white picture was available to any of the men, for a price. Jim bought one and later had an enlargement made of it.

By the time the picture was taken, many of the POWs were out of the camp roaming the countryside and Niigata with their airdrop "goodies." The photograph shows an assortment

Japanese Prisoner of War Camp Niigata 5B on or about 29 August 1945. The sand hills where pine firewood was collected can be seen in the background behind the prison camp fence with its newly cut door. Part of the large painted 5B on the roof of the middle two-story/tiered barracks can also be seen in the background. Jim Allen is slightly to the right of the center in the middle row of standing men. (James A. Allen Collection)

of men, mostly in working uniforms and hats of various military backgrounds. One man stands out wearing a white shirt and tie. Some are wearing undershirts, one man plainly seen is barechested, and a couple of the POWs seem to be smiling as they squint against the sunshine, but most all wear an expression of non-emotion. Their captors are still in control, this time with a camera. The reality of their situation is that they are still prisoners in a POW camp whose gates are opened, but the men haven't made it home yet.

In addition to the men in the picture, this souvenir of Jim's allows the viewer to catch a glimpse of the sand hills that were behind Camp 5B. On the roof of the center building, Jim's barracks, part of the giant white 5B that was painted on the roof can be seen. Even thought the photograph is in black and white, which adds to the dreariness of the scene, the spartan surroundings are clear: dirt or mud to walk in, spare, plain buildings, the eight-foot high wooden fence in the background.

As the time lengthened for the POWs to be liberated, some became quite bold. "An awful lot of guys got their [identification] pictures the Japanese took at the end of the war. Went into the [camp] office and took them! Kenny Newton for one and Rod McMahn." McMahn was in the Woosung and Kiangwan POW camps, but had been moved with other prisoners to the city of Kawasaki near Tokyo to work in a steel mill. He remained there until the mill was destroyed during an American bombing raid. McMahn was then moved to Niigata. Several of the POWs that were moved out of Kiangwan before its closure had eventually been transferred north to Niigata where Jim became reacquainted with them.

As the waiting continued, Jim began to give some thought to the journey home. Since he had been such a packrat with all his souvenirs, Jim realized he needed to have some sort of additional luggage than his backpack and Red Cross box and began to make travel bags to carry his belongings in. Raw materials were readily available thanks to the straps, fabric, and line from the airdrop pallets. Each pallet had a parachute attached with long, strong shroud lines, and strong webbed cloth straps securing everything to the pallet. Attached to each parachute was a pilot chute made of a strong green canvas that when opened pulled the heavy main cargo parachute from its backpack. Jim fashioned the first two "airline carry-on bags," as he calls them, from this material and its shroud lines. Hand sewn, the sides of the two sturdy bags were made from the pilot chute material. Pieces of the thick straps that held the cargo in place were hand sewn onto the cargo chute material for handles. In order to fasten one of his "carry-ons," Jim sewed on a zipper from a winter coat. "I was pretty proud of it. Right nice, sharp looking deal when it was brand new." He used shroud lines to lace up the sides of the other bag in order to close it. The second "one I didn't get fancy with; I just laced it up here." The small but strong canvas bags were ahead of their time, faintly resembling carry-on luggage used by the travelers of the 1990s. "I did this for food. I had one of these full of food just to go overnight to Tokyo." That's the way Jim had learned to survive while a POW: plan ahead and if food was available, take it with you. Jim was taking no chances in case the overnight journey became a much longer one.

Jim sorted through his belongings and packed them into his other carry-on bag and a canvas bag that once held a cargo para-

Jim Allen in May 1999, displaying his two "carry-on" bags he made at Niigata 5B POW Camp from the parachute material left from supplies being airdropped into Niigata 5B in the last half of August 1945. (L. A. Magnino)

chute for the airdrop pallets. This bag was to be tied onto his primitive strap backpack. Jim packed his two blue Red Cross wool blankets and overcoat, clothing, more food, and some of his souvenirs. As with the earlier trip to Japan, he prepared boiled water. The remaining scraps of paper with drawings of work orders for the Carpenter Shop were put into their shoestring tied paper covering and then placed into one of his bags. Jim neatly packed away his "rice shovel" metal spoon along with the opium pipe used to smoke tusami, Red Cross box Gillette razor blade packages, a Chinese razor, and many other mementos. The guitar was to be carried along on his back with the strap backpack, as they had previously traveled all the way from Kiangwan. When the day of departure from Camp 5B came, Jim would be loaded down, but prepared for anything.

After more than three-and-a-half years of prisoner of war life, Jim still had the black and blue plaid cloth tobacco pouch that held the thirty-five cents worth of airmail stamps, the wooden Dixie Cup spoon, Carpenters' Union card, Navy physical paper, and the pictures from the SS *Matsonia*. Throughout his wartime journey, Jim had "carried them all the way," never leaving his precious mementoes of freedom.

On the morning of 2 September while Jim worked on preparations to leave Niigata and Japan, another important event took place. On board the United States Ship *Missouri* at anchorage in Tokyo Bay, Allied and Japanese representatives met and formally signed at 0941, the treaty of peace between the warring countries. Now with the formalities taken care of, the POWs held in Japan could be returned to their homes and waiting loved ones. That was now only three days away for those at 5B.

There were to be two groups of POWs for the final departure from Niigata Camp 5B, one leaving 4 September, while the other group would leave 5 September. As a group leader of fifty POWs, Jim was to select men from his group for each day. Always trying to be fair, Jim drew numbers from an old hat. In recalling that lottery, Jim says, "I drew the first number out and drew [#995] Kenny Johnson." Johnson had been with Jim the entire war. They had worked together those long years of internment in the POW camps' carpenter shops and in his retelling of the lottery, Jim's voice gave away his pleasure at having selected someone that he liked and knew for so long.

Finally, 5 September arrived and it was time for Jim to leave Niigata. It had been a long day as POWs had been loaded up into buses and driven off, with Jim, as a honcho, helping to ensure all were aboard and accounted for. Now at 9:00 PM, late summer darkness had descended on Camp 5B. One last bus stood with its Japanese driver patiently waiting. Jim and another POW, a "Music" or Marine Corps musician whose name Jim cannot recall, went through each of 5B's barracks, "hollering if there's anyone left. In the last barracks where the Bataan Death March boys from the Philippines were, we found one [POW] back in there with some blankets and what-have-you. How we ever seen him, I'll never know. But somehow we managed to get him out" from under the blankets and jumbled mess inside the building and out of the barracks. With the "Music" and Jim working together on the drunk, passed out POW, they were able to finally "pour him in the bus."

Now, all were present and accounted for and it was time to leave the last of the POW camps Jim had spent half of his adult life in. Under the still darkness of the Niigata night sky, the "Music" commenced to play "Taps." A slight wind blew, causing the doors of the now abandoned Camp 5B's buildings to creak as they moved slowly as if pushed by invisible hands. "It was real quiet," Jim remembers, the sound of the bugle playing taps reverberated from the buildings in a hauntingly sad way. "Of course, every time I go to an interment [burial] at the National Cemetery in Riverside, California, they always play taps there and on Memorial Day . . . and it always brings back my last moments as a prisoner of the Japanese. Three years nine months and a few days." Twenty-five days to be exact.

After Jim and the "Music" climbed aboard the bus, the Japanese driver pulled out of Camp 5B and headed for the railway siding in Niigata proper. With the last three passengers, Jim, the "Music," and the passed out Bataan Death March survivor, the prisoner of war repatriation train was ready to start the overnight journey to Tokyo.

17

Homeward Bound —
Look Out Uncle Sam!

At the Niigata train siding, Jim happily discovered that the transportation would be much nicer than his previous trips planned by the Japanese. This time the POWs rode in the luxury of real passenger cars, not cattle cars or converted boxcars. Although Japanese Army soldiers accompanied them, they basically left the POWs alone during the overnight journey.

The main recreation on the train that night was drinking saké. By morning, the train cars were full of drunks. "Oh boy, there was a lot of saké on that train that night," Jim recalls. "And we was mean, really. Next morning, we'd go by a train depot and a Japanese civilian would be standing out there on a concrete platform. . . We used to throw them empty saké bottles out [the train windows] so they just hit [the civilians] on their feet and watch that glass go through them. We was having a ball," Jim chuckles as he remembers.

Without restraints by the Japanese guards, and their inhibitions loosened by the saké, the POWs let fly their pent-up hostility toward their captors. But Jim admits now that it wasn't necessarily the appropriate thing to have done. "Yeah, yeah, looking back in time, we shouldn't have done it," but on that September morning in 1945 after being a prisoner of the

Liberated POWs arriving at the Tokyo train depot. American bombs made the holes in the train platform's canopy, according to Jim. (Victor Lane/James A. Allen Collection)

Newly liberated POWs milling around the Tokyo train station to board a train to Yokohama. At the time, Jim remembers, they didn't know where they were headed, similar to when they traveled during their imprisonment. (Victor Lane/James A. Allen Collection)

Japanese for over three years, throwing empty saké bottles at those on the train station platforms was a "swell" activity.

At 9:00 AM, Jim and his train mates arrived in Tokyo feeling the effects of the previous night's saké, but filled with anticipation and excitement at the prospect of seeing Americans who had not been prisoners of war. At the Tokyo train station, Jim and the other POWs were met by United States Army representatives and officially left the supervision of the Japanese.

Before leaving his liberated charges behind, one of the Japanese guards from Niigata, the vile Sergeant Ito, came around shaking the now ex-POWs hands, Jim heard later. Leo R. Gilmore, a rough Wake Island CPNAB civilian, "didn't care to have his hand shook and hauled off and hit Ito in the face. Sergeant Ito's teeth were on the ground or concrete, he loosened a bunch of them." Jim says he would have loved to have seen Gilmore knock Ito for a loop. No one did anything about the assault. According to Jim, there was a "short period of time where you could do anything you were big enough to do," including paying back in kind.

Now in United States Army hands, Jim saw his first American woman in almost four years, a WAC standing at rigid attention along the siding. He tried to engage her in conversation by saying "Good morning," but was completely ignored. "I spoke to her, but hell, she just looked straight ahead." The woman had either been ordered not to speak with the arriving men or possibly had been propositioned so much that she chose not to respond to any of them. Jim, for one, was very disappointed

Quickly Jim and the others were moved along down different train platforms to another train,

The remains of a building is seen from the window of Jim's train as it approached Yokohama from Tokyo. There was not much left standing after the Allied air bombing earlier in the war. (Victor Lane/James A. Allen Collection)

which stood waiting to take them to the nearby city of Yokohama and processing for repatriation. Between the train stations of Tokyo and Yokohama little remained standing; Uncle Sam's flying forces had done their work well. Upon arrival in the burned out industrial city of Yokohama, Jim and the others were transported to the Yokohama docks on Tokyo Bay, where the United States Army was processing the POWs for travel back to the States. Instructed to toss all he had, Jim followed those instructions to his everlasting regret because he lost many of the souvenirs that he had held onto for so long. Among them were his two Red Cross blue wool blankets, clothes, and "a silk deal that hung on a wall. It was white silk with a tree branch with a bird on it like the Japanese hang on the wall, four to five feet long and sixteen inches wide. It had a white yoke on top to hang on the wall. Threw it away at Yokohama [as well as] all the food, or a lot of it." Jim left a parachute bag upon the mountain of items being thrown away by the newly liberated prisoners of war. Most of them did not

Another view from the train traveling between Tokyo and Yokohama, showing the devastation that conventional bombing had upon the two Japanese cities and surrounding area. Not many buildings were intact or left standing, according to Jim, and many cities they traveled through looked like the photograph above. (Victor Lane/James A. Allen Collection)

want souvenirs of the war. Jim was different about his memories and experiences. His souvenirs were physical evidence of what he had endured, learned, and grown from, although at the time, he probably did not realize it.

Sadly, one item lost was the hometown address of baby Nishegawa Roosevelt-san, the tiny son of the interpreter Nishegawa of Kiangwan Camp and the surrogate for the nephew Jim had yet to see. The sentimental piece of paper was in the pocket of one article of clothing Jim added to the castaway mountain along the docks. Now Jim would not be able to find out what happened to the child during the post-war occupation period. In spite of the fact that he was able to hang onto most of his "souvenirs" while passing through the gauntlets of the United States and the Japanese militaries, Jim is still bitter as he remembers "at Tokyo Bay or Yokohama, when the good old United States Army told us to throw everything away; they'd give us new stuff." Jim followed the Army's instructions, but remains bitter about losing Roosevelt's address and other items. "I got to where that if the Japs wanted it, they took it. I NEVER willingly gave up NOTHING! I believed the American Army and that was a big mistake, a big mistake! I should have kept my guard up and thought [the] American Army was all the same as the Japanese Army." As a civilian, Jim was more than ready to be rid of military restrictions.

Jim was processed through Unit 58 with Infantry Second Lieutenant Robert J. Holloway as the processing officer. Jim filled out an American Forces Pacific Form #112 entitled AF-FIDAVIT OF RECOVERED CIVILIAN. The United States government had prepared and published the four page form on 10 August of that year in anticipation of the gigantic operation of processing the hundreds of civilian prisoners of war in addition to the military ones.

After Holloway had Jim affirm that the information on the form was correct to the best of his knowledge, the lieutenant went over the document with Jim. The first question was whether or not Jim wanted to be repatriated (returned to the United States), the reply to which could be interpreted as a resounding yes, for Jim had scratched through the "not desiring repatriation" statement boldly several times. The next five were the usual questions about name, date of birth, birthplace, and nationality. The next question asked for a passport for proof of nationality and, if none, the following question was to be answered with any other acceptable documents. Carrying his United Brotherhood of Carpenters and Joiners of America (Local 1507) card with him in the tobacco pouch the entire war paid off for Jim. "I used that on my affidavit to get back home in the United States." The Japanese had taken the leather wallet containing his driver's license on Wake Island. That left his Carpenters Union card and Contractors Pacific Naval Air Bases (CPNAB) contract as his only claim to United States citizenship. Some of the POWs with Jim didn't have that much, but he doesn't recall what happened to those in that situation.

At the line for identification marks to be written in, Jim neatly printed Scar-Left-Back-Deformed-Fingers, putting hyphens between the words as he had done with his letters home when writing under the careful watch of the Japanese Army. The prison behavior had become a deeply ingrained habit that Jim reverted to naturally, even though he no longer needed to. The identifying scar was a reminder of the 8 December 1941 air attack back on Wake Island. Several lines Jim had to leave blank since they concerned marriage and children. When asked for relatives' names, Jim wrote in his mother and his grandfather, Amos Bennett. They were the two most important people in his life and ones he hoped to see soon.

Where required to write about his activities from 7 December 1941, until his internment, Jim wrote "USMC 1ST Defence-Battalion Battery-E-3" A.A.-Gun-Crew" of his sixteen days as a volunteer Marine. He filled in "Camp-Maintenance-

Carpenter-China-5B-Coal-Yard-Labor" about his employment while held by the Japanese. The form asked when Jim was originally interned to which he filled in the following:

> Dec. 23ʳᵈ 1941 at <u>Wake-Island</u> and was released on <u>Sept–6ᵗʰ</u> 1945 at <u>58-Yokohama</u>. If released, state under what circumstances and conditions. <u>By Peace</u> .

It was a peace that was available to Jim only by the grace of God and by much loss of life on the part of the many who worked to bring it about.

When Lieutenant Holloway finished inspecting Jim's form, he wrote on the top of the first page, "OK for repatriation to USA," and signed his name and rank below. Jim was passed on to the next station in the processing gauntlet. Here Jim filled out more paperwork, this time on a claims form entitled, "American Civilians Who Were Held" by the Japanese, in hopes of recovering some compensation for his lost Wake Island tools and wages. Jim and the other POWs with him were moved along toward a shower and physical examination. It was his first real shower since Fusan two months earlier. Jim discovered his weight had climbed from 138 pounds in Kiangwan to 160 pounds, thanks to the food from the bountiful U.S. airdrops. Finally, a U.S. Army doctor examined Jim, "and that's when he checked me over and give me that slip to fly out of Tokyo with, which I still have!" Jim exclaimed over fifty years later. "All I had to do was take that [chit] and get on an army truck and they'd took me out to the airport." On the small piece of white paper the doctor had written, "Atzugi Air Strip, Civilian," in lead pencil. The little chit offered a quick trip east across the wide Pacific and home.

However, relatively healthy and fit, all things considered, Jim wasn't in any hurry to get home at the moment. Feeling euphoric and free after 1,368 days of imprisonment, Jim enjoyed talking to anyone who would speak to him. He wanted to catch up on everything he'd missed since December 1941. Although Jim lost some of his belongings, he still had his handmade guitar, the Don Ludington-made backpack, his cardboard Red Cross box, and the two carry-on bags that held a bit of food. Even if the war was really over, Jim was determined to be ready to provide for himself. It was hard not to be concerned about food and to trust others to feed him. Since he had his own supply of foodstuffs available whenever he wanted them, Jim was more interested in talking with other Americans about what had happened in the last few years than taking a quick trip home on an airplane. "No, I was really in no hurry. And I had my guitar and anybody who'd talk to me, other than a damned prisoner of war, I'd go ahead and talk to them."

Jim wandered about the Yokohama dock area enjoying the freedom and the conversations in which he eagerly engaged. Even the heavy load of all his belongings didn't bother him or slow him down. The overwhelming joy of being free gave buoyancy to Jim's feet, and he felt he could go on forever. It was a warm September afternoon in Yokohama, very different than his previous visit in 1942. Two people from Newsreel Pictures, Nick Welch of Rock Island, Illinois, and D. T. Hiller of Brooklyn, New York, took Jim's picture holding the purloined *Freedom* magazine and his handmade guitar.

At 8:00 that evening an announcement was made over the loudspeakers at the dock that the last launch for the POW repatriation ship in the harbor, the USS *Ozark* LVS-2, was about to leave. The name of the ship was fitting for one born in Missouri. "So like a damn fool, I went out and that was the end of the fun!" To Jim's dismay, once on the *Ozark* he found that he couldn't return to the Yokohama docks. He was now subject to the operations of the United States Navy and was not totally free to do as he wished as he had been earlier in the day. In some ways, Jim thought, it was like being back in prison camp. The fun was over too quickly.

Known as a Higgins Combat Landing Craft, the U.S. Navy launch from the *Ozark* headed out toward the much larger waiting ship, her lights beckoning the weary men like the lights of home. The 453 feet long *Ozark* had a beam, or width, of sixty feet and was a new type of ship called a Landing Vehicle Ship (LVS). Commissioned on 23 September 1944, she had a rear door, or ramp, that dropped down into the water to facilitate amphibious landing operations. As the Higgins boat bearing Jim and many other liberated men approached the stern of the massive *Ozark*, they could see that she already had her ramp lowered in anticipation of their arrival. As the smaller boat made its approach to the stern of the *Ozark*, they could see into the cave-like loading bay of the mother ship. The landing procedure called for the Higgins boat to advance on the stern of the *Ozark* until it was to the edge of the lowered ramp and then drop it's own bow ramp to allow its passengers to walk from one vessel to the other. Unfortunately, the bo's'n steering the Higgins came onto the lowered ramp too fast. As the *Ozark's* and the Higgins' ramps met abruptly, fellow CPNAB civilian POW Charles Mayberry and Jim collided, which resulted in the breaking of Jim's guitar strings; the rest of the sturdy guitar held together. Although Jim knew it wasn't Mayberry's fault, he still "growled" at him angrily about breaking the strings. "Hell, I carried it all the way from Kiangwan, China, clear to there [without damage]," Jim declares, still irritated decades later. "I kept it dry in a rainstorm in Fusan, too!" His personal VJ trophy, Jim was very protective of his priceless guitar.

When the launch finally became stable, the men walked off the ramp and onto the *Ozark* proper. Jim and his group were met by the Officer of the Day and given a round tag of yellow and white with their assigned stateroom number and bed number as

Jim's assignment tag from the *Ozark*. (James A. Allen Collection)

well as the ship's name. Jim was given C deck, stateroom 304, bunk 102. Jim and the others were escorted to their staterooms. Although Jim was not happy about being unable to leave the ship again, his arrival was perfectly timed to receive some of the better accommodations aboard a Navy vessel. Unlike his USS *Regulus* voyage to Wake Island, on the new USS *Ozark,* Jim found that C-304 was an air-conditioned stateroom. His tag had also indicated the top bunk, 102. "A fine bed" stated Jim, especially after the brick floors and wooden platforms with straw mattresses he had used for over three years. A "real" mattress was swell!

The next day, as other liberated POWs came aboard and the available staterooms were filled, the remaining men were given canvas cots on open deck space in the ship's hold and large vehicle deck. Without air-conditioning, the voyage would be hot and miserable for those assigned there. Remembering the wretched cruise to Wake Island four years earlier, Jim felt better about having left the dock area the night before.

Having a good bed in a cool, comfortable room, Jim spent hours on his bunk reading all the available magazines, news-

Tokyo Bay and Allied naval vessels as the USS *Ozark* sails for Guam.
Although he knew many of the ex-POWs on board, Jim preferred to
read below decks for most of the voyage since he had a "hell of a
good bed down below!" (Victor Lane/James A. Allen Collection)

papers, and books that he could find on board the ship. "Any-
time I could find a book, I read it. I read everything I could get
ahold of. I laid in there and read too long," recalls Jim, which
resulted in his missing meals. "I missed more meals by laying
down there [in his stateroom] and waiting and by not getting
in that damn line than I missed with the Japanese." By the
time Jim would stop reading to get in the chow line, the cooks
had served all the food available and the doors to the mess
deck would be closed until the next scheduled meal. Some of
the 950 ex-POWs on board the *Ozark* would sit on the deck by
the mess doors and wait for them to re-open at the next mealtime. Food was the most important thing for those ex-POWs
and they never seemed to get enough of it. Apparently this
was something the military had not foreseen.

Jim was not the only one to find himself shut out of the mess
deck. Some of the ship's 400 crew members did also, resulting in
complaints to the captain. An investigation discovered some of
the ex-POWs aboard were so hungry that after they went through
the chow line, they'd gobbled the meal and gotten back in line for
more, sometimes three or four times. This resulted in the galley
running out of food before everyone was fed.

By the time the ship left Yokohama on the eighth the problem had been identified and all men aboard the *Ozark* were

given tickets. An armed guard was posted to stand watch at the door and another stood nearby to punch each man's ticket for the appropriate meal. This resulted in a smooth operation. Jim recalls then he "could wait till the line had gotten [inside the door] and walk right in, get [my] meal, eat it and carry on; go back and read," which suited Jim just fine.

With his reading, Jim was able to catch up on the last few years' newsworthy events during the three week Pacific crossing to San Francisco via Guam and Pearl Harbor. Unlike some of the returning ex-POWs, Jim was not surprised or indignant that women were actively engaged in industrial jobs. Discovered in one of his magazines, Jim was intrigued by a particular cartoon, of "the gal working on an airplane engine. She [had] lost a bobbie pin and she was tearing the damn airplane engine up to find the bobbie pin!" By the time he docked in San Francisco, Jim "was in pretty good shape" on knowing what had occurred during his imprisonment.

Periodically during the four day voyage from Yokohama to Guam, there would be announcements over the ship's public address system. These messages informed the liberated men that the ship's personnel "were giving away something, cold drinks, toiletries, something down in the bowels of the ship someplace," Jim recalls. "Everyone lined up and they would give it to you." Everything was free for the ex-POWs during that short voyage. Jim and his peers enjoyed all the treats.

On Tuesday morning, 12 September, the USS *Ozark* docked at the United States Naval Station on the island of Guam in the U.S. Territory of Hawaii, as it was then known. The Recovered Allied Military Personnel (R.A.M.Ps), as the ex-POWs were officially known, were shuttled to Base Hospital #103 for tests.

Jim arrived at 10:00 AM and began the physical exams that were required before being allowed to continue on to the States. Jim and the other ex-POWs had their individual information recorded on three by five cards entitled HEADQUARTERS, ISLAND COMMAND, GUAM. According to that little card, Jim was officially an ALLIED PRISONER OF WAR UNDER NAVAL JURISDICTION as recorded by the personnel officer, M. A. Christensen, a pharmacist in the regular Navy. On the upper right hand corner of Jim's card, E1-2 (enlisted grade 1 or 2) was written in pencil. This was the United States Navy's way of classifying the civilians as they related to the Navy hierarchy — as low as possible.

During his early September stay on Guam, Jim sent a Western Union Telegram to his mother, letting her know he really was on his way home. It had a short but pertinent message.

WASHINGTON DC 1042 P.M. OCT 9 1945
THE FOLLOWING MESSAGE RECEIVED
QUOTE AM FREE WELL HAPPY WILL SEE YOU
SOON LOVE
JAMES A ALLEN
LERCH PROVOST MARSHALL GENERAL
9:13 A.M.

Viola received Jim's telegram of good news on 9 October, the same day it had arrived in Washington, D.C. This was seven days after Jim had already arrived safely back in California. The telegram must have taken a much slower boat than the *Ozark*.

While on Guam, the men were given five beer chits, or tickets, which could be exchanged for the real thing, only one can per day though. Jim still has all five of his faded yellow, heavy construction paper beer chits. "I didn't get no beer. I didn't want no beer. There was a big long line. I didn't care about a long line. I wouldn't get in a long line for food [on the *Ozark*], so why would I get in a long line to get a beer?"

What Jim did want was time to build a wooden shipping box in order to send some of his belongings ahead to California. Jim received permission to go to the base hobby shop. Once there, Jim built him-

Ex-POWs milling around the dock at Guam waiting to re-board the *Ozark* (in the background) after their medical exams. (Victor Lane/James A. Allen Collection)

self a box large enough for his guitar and most of his souvenirs. After sealing it, Jim wrote the last address he had for his mother, Weaver Street in El Monte. By examining postmarks on his letters, Jim was aware that his family had moved several times in his absence and could only hope that they were still in residence at that last address.

In order to mail the box, Jim needed U.S. dollars, not the Chinese Republic Bank (CRB) notes, Japanese Yen, or Philippine dollars that had been used as currency in the prison camps. On the ex-POWs' arrival at Guam, all military personnel received one hundred dollars cash from their accumulated back pay from the government. The American civilians were given five dollars each from the Red Cross on Guam. The civilian repatriates were not given any money from the United States government. Jim used most of his five dollars to mail his box of mementos home to California.

The next day, 17 September with Jim and the others again in their same assigned beds, it was anchors aweigh as the *Ozark* continued its journey east toward North America. This leg of the trip was far different from the first, especially for the civilians. Jim relates that, "There was nothing free on anymore, other than the meals. We had Canadians on board, and periodically they'd line up and go down and get ice cream, a cold drink or toiletries or something. But if the Americans wanted anything, if an American civilian wanted anything, they had to pay for it!" Jim says with the bitterness in his voice not diminished with time.

On the first day of the middle leg of his journey home, Jim was able to secure a V-mail form to write his mother. The small (four and one-quarter inches by five and one-quarter inches) letter Viola received resembles a modern day photocopy which had been reduced from its original size. The letter gives a succinct report of his health and experiences as well as informing his mother of his desire for information.

After leaving Guam, the *Ozark's* route took her to the south of Wake Island. As the gray-hulled ship passed by the tiny atoll, Jim and many other men stood along the deck railing watching the lights twinkling in the distance. What thoughts passed through each man's mind can only be speculated.

A landmark point was crossed on the twenty-second, the International Date Line. Traveling west to east, the *Ozark* moved back in time from Friday, 22 September to Thursday,

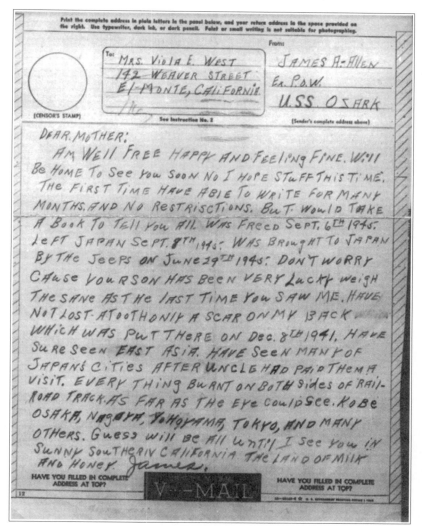

Jim's V-MAIL letter to Viola. (James A. Allen Collection)

21 September, reliving the previous day. Now the liberated men were experiencing the same day as their families instead of always being a day ahead of them.

With some of the money remaining after sending his memento box, Jim bought a six cent airmail stamp to send a letter to Viola. Jim posted it at the *Ozark*'s mailroom where it would be transferred in Hawaii for a flight to California. Upon the front and back of a sheet of Red Cross stationary, Jim wrote:

September 23, 1945

Dear Mother:
Another letter to let you know I am alright and on my way home. As I have not received a letter from you for many months (the last post marked in 1943). I do not know much as to what has happened since I have left home. Please write a long letter or letters telling me all the news death's and what nots so that I won't be tripping up when I get home or in writing letters. Everything has changed so much it seems like a new world. I am at a lost so if you'll write the news it will help a lot.

And please don't worry about me I am in very good health as have had a medical exam in Guam and am alright. Left Guam 17th of Sept. when I'll be home I don't know but will be as quick as possible so just sit tight. And don't go to any extra trouble for me because if you do I'll be unhappy.

Have sent a box to 142 Weaver with some of my junk so try and locate it as there is some things I would not like to lose. Tell all hello and little Jimmie to And tell all to write now as the only people I received letters from in Japan was you and Mrs. Sayre in Downey. If they don't write now look out. Am not having a very enjoyable trip home had [expected] much different. But how things have changed.

Well this will be all for now but we will talk for sometime when I get home.

Your wayward.
Son
James

When Jim wrote this letter he believed that he may be held somewhere and still wanted to receive news from home. As it turned out, Viola received the letter the first of October, the day before Jim sailed into San Francisco Bay. It was too late to write any more letters and also unnecessary.

Just after lunch on the twenty-fifth, with a favorable tide, the *Ozark* sailed into Pearl Harbor. There were many battle weary ships tied at the harbor's piers and moorings. None of the ex-POWs were allowed off the ship, officially, for the overnight stay. However, the ex-POW civilian Jim had shared the lavatory with on the train to Niigata did get ashore and returned with the information from his old skipper about how the ferry from Fusan had almost been hit by an American torpedo.

CPNAB construction worker Allan A. O'Guinn sitting on the deck of the USS *Ozark* as she steams toward the States. O'Guinn was a plumber on Wake Island. (Victor Lane/James A. Allen Collection)

The news brought a chill to the warm Hawaiian air.

Jim's second visit to Hawaii was far different than the first one. Sunset was not observed under a banyan tree with a drink and young lady, but by standing at the *Ozark's* railing with other men and looking past a mass of drab Naval scenery beyond. Just twenty-four hours after arriving at Pearl Harbor, the *Ozark* began the last leg of its voyage to San Francisco. Home was now only seven days away.

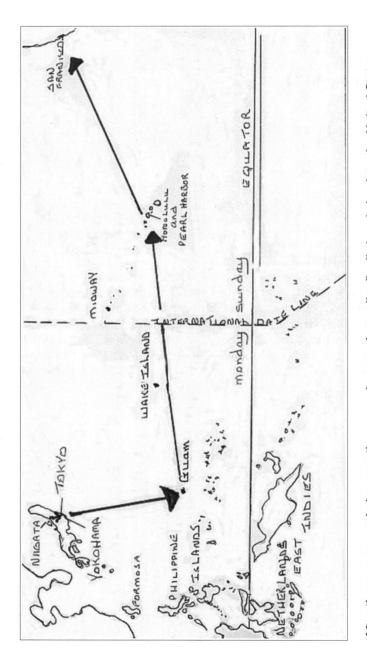

After three years and nine months as a prisoner of war, Jim finally heads back to the United States via the islands of Guam and Oahu.

18

On the Homefront

While Jim and his fellow POWs celebrated the war's end and began heading toward the States, their loved ones were also celebrating and anticipating a homecoming celebration. The days were no longer filled with questions of when the war would end or when the sons, brothers, fathers, and neighbors would be home. Each hour brought new information as telegrams and letters came to families and calendars finally could be marked with the expected dates. Many hearts beat lighter as the load of the war began to peel away and was replaced by the anticipated joy of forthcoming reunions.

Both sorrow and joy, though, would be visiting some families. Two McDonald families especially, would experience one emotion swiftly replacing the other. The honcho of the 150 POW group Jim was in at Niigata, Joe McDonald, had been reported dead from the 1941 battles on Wake Island. His Reno, Nevada, "family, folks had a funeral and everything. Then he showed up alive at the end of the war." Their three-plus years of mourning instantly vanished and tears of sadness transformed to joy. Unfortunately for the Cody, Wyoming, family of the other Joe McDonald, Joseph Thomas, who had worked on Wake Island, the anxiously awaited-for reunion with their son would not be taking place.

The home Jim remembered was no longer the same one he had left in September 1941. His family had changed resi-

Viola Allen West, seated in her wheeled chair, outside her home in Manteca, California. (James A. Allen Collection)

dences and grown smaller with the war years, and his mother's health had further deteriorated. Viola's rheumatoid arthritis progressively grew worse until it affected her entire body. Sitting motionless for hours by the radio while intently listening for war news relevant to her James had not helped her condition. By September 1942 she had to use a wheeled chair to move about. Someone took a supermarket grocery cart, which were much smaller in the 1940s, cut the front and sides off, and welded it together for strength. The wheeled chair had no arms and a hard wooden seat with a cushion. It looked nothing like a present day wheelchair. Viola got around by pushing backwards with her feet to move the chair, which had four small, hard rubber wheels. Her wheeled chair worked well, as long as there were not any large bumps or obstacles to go over; the four small grocery cart wheels became easily stuck. In the 1940s, there was little public recognition of those with handicaps, and sidewalk cutouts and barrier free entrances to public buildings were unheard of. Even with her chair, it was difficult for Viola, and others who were disabled, to get around.

Viola had written her carpenter son on 3 September 1942, "wish you was here to make me a runway off the porch for my chair . . . ." By mid-November the same year, Viola wrote, "sure can make my chair walk," possibly as a way of making light of her condition in order not to worry her absent son.

Other changes in the family had taken place. Jim's sister Hazel married in May of 1942 and gave birth to a son in August of the following year. Although Viola had written many times with the news of the two events, it was the spring of 1944 before Jim had finally received the letters that told of his sister's marriage and the arrival of his namesake nephew, Jimmie. As Jim says, "I was an uncle long before I knew it." Many of Viola's and Jim's letters contained the same information, repeated again and again in hopes that one letter might make it through.

Jerald, the older of Jim's two younger brothers, had left home and had been serving as an enlisted man in the United States Navy since 15 October 1942. Viola had written saying that Jerald was near him as a way of letting Jim know what was happening to his brother. Jim wrote back that he guessed Jerald was no longer working for the railroad as a way of telling his mother he understood her message. Jim also understood when his mother wrote that Jerald was in good health that she meant his ship had not been sunk. Jerald made three Pacific cruises aboard an ammunition ship and two destroyers, safely, during the war. Jerald had also married during Jim's absence. Although time was in some ways standing still for Jim, it was marching along rapidly for others.

In her letters, Viola also mentioned to Jim that his "little" brother Billie, now called Bill, had grown to be 5'11" tall and was captain of the school basketball team. "Bill got his name in the paper playing basketball," she wrote in a letter dated 26 February 1943. "He is some boy. Has a job for the summer." But frustration with the lack of communication only grew for Viola, as she had to shorten her long chatty letters to brief ones of twenty-five words with hyphens between by the autumn of 1943. The short, printed letters required by the censors had made it harder to let Jim know how things were going at home.

Jim had left his three siblings as children, in his way of thinking, since he was the oldest and had shouldered some of the responsibility for caring for them since the age of eleven. During his absence, his sister and brother Jerald had matured into adults, while Bill was close to becoming one. In his last letter home, dated 14 September 1944, Jim acknowledges the changes he knows have taken place at home, writing, "WILL-BE-GLAD-TO-GET-BACK-TO-THE-OLD-U.S.A.-WHEN-IT-BE-I'LL-NOT-KNOW-THE-PLACE-NOR-WILL-IT-KNOW-ME. As he wrote the letter, Jim still saw no foreseeable end to his imprisonment and wrote his mother that he "WOULD-LIKE-VERY-MUCH-TO-HAVE-SOME-PICTURE'S-OF-YOU-

ALL-YOU-ANYWAY-SOME-OF-THE-FELLOWS-RECEIVE-
THEM-BUT-MOST-DON'T." Current photographs were a big
help to the POWs to keep them up to date on the situation
back home. This was especially true when things were substantially different than they remembered them.

Viola had written a letter every week since he had left as well
as sending numerous packages. Jim only received some of his
mother's letters and one from Mrs. Sayre, whom he did yard work
for while in high school. He never received any letters that others had written or his mother's packages and photographs.

But Jim was optimistic about coming home alive and was
still planning on having a future life after prison camp. Although the order of events may be a bit off, Jim closes his
letter of 14 September with, "AS-YOU-KNOW-IT-WILL-BE-
A-LONG-TIME-BEFORE-I-GET-MARRIED-I'LL-HAVE-TO-
FIND-SOMEONE-TO-MARRY-AND-GET-HOME."

In 1945, Viola and Jim's stepfather, Carl West, moved to the
central California town of Manteca, a farming community where
Carl was employed in a vineyard. Bill chose to stay behind in El
Monte and live with his sister's family in order to play basketball and finish his senior year in high school; he would graduate in June of 1946. Viola's move north caused confusion and
delays with returned mail from the Shanghai War Prisoners
Camp having to be forwarded through several previous ad-
dresses in Southern California before being sent north. A letter
mailed from El Monte on 15 June 1943 was eventually returned
to her in Manteca on 29 June 1946. She received the last letter
Jim wrote from the Kiangwan camp, dated 14 September 1944,
a year later on 8 September 1945, after the war was already
over, but before her son had returned home.

As the fighting dragged on, the last year of the war was
very difficult for the Allen family. When Viola heard reports of
American troops pushing into Japanese held areas, she could
only pray that her James' Shanghai prison camp would be
liberated soon, if not already. Viola did not, however, have word
about her son's condition and location during the entire last
year of the war, adding to her anxiety for her son's life. But all
that soon became concerns of the past as the war ended. The
present held much promise for the future, but the future would
not begin until her James was home.

19

Home At Last!

Finally, on 2 October 1945 the United States Ship *Ozark* came into sight of the coastal mountains of California. The excitement of being home grew among the ex-POWs as the big gray ship slipped under the Golden Gate Bridge and into San Francisco Bay. It had been four years and twenty days since Jim had sailed under the orange painted bridge, heading west into the Pacific towards Hawaii aboard the SS *Matsonia*.

While off the California coast, Jim was approached by a United States Army Captain, James W. Hamilton, TC, O/C, Positive Intelligence, Sub Section, Intelligence, Security and Technical Information Division, who was stationed at Fort Mason in San Francisco. He had learned of Jim's various souvenirs and asked him if he could borrow two of them: the Regulations for Prisoners from the *Nitta Maru* voyage and the pencil sketch of the prisoners' bunks that civilian Ernest B. Archer had drawn at the Woosung camp. Jim was agreeable and handed them over to Captain Hamilton. Hamilton mailed them back to Jim on 3 October as promised, having gleaned whatever information he needed.

As the early morning October sun rose, the USS *Ozark* made her way to the civilian San Francisco shipping terminals. She eventually docked at 9:00 AM alongside a commercial pier with a warehouse. The pier was empty except for the stevedores and line handlers awaiting the *Ozark's* arrival. After the *Ozark's* lines were securely tied to the pier, the gangway was moved into place and the anxious ex-POWs finally disembarked and touched United States soil.

Jim joined the long line that moved slowly down the gangway. Once on the pier, the line moved towards a table manned by the Red Cross. Donuts and orange juice were being passed out to the men before they moved on to the other tables for processing and possible transportation to government hospitals. As Jim made his way down the gangway, a familiar face caught his eye. Inside the pier's warehouse his Uncle Arthur Bennett was standing behind a barricade. Ecstatic at seeing his mother's older brother, Jim immediately left the line of disembarking men and went over to him. After greeting Jim, Uncle Arthur led him over to where his Aunt Ollie and Viola were patiently waiting in Arthur's car. They were the only family members of any of the POWs there. Jim has never learned how his family knew he would be on the *Ozark* and when it would arrive when other families, especially those close by in the San Francisco area, did not.

Since Viola could not walk and was confined to her wheeled chair, Arthur had received permission from the pier authorities to drive inside the pier warehouse and park near the Red Cross stand. Thus the disabled Viola could remain in the car and still see her James disembark the big, gray ship. Jim leaned into the car, hugging and kissing his mother as, with tears in her eyes, she tightly held her long missing son in her crippled arms. Her James was home at last!

After all the hellos and hugs to his mother, aunt, and uncle, Jim was excited and ready to leave the pier; he'd had enough of the military, Japanese or American! As the shipload of former POWs continued to file over to the Red Cross area to be processed, Uncle Arthur and Jim climbed into the waiting car. Turning the car around, Arthur drove toward the street at the end of the pier. As the San Francisco sun shone through the car's windshield, Jim felt truly free of the restrictive military life.

Since Jim didn't have any clothes other than ones from the American military's government issue (GI), Arthur drove through San Francisco until he reached Hastings Men's Store. The large selection of new merchandise was the same to Jim as a candy store would be to a child. Before he left, Jim bought shoes, socks, shirts, and pants, as well as two ties, which he still has after almost sixty years. Some possessions hold too many memories to just toss them away.

Feeling normally attired for the first time in years, Jim and his folks left San Francisco and headed toward his mother and stepfather's home in Manteca, which was about seventy-five miles away on four lane roadways. Carl West was working at a thirty-five acre grape vineyard and rented a small house on its perimeter. Several members of Jim's extended family resided in Manteca including his Uncle Arthur and Aunt Ollie. Manteca

With his mother seated in her wheelchair, Jim posed for a picture shortly after his return from the Japanese POW camps in October 1945. (James A. Allen Collection)

was a real homecoming for Jim with more hugs and handshakes as well as stories about the war years to be exchanged with cousins and others.

During the exchanges of information, Viola gave Jim the letters that the censors had returned to her. Jim had never received all of the letters she had written faithfully each week, nor any of her packages. Although others had written him, Jim had only received those from his mother and one from a former yardwork employer and neighbor, Mrs. Sayre.

After a great American home cooked meal of venison, Jim was content just to sit around and talk with his folks and the other relatives who lived nearby. Later that evening, between 7:00 and 8:00, a very tired Jim happily crawled into a real American bed, only to be awakened at 1:00 in the very early morning by his "little" brother Bill who had just arrived from Southern California. The sleepy Jim unknowingly insulted Bill when he failed to recognize him; Bill was no longer the gangly thirteen-year-old Jim remembered. Bill, Hazel, brother-in-law Bob and two year-old nephew, Jimmie, had all traveled north

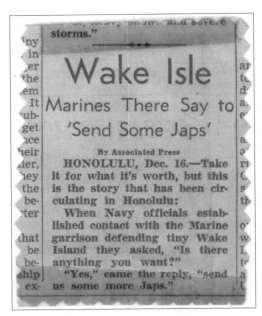

storms."

Wake Isle

Marines There Say to 'Send Some Japs'

By Associated Press

HONOLULU, Dec. 16.—Take it for what it's worth, but this is the story that has been circulating in Honolulu:

When Navy officials established contact with the Marine garrison defending tiny Wake Island they asked, "Is there anything you want?"

"Yes," came the reply, "send us some more Japs."

Viola had saved this newspaper clipping from 1941 for Jim. It contains the famous, though erroneous, "Send more Japs" quote that was never sent from Wake Island. At least the AP reporter says to "Take it for what it's worth." (James A. Allen Collection)

from El Monte by car that night. Seeing his little nephew for the first time, Jim finally felt like the uncle he was.

During Jim's absence Hazel had dutifully looked after Jim's car, making the loan payments, paying the garage rent, and occasionally cleaning it. Her husband Bob had been able to "wrangle," as Jim puts it, four new tires and a new battery for the "1940 dark green four-door Ford sedan with a Columbia axle," not an easy task with wartime rationing of such products still going on. Jim was ecstatic about getting his pride and joy back.

The next morning, Jim's brother and brother–in–law returned home for school and work while Jim and his beloved Ford were off on the road heading west. He retraced his travel route of the previous day, heading towards Oakland and a Contractors Pacific Naval Air Bases (CPNAB) office where a $1,000 voucher was waiting for him. This was a considerable sum of money in 1945 when a Hershey chocolate bar was a nickel and gasoline cost seventeen cents a gallon.

The $1,000 voucher represented a portion of Jim's pre-war pay and overtime from working on Wake Island. The remainder would be paid in the near future. The voucher also represented some of the money that the CPNAB, along with other groups, had been able to attain for their employees through Congress. In early 1942, the Pacific Island Workers Association was created by the families of the captive CPNAB workers as a way of obtaining information about what was happening to them and passing it along to the POWs' loved ones. Then in June of that same year, the CPNAB contractors incorporated the nonprofit Pacific Island Employees Foundation (PIEF) to help with financial assistance for POW families. The CPNAB contractors donated money for the foundation and stipulated that any left over after the war be given to some other charitable organization. PIEF helped many families during the war by making 4,923 donations for various needs from school tuition to shoes, eyeglasses, groceries, and burial expenses. Over $94,000 was given out. Also, PIEF served as a clearinghouse for information for the relatives and friends of the CPNAB POWs. Viola had participated by sending Jim's letters to the Foundation to be searched for new information or clues to other POWs whereabouts and health.

Another group formed to help the Contractors Pacific Naval Air Bases prisoners was The Women of Wake. Comprised of the wives of those captured on Wake Island, The Women of Wake organization was led by May Ward. According to Jim, "May Ward was some kind of wheel on the Alaskan Highway Project and knew her way around [Washington] D. C.," which apparently helped get the ear of legislators. During the war The Women of Wake worked toward reparations for the captured CPNAB employees and lobbied Congress on bills to give back wages for the time lost while a POW. Because of their efforts and those of others, several bills were passed by Congress, including Public Law (PL) 77-784. Signed by President Roosevelt on 2 December 1942, PL 77-784 provided a missing or detained civilian employee with a credit of $108.33 per month, retroactive from 1 January 1942, until his return to the continental United States. Effective the first of January 1944, Public Law 78-216 stated that any benefits to which the person was entitled would be credited at a rate of 100% of the wage that a similar civilian occupation might receive, but couldn't exceed what the POW earned as an average weekly wage before he was captured. Unfortunately due to a "legalese" glitch, the CPNAB workers' wages could not be computed with their pay rate on Wake Island, but had to be taken from a similar occupation as classified in the 1940 *Civil Service Schedule* for government employees. Not many jobs listed were for masons, ironworkers, carpenters, crane operators or other heavy construction work.

The men working for the Contractors Pacific Naval Air Bases had received only a portion of their pay on the island while the rest of their pay and overtime was banked for when they returned to the mainland. Because of this, the CPNAB distributed a portion of the employee's pay and overtime as well as government dollars awarded, to the civilian POWs' dependent families during the war years. Viola, however, never touched any of Jim's money. The full amount was waiting for him upon his return to the States.

As Jim stood in line at the Oakland CPNAB office, he was feeling great dressed in his new suit of clothes, especially when he compared himself to the other POWs in line. Many of them still wore the GI clothing from the airdrops in Japan. "They looked lost and woebegone to me," says Jim. The CPNAB office handed the POW employees a thin, blue hardcover book entitled *A REPORT to Returned CPNAB Prisoner of War HEROES and their Dependents*. Within the book could be found what had been done to date about the financial reparations for the POWs. There were also pages of photographs sent by families of the captive men that had been printed in newsletters during the past three years. "I really appreciated it tremendously, what [CPNAB] had done at the time," says Jim.

After receiving his voucher, Jim walked across the street to a bank and redeemed it for cash. The feeling of American money in his pockets after such a long absence was a good one. So good that the additional feelings of freedom and independence overcame Jim, and he found himself driving around Oakland and the nearby University of California at Berkeley for no reason at all. For quite a while, Jim drove just where he wanted with no specific purpose in mind, but with an exhilarating feeling of being able to do as he pleased. He was truly free at last!

Finally heading back to Manteca via Stockton, Jim came upon an unusual sight on the highway. Traveling in the opposite direction was a large U.S. Army convoy of amphibious vehicles called Ducks, which were capable of moving in water or on land. This was an unknown vehicle to Jim since they had been developed and built during the war. Even more unusual than the Ducks, though, was the fact women were driving them. Although his reading had prepared him somewhat for the changes in American society since the war began, Jim says, at the time, "That was quite a sight for me!"

In the afternoon, Jim located a Department of Motor Vehicles office in Stockton. Taking the written test, Jim earned a 100%. Next was the driving test, but as Jim recalls, "That was a breeze because the old boy, all he wanted to know was about prison camp." Jim laughs heartily as he tells the story. "So we just chatted and talked and drove."

A few days after Jim was in Manteca, while at a gas station filling up, a man offered Jim $1,800 for his basically new 1940 car. Jim had paid only $750 for the car in the spring of 1941, but it had cost the original owner $1,080 since it was a Ford Deluxe with radio and heater, two items considered luxuries at that time. The need for tanks, airplanes, and other war products had caused a shortage of personal vehicles and those available had many miles of hard use on them by 1945. Viola had been under a lot of pressure to sell the green sedan, but had resisted in order for Jim to have the car when he returned home. The young Jim was very happy to have it waiting for him in September of 1945, but by the turn of the century he had changed his mind. "That's when two fools met; him for offering [the money] and me for not accepting!"

Within a few days, Jim, his sister Hazel and nephew Jimmie returned to El Monte. Viola was sorry to see them go, but realized Jim needed to go back to the area he remembered as his last home. Telling his mother he would be back before Thanksgiving, Jim began the long drive south along the dusty, unpaved rural two lane roads. After traveling about 150 miles Jim and his passengers turned off the unpaved gravel Highway 33 and pulled into the small town of Coalinga. This was where Jim's good buddy Bill Goodman's mother and stepfather, Alice and George Smith lived, and Jim wanted to stop and visit. He was well acquainted with them from his friendship with Goodman. The two had had many boyhood adventures and escapades. Goodman had not yet returned home from his war experiences. Right after Pearl Harbor's bombing, Goodman had enlisted in the Navy. Goodman was offered an officer's job since he had some college studies behind him. However, he turned it down and was instead sent to Purdue University to study the relatively new electronic detection system called radar (radio detecting and ranging), which used radio waves for measuring the location and distance of an object. Sent to use his new knowledge in Navy planes over Central America, Goodman later told Jim the only thing he found on radar was a floating orange crate.

On his way east to Missouri, in the autumn of 1945, Jim Allen stopped in Oklahoma City, Oklahoma, to see fellow ex-POW Victor Lane at his home. In the photo, Jim is wearing for the first time his new double-breasted suit he bought on 4 April 1941, before he left to work on Wake Island. (Victor Lane/James A. Allen Collection)

After spending the night in Coalinga, Jim, Hazel, and little Jimmie continued their journey. South of Coalinga, Highway 33 was paved and easier going, but there were still almost 400 miles to go on the winding two lane highway. California's famous freeways were yet to be built. Once in El Monte, Jim checked in with the carpenter's union and then made plans to go east. He'd been behind barbed wire and brick fences too many years to remain stationary for long. Jim also had a powerful urge to see more of the country he had defended and suffered for. He had promised Viola before he'd left Manteca he would be back by Thanksgiving, but that still gave Jim plenty of time to tour "from sea to shining sea."

The next morning, Jim and his youngest brother, Bill, headed east in Jim's Ford. The final destination was Washington, D.C., where Jim's brother Jerald was now living with his wife, Cecilia, whom Jim had yet to meet. Jim first made a mid-continental stop in northeastern Missouri to see his grandparents and many aunts, uncles, and cousins. Barbary and Amos Bennett had celebrated their sixtieth wedding anniversary during Jim's imprisonment. They did their best to make Jim's Missouri homecoming a joyous occasion. With picture taking and getting all the relatives together with lots of food, especially Grandpa Amos' homemade molasses on top of biscuits, which Jim loved, it was a real old fashioned affair. Within a few days, the restless Jim resumed his journey to D.C. Brother Bill took a bus back to California and school, so his cousin Bob

Carey and his wife, Shirley Mae, accompanied Jim as he continued east.

Arriving in the city of Washington, Jim and his traveling companions immediately looked up his brother Jerald. Married to Cecilia in 1944, Jerald had mustered out of the Navy now that the war was over and was employed as a beer truck driver. Having seen action on several Pacific Ocean cruises as well as an Atlantic one, he was now enjoying life as a civilian and husband. Swapping war stories with each other, Jerald told Jim about being on a destroyer during the Battle of the Philippine Sea. His ship was

While in Missouri Jim had his picture taken with his grandparents, Amos and Barbary "Barbara" Bennett on their daughter Tina Carey's farm in Perry, Missouri. Amos' early influence on Jim helped him to survive prison camp as well as he did. (James A. Allen Collection)

caught in a typhoon and its main deck broke. Water poured into the lower decks, and the crew stuffed mattresses and anything else they could find into the holes in order to prevent the ship from flooding and possibly sinking. Jerald's ship was in a terrible predicament; if they stayed in the typhoon, they might sink, but if they tried to break out of the severe storm, the Japanese ships waiting outside of the storm would get them. Fortunately, neither the typhoon nor the Japanese were able to submerge them.

Jim's cousin Frank Carey, Jr. (Bob's brother) was also in Washington. Still on active duty as a Marine, Frank was stationed at the Naval Observatory, now known as the Vice President's Residence. They, too, had a fine visit, swapping war adventures, trials, and tribulations.

During the war, Washington had been a lively place, and it still had an air of excitement about it even after the war was officially over. There was a lot for a young man to take in and Jim walked "through the National Art Galleries, Smithsonian Institute, the Capitol; I looked it [all] over" he recalls with a chuckle.

At the Smithsonian Institute Jim first saw some of the simplest, yet effective, wartime long distance aerial bombs created by the Japanese. Because of the U.S. government's wartime secrecy and the cooperation of news agencies, knowledge of these bombs was never widespread. Since they failed to hear of any destruction caused by them, Japanese intelligence dismissed the balloon-laden bombs as being ineffective. In reality, they were far from ineffective compared to their cost. According to Jim, one Japanese lieutenant with very little money made trans-Pacific aerial bombs using dynamite and weather balloons inflated with the hot air created by a steamboiler. Using the prevailing westerlies and jet stream wind currents, which were little understood at that time, the Japanese lieutenant launched the balloons and their deadly cargo by the hundreds. Quite a few of the bomb carrying balloons made it across the Pacific Ocean to land in the Pacific Northwest and start forest fires that created concern and a news blackout; the government explained away the fires as lighting strikes. A few of the balloons apparently caught just the right winds and made it all the way to the Dakotas. These silently flying bombs caused a lot of damage, but luckily not in heavily populated areas of the United States. If they had, it could have had a tremendous psychological effect on Americans in addition to any physical damage sustained.

After a short stay in D. C., Jim started the long drive back to the West Coast with his cousins, Jerald and Cecilia traveling with him. Again there was a stop in Missouri to drop off the Careys and visit family. A few days after arriving back at his relatives, Jim set off for St. Louis to pick up his old high school buddy Bill Goodman, who was now stationed in Nashville, Tennessee. Bill had a liberty pass, but he was only allowed to travel as far as St. Louis. By going with Jim to Perry, Missouri, Goodman was officially out of bounds. That did not seem to bother him much; seeing his old buddy and getting a home cooked meal would be worth the risk!

Jim and Goodman arrived back at Jim's Aunt Tina (pronounced Tie-na) and Uncle Frank Carey's (Bob and Frank

Jr.'s parents) farm in rural Perry late that cold autumn Saturday night, but still full of energy. Having seen multitudes of rabbits sitting along the roadside on the drive from St. Louis, the young men borrowed Uncle Frank's .22 single shot rifle and set off for some nocturnal rabbit hunting.

Wild rabbits, a farmer's enemy, were hard to find in Missouri in the years preceding World War II. During the Depression, rabbit stewed or fried, was the salvation for many impoverished families; sometimes the only meat they might have, save squirrel. With the advent of the war, many young men, the main rabbit hunters, left the area for service or war related jobs in cities. Left alone, the rabbits rapidly multiplied and in a few years had bred themselves into thousands of four-legged crop destroyers, which the farmers, like Jim's Uncle Frank, were anxious to have annihilated.

Jim drove while Goodman sat on the Ford sedan's right front fender with his feet resting on the bumper. Although the "farm market" road was not as smooth as a paved highway, Goodman was quite the sharpshooter that night. "That's the amazing thing about him," says Jim. "The road wasn't all that smooth, and he hit rabbit after rabbit."

Once they returned to the Carey's farmhouse to warm up with hot coffee, Goodman opened a photograph album and revealed a beautiful dark haired woman's picture. The photograph was of Goodman's cousin, Margie Glitten, who lived in Kansas City, Kansas. Goodman had a proposal for Jim: wouldn't it be great if Jim waited until Goodman was discharged in the near future, but surely by Christmas, and then the two of them drive through Kansas City where Jim could be introduced? Goodman had been on leave a few days after Christmas of 1944 and had visited with his cousin and her parents. The native Californian was intrigued by the large amount of snow, so one night Margie took him for a walk through the "squeaky," crunchy snow, much to Goodman's delight. They ended up visiting Margie's friend Elnore "Nora" Milberger. Home for the holidays to visit her parents, Nora was living in California and working as an elementary school teacher. Smitten, Goodman told his cousin on the walk back to her house, that he was going to look up that girl and marry her. A year later, Missouri was as close to Nora as Goodman had been able to get and he hoped his Jim would help him out. Anxious to return home for Thanksgiving as he had promised his mother, Jim declined the Kansas excursion, taking Goodman back to St. Louis the next evening. A couple of days later, Jim, along with Jerald and his wife, headed west for California.

When Jim arrived back at his mother's, he found that the belongings he had mailed from Guam had arrived. Opening the wooden shipping box, Jim sadly discovered the guitar had fallen apart. Lacking a lacquer or other finish to help protect it, the humidity and salt air during the shipboard crossing of the Pacific Ocean had compromised the prison camp glue, allowing the instrument to collapse into a heap. Gathering up the pieces of wood, metal. and bone that represented several years of his life and the trials he had endured, Jim put them into a black cardboard suitcase he had used when he was a deckhand on the *John James*. There it would remain undisturbed for the next twenty-one years.

After Jim returned to California, he received a letter from Joseph Tettelback, the aircraft carrier pilot who had thrown cigarettes wrapped in a newspaper out of the cockpit while over Niigata Camp 5B. He had received Jim's letter and wrote of being currently "anchored in Tokyo Bay and it sure is a wonderful sight to see all of these ships anchored here and knowing they're ours." Apparently Tettelback didn't realize Jim was a civilian POW, for he hoped Jim was in the best of health after his imprisonment and become "a civilian by this time.

Jim's letter from Joseph Tettelback, the pilot who threw him cigarettes and a newspaper from the carrier plane's cockpit as it flew over Niigata 5B. (James A. Allen Collection)

for I know you boys must have went through hell being under such conditions."

As the Christmas and New Year's holiday season approached, greetings began to arrive from several of Jim's companions of the previous four Christmases.

Workers of Wake Christmas card. (James A. Allen Collection)

Californians Miles Glaze and family, Marine Sergeant Walton "Wally" Matkin, and Mr. and Mrs. Edgar A. Peres sent greetings, as well as Marine, now Master Gunnery Sergeant, Charles A. "Charlie" Holmes from Texas. The note Holmes wrote in his card probably summed up the sentiments of most of the Wake POWs: "This Beats the last 4 Xmas. Doesn't It, Jimmie?" Tinsmith Don Ludington, now living in Boise, Idaho, greeted Jim with "Hello Chum" on his card of an angel trying on a wreath as a halo and signed it, "Big Tin Shop Don." Ludington also wrote, "Drop me a line in your spare time."

The need to stay in touch with each other was very strong for some of the ex-POWs. Perhaps this was because these men felt once they returned home only those that had shared the pain of prison camp could appreciate what a Christmas at home felt like.

Russell Mace of Four Lakes, Washington, wrote a short note on the back of his card asking how Jim was and to say hello to any of the ex-POWs Jim might run into in Southern California. He ended his note with the 1940s advice, "don't take any wooden nickels. Ha, Ha. Your friend Curley Mace." After the horrors of their internment, lighthearted slang seemed to take an edge off the hard won peace they now lived in. Mace also inserted a manila colored card with brown script from the Workers of Wake Island with the dates, 1941 and 1945 in two different corners. The following was found inside:

1942

From our isolated pinnacle we watched across the sea.
We saw the flickering lights go out, the beams of liberty.
The torches fell at Singapore, at Wake and far Hong-Kong;

So now behind drawn blinds we sit, as wartime rules
  behest us;
Remembering a year ago the fall of Wake obsessed us.
Let's look ahead to other years, to Christmas once more
  glowing,
A season when we'll see the lights across the ocean
  showing.
And when those beacons burn again, and our men back
  from war,
Let's light the tapers from the Flame that once came
  from a Star.
                                        — Marion Pratt.

                        1946 ?
We the "Workers of Wake" Greet you on our first
Christmas of Peace. We request your consideration and
support of Bill S I 561 which provides full salary for
Contractors' Employees of Wake Island imprisoned by
Japan three years and nine months. Present legislation
only provides full salary for the final twenty-one months
of that time. Your support is solicited to enable us to
receive full salary for the entire period. This will enable
us and our families the comfort of physical and
economic rehabilitation.
                THE WORKERS OF WAKE.
                Rt. 3 — Boise, Idaho

    Because of that strong need to stay in touch as well as help
each other receive reimbursement for the time lost while interned, a group of ex-POWs Jim knew were involved in estab-
lishing an organization of other CPNAB ex-prisoners of war.
This organization, Workers of Wake was begun in the late 1945
as a way of keeping in touch with other ex-POWs and also so
they could be contacted about monies to be paid for lost tools,
clothes, equipment, and wages. The Workers of Wake organization would become a dynamic proponent for compensation.
Although agreeable to the organization's motives, during the
winter of 1945-46 Jim personally had two more important objectives on his mind.
    Following his return from Missouri and Washington,
D. C., Jim continued to enjoy his freedom, something those
who have never lost it can never truly appreciate. Spending

his CPNAB back wages prudently, Jim was not forced to immediately find a job, but to keep busy he began building a small home for his mother's brother Martin and wife Dayma with whom he was living. It was good rehabilitative exercise for the war-weary Jim, which he could complete at his own pace. While residing with them in El Monte, Jim received a check for $6,000.00 (equal to $54,020.72 in

Jim Allen and check. (James A. Allen Collection)

1999 dollars), thanks to the efforts of The Women of Wake organization and other groups lobbying Congress to give those entitled back wages for the entire time lost while a POW. Planning for the future, Jim tucked away his money to buy the home he said he would have before he married.

With his nest egg in place, Jim got busy as many young men after their war experiences, looking for a woman to settle down with. By this time Bill Goodman had been honorably discharged from the Navy and had returned to Southern California. Jim had not forgotten the lovely young woman in Goodman's photograph album and learned the cousin from Kansas City was now living nearby in the town of Montebello. Employed in a defense plant and a volunteer for the Civilian Defense during the war, Margie was now teaching at an Arthur Murray Dance Studio. Cousin Margie also happened to be rooming with her friend Nora, whom Bill Goodman himself was still very interested in. Officially, Goodman was taking Jim over to the young women's apartment to pay respects to Goodman's Great Aunt "Nannie" who was staying with Nora, and had traveled west from Kansas as chaperon to Margie.

Twenty-four year-old Margie had already traveled to California from Kansas twice during the war, once with family friends and once with her mother. Wartime train travel demanded a thirty-day stay before a return trip was made in order to keep war material and troops moving effectively and efficiently, so Margie was able to have extended visits on the West Coast. By Margie's third California visit, she was ready to leave the Midwest behind for good, trading snow, ice, and prairie for warm sunshine and ocean waves.

Arriving at the women's apartment on a cool January Friday night, the two young men were warmly welcomed and before leaving, a double date was arranged for the following day. However, shortly after arriving the next day, Goodman found himself in rougher seas than when he was in the Navy after he told his cousin Margie she was a Midwesterner and should not live in California. (Apparently Goodman overlooked the fact that Nora was also from Kansas since he was interested in her.) Angry with her cousin, Margie immediately left for a bus to take her to the train station and eastbound transportation. Jim and Nora, along with a scolded Bill Goodman, drove down to the bus stop and talked to Margie from the car window as they drove alongside the bus. Goodman managed to repair the damage he had done and when the bus halted at the next stop, Margie got off. The two couples returned to the women's apartment.

After bidding goodbye to Great Aunt Nannie, they headed east in Jim's four door sedan down the two lane Highway 99 (now eight lane Interstate 10) towards Palm Springs, about one hundred miles away. The two couples enjoyed a delightful lunch and the warm January desert sun before they continued to drive through the desert, south through the agricultural fields of the sand and sagebrush bedecked Coachella Valley. Stopping at a quaint local restaurant called "Valerie Jean's", they sipped cold date shakes, enjoying the fruit of the local date palm trees before driving on through groves of date palms and citrus trees.

Having traveled about as far south as they could and still remain in the United States, Jim turned the car west and climbed up over the coastal mountains. The foursome drove until they reached the Pacific Ocean and Highway 101, which hugged the coastline as it wound toward the Los Angeles area. As the fiery sun sank into the ocean waters, they stopped by the beach in the small town of Laguna. There the two couples sat upon the rocks with the waves lapping up as a full California moon cast its magical light upon them.

Having driven in one rather large circle with a circumference of 228 miles, they arrived back at the young women's apartment at midnight, much later than they were expected. Great Aunt Nannie was waiting for them by the door in her nightgown. The late hour apparently did not diminish the seventy-six year old Nannie's good impression of Jim, for upon her return to Kansas she spoke well of him to Margie's parents. Desert sun and ocean moonlight had worked their romantic magic, for after their Palm Springs excursion, Jim and Margie continued to see each other.

Jim and Margie on a Carmel, California, ocean cliff while on their honeymoon.
(James A. Allen Collection)

The romance moved into high speed. Like many postwar couples, Jim and Margie had a short engagement. Having met on 11 January, they were engaged by Valentine's Day and married Sunday, 7 April 1946. Future high school principal Bill Goodman married elementary teacher Nora Milberger the following Thursday, with each couple participating in the other's bridal party. The friendships continued for another forty-three years, with Jim and Margie still visiting with Nora long after Bill's death in 1989.

Once he was engaged, Jim put a down payment on a small two-bedroom house with part of his $6,000 compensation money. He had done just as he had told his mother he would do before leaving for Wake Island: he owned his own home before he married, something Viola thought was impossible.

With his Uncle Martin's home completed and now a husband and homeowner, Jim returned to his occupation as a carpenter a week after his wedding. He began by working

The Allen Family, May 1952, standing in front of the house Jim built for them in 1950. (James A. & Margie Allen Collection)

on a four-story addition to the already imposing six-story Sears Roebuck warehouse located behind the main store at Olympic and Soto Streets in Los Angeles. With the postwar building boom beginning, there would be plenty of construction work for Jim in the years to come. As time passed, the newly married couple joined thousands of other postwar couples and began to raise a family. Their first child, a son, was born at high noon, appropriately, on Independence Day 1947. A daughter would follow several years later. The postwar "American Dream" era was underway, and Jim and his family were a part of it.

As Jim settled into his new roles as husband and father, there were still ongoing efforts being made toward reparations for him and the other eligible POWs. In the 1950s, The Workers of Wake morphed into a new organization, The Survivors of Wake, Guam and Cavite. Shortly after its inception, Jim became a member. He has remained so ever since paying the few dollars per year dues and attending conventions and get-togethers as often as he can.

Although a surrender agreement had been formally signed, a treaty of peace had yet to be agreed upon between the Allied powers and Japan. Until the expensive occupation of Japan was deemed no longer needed, the drafting of a Japanese Peace Treaty was put off. Finally in September of 1951, a conference was held at which forty-eight of the fifty-one nations attend-

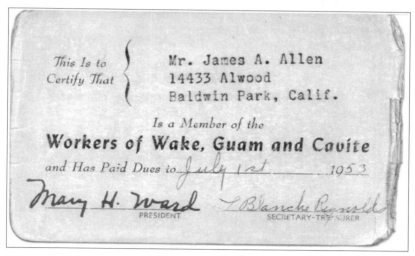

This Is to Certify That

Mr. James A. Allen
14433 Alwood
Baldwin Park, Calif.

Is a Member of the

Workers of Wake, Guam and Cavite

and Has Paid Dues to *July 1st* 1953

Mary H. Ward
PRESIDENT

Blanche Reynold
SECRETARY-TREASURER

May Ward, president of the Workers of Wake, Guam and Cavite, was instrumental in making Congress aware of the civilian POWs' plight during the war and having them receive some of the benefits. (James A. Allen Collection)

ing agreed upon and signed the treaty. It became effective on 28 April 1952.

The treaty allowed for Allied seizure of enemy assets, according to Ernest R. May, an assistant professor of history at Harvard. It also permitted the Allies to keep the assets of specific Japanese citizens. Neutral countries were encouraged to follow suit with Japanese holdings in their countries, using the funds to benefit the former POWs and their families via the International Red Cross. By the middle of the 1950s, through the united effort of the Survivors of Wake, Guam and Cavite and others, Jim and many more civilian ex-POWs received final payment for lost goods, wages, and time. The seized enemy war assets comprised much of the money. "Last check I got for my stay over there was in 1956, two-dollars-a-day for all the time over there" (around $2,700, equal to $16,329.90 in 1999 dollars). Without overtime, potential promotions or the cost of lost tools, clothes, etc., figured in, at two dollars an hour Jim would have earned approximately $17,000 during his years of internment if he had been in the United States. Jim received a total of about $18,000, piecemeal, over a ten-year period ending in 1956.

By the time he had returned home, one-seventh of Jim's life had been spent as a prisoner of the Japanese. But all that time it was as a civilian, not as a member of the United States Armed Forces with its benefits and GI Bill. Jim was not officially recognized for his defense of Wake Island, fighting side-by-side with the active-duty Marines. He was still officially just a bystander in the wrong place at the wrong time. It would be only through a united effort and the tireless leadership of many in the Survivors of Wake, Guam and Cavite and other veteran's groups that the civilian POWs would receive any recognition of their wartime service and sacrifices.

20

The Long Road to Recognition

Many stories, especially those tales that become epics, end with the protagonist's return home from battling and/or slaying whatever foe they many have encountered. In the case of a prisoner of war, the original foe may be defeated, but new foes may emerge to haunt the ex-POW for life. The greatest battle for some individuals only begins with the return to normalcy, or what is generally referred to as normal. For an ex-POW, a normal life is not quite the same. Imprisonment, as well as battle, leaves lasting, yet usually unseen scars upon the individuals. Although the war was over officially in 1945, it would continue to be fought in different ways for the rest of many of the ex-POWs' lives.

Young men like Jim Allen would outwardly recover quickly from their experiences with the availability of plentiful food and rest. But within many of them was a time bomb waiting to go off. And since the Wake Island civilians like Jim were not officially recognized as having served their country during the war, these men were not publicly acknowledged as having done their share to win the war except in their local area by friends and families. After they returned home, few would know of their experience unless it came up in conversation. Although the hard-fought monetary compensation received was welcomed, it could not eliminate the mental and physical damage hidden within the men themselves from the years of starvation, disease, beatings, and horrors that they had endured. No amount of money could make up for the loss of their pre-war physical and mental health or the loss of several years of their lives, and not just the war years, but the years afterward. According to author Gavin Daws in the *Prisoner of the Japanese*, men held as POWs for as long as Jim was, physically aged at a rate faster than the norm. Therefore, when Jim was freed in 1934 at the chronological age of twenty-seven, his body had actually aged closer to that of a man in his mid-thirties.

As the ex-POW reaches old age, the calendar may show eighty years have passed, but his body may actually be closer to ninety-three, a decade or more difference. This means that a POW has been robbed not only of the actual time spent in captivity, but also some of the years in his future.

The missing arms, legs, or other physical scars of war were relatively easy to acknowledge and work with. But the unknown, hidden scars of the psyche are harder to spot and treat. This is not a new phenomenon; emotionally damaged individuals have been common following conflicts throughout history. Previously known by other names such as shell shock, battle fatigue, or even melancholia after the American Civil War, Posttraumatic Stress Disorder (PTSD) is the current psychological term for identifying those individuals who suffer from experiencing extremely traumatizing events. These events can be manmade, such as the 1995 bombing of the Alfred P. Murrah Federal Building in Oklahoma City, car or plane crashes, violent criminal attacks, or wartime experiences. They may be natural disasters such as tornadoes, severe floods, or extreme wind and rainstorms like 1992's Hurricane Andrew. Whatever the stimuli, the lasting imprint of the traumatic event is left burned onto an individual's psyche, becoming a part of who they now are. In the case of a war experience, those friends and family who were never near a battlefront, or as in Jim Allen's case, a Japanese POW Camp, have no clue as to what the affected individuals have truly experienced and continue to experience for the rest of their lives. Since they themselves have not experienced the trauma, family, friends, and coworkers cannot truly understand how their loved one, friend, or coworker's trauma has impacted him/her. They could only listen to stories of events as related by Jim, or other ex-POWs, and try to imagine the fear, brutality, suffering, anxiety, and hardship, falling far short of the real thing. Unsuspecting associates may dismiss the peacetime actions of an ex-POW as eccentric or irritating.

PTSD is insidious in the way it can be hidden in a POW like Jim. The individual is set up for continuing problems, especially if there is not intervention by trained specialists. Jim, for one, struggled for decades with the after-effects of his war experience, especially the visible physical effects of periodic malaria attacks, which sometimes forced him to remain in bed until they abated. He did not realize some of the problems he was experiencing in his work and his personal life were related to his long imprisonment. Young and appearing reasonably healthy, save for his malaria, it was hard to believe that Jim, or others like him, had problems. The years of deprivation and starvation took their toll in different ways for different people. For some, the invisible scars they bore became too much and suicide was their release from the mental imprisonment they were suffering during the years following their 1945 repatriation. Alcohol, drug, or nicotine abuse became other POWs' ways of coping with the anguish they felt.

Unlike the 1990s, mental health therapy during most of the last half of the twentieth century was looked down upon and/or misunderstood by society. Those who needed psychiatrists were construed as being weak or crazy, or both. But the ex-POWs were anything but weaklings after having survived the horrors of living for several years in a prison camp. Jim Allen and other Wake Island defenders were, and are, survivors. But for some, after years of surviving, day to day living became a kind of prison for them.

After Jim returned home, he became very involved with the Carpenters Union Local 1507 in El Monte, California. He served as Business Agent for a short time in the late 1940s and President of his local in the 1950s for a few years. Not knowing much about the politics of these positions, Jim says, "I watched and listened. [I had] a lot to learn." Eventually the associated stress bothered him and forced him to give the positions up. "That's why I had so many employers," says Jim.

Robert C. Carson in the text, *Abnormal Psychology & Modern Life*, writes that individuals who have endured imprisonment in concentration or prisoner of war camps generally have had their ability to handle stress diminished as well as other physical and psychological damage of varying degrees. This is true in Jim's case, especially as he aged. Increased stress in his life became harder and harder for him to deal with. When

Jim returned from Japan, he had money from his reparation checks in the bank. That money served as a buffer, which gave him a bit of independence. If he didn't like the boss of a particular job site, he'd go find another construction job or when the job was finished, he then would move on and find another employer; he worked for sixty-four during his construction career. "Couldn't stand the heat!" is how Jim expresses his moving from job to job during the post-war building boom. As in the POW camps, Jim's leadership ability and carpentry skills propelled him into positions of authority.

However, with its increased responsibility, the stress of being in charge as foreman and eventually construction site superintendent led to more stress, which presented Jim with making a life changing decision based on two choices. He could retire in his fifties with very little to live on, or as he puts it, "end up in a mental institution." Jim chose to retire. Jim's stress reliever became his raised bed vegetable garden. Working at a slow pace, Jim used his considerable construction skills to create twenty-five rectangular reinforced cement containers with apparatus for trellis, shade and irrigation in which to grow hundred of pounds of vegetables, tomatoes especially. During these early years of retirement, the family lived on what Jim grew in his garden. Jim even canned tomatoes for later use just as he had in the Kiangwan camp. Jim would spend hours fixing and fussing over his plants, losing himself in his work while the stressors affecting him were lapsed from consciousness.

Meanwhile, television coverage of the Vietnam War, with its graphic visual reminders of war's horrors, came into "safe" living rooms each evening during the late 1960s and early 1970s, regenerating Jim's prisoner of war memories. This was especially true when he saw the television coverage of Vietnam's POWs being repatriated and rapidly flown home, to their individual detriment, Jim vehemently claims.

For Jim, television's electronic images of Vietnam survivors dredged up many buried memories as the TV images appeared before him or when he read news reports in the daily papers. Mental anguish combined with stress of family responsibilities and work created more stress as Jim struggled with his as yet unrecognized PTSD and physical problems resulting from forty-five months as a prisoner of the Japanese. The effects of his imprisonment were like an invisible brick wall and/or electrified barbed wire fence, surrounding Jim at all

Jim in June 1991, holding the guitar he made in the Shanghai War Prisoners Camp at Kiangwan after it was rebuilt a second time. (Margie Allen)

times, inflicting pain whenever he struggled to cast them off. Worse yet, Jim did not fully realize that this invisible fence continually enveloped him. Neither did those close to him.

What appeared to his family to be a very simple task for the skillful Jim to accomplish could in reality produce an extremely stressful situation. Around 1966, with the era's folk music revival and rock and roll, Jim was pestered by his teenage daughter to repair his guitar so she could learn to play it. Reluctant at first, Jim began the tedious task of cleaning joints of old glue, making repairs and re-gluing his prison camp guitar back together. Although his daughter did learn to play a few chords and simple tunes, it was not easy. Jim had put the guitar back together in such a manner that the bridge left the steel strings misaligned and much too high off the fret board, making it extremely uncomfortable to play. "I didn't have patience enough," Jim says. It would be many more years before Jim would have the free time and ability to cope with putting the guitar back together properly.

The guitar was destined to sit in a corner, silent except for the occasional off-key plunking of young grandchildren, for another twenty-eight years until Jim's teenage grandson pestered him about fixing the guitar. Jim was now retired from the construction profession and working in his stress-relieving garden.

He had much more time at his disposal than he had had when he had put the guitar together for his daughter. Taking the guitar completely apart this time, Jim patiently worked on his creation in an effort to have the pieces fit properly together. His determination to get it right paid off. This second time, the strings now rested at the proper position across the instrument's neck. Also, the guitar was finally given a finish; until now it had been just raw wood. Jim's grandson, an accomplished musician, was able to play it with ease and once again music could be heard from the clandestinely crafted fifty-one year-old guitar.

How does one explain an experience that redefines who you are and why you do things when you yourself do not fully understand why? This is a hard question for anyone to answer, not just a former prisoner of war. Unexpectedly the marriage of Jim's daughter to a Naval aviator while the Vietnam War was being replayed on the nightly news programs broke a dam of some memories long held back. Jim found a strong urging to impart some of his collected POW experience wisdom upon the groom in case he, too, became a prisoner of war in the future, and Jim verbalized what he considered to be important tips for a potential prisoner of war to know. With the passage of additional years and encouragement from family members and others, Jim began to speak more openly about his experiences in a more orderly fashion instead of just the snippets of information that escaped in reference to some current situation present in his family or work life. Still, Jim was caught in a limbo of being an ex-POW but not an ex-serviceman. The lack of recognition of his defense efforts as the reason for his imprisonment only added to his anxiety and stress.

For Jim and many of the defenders of Wake, civilian and military, keeping in contact with each other became a band-aid for their mental anguish. Jim says that he always felt someone was looking out for him during the war as a way of explaining his "luck" at coming through his experiences alive and relatively unscathed, or so it appeared. Whatever constituted Jim's luck remained with him after the war and steered him toward some of the organizations that were forming to help former civilian POWs receive reimbursements for lost tools and wages. These groups kept the ex-POWs in touch with each other and became a therapy of sorts for Jim, allowing him to meet with those who could understand what he was going through and help chase away the ghosts of the past by talking about it.

The Survivors of Wake, Guam and Cavite kept the former POWs in contact, especially through newsletters and reunions. The reminiscing helped Jim release some of the emotional energy that was stored up within him, and drain it away as he talked with other former POWs. Family may never truly know the ex-POW's anguish over his experiences, but those ex-POWs who were at the Survivors of Wake, Guam, and Cavite Conventions did; they comforted each other within the boundaries of America's social codes for men's behavior during the last half of the twentieth century.

The conventions also allowed the ex-POWs to display their humanitarian side and aid those they knew in the war, even if they happened to have been on the other side. In late October 1961 the Survivors of Wake, Guam, and Cavite held their annual convention in Boise, Idaho. During one of the last day's sessions, it was brought to everyone's attention the Japanese doctor at the Woosung, Kiangwan and Fengtai POW camps, Dr. Yoshiro Shindo was in need. Carpenter Kenny Johnson's Air Force brother serving in Japan had located the good doctor living frugally in Tokyo. Dr. Shindo had done all he could for the POWs with what little resources he had. Joseph Astarita immortalized Shindo in one of his drawings, writing the caption, "He did what he could to help us but the high brass had their thumbs on him." According to one of those present at the 1961 convention, Shindo "went by his doctor's principles instead of by the Japanese military." Another attendee recalled that Dr. Shindo "saved a number of the boys' lives. And besides that he was able to restrain the Japanese officers from making things tougher for us." The gratitude for the aid the compassionate doctor had given to his adversaries had not diminished with the passage of time. The Survivors of Wake, Guam and Cavite took up a collection, which they forwarded to Dr. Shindo in Tokyo. Though some might question their action, it was appropriate to the ex-POWs.

Years of work petitioning the government paid off for the Civilian Defenders of Wake Island. The Ninety-fifth Congress once again considered the position of civilians, like Jim, who had helped to defend their country and had not been in a position to be in the American military. Eventually Public Law (PL) 95-202 was placed in effect. Jim and any other civilians who could produce proof of their personal efforts defending the United States of America or its territories were to be declared veterans.

In early 1982, Jim's Naval officer son-in-law informed him of a routine unclassified naval message that had come across his desk referencing PL 95-202. The time had finally come for Jim to be a veteran officially. Jim gathered up all the materials he had saved through the years that could prove his service to his country.

Fortunately, back in the spring of 1946, The Workers of Wake sent out a form letter for the civilian ex-POWs to fill out. The letter stated that the person identified on the document had been an employee of Contractors Pacific Naval Air Bases on Wake Island and "did participate actively in the siege of Wake Island from December 8, 1941 to December 23, 1941." In the space following, the ex-POW was to then write out a description of his service, which Jim did. He also filled in the names of those Marines with whom he served at Battery E. When completed, this testament of service was notarized for future use in gaining recognition for defending their country and on 18 May 1946, Jim did just that. Now, thirty-six years later, the Workers of Wake's forethought aided Jim in his quest for recognition of his service.

Jim also had his *Affidavit of a Recovered Civilian* form he had filled out at the Yokohama docks so long ago as well as a 2 July 1946 letter from now Lieutenant Colonel Wally Lewis who was then assigned to the Command Staff School at Quantico, Virginia. Lewis' letter contained a list of names, including Jim's, of those who were in Battery E under Lewis' command. Additionally, Jim had kept a letter from the now retired Marine Sergeant Tallentire written on 17 August 1971, which affirmed Jim's role on Gun One of Battery E.

Unknown to Jim until many years after it was written, a memo by Colonel James P. S. Devereux, the Commanding Officer of the Marine Detachment on Wake Island, listed James A. Allen as one of fifty-seven civilians who fought alongside the Marines. This was in contrast with the majority of the 1,200 civilian construction workers who did nothing to help out during the entire sixteen-day siege. This memo was dated 13 September 1946, only a year after the surrender agreement was signed in Tokyo Bay. Addressed to "The Board of Awards, Navy Department, Washington, D. C.," the memo concerned the subject of giving those worthy civilians the recognition they merited.

Following the procedures delineated on the Naval message, Jim obtained military form DD2168, application for discharge, from his son-in-law and filled it out along with a *Statement in*

Support of Claim form for the Veterans' Administration. When everything was completed and double-checked, the forms and letters were forwarded to the Department of the Navy's Naval Military Personnel Command in Washington, D.C. for action.

Because of his skill for keeping papers and records, Jim's application for discharge took less than a month for approval. Since the United States Marine Corps is part of the United States Navy, Jim was officially Honorably Discharged from the United States Navy as an E4 Enlisted Man with a specialty rating of Construction Man Third Class. This specialty group is commonly known as Seabees, a nickname for Construction Battalion, or CB. The Seabees were organized after the need for armed construction workers was recognized with the capture of Wake Island. The Seabees were a vital part of the Navy's amphibious assaults during World War II, building landing strips and support bases on South Pacific islands.

As a Navy veteran, Jim's dates of service are recorded as being from 8 December 1941 to 2 October 1945, from the Wake Island Siege to his return to United States soil. On 27 April 1982 Captain W. P. Behning wrote he was, "enclosing the WW II Victory Medal, the American Campaign Medal and the Asiatic Pacific Campaign Medal to which you are entitled by virtue of your active duty naval service, and the Purple Heart medal and Certificate for injuries received in defense of Wake Island." In closing, Behning wrote:

On behalf of your many shipmates, both past and present, I would like to express a long-overdue, sincere thank you for your patriotism, extraordinary service and dedication to the U.S. Navy. By your fighting spirit, courage, and devotion to the common cause in the face of severe personal risk, you have upheld the highest tradition of the United States Naval Service.

Receiving Captain Behning's letter meant a lot to Jim. It signaled the reality of his being an official veteran of World War II, not just a bystander. He had finally reached the end of the long road to recognition. Today Jim proudly displays his medals in a shadow box case on a wall of his home.

On 16 September 1988, Jim received the newly designed Prisoner of War Medal, in a public ceremony hosted by the Jerry L. Pettis Memorial Veterans Hospital and the City of Redlands, Cali-

In July 2000, Jim Allen posed with his medals awarded for his service. (L A. Magnino)

fornia. Held in an outdoor amphitheater under a sunny sky, 283 ex-POWs were honored: 110 from the Pacific Theatre of WW II, 152 from the European Theatre, 15 from the Korean Police Action, and 5 from the Vietnam War. Those present were addressed by then California Senator Pete Wilson. Representatives of the United States Navy, Marines, Army, and Air Force presented the Prisoner of War Medals to the ex-POWs for their "honorable service while a prisoner."

Encircled by barbed wire, an eagle stands proud and defiant in the center of the Prisoner of War Medal. He is "alert for the opportunity to seize hold of beloved freedom," according to designer Jay Morris of the U. S. Army's Institute of Heraldry. Proud definitely applied to Jim that late summer evening when he received his medal from Admiral Higginbee, the Navy's representative for the occasion. The last "sailor" to receive the medal that night, Jim "seized the opportunity" and bowed low, Japanese style, to the admiral. It was Jim's way of symbolically bringing the past and present together visually. With an impish grin upon his face, Jim joined the rest of those present in laughter.

Since he was now officially a veteran, the sixty-four year-old Jim became eligible for Veterans Administration (VA) benefits. For Jim, who was on the small fixed income of his carpenter's pension and Social Security, this was a beneficial bonus. "Like winning the lottery," Jim has said. Before the award, health care costs were a problem for Jim and Margie. Many of the physical problems that Jim had suffered from since the 1940s were found to be related to his prison camp experience, including some loss of feeling and tiredness in his legs, back problems, and general fatigue. Receiving help from the Veterans Hospital has extended Jim's life by several years with the expert care administered by those knowledgeable of POW injuries, both physical and mental.

A dark cloud that passed over Jim in 1995 tempered the excitement of being an official veteran. While in West Virginia for his oldest grandchild's graduation from Bethany College, Jim experienced an odd weakening sensation and felt the need to lie down. Feeling fine later in the day, Jim dismissed the episode as his excitement and pride for his granddaughter.

Shortly afterward, while at the VA hospital for a scheduled routine check up, a heart problem was noted and a series of tests conducted. Another hidden effect of imprisonment was finally identified. Jim was suffering from the residual effects of beri beri, a legacy of his poor POW diet, which lacked thiamine, commonly known as vitamin B1 and is not found in white rice. Over a prolonged period of time, problems with one's heart, nerve, or brain function can occur without vitamin B1 in the diet. The POW years of eating a mainly white rice diet had taken their toll silently, undetected until now. Jim was told his heart was ischemic; part of the heart muscle was no longer functioning because of an insufficient blood supply. His heart was pumping around thirty-five percent output. "Part of my heart is dead," is the way Jim simply puts it. This could lead to a heart attack if not properly cared for and was also a cause of his fatigue. Jim claims that many fortunate things have happened to him in his life, but he says he really is fortunate for the great care and attention he has received from the Jerry L. Pettis Veterans Hospital in Loma Linda, California. "The VA has been like I hit a jackpot in Las Vegas," Jim says.

The VA Hospital has also given Jim an outlet for his people skills. A volunteer once a week at the hospital, Jim talks with other POW's waiting for appointments to help ease their stress or answer questions. He also participates in group discussions once a month with other World War II POWs associated with the Veterans' Hospital in Loma Linda. Always helpful, Jim has aided others in their quest for benefits by looking up information and explaining forms. His association with the VA hospital has also helped renew old friendships and acquaintances with other Wake Island defenders who came to the Loma Linda hospital for treatment.

It has been said that time heals all wounds, and by 1985 the Marines did not begrudge the civilians their role in Wake Island history. That year the Wake Island Marines had a reunion in Buena Park, California, and the Wake civilians were graciously invited to attend. At this time his invalid mother-in-law required his help with her care. Yet, so strong was the urge to see his comrades in arms, the sixty-five year-old Jim willingly traveled the seventy-mile round trip from his home for each day's session. Although only thirty-five-miles one way, the trip could take up to two hours in the congested Southern California traffic. Jim's family by now had become much more understanding and appreciative of what the ex-POW had been through and wanted to share some of the convention's activities with him, although it was physically difficult for his mother-in-law in her wheelchair. With pleasure, Jim drove his round trip twice on the day of the convention's banquet in order for his wife and mother-in-law to also attend the evening's festivities.

Prior to being better restored in 1994, Jim's Kiangwan camp guitar did have one quick excursion out of its corner, for old times' sake. During one afternoon of the convention, Jim remembers, "why up on the sundeck at the Holiday Inn, why they were up there, the Marines and there were officers and GIs, enlisted men. They were everywhere, even Devereux was there." The lieutenant for whom Jim had volunteered to practice on the five-inch gun while working on Wake Island, Clarence "Barney" Barninger, now a retired lieutenant colonel, was there with his wife. Jim met with them and as a result of their conversation, left to go to his car, returning shortly with his prison camp guitar that he had carefully stowed away in the trunk. Jim placed the guitar face down on the table in front of himself and the Barningers. Jim asked if Barninger recognized his and Wally Lewis' old table from their barracks at the Kiangwan camp. While they continued to reminisce about the past, Mrs. Barninger and the two ex-POWs placed their drinks on the raw wood back of the guitar, using it like a table. "It would have been great if Lieutenant Lewis [now Lieutenant Colonel Lewis] had of been there with his spouse," says Jim. "It'd been great. It would have been perfect. Wasn't to be, I guess. [Have] to be satisfied with what I had."

While at the same reunion, the Wake Island Civilian Defenders were asked to join the United States Marines in nearby Costa Mesa as guests of Wake's old fighter squadron. VMF-211, then stationed at the El Toro Marine Air Station (now closed), invited the survivors to witness a memorial ceremony honoring those who defended Wake Island. The commanding officer at the time, Lieutenant Colonel Jeff McAnally, was the son of Marine Corporal Winford J. McAnally who was stationed on Wake Island in Decem-

The Wake Island Marines & Civilians posed in 1985 in front of an F6 fighter plane, similar to the one flown by VMF 211 in 1941. Jim Allen is on the far right, standing. Jim identified Lieutenant Tharin (now General, retired) in the back row by writing his name in. (James A. Allen Collection)

ber 1941, and subsequently became a prisoner. The men, as well as their wives, were honored guests and a photograph on the flight line with a vintage F-6 aircraft was taken to mark the occasion. It had been 15,279 days since they had left Wake Island according to Rudy Slezak, who had been at Battery E Gun One with Jim.

As the years have passed and more people have become aware of the Civilian Defenders of Wake Island, Jim and his peers have been invited as guests to witness various ceremonies and memorials. Not long after becoming a veteran officially, for example, Jim and others who were attending a Survivors of Wake, Guam, and Cavite reunion in San Diego were invited to attend a graduation ceremony at the nearby Marine Corps Recruit Depot. After the main graduation ceremonies, there was a dedication of a bronze plaque, which was inscribed as follows:

> DEDICATED TO THOSE
> MARINES, SAILORS AND
> SOLDIERS WHO DIED IN
> THE HEROIC DEFENSE OF
> WAKE ISLAND AND IN
> PRISON CAMPS. AND TO
> THOSE WHO SURVIVED.
>
> DECEMBER 8, 1941
> TO
> SEPTEMBER 2, 1945

Jim Allen standing in front of the newly dedicated bronze plaque for the Wake Island Defenders. (James A. Allen Collection)

Now as true veterans, Jim and the other Wake Island Defenders were included in the inscription. But some Wake Island Marines, claims Jim, didn't always look favorably upon the civilians and felt they were the reason the island was surrendered. "Lots of the Marines have changed their attitude [toward the Wake civilians] over the years," says Jim. Originally, "They were angry about having civilians on Wake Island. They were brainwashed; they would have fought to the death!" save for having the hundreds of civilians with them on the atoll. The United States Marines were, in Jim's opinion, as "Bad as the Japanese! [The Marines] were bad then [about continuing to fight while overwhelmingly outnumbered], but they were well trained — they knew what they were doing," Jim emphasizes, of their skill in combat.

A sentimental journey was in store for Jim and approximately fifty Defenders of Wake Island, military and civilian, in November 1985. The men, along with wives, relatives, and friends, made a pilgrimage to the tiny atoll on a chartered DC-8 flight from Honolulu. This time Wake was first spied through a plane window instead of from sea level on the deck of a ship. As the plane flew closer, the lighter azure blue lagoon in the heart of the coral atoll stood out in contrast to the darker blue of the Pacific's water. From the air, the surf of the coral reef appeared like a lacy necklace around the three tiny islets of the atoll. Upon arrival, the first obvious change noticed on the island was the vegetation. Tall palm trees and Australian pines were thick in contrast to 1941's short, scrubby brush. Jim and the others, including Marines Rudy Slezak, Robert Curry, and civilian Albert L. Brueck found only ruins where warehouses, gun emplacements, and barracks stood. Newer buildings stood by the runway, which was owned and operated now by the U.S. Air Force. Although only on Wake Island for an overnight stay, it was long enough for ceremonies and for the civilians to create a new memorial made of a concrete slab and decorated with the ever-plentiful coral. In the wet cement was written with a stick:

The Wake Island Civilians' 1985 memorial. (Al Brueck/James A. Allen Collection)

CIVILIAN WORKERS OF WAKE 12 –23 – 41.

The day's date, 11-4-85, was written in the lower left-hand corner of the cement slab. The new memorial represented not only those in 1941, but the survivors who made it back to the spot where their lives began a much different journey from the one they had planned and looked forward to.

While not planning another return trip to the Wake atoll, the Survivors of Wake, Guam and Cavite still come together formally each year, but with fewer members. Many widows continue to attend, but some of the Survivors are no longer able to make a several hundred-mile journey. Jim made it to Boise, Idaho for the fortieth reunion in 1998, but was unable to travel the following year. As the ranks thin, those still in attendance carry on for their absent shipmates.

Slow in coming, the recognition of what Jim and the other POWs sacrificed for other Americans, has been validated in the last few years. The recognition of what those in World War II did was increasingly recognized in the 1990s as the twentieth century wound down. Many, young and old alike, have finally been able to cast aside the guilt of Vietnam and appreciate the veterans of all conflicts for the service they performed. It may not have been just or right; it may have been cruel, horrible, or chaotic; it may have had meaning and purpose and then again, it may not. But for whatever reason, the common veteran, military or civilian, did go on and perform their duty in a time of need, and for that alone, they should be hon-

The returning Wake Island Survivors & Defenders look through the barred doorway into one of the deteriorating ammunition bunkers, the thick cement baffle still in place protecting the entrance. It was to one of these bunkers the hospital was moved during the siege and where Jim Allen and other POWs were first held by the Japanese, 23 December 1941. (Al Brueck/James A. Allen Collection)

ored as a valued member of our society. One only realizes the true value of something after it has been lost. This is especially true of freedom. For those who have never lost their freedom, or had their freedom challenged, they can never truly appreciate its worth.

Wake Island was a pivotal point in Jim Allen's life. Increments of time are measured before and after Wake Island and later expanded to before and after prison camp. Jim's POW experiences reshaped his persona, his being, influencing everything in his life from that point onward. Jim is still on his journey, but traveling at a much slower pace. Still an avid reader and lifelong learner, he says he's too old to use the GI Bill for college classes, but he continues to learn from life. Jim strongly promotes education like his mother before him. Although Viola died in 1961, her education legacy continues. Three grandchildren and seven great-grandchildren have received undergraduate and/or

The ex-POWs present at the 1998 reunion pose for their annual group photograph. Jim Allen is seated in the front row, the third man from the right. The woman on the far left is Lena Swanson, an attorney "who has helped many a POW get benefits and their widows Dependent Indemnity Compensation," claims Jim. "Sweetheart of the POWs," she is considered part of their group. (Karen Miner/James A. Allen Collection)

graduate degrees. Since several of the great grandchildren are still quite young, there is the possibility of still more in the future.

Perhaps because Jim remembers what it was like to be stripped naked with nothing to claim as his own but what was stored in his mind, education is important to him. He tells the young to keep their eyes and ears open and their mouths shut and learn as much as they can because they never know when all they'll have is what's in their head.

Even in his eighties, Jim continues to do what he can to help others, young and old, learn more as he always has, though not always in conventional ways. In December 1999, encouraged by his only grandson, Jim participated in an on-line education program, being interviewed and featured on the California Department of Education website *SCORE.Rims.k12.ca.us* "Memoirs of a POW." With the aid of technology, a younger generation has learned more about World War II as well as Jim's personal tale. Ready to encourage further learning, Jim thoughtfully answered questions by e-mail asked by students at all grade levels. Questions were also posed to him by adult Internet users, including a woman whose grandfather and uncle had also been civilian workers on Wake Island.

The interest in the Second World War by younger generations has heartened Jim and other ex-POWs. Perhaps what they experienced served a purpose for others to learn from and their service and sacrifices won't be forgotten as the years, and men, slip away.

Jim's survivor spirit carries him on. He continues to live life to the best of his ability, just as he always told his children and their children to do, finding alternative routes when his current pathway is blocked. Reflecting on his long journey through life as he began its eighth decade, Jim summarized it this way: "Traveling through life's minefields, of which there are many, I've managed to not step on any yet. I've been very fortunate."

Epilogue

This book is one that doesn't seem to want to end. With each new conversation I have with a Wake Island civilian ex-POW, I learn about many more interesting stories from those who experienced them. There is so much more to tell than the pages of one book can hold.

I had the pleasure of joining the Survivors of Wake, Guam and Cavite for their reunion in September 2000. Many of the men, along with even more family members, made the trek to Reno, Nevada, in order to see their fellow survivors once more. Not all could make it, but 200 people did attend. One ex-POW was in an accident on his way to the reunion and announcements were made as to where he was and that he and his wife were both fine, but going home.

Another gentleman was taken ill outdoors in the extreme Nevada summer heat and taken to a hospital. It was feared he would not be joining the other Survivors at the banquet that evening, but it takes a lot to keep a Wake Island Survivor down. He arrived at the banquet only a few minutes late as the president of the group was lamenting his absence to those in attendance. A round of applause and cheers greeted the latecomer.

But there is so much more to tell. Like the radio made from spare parts and stolen earphones. Former prisoner of war Oral Nichols recalls listening to radio station KGI San Francisco for an hour the Sunday after he stole the earphones from the Japanese offices he worked in. The American voices made home seem not quite as far away or out of reach with thousands of miles of ocean in between. Another ex-POW, Charles Nokes, told of traveling uncomfortably in a boxcar on the journey to Japan. He passed some of the time by counting the tunnels the train passed through in Korea — 108. These are little mundane, insignificant things to family, friends, or acquaintances, but they are incredibly significant to an ex-POW. This is especially true when positive things to remember are hard to come by as you spent each minute wondering if death waited to greet you around the next corner.

These stories go on and on and all deserve to be told. But if they can't be written down, hopefully someone will listen and appreciate what the speaker had to endure then, and during the ensuing years after, to be able to tell the stories now.

We must search ". . . the Library of Our Minds to find information!" — Charlie Nokes

Miscellaneous Notes

Jim Allen was not the first prisoner of war in his family. Unknown to him until recent years, his great grandfather, Private Hiram Chittenden Allen of the 8th Cavalry of Illinois, was a prisoner of the Confederate Army when he was captured in Mississippi during the spring of 1863. Private Allen was repatriated a month later just outside of Richmond, Virginia. He continued to serve the Union until the end of the Civil War.

Chapter 4

During the first attack on the Wake atoll, the Japanese planes were from Air Attack Force 1, which was a part of the Twenty-fourth Air Flotilla. These land-based bombers were from the Marshall Island of Roi, which lay 720 miles south of the tiny Wake atoll. According to Heinl in his book, *The Defense of Wake*, Air Attack Force 1 was later joined by Air Attack Force 3, a squadron of four-engined bombers based on Majuro, another Marshall Island, 840 miles to the south of Wake.

During the 23 December 1941 landing preparations, planes from the Japanese carriers *Soryu* and *Hiryu* participated in the softening up of Wake prior to the landing of Japanese troops. These were the same planes that had participated in the bombing of Pearl Harbor.

On the night of 9 December, Battery E was moved 600 yards to the Northeast of its original location on Peacock

Point. The move, which included not only the four large an-
tiaircraft guns and the stockpiled ammunition, but also all
the sandbags that were used for entrenchment, took all night.
The working party finally finished at 0500 the next morning
as dawn was breaking.

According to Heinl, it was at 0800 on 23 December that
Major Devereux "moved southward down the shore road to
deliver Wake to the Japanese enemy." It was shortly after that
when Jim and the Battery E men would have met up with
Devereux. However, the fighting, which began around 0230
would continue for another five-and-one-half hours before the
last defenders on Wilkes Island surrendered at 1330.

Chapter 5

Two ammunition bunkers became hospitals during the
siege of the Wake atoll. Each had twenty-one beds. The makeshift hospitals were on either end of the row of ammo bunkers, which were located along the eastern shore of Wake Island proper. Civilian Dr. Shank oversaw the northern bunker,
while Navy Dr. Kahn attended those in the Southern bunker.
Each bunker, a Quonset hut shape covered with earth, was
twenty feet wide by forty feet long with a height of fifteen feet
on the centerline.

"The main reason for the fall of Wake seemed obvious
at the time, and remains so: the enemy in greatly
superior strength, supported by ample surface and air
forces, was able to effect a lodgment on Wake and then
to apply his ground superiority so as to overwhelm the
defenders at any and virtually all given points. Had it
been possible at any time for United States surface
forces to intervene, or for substantial reinforcements
to reach Wake, the results might have been entirely
different." (Lt. Colonel R. D. Heinl, Jr., *The Defense of
Wake*)

Chapter 7

As a POW Jim Allen had several nicknames including
Honcho after he was made supervisor of the Carpenter Shop.
But according to ex-POW T. Truman Cope at the Survivor's of
Wake, Guam and Cavite's 2000 Reunion, Jim's best nickname
was "Knowledge."

Thirty-six men were assigned to Barracks 4 Section 4. Of those POWs who were assigned there, only nineteen names can be recalled:

"Pop" Albertoni (steelworker), James A. Allen, Faye Belnap, Orville Berry (carpenter), Earl Burge, Joe Cope, H. T. Cope, T. Truman Cope, Ray Forseyth, Gene Henderson, Frank Mace, Homer May (trucker), Carl Nelles, Oral Nichols, Forest Packard, Edgar Peres, Pete Perrine, Arnold Robinson, Les Turner.

Chapter 8
Entrepreneur Jimmy James had lived in the Shanghai area for many years after his discharge from the United States Army in December 1922. He had owned several businesses in China over the years, including several restaurants. On 3 March 1943, two-and-one-half months after the POW Christmas dinner he provided to Jim Allen and the others of the Shanghai War Prisoners' Camp at Kiangwan, the Japanese interned Jimmy James in the Chapei Camp. Located five miles to the west of Shanghai, James remained there until the war's end two-and-one-half years later in August 1945. Jimmy James was back at his businesses immediately. While on a trip to the United States in November 1948, James lost all his holdings in China when the communist regime took over during his absence.

Chapter 9
Leo Patrick Driscoll, for whom the first grave marker cross was crafted at the Carpenter Shop, was also on the S. S. *Matsonia* voyage to Honolulu with Jim Allen.

Chapter 12
There apparently was a second secret radio at Kiangwan operated by the civilian POWs. Supposedly, it was used in the attic of the hospital and hidden in the ward below in the thick bandages of one of the patients.

Chapter 16
According to the *Encyclopedia of World War II*, volume 22, page 3014), during the final planning for the delivery of the second atom bomb on 9 August 1945, Niigata was decreed too far off for the planes carrying the nuclear payload. The south-

ern Honshu city of Kokura was designated the target instead with Nagasaki as the backup.

Chapter 20

At the 2000 Reunion of the Survivors of Wake, Guam and Cavite a group picture was not taken as was done in the past. The increasingly smaller group picture each year is a grim reminder of how time is passing.

Appendices

Jim Allen's Log of World War II Travels
— as remembered and recorded by him —

	1941	
Sailed from Port of Los Angeles, San Pedro, California	September 11	1:30 PM
Arrived in San Francisco, California	September 12	7:00 AM
Sailed from San Francisco, California	September 12	5:00 PM
Arrived in Honolulu, Territory of Hawaii (T.H.)	September 17	8:00 AM
Sailed from Honolulu, T. H.	September 19	10:30 AM
Arrived at Wake Island, T. H.	September 30	3:00 PM
Began working on Wake Island, T.H.	October 1	7:00 AM
Quit working on Wake Island, T.H.	December 8	Noon
Became a prisoner of war	December 23	10:00 AM
	1942	
Sailed from Wake Island, T.H.	January 12	11:00 AM
Arrived in Yokohama/Tokyo Bay	January 17	unknown
Sailed from Yokohama/Tokyo Bay,	January 20	unknown
Arrived and sailed from Shanghai, China	January 23	unknown
Arrived at Woosung, China	January 24	3:00 PM
Arrived at Woosung War Prisoner's Camp	January 24	5:30 PM
Left Woosung War Prisoner's Camp	December 3	1:00 PM
Arrived at Kiangwan War Prisoner's Camp	December 3	5:00 PM

	1945	
Left Kiangwan War Prisoner's Camp	May 9	5:30 AM
Arrived Fengtai, China & Fengtai (Transit) Camp	May 14	Noon
Left Fengtai Camp	June 19	6:00 AM
Arrived at Fusan, Chosen (Pusan, Korea) (Transit) Camp	June 23	6:00 AM
Left Fusan Camp	June 27	11:00 PM
Sailed from Fusan, Chosen	June 28	6:00 AM
Arrived Susa, Japan	June 28	4:00 PM
Left ferryboat at Susa, Japan	June 29	1:00 PM
Left Susa, Japan	June 30	8:00 AM
Arrived at Shimonseki, Japan	June 30	3:00 PM
Left Shimonseki, Japan	June 30	8:00 PM
Arrived at Niigata, Japan	July 2	9:00 PM
Left Niigata, Japan	September 5	9:00 PM
Arrived in Tokyo, Japan	September 6	
Arrived in Yokohama, Japan, liberated, ex-POW	September 6	9:00 AM
Boarded U.S.S. Ozark	September 6	8:00 PM
Sailed from Yokohama, Japan	September 8	11:00 AM
Arrived at U.S. Navy Fleet Hospital 103, Guam	September 12	10:30 AM
Left Fleet Hospital 103	September 16	8:00 AM
Sailed from Guam on U.S.S. Ozark	September 17	6:30 AM
Crossed the International Date Line, heading east	September 22 now September 21	
Arrived Pearl Harbor, T.H.	September 25	12:30 PM
Sailed from Pearl Harbor, T.H.	September 26	12:30 PM
Arrived San Francisco, California	October 2	9:00 AM

S.S. MATSONIA

...*Cabin Class*...

★ SOUVENIR PASSENGER LIST ★

Sailing from San Francisco to Honolulu
September 12, 1941 at 5:00 p.m.

SHIP'S OFFICERS

CAPTAIN FRANK A. JOHNSON, U.S.N.R., Commander

F. E. DIGGS, U.S.N.R., Chief Officer

G. R. GRONVOLD, U.S.N.R., Chief Engineer

G. V. NOYES, Asst. Chief Engineer

C. L. CHRISTIAN, Chief Steward

H. L. SCHURTZ, Executive Chef

L. E. THOMPSON, Cabin Class Steward

W. B. HODGKINSON, Chief Purser

E. H. LUNDGREN, Senior Asst. Purser

W. J. MATSON, Cabin Class Purser

E. N. TURKUS, Surgeon

Adams, Mrs. Dorothy
Adams, Mr. James O.
Alapa, Mrs. Tamar
Allen, Mr. James A.
Ambrose, Mr. J.
Ambrose, Mrs. J.
Ambrose, Master Dennis P.
Ambrose, Master John F.
Ambrose, Master James E.
Andrew, Mrs. Mary Ann
Andrus, Mr. Verdun
Arledge, Mr. Arthur E.
Arledge, Mrs. Clara B.
Atkins, Mr. Robert F.

Bahruth, Mr. Clarence R.
Bailey, Miss Mary Elizabeth
Bair, Mr. Guy J.
Bartlett, Mr. Ray W.
Bickford, Mr. Donald D.
Blakeney, Miss Earline
Bowman, Mr. Howard L.
Boyrie, Mr. F. Y.
Boyrie, Mrs. F. Y.
Brause, Mrs. Walter
Brechbiel, Mrs. Wayne
Brentin, Mr. A.
Brickner, Mr. Francis
Bromilow, Miss Barbara
Brown, Miss Barbara
Brown, Mr. Fred C.
Bryant, Mr. R. E.
Bryant, Mrs. R. E.
Bryant, Miss Barbara Jean

Cameron, Lt. Col. H. F.
Campbell, Master James S.

Cannon, Mrs. Glen
Cantry, Mr. Charles A.
Casteel, Mrs. H. A.
Casteel, Miss Donna Belle
Casteel, Mstr. Vernon Meade
Chenot, Mr. Harry E.
Chew, Mr. Buck T.
Ching, Mr. Henry K.
Ching, Mr. W. C.
Ching, Mrs. W. C.
Chin, Mr. Wing Fong
Cho, Mr. Edward
Chong, Mr. Francis Paul
Christy, Mr. Arthur W.
Chuck, Mr. Kam C.
Chung, Mr. Allan
Clark, Mrs. C.
Clark, Miss C.
Clubb, Mr. William F.
Cornwall, Miss Dorothy
Crittenden, Mrs. Cleo
Crogan, Mr. Robert L.
Culter, Mr. Douglas M.

Dailey, Miss Gayle
Dean, Mr. Glen D.
Dean, Miss Peggy
De Coito, Mr. Lionel
Delap, Mr. Wesley F.
Dilly, Mrs. Dyann
Divin, Mr. Fred J.
Dole, Miss Priscilla M.
Drake, Mrs. Elena
Driscoll, Mr. Leo P.

Eilers, Miss Clemence M.
Elder, Mrs. W. C.

Eugenio, Mr. Antone
Eugenio, Mrs. Antone
Evans, Mrs. James G.
Evans, Mr. Clifford A.

Faulkner, Mr. Theodore Alvin
Fisher, Miss Betty
Fong, Mr. Ginn S.
Fredrickson, Mr. Melvin C.

Gage, Mr. Ivan
Gantt, Mr. L.
Gerard, Mr. Morris K.
Giddings, Mrs. Edith
Glasscock, Mr. Charles W.
Glenamen, Mr. Francis D.
Goembel, Mr. Clarence E.
Grant, Miss Marion
Gregory, Mr. Bert D.
Gunnerud, Mr. H. F.
Gunnerud, Master Robert
Gushiva, Mr. Frank

Haas, Mrs. A.
Hanson, Mr. Carl E.
Hartman, Mr. Edward
Helms, Mr. L. J.
Hemphill, Mr. Clyde F.
Henderson, Mr. Charles
Hillyard, Mrs. H. S.
Hobart, Mrs. May F.
Hom, Mr. You Sang
Hormann, Mr. Bernhard L.
Hormann, Mrs. Bernhard L.
Hormann, Miss Pauline
Hormann, Miss Sylvia
Hulick, Mr. Charles W.

Huschke, Mrs. R.
Huschke, Miss L.

Ishimoto, Mr. Hisao

Jader, Mr. Gust A.
Jakobsen, Mr. Oscar D.
Jaouen, Mr. Y. M.
Jaouen, Mrs. Y. M.
Jee, Mr. Nee Pon
Johnson, Mr. Chuck
Johnson, Miss Patricia
Johnson, Miss Tillie
Joos, Mr. C. F.

Kasper, Miss A.
Knight, Mrs. Stewart
Knight, Miss Janice Louise
Kosasa, Mr. Neil

Landa, Mr. Daniel
Lee, Mr. Ben Y.
Leong, Mr. Mon
Lim, Mr. On
Lindstrom, Mrs. Madeline T.
Loomis, Mr. Charles
Lowman, Mr. Joe L.
Lyons, Mrs. Eulalie M.
Lyons, Miss Lois E.
Lythgoe, Mr. Gene

MacKay, Dr. Donald C. G.
MacKay, Mrs. Donald C. G.
Mackinga, Mr. Allen B.
Maddock, Mr. Bill
Malle, Miss Joyce
Mallery, Mr. Ray F.
Manjarrez, Mr. Joseph W.
Marr, Mr. William G.
Marsh, Mr. Benjamin J.
Marsh, Mr. John
Mark, Mrs. Nora
Marriott, Miss Margaret
Martin, Mr. George
Martin, Mr. Tony
Massey, Mr. Garlin
McCombs, Mrs. Ruby H.
McDonald, Miss Jessie E.
McGlochlin, Mr. Richard
McIntosh, Mr. Robert
McKim, Mr. James C.
McMorrow, Miss Catherine
    Teresa
McMurphy, Mr. P. E.
McQuitty, Mr. Frank L.
Merchant, Mrs. H. W.
Merritt, Mrs. J. A.
Merritt, Master John Gilbert
Messner, Miss Pearl
Michael, Mr. Theodore
Moore, Mr. Charles A.
Moore, Mrs. Charles A.

Moore, Master Charles A., Jr.
Morimoto, Mr. Akira
Motada, Mr. Francis
Munroe, Mrs. Anne M.

Nead, Mr. Ralph E.
Neblett, Mr. N. H.
Neil, Mr. Chas. H.
Newhart, Mr. Dencil M.
Nicholas, Miss Pearl
Nichols, Miss Wylma
Nokes, Mr. Charles H.

Ockel, Mr. William R.
O'Neal, Mr. John H.
Ortendahl, Mr. Leonard L.

Pallette, Mr. D. B.
Penner, Mr. Omer A.
Peschke, Mrs. Mary E.
Pittman, Mrs. Velma
Polinsky, Mr. Alex E.
Porter, Mrs. Howard L.
Porter, Master Allan
Porter, Master Glenn
Porter, Mr. Richard
Purcell, Miss Helen

Ralston, Mr. Doris L.
Reynolds, Mrs. H.
Rice, Mr. Frank W.
Rich, Mr. Stewart C.
Rich, Mrs. Stewart C.
Richards, Miss Ruth
Riddle, Mrs. Mae
Riffel, Mr. John H.
Roberts, Mrs. Charlotte
Roberts, Master Donald
Robinson, Mr. Jackie
Roth, Mr. Fred P.
Rovitzky, Miss Ethel
Rucker, Mr. Raleigh K.
Rudinger, Mr. Richard
Ryan, Miss Margaret

Sacks, Dr. Norman
Samuel, Mrs. T. W.
Sanders, Mr. Harry
Sappington, Mr. Clinton
Scarper, Miss Ruby
Schumacher, Mrs. William J.
Seaman, Mr. John James
Shafer, Mr. Fred H.
Shellhart, Mr. Cleighton C.
Shields, Mr. Hugh J.
Short, Miss Helen E.
Slover, Mr. Allen L.
Smith, Mr. Eugene
Smith, Mr. John N.
Smith, Mrs. John N.
Starnes, Mr. Elie R.
Steele, Mrs. Warren L.

Stegemann, Mr. Joseph J.
Steggs, Mrs. Madeline
Stiglic, Mr. Frank
Spurlin, Mr. William D.
Suey, Mr. Jack Young
Swanson, Mr. Norman
Sylvester, Mrs. F. M.

Taylor, Miss Emily
Tebo, Mr. Judd
Terrell, Mrs. W. R.
Terrell, Miss Jean
Thompson, Mr. Glenn H.
Truy, Mr. Joseph D.

Verbarg, Miss Frieda
Volberg, Mrs. Kathryn Ludloff
Volberg, Master Harold
Volberg, Mr. Herman William

Wagner, Mr. Lloyd A.
Walden, Mr. Glenn C.
Walters, Mr. Kenneth
Ward, Mr. William C.
White, Mr. David K.
White, Mr. Raymond
Wieler, Mr. Paul E.
Williams, Mrs. Anne
Williams, Mr. Donald M.
Williams, Mr. Lloyd H.
Wilson, Mr. Kenneth L.
Wong, Miss Irene
Woods, Mr. Charles
Woods, Mr. Charles E.
Wong, Mr. Bing S.
Wong, Mr. Chin C.
Wong, Mr. Kwok H.
Wong, Mr. Thyn
Wong, Mr. Yin
Woody, Mr. Taylor
Woody, Mrs. Taylor
Wright, Mr. Norman J.

Yuan, Mr. Quock J.

Contractors Pacific Naval Air Bases
CPNAB

W.A.Bechtel Company of San Francisco, CA
Byrne Organization, Norfolk, VA
Hawaiian Dredging Company, Limited, Honolulu, T.H.
Morrison Knudsen Company, Incorporated, Boise, ID
J.H. Pomeroy and Company, Incorporated, San Francisco, CA
Raymond Concrete Pile Company, New York, NY
Turner Construction Company, New York, NY
The Utah Construction Company, San Francisco, CA

Pacific Island Work Sites

Guam
Hawaii
Johnston
Midway
Palmyra
The Philippines
Samoa
Wake

U. S. CIVILIAN POWs
EXECUTED BY JAPANESE
Oct. 7, 1943

Cyrus Abbott
Horace Allen
Norman Anderson
Roland Andre
Allen Anwick
Carl Alfred Baasch
George Bellanger
Don Bowcutt
David M. Boyce
Charles Cantry #
Stanley A. Carlson
Allen Cavanagh
David Chambers
Donley Chard
Carleton Church
Louis Cormier
Karl Cox
David Cummings
James Cunha
Joseph Davis
George Dean
Harold Dobyns
Martin Dogger
Henry Dreyer
Joseph Dunn
Jack Fenex
Howard Flint
Glen Fontes
Floyd Forsberg *
Dale Francis
Albert French
Lawrence G. Froberger
William Gerdin

Charles A. Gibbs
Clarence Goembel
Ralph Haight
William Haines
John Vernon Hansen
George Harris
Wilbur Harvey
Frank Hastie
Howard Hettick
Ernest Hochstein
George Jenson
Alfred Jones
Ora Keeler
Martin Kelly
Tom Kennedy
Charles Kidwell
Woodrow Kroeger
Rolland Light
Henry Ling
Gene Lythgoe
Irving Marshall
John Martin
James McDaniel
Tom McInnes
Frank Migacz
Melvin Migacz
Irwin Miller
Howard Mitchell
Wayne Mitchell
Joseph Mittendorf
Carl Mueller
Richard Myers
Cliff Olmstead

Gordon Pease
Archie Pratt
Donald Preston
Morton Rankin
William H. Ray
William Reynolds
Sheldon Robbins
Charles Schemel
Herman Schottler
Lawton E. Shank, M.D.
Orbin R. Shepard
Glenwood Sherman
Gould Shriner
Russell J. Sigman
William Simpers
Charles Smith
Francis St. John
Willis Stone
Alvin Streblow
Wesley Stringer
Arthur J. Susee
Leroy F. Tart
Glenn Thompson
Karl E. Tucker
Vernon Vancil
Ralph Van Valkenburg
Glen Vent
Charles Villines
Frank E. Williamson
Redmond Wilper
Charles Woods
Harry Yuen

— One of Jim Allen's cabinmates on the *Matsonia*
* — One of the Battery E Gun One volunteers

The names of the 98 civilian prisoners who never left Wake Island as
they are inscribed on a memorial located on Wake.

REGULATIONS COVERING TRANSFER OF PRISONERS

1. Any disobedience of orders issued by Japanese Authorities during this transfer will result in strict punishment.

2. Prisoners must keep as quiet as possible and engage in conversation only when absolutely necessary.

3. In case of unexpected accident, prisoners must follow orders given by those in charge as quickly and quietly as possible. Anyone disobeying at this time will be shot.

4. Company Leaders and Section Leaders will be in complete charge, under the Japanese, and must be obeyed without hesitation.

5. Prisoners must salute all Japanese Military men.

REGULATIONS ON BOARD SHIP

1. Prisoners must not go outside of assigned areas.

2. Prisoners must smoke only at assigned place and not walk around with lighted cigarettes in mouth or hands.

3. Prisoners are not allowed to touch fixtures or any device without permission.

4. Prisoners will go on deck only at specified time and then to specified place.

5. Company Leaders and Section Leaders are responsible for the cleanliness of rooms, which are to be kept clean at all times.

6. Company Leaders must report any case of sickness or accident to the Authorities as soon as possible.

7. Do not waste water at any time and do not drink water other than that issued for drinking purposes.

8. Men in each section will be appointed to handle food and clean all dishes.

Sheet of regulations for the POWs transferred to Japan in 1943. Eddie Peres was one of the transferred men and was taken to a camp in Osaka, Japan. (James A. Allen Collection)

Bibliography

Allen, James A. Memorabilia Collection, 1941-1999.

———— Audio and personal interviews, 1995-1999.

———— Videotapes of memorabilia and recollections, 1996.

Almanac of America's Wars. New York: Brompton Books Corporation, 1990.

Astarita, Joseph J. *Sketches of P. O. W. Life*. Brooklyn, NY: Rollo Press, 1947.

Bergamini, David. *Japan's Imperial Conspiracy*, Volume I & II. New York: William Morrow and Company, Inc., 1971.

Bliven, Bruce, Jr. *From Pearl Harbor to Okinawa The War in the Pacific: 1941-1945*. New York: Random House, 1960.

Browning, James S. *Documented Facts Regarding the Defense of Wake Island, Dec. 8-23, 1941*, privately printed papers, Tuscaloosa, AL, circa 1990.

Buck, Jane Floyd. "Wake Island Wife," *The Saturday Evening Post*, July 21,1945, pages 20, 60 & 62.

Calvocoressi, Peter and Wint, Guy. *Total War*. Harmondsworth, Middlesex, England: Penguin Books, Limited, 1972.

Carson, Robert C., et al. *Abnormal Psychology and Modern Life*. Glenview, IL: Scott, Foresman and Company, 1988.

Chesneau, Roger. *Aircraft Carriers of the World, 1914 to the Present*. Annapolis, MD: Naval Institute Press, 1984, page 173.

Cohen, Stan. *Enemy On Island. Issue In Doubt. The Capture of Wake Island December 1941*. Missoula, MT: Pictorial Histories Publishing Company, 1985.

Compton's Interactive Encyclopedia, Compton's NewMedia, Incorporated, 1993/1994.

Cowie, A.P. and Evison, A. *Concise English-Chinese Chinese-English Dictionary*. Quarry Bay, Hong Kong: Oxford University Press, 1986.

Cressman, Robert J. *"A Magnificent Fight" The Battle for Wake Island*. Annapolis, MD: Naval Institute Press, 1995.

Cunningham, Commander Winfield Scott, Rear Admiral USN (Ret.). *Wake Island Command*. Boston: Little, Brown and Co., 1961.

Davis, James Martin. *Top Secret The Story of the Invasion of Japan*. Omaha, NE: Ranger Publications, 1986.

Daws, Gavan. *Prisoners of the Japanese,* New York: William Morrow and Company, 1994.

Devereux, James P.S., Colonel USMC. *Wake Island*. New York: J. B. Lippencott Company, 1947.

———. Memo to the Boards of Awards, Navy Department, Washington, D.C., concerning the recognition of services of certain civilians. Written while attached to the Post Service Battalion, Marine Barracks, Quantico, Virginia, 13 September 1946.

Emperor Hirohito. *Emperor Hirohito, Accepting the Potsdam Declaration, Radio Broadcast,* http://www.mtholyoke.edu/acad/intrel/hirihito/htm [Accessed December 6, 1999].

Epstein, Beryl and Sam. *The Story of the International Red Cross*. New York: Thomas Nelson and Sons, 1963.

FAA Welcomes You to Wake Island, Public Affairs Office, Federal Aviation Administration Pacific Region, Honolulu, HI, March 1969.

Freedom, Shanghai: Asiana Publishing House, 1942.

Galuppini, Gino. *Warships of the World*. New York: Times Books, 1983.

Gray, Paul. "Doomsdays," *Time Magazine,* August 7, 1995, pages 48-53.

Goode's World Atlas. New York: Rand McNally and Company, 1986.

Heinl, Robert D. Jr., Lieutenant Colonel, USMC. *The Defense of Wake*, Headquarters, United States Marine Corps, Washington, D.C., 1947.

History of the USS Ozark LSV 2 Unit History, http://members. aol.com/famjustin/LSV2his.html [Accessed 7 January 2000].

James, Jimmy. *Jimmy James' History,* privately printed paper, circa 1989.

Jansen, Marius B. *Japan and China: from War to Peace 1894-1972.* Chicago: Rand McNally College Publishing, 1975.

Japanese Surrender Documents of World War II, The University of Oklahoma Law Center, http://www.law.ou.edu/hist/japsurr.html, [Accessed 27 September 1999].

Kephart, Rodney. *Wake, War and Waiting . . . .* , New York: Exposition Press, 1950.

Kinney, Brig. Gen. John F., USMC (RET.), with McCaffrey, James M. *Wake Island Pilot.* Washington, DC: Brassey's, 1995.

Kludas, Arnold. *Great Passenger Ships of the World, Volume 4: 1936 – 1950*, trans. by Charles Hodges. Wellingborough: Patrick Stephens, Ltd., 1975.

Layton, Read Admiral Edwin T. USN (Ret.), with Pineau, Captain Roger USNR and Costello, John. *"And I Was There" Pearl Harbor and Midway — Breaking the Secrets.* New York: William Morrow and Company, Incorporated, 1985.

The Marshall Cavendish Illustrated Encyclopedia of World War II, Volume 22. New York: Marshall Cavendish Corporation, 1972.

May, Ernest R. *Japanese Peace Treaty,* http://gi.grolier.com/wwii/ wwii_15.html [Accessed December 11, 1999].

The Merck Manual of Medical Information. White House Station, NJ: Merck Research Laboratories, Merck and Company, 1997.

McCune, George M. *Korea Today.* New York: International Secretariat, Institute of Pacific Relations, 1950.

"MK Honors Heroes of Wake Island," *The Emkayan Magazine.* Boise, ID: Morrison Knudsen Corporation, Volume53/Fall 1995, pages 12-15.

Morison, Samuel Eliot. *History of the United States Naval Operations in World War II, Volume III, The Rising Sun in the Pacific 1931 – April 1942.* Boston: Little, Brown and Company, 1958.

———— *The Two-Ocean War*, Boston: Back Bay Books/Little, Brown and Company, 1963.

Norwood, Captain James I. and Shek, Captain Emily L. *Prisoner of War Camps In Areas Other Than The Four Principal Islands of Japan, Woosung, China*, Liaison and Research Branch American Prisoner of War Information Bureau, July 31, 1946.

——— *Fengtai, China*, July 31, 1946.

——— *Kiangwan, China*, July 31, 1946.

Translations of two leaflets dropped on Japanese cities shortly after the first atomic bomb was dropped, ca. August 6, 1945, Hiroshima and Nagasaki Documents, Nuclear Files Archive, www.nuclearfiles.org/docs/1945/450806-flyers.html [accessed 25 September 2000].

Oliver, J. Charles. *Memoirs of J. Charles Oliver*, privately printed, circa 1973.

Pacific War Research Society. *Japan's Longest Day*. New York: Ballentine Books, 1968.

Peterson, Christopher. *Personality*. New York: Harcourt Brace Jovanovich, Incorporated, 1988.

"POW Survivors Pass Hat For Japanese Physician," *The Idaho Sunday Statesman,* October 29, 1961, page 8.

The Random House College Dictionary. New York: Random House, Inc., 1982.

A Report to Returned CPNAB Prisoner of War Heroes and Their Dependents. Boise, ID: The Pacific Island Employees Foundation, Incorporated, 1945.

Reynolds, Quentin. *Officially Dead, The Story of Commander C. D. Smith*. New York: Random House, 1945.

Rossner, Nigel. "Wartime documents reveal Japan ordered massacre of every POW." *South China Morning Post,* Volume XLIV number 167, Hong Kong, June 17, 1988.

Ross, Bud. "Branch Camp No. 5B — Niigata," *Ex-POW Bulletin*, American Ex-Prisoners of War, Largo, FL, March 1995.

Schultz, Duane. *Wake Island The Heroic Gallant Fight*. New York: St. Martin's Press, Inc., 1978.

The Simon and Schuster Encyclopedia of World War II. New York: Simon and Schuster, 1978.

Smith, J. B. *The Last Mission*. Mount Pleasant, IA: J. B. Smith Enterprises, 1995.

Smith, Robert J. *Japanese Society*, New York: Cambridge University Press, 1985.

Spector, Ronald H. *Eagle Against the Sun*. New York: The Free Press, Division of Macmillan, Incorporated, 1985.

Stars and Stripes, (Pacific edition) U. S. Armed Forces Daily, 8 October 1943

Taylor, William. Personal picture story of his escape in China during 1945, privately printed.

Urwin, Gregory J. W. "The Wake Island Militia," *Naval History*. Annapolis, MD: U. S. Naval Institute, December 1997.

Warner, Philip. *World War II The Untold Story*. London: The Bodly Head, 1988.

Webster's New World Compact Japanese Dictionary. New York: Macmillan, Incorporated, 1983.

Weld, Staff Sergeant George F. *Flying Tigers' Guide to Shanghai,* Headquarters Fourteenth Air Force, November 1945. Reproduced by Eastern Web Services, http://www.shanghai-ed.com/tales/t-tigmap.htm [Accessed 26 April 2000].

White, Theodore H. and Jacoby, Annalee. *Thunder Out of China*. New York: William Sloane Associates, Inc., 1946.

World History Review Text. New York: AMSCO School Publications, Incorporated, 1990.

Yoshida, Jim. *The Two Worlds of Jim Yosida*. William New York: Morrow and Company, Inc., 1972.

Index